D0849741

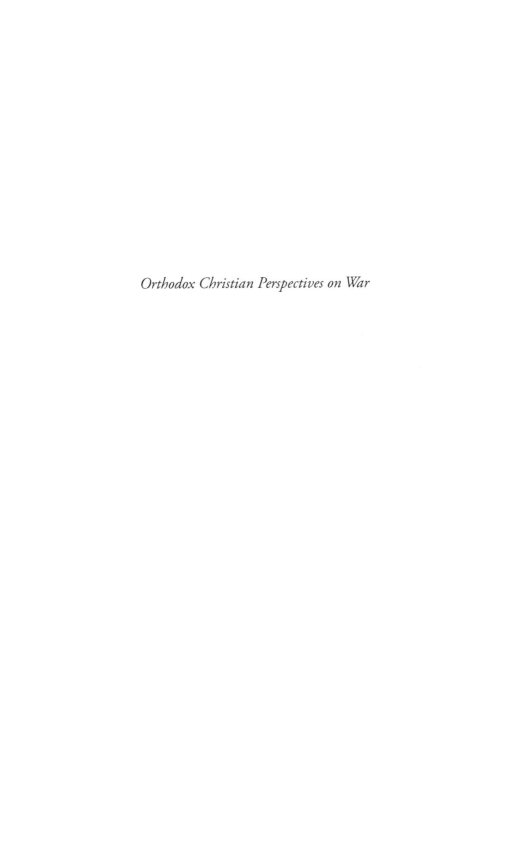

Orthodox Christian Perspectives on War

ORTHODOX CHRISTIAN PERSPECTIVES ON WAR

edited by
PERRY T. HAMALIS
AND VALERIE A. KARRAS

University of Notre Dame Press

Notre Dame, Indiana

University of Notre Dame Press
Notre Dame, Indiana 46556
undpress.nd.edu
All Rights Reserved

Copyright © 2018 by University of Notre Dame

Published in the United States of America

Library of Congress Cataloging-in-Publication Data

Names: Hamalis, Perry T., 1970- editor. | Karras, Valerie A., editor.
Title: Orthodox Christian perspectives on war / edited by Perry T. Hamalis
and Valerie A. Karras.
Description: Notre Dame : University of Notre Dame Press, 2017. |
Includes bibliographical references and index. |
Identifiers: LCCN 2017035136 (print) | LCCN 2017037605 (ebook) |
ISBN 9780268102791 (pdf) | ISBN 9780268102807 (epub) |
ISBN 9780268102777 (hardcover : alk. paper) |
ISBN 0268102775 (hardcover : alk. paper)
Subjects: LCSH: War—Religious aspects—Orthodox Eastern Church. |
Orthodox Eastern Church—Doctrines.
Classification: LCC BL65.W2 (ebook) | LCC BL65.W2 O775   2017 (print) |
DDC 261.8/730882819—dc23
LC record available at https://lccn.loc.gov/2017035136

∞ *This paper meets the requirements of*
ANSI/NISO Z39.48-1992 (Permanence of Paper)

To the Lelon Family

whose vision and support made this book possible, the second in an ongoing effort by the Lelons' Zacchaeus Ventures to promote the voices of younger Orthodox Christian scholars in important contemporary conversations

CONTENTS

ABBREVIATIONS

ANF   *The Ante-Nicene Fathers.* Edited by Alexander Rob-
                     erts and James Donaldson. 10 vols. Peabody, MA:
                     Hendrickson, 1994. First published 1885–87.

CSEL   Corpus Scriptorum Ecclesiasticorum Latinorum.
                     Vienna, 1866–.

FC   The Fathers of the Church. New York: Cima,
                     1947–49. New York: Fathers of the Church, 1949–60.
                     Washington, DC: The Catholic University of
                     America Press, 1960–.

*NPNF*¹/*NPNF*²   *The Nicene and Post-Nicene Fathers.* Series 1 and 2.
                     Edited by Philip Schaff. Peabody, MA: Hendrickson,
                     1994. First published 1886–89.

ODB   *Oxford Dictionary of Byzantium.* Edited by Alexander
                     Kazhdan. 3 vols. Oxford and New York: Oxford
                     University Press.

PG   Patrologia Graeca. Edited by J.-P. Migne. 162 vols.
                     Paris, 1857–86.

SC   Sources chrétiennes. Paris: Éditions du Cerf, 1943–.

INTRODUCTION

PERRY T. HAMALIS AND VALERIE A. KARRAS

The reality of war, the fragility of peace, and both the uses and abuses of moral and religious reflection on these perennial phenomena have spurred a flurry of recent studies from a variety of religious traditions.[1] Yet, despite the relevance of the topic and the ongoing expansion of scholarship engaging it, there remains a paucity of resources available in English that draw directly from Eastern Orthodox Christianity's history and theology.[2] This is troubling for a number of reasons, ranging from the lost benefits that Orthodoxy's historical, ethical, and theological traditions could offer to current debates among political leaders and scholars, to the convicting acknowledgment within Orthodox communities that our present-day witness is falling short. Given the perennial significance of war and peace, as well as the current global challenges posed by nations and ethnic groups that include massive numbers of citizens who self-identify as Orthodox Christians—from Russia and Ukraine in Eastern Europe, to Syria, Lebanon, and Palestine in the Middle East, to Egypt and Ethiopia in north Africa, to Greece and Cyprus in the eastern Mediterranean—the acute need for fresh, authentic, and sound resources lies beyond question.

1

The collection of essays in this volume helps substantially to fill the gap in the existing scholarship and enhances available Christian resources by engaging the subject of war through a prismatic lens. We use the term *prismatic* because, first of all, as light when passing through a prism is broken down into the individual colors of the spectrum, the vast topic of "war" is deconstructed in this volume into a number of its constitutive elements, with the contributors examining one or more of these elements from the perspective of their own areas of academic expertise: political science, history, biology/medicine, ethics, biblical studies, patristics, and systematic theology.[3] All, nonetheless, are committed both to standing within the Orthodox Church and to practicing rigorous academic inquiry and research. Since war is such a complex phenomenon, and since Orthodox tradition includes numerous interwoven threads, we believe that a constructive work requires an interdisciplinary approach. Second, this volume is prismatic in nature because the contributors' aim is not to reconstitute the spectrum into a unified whole, so to speak. In other words, the purpose is not to advance a single theory of "the meaning of war" or a comprehensive and normative stance purporting to be "*the* Orthodox Christian teaching on war." To do so, we believe, would restrict—and even distort—a tradition whose value lies, at least in part, in its diversity of pertinent experiences and teachings.

In point of fact, Orthodoxy is theologically and ecclesiologically distinguished from its historical sister, Roman Catholicism, in part because it has no unified ecclesiastical structure with a single bishop recognized as having the authority to speak decisively for the entire church on moral issues, nor is there the concept of a *magisterium*, that is, a specific and infallible teaching authority vested in and, more importantly, restricted to certain persons (e.g., bishops, patriarchs, or popes) within the church. The joint encyclical issued in 1848 by the "Patriarchs of the East" argued this point in response to the First Vatican Council's declaration of papal infallibility, and renowned Orthodox theologian Fr. Georges Florovsky referenced this encyclical in his identification of infallibility with the church in her fullness: "The Church alone possesses the capacity for true and catholic synthesis. Therein lies her *potestas magisterii*, the gift and unction of infallibility."[4]

While a more diverse and less reified set of perspectives on war characterizes Orthodox tradition, the contributors share at least three basic convictions that drive this work. First, the Eastern Orthodox tradition includes insights and teachings on war that are nuanced, relevant, and illuminative. While these insights and teachings do not present a systematic and wholly consistent witness, they express distinctively Orthodox perspectives on war. Orthodox Christianity's liturgical, exegetical, patristic, ascetic, theological, canonical, hagiographic, ethical, and artistic resources respond to war's challenges with teachings and practices that in some ways overlap and in other ways are sharply different from the teachings and practices of non-Orthodox Christian communities.[5]

Consider, as just one example, the following passage from a homily of the late fourth-/early fifth-century archbishop of Constantinople, St. John Chrysostom, on the meaning of the biblical verse, "that we may lead a quiet and peaceable life in all godliness and dignity" (1 Tim. 2:2b NRSV): "For there are three very grievous kinds of war. The one is public, when our soldiers are attacked by foreign armies: The second is, when even in time of peace, we are at war with one another: The third is, when the individual is at war with himself, which is the worst of all."[6] One sees, first, that the most common meaning of *war* (armed conflict between states) is immediately complemented by two additional meanings in St. John's lesson, one interpersonal and one intrapersonal.[7] Furthermore, and perhaps most surprisingly, Chrysostom contends that it is the intrapersonal that is "worst of all." This claim not only underscores a prioritization of the interior life; it also expresses his belief that all wars are, at root, caused by spiritual conditions.

In the passage one also notices that the only type of transnational war acknowledged by St. John occurs when "our soldiers are attacked by foreign armies," indicating an essentially defensive perspective. We offer this brief gloss on a late-fourth-century homily without further historical contextualization or analysis in order simply to hint at the kinds of insights that can be mined from the Eastern Orthodox tradition on the subject of war.[8] Not only do the essays that follow draw expertly upon Eastern Orthodoxy's vast tradition, but they do so in dialogue with recent scholarship in Western Christian ethics, the humanities, and the natural and social sciences.

Second, the contributors all agree that the history and experience of the Orthodox Church provides an alternative viewpoint to that of Roman Catholicism and of various Protestant denominations. Orthodoxy's roots in early Christianity and its persistent adherence to those roots, its connections with the Roman emperor Constantine and the Byzantine Empire, its historical relationships with Muslim communities in the Balkans, North Africa, and the Middle East, its predominance within Russia and other Slavic nations, its complicated role in many Balkan and post-Soviet states' developments, and its increasing though still limited visibility in the Americas, Asia, and Australia all testify to Orthodoxy's historical significance for reflection on war. All of these unique elements factor into the characteristically "Eastern" perspective of Orthodox Christianity vis-à-vis the "Western Christianity" of Roman Catholicism, Anglicanism, and Protestantism. To provide just one example, the viewpoint of Arab Orthodox Christians toward the Crusades was often considerably different from that of the Frankish and other Western Christian crusaders attacking Jerusalem and other cities in the Holy Land.

Third, this work's contributors share the conviction that the English-speaking world has largely overlooked or dismissed Orthodoxy's potential contribution to critical reflection on this timely subject. With very few exceptions, courses, conferences, and conversations on "Christianity and war" in the United States tend either to restrict their scope to Catholic and Protestant perspectives, seemingly unaware of Eastern Orthodoxy, or simply to caricature the Christian East as the tradition responsible for "Constantinianism," understood simplistically as the inauguration and perpetuation of Christianity's sellout to political power and to justified war-making.[9] Several of this volume's essays demonstrate that, even within its original historical context, Constantinianism was much more complex than typical Western perspectives acknowledge, and the Byzantines' efforts to balance a strong defensive militarism with a theologically grounded nonaggression policy are rarely noted outside of Byzantine history circles. Deeper questions of how Orthodox Christian cultures, both historically and contemporarily, develop positive or negative views of non-Orthodox or non-Christian cultures and, hence, develop cooperative or antagonistic relations with them, are often similarly ignored or stereotyped. Having said this, the contributors to this work also realize that we cannot expect others to include an Orthodox perspective or to treat Orthodox tradition's many threads with care if so few scholarly Orthodox resources are available. We humbly hope that our offering here helps to rectify this state of affairs.

Orthodox Christian Perspectives on War speaks to two audiences. It aims, first, to present non-Orthodox readers with the breadth and depth of Orthodox Christian thought on the phenomenon of war with the hope of dispelling myths and contributing constructively to current scholarship in political science, ethics, history, biblical studies, patristics, and theology. Part of this task lies in showing that the dominant categories that currently structure Christian reflection on war cannot be appropriated easily within an Orthodox perspective, and in identifying untapped possibilities for constructive exchanges. Within the discipline of ethics, for example, many contributors to this volume show that "just war," "pacifism," "holy war," and "political realism" are problematized when applied to the layers of Orthodox tradition. They constitute a foreign moral language that cannot be assimilated easily or without compromising, to some extent, the tradition's integrity.

Secondly, this volume seeks to make Orthodox readers around the world more aware of the complexities and nuances of their own tradition. Due to the relative paucity of Orthodox works on this subject, especially in English, combined with the dominance of Western Christian rhetoric and models, many Orthodox leaders and thinkers have erroneously extrapolated from predominant Western Christian paradigms to Orthodoxy, not recognizing the incongruity—and at times, total incompatibility—of the two perspectives. We hope, therefore, to make contributions that are authentic, scholarly, theological, pragmatic, and pastoral for Orthodox and non-Orthodox readers alike.

The essays collected here are structured under three headings. In part 1, "Confronting the Present-Day Reality," the relevance and immediacy of the question is illuminated in two essays. First, the challenges of war are explored from the raw, personal level of soldiers and their families in Aristotle Papanikolaou's "The Ascetics of War: The Undoing and Redoing of Virtue." Second, in "Exposing the State of the Question: A Case Study of American Orthodox Responses to the 1999 War in Kosovo," Andrew Walsh provides an analysis that helps readers to discern the nature of the challenges that Orthodox communities in the United States face in striving to respond to the reality of war. Part 1 thus spans the personal to the political and proffers an engaging foray into the topic through concrete examples.

In part 2, "Reengaging Orthodoxy's History and Tradition," seven contributors offer their critical and constructive interpretations of authoritative sources within Orthodoxy's historical tradition. Beginning with the Old Testament, Nicolae Roddy's essay, "Chariots of Fire, Unassailable Cities, and the One True King: A Prophetically Influenced Scribal Perspective on War and Peace," reminds readers of a basic insight from the prophetic corpus: no matter how advanced a nation's offensive weapons and defensive armor are, the only sure path to preservation lies in faithfulness to the true God. Picking up the topic in first-century Palestine, John Fotopoulos, in his essay "Herodian-Roman Domination, Violent Jewish Peasant Resistance, and Jesus of Nazareth," examines the significance of the "popular king/bandit" phenomenon and trope within Jewish tradition to illuminate how both Palestinian Jews and their Roman occupiers perceived and responded to Jesus and to interpret Jesus' teachings on war and violence in that context.

Straddling pre- and post-Constantinian Christianity, Valerie A. Karras's essay, "'Their Hands Are Not Clean': Origen and the Cappadocians on War and Military Service," compares and contrasts the views toward Christians in the military of the third-century Alexandrian theologian Origen with the fourth-century Cappadocian bishop St. Basil of Caesarea and his contemporaries St. Gregory of Nyssa and St. Gregory of Nazianzus. In "Constantine, Ambrose, and the Morality of War: How Ambrose of Milan Challenged the Imperial Discourse on War and Violence," George Demacopoulos moves the investigation of war firmly into the fourth-century Byzantine Empire and offers the first of several essays focused on the post-Constantinian church's teachings and witness on war. For Demacopoulos, one of the most significant sources for advancing our understanding of the shift from pre-Constantinian Christianity to post-Constantinian Christianity is Ambrose of Milan, and his reading of Ambrose paints a picture that is significantly different from predominant interpretations within and outside of Orthodox circles. The hagiographic tradition's fascinating witness, which contrasts sharply with popular notions of "holy warriors," comes into focus in James C. Skedros's essay, "Lessons from Military Saints in the Byzantine Tradition." Finally, a co-authored essay by Alexandros K. Kyrou and Elizabeth H. Prodromou, "Debates on Just War, Holy War, and Peace: Orthodox Christian Thought and Byzantine Imperial Attitudes toward War," rounds out part 2. Blending their respective specialties in Byzantine military history and international relations, Kyrou and Prodromou advance both a corrective reading of Byzantine attitudes toward war and a constructive proposal for how Orthodoxy's Byzantine legacy can contribute positively to current global challenges and discourse on peace and war.

Part 3, "Constructive Directions in Orthodox Theology and Ethics," begins with two essays that center on the theme of providence and war. In the first, "War and Peace: Providence and the Interim," Peter C. Bouteneff mines Greek patristic sources for teachings on good and evil as they pertain to the phenomenon of war and relates them to current debates on war as a "lesser good" or a "necessary evil." In the second, "A Helper of Providence: 'Justified Providential War' in Vladimir Solov'ev," Brandon Gallaher examines the writings of one of the most influential and creative voices from nineteenth-century Russia, Vladimir Solov'ev, discerning his distinctive approach to good and evil and expressing his normative teachings on war vis-à-vis the—by then—predominant categories of holy war, realpolitik, pacifism, and just war. Following these, Gayle E. Woloschak, in "War, Technology, and the Canon Law Principle of *Economia*," centers her analysis upon the concept of *economia* and its constructive value for engaging in deliberations regarding both decisions to go to war and decisions on the use of various war technologies. And in his concluding essay, "Just Peacemaking and Christian Realism: Possibilities for Moving beyond the Impasse in Orthodox Christian War Ethics," Perry T. Hamalis argues that the best next step for Orthodoxy's representatives is not to insist on the utter distinctiveness of our tradition of reflection on war, but rather to embrace and adapt two lesser-known but established approaches that comport more organically with Orthodoxy's witness on war: just peacemaking and Christian realism.

As editors, we appreciate the patience of our contributors and ask for our readers' understanding as the publication of these essays was delayed due to multiple personal matters in both of our lives. We conclude now with a word of humble gratitude to the Dr. Thomas Lelon family, the visionary leaders who brought us together as "LOGOS," an interdisciplinary community of "next generation" Orthodox scholars, and generously supported this project. For most of the volume's contributors, in fact, this is our second shared project completed as LOGOS; we began work after the successful release of *Thinking through Faith: New Perspectives from Orthodox Christian Scholars*, edited by Aristotle Papanikolaou and Elizabeth H. Prodromou (St. Vladimir's Seminary Press, 2008). Dr. Lelon, Mrs. Alexis Lelon, and their son, Charles T. (Chuck) Lelon, together with other supporters they gathered, not only encouraged us enthusiastically and patiently throughout the process, but provided the funding that enabled us to meet face-to-face as collaborators on multiple occasions in order to read together some of the existing literature, present our ideas, discuss one another's draft essays, and learn from each other's disciplinary expertise and critical feedback. It was an atmosphere that nurtured scholarly insights, deepened friendships, and renewed faith. And so, we also want to thank our fellow contributors to this volume, all of whom, despite the teaching and research responsibilities of their academic posts, committed to offering this collection as a labor of love and with the prayerful hope "for the peace of the whole world, for the stability of the holy churches of God, and for the unity of all."[10]

NOTES

1. A limited sampling includes Ahmed Al-Dawoody, *The Islamic Law of War: Justifications and Regulations* (New York: Palgrave Macmillan, 2011); Karen Armstrong, *Fields of Blood: Religion and the History of Violence* (New York: Anchor, 2015); Nigel Biggar, *In Defence of War* (New York: Oxford University Press, 2013); Alan Billings, *The Dove, the Fig Leaf and the Sword: Why Christianity Changes Its Mind about War* (London: SPCK, 2014); Caron Gentry, *Offering Hospitality: Questioning Christian Approaches to War* (Notre Dame, IN: University of Notre Dame Press, 2013); Stanley Hauerwas, *War and the American Difference: Theological Reflections on Violence and National Identity* (Grand Rapids: Baker Academic, 2011); James Turner Johnson, *Just War Tradition and the Restraint of War: A Moral and Historical Inquiry* (Princeton: Princeton University Press, 2016); John Renard, ed., *Fighting Words: Religion, Violence, and the Interpretation*

of Sacred Texts (Berkeley: University of California Press, 2012); Matthew Allen Shadle, *The Origins of War: A Catholic Perspective* (Washington, DC: Georgetown University Press, 2011); Ronald J. Sider, *The Early Church on Killing: A Comprehensive Sourcebook on War, Abortion, and Capital Punishment* (Grand Rapids: Baker Academic, 2012); Timothy Sisk, ed., *Between Terror and Tolerance: Religious Leaders, Conflict, and Peacemaking* (Washington, DC: Georgetown University Press, 2011); and Tobias Winright and Laurie Johnston, eds., *Can War Be Just in the 21st Century?* (Maryknoll, NY: Orbis Books, 2015).

2. Existing books in English include Semegnish Asfaw, Alexios Chehadeh, and Marian Gh. Simion, eds., *Just Peace: Orthodox Perspectives* (Geneva: WCC Publications, 2012); William Joseph Buckley, ed., *Kosovo: Contending Voices on Balkan Interventions* (Grand Rapids: Eerdmans, 2000); Lucian N. Leustean, ed., *Eastern Christianity and the Cold War, 1945–91* (London: Routledge, 2010); Timothy S. Miller and John Nesbitt, *Peace and War in Byzantium: Essays in Honor of George T. Dennis, S.J.* (Washington, DC: Catholic University of America Press, 1995); Radmila Radić, *Religion and the War in Bosnia*, trans. Paul Mojzes (Atlanta: Scholars Press, 1998); Alexander F. C. Webster, *The Pacifist Option: The Moral Argument against War in Eastern Orthodox Moral Theology* (San Francisco: International Scholars Publications, 1998); and Alexander F. C. Webster and Darrell Cole, *The Virtue of War: Reclaiming the Classic Christian Traditions East and West* (Salisbury, MA: Regina Orthodox Press, 2004). In addition, volume 47 (2003) of the *St. Vladimir's Theological Quarterly* is entitled *Justifiable War?* There are also two collections of source materials, both running the gamut from early church canons and commentaries through Byzantine and imperial Russian ecclesiastical literature and from civil legislation to modern synodal and patriarchal statements: Fr. Hildo Bos and Jim Forest, eds., *For the Peace from Above: An Orthodox Resource Book on War, Peace and Nationalism*, rev. ed. (Rollinsford, NH: Orthodox Research Institute, 2011; 1st ed. 1999), also available at http://incommunion.org/2004/10/18/table-of-contents-for-the-peace-from-above-an-orthodox-resource-book-on-war-peace-and-nationalism/; and, including helpful commentary and analysis, Yuri Stoyanov, "Eastern Orthodox Christianity," in *Religion, War, and Ethics: A Sourcebook of Textual Traditions*, ed. Gregory M. Reichberg and Henrik Syse with Nicole M. Hartwell (New York: Cambridge University Press, 2014), 164–234.

3. See the detailed contributors' biographies at the end of this volume.

4. Georges Florovsky, "The Authority of the Ancient Councils and the Tradition of the Fathers," in *The Collected Works of Georges Florovsky*, ed. Richard S. Haugh, 14 vols. (Belmont, MA: Nordland Publishing Co., 1975–88), 1:103;

cited in Paul L. Gavrilyuk, *Georges Florovsky and the Russian Religious Renaissance*, Changing Paradigms in Historical and Systematic Theology (Oxford: Oxford University Press, 2014), 222. For the patriarchal encyclical, see "Encyclical of the Eastern Patriarchs, 1848: A Reply to the Epistle of Pope Pius IX 'To the Easterns,'" Internet Modern History Sourcebook, Fordham University, http://www.fordham.edu/halsall/index.asp.

5. *Liturgical* refers to the worship services of the church, *exegetical* to biblical interpretation, *patristic* to early Christian theologians (the church "fathers"), *ascetic* to monastic and other similar traditions and practices, *canonical* to the church's religious law, and *hagiographic* to writings about the saints.

6. John Chrysostom, *Hom. 7 in epistolam primam ad Timotheum* (PG 62:554); English translation in *NPNF*¹ 13:429.

7. This is not, of course, unique to Eastern Christianity. Within Islam, e.g., there are similarly varied levels of spiritual and military meanings distinguishing between the "greater" and "lesser" jihad. See Rudolph Peters, *Jihad in Classical and Modern Islam* (Princeton: Markus Weiner, 1996).

8. For a fuller treatment of St. John Chrysostom's teachings on war, see Perry T. Hamalis, "Peace and War in the Thought of St. John Chrysostom," in *Proceedings of the International Symposium "St. John Chrysostom, Archbishop of Constantinople: 'Yesterday and Today'"* (Seoul: Orthodox Metropolis of Korea, 2007), 73–81. The symposium was held in Seoul on November 10, 2007.

9. For one of the best existing exceptions from a representative of Eastern Orthodoxy, see John A. McGuckin, "Nonviolence and Peace Traditions in Early and Eastern Christianity," in *Religion, Terrorism and Globalization: Nonviolence; A New Agenda*, ed. K. K. Kuriakose (New York: Nova Science Publishers, 2006), 189–201. A non-Orthodox, A. James Reimer, in *Christians and War* (Minneapolis: Fortress Press, 2010), 65–75, provides a helpful and accessible account of the "Constantinian Shift" and its impact on Christian war ethics that is more balanced than most, sidestepping the typical rhetoric of the "Constantinian fall" and acknowledging both the positive and negative ways of interpreting the emperor's conversion and the development of the justifiable war tradition by St. Augustine.

10. Petition from the "great litany" found in most worship services of the Orthodox Church, including *The Divine Liturgy of St. John Chrysostom* (Brookline, MA: Holy Cross Orthodox Press, 1986).

PART ONE

CONFRONTING THE PRESENT-DAY REALITY

CHAPTER 1

THE ASCETICS OF WAR

The Undoing and Redoing of Virtue

ARISTOTLE PAPANIKOLAOU

Contemporary discussions of just war theory in Christian ethics focus on whether Christians should be in the business of defining criteria for the decision to go to war and for the proper engagement in combat. There is very little attention to the way in which, debates about just war criteria notwithstanding, combat soldiers are forced to engage in practices, both in training before war and during war, that fine-tune the body to the constant threat of violence—what I term the ascetics of war. If war is seen as fostering a certain ascetics on the body, then the Orthodox notion of divine-human communion (*theosis*) is relevant to discussions of war insofar as divine-human communion is itself linked to an ascetics of virtue. Understanding the human as created for communion with God shifts the focus of the discussion from just war versus pacifism to the effects of war on the human person and the practices that undo such effects. After briefly discussing the current debate within contemporary Orthodox theology on just war theory, I will draw on the work of Jonathan Shay to illustrate the effects of the ascetics of war on the body. I will then argue that the ascetics of virtue that involves the particular ascetical practice of truth telling has the power to undo the traumatic effects of war on the combat veteran. Insofar as this undoing is an embodiment of virtue, it is also an embodiment of the divine—*theosis.*

FORGETTING VIRTUE

When it comes to the question of war, the Orthodox are probably most well known for asserting that there is no just war theory in the Orthodox tradition. Beyond that negative assertion, it is very difficult to discern what the Orthodox think about war. For the just war naysayers, it would not be difficult to find among the Orthodox such statements as, "There is no just war, no just violence, no just revenge or recompense, no just accumulation of wealth."[1] In this statement, it is a little unclear why—other than for rhetorical effect—war, violence, revenge, and accumulation of wealth are grouped together, since the whole point of the idea of just war is to differentiate morally sanctioned forms of violence from those that are clearly immoral, such as revenge. From one of the leading Orthodox voices in ethics in the past fifty years, one hears how

> these two seminal writers [Ambrose and Augustine] led the Western Church not only to an acceptance of the military role by Christians, but to its enhancement into a positive virtue through the development of criteria by which a war could be distinguished from an unjust war, and be called "just." It is my contention that the East developed a different approach to the issue. Rather than seek to morally elevate war and Christian participation in it so that it could be termed "just," the East treated it as a necessary evil. . . . Contrary to Augustine . . . the Eastern Patristic tradition rarely praised war, and to my knowledge, almost never called it "just" or a moral good. . . . The East did not seek to deal with just war themes such as the correct conditions for entering war [*jus ad bellum*], and the correct conduct of war [*jus in bello*] on the basis of the possibility of the existence of a "just war," precisely because it did not hold to such a view of war.[2]

This denial of any form of just war theory in the Christian East is often extended to some form of praise for the Christian Roman Empire for embodying a primarily defensive, nonaggressive ethos in relation to war.[3]

One is tempted to attribute this denial of a just war theory, together with its praise of the Christian Roman attitude to war, as another example of self-identification of the Orthodox vis-à-vis the proximate other—the "West."[4] Even though something like this distorted apophaticism—Orthodoxy is what the West is not—may be operative in some Orthodox denials of just war theory, it is irrefutable that a "theory" of just war, consisting of distinctions between conditions for entering war and conditions for conducting war, together with their respective criteria, is nowhere to be found in what has come to be known as the Orthodox trajectory within the Christian tradition. Such an absence makes Fr. Alexander Webster's defense of a justifiable war tradition within Orthodoxy something of an anomaly.[5] While admitting that the Orthodox tradition never developed a just war theory—on this point, there seems to be a consensus—Webster argues against the position that the Orthodox consistently saw war only as a necessary evil and never as a moral good. Webster amasses a pile of citations from biblical, patristic, canonical, liturgical, and imperial sources, which he believes point collectively to an affirmation of the moral value of war under certain conditions. As Webster argues, "We hope the abundant textual and iconic evidence adduced in the present volume will restore among them [Orthodox bishops, theologians, and activists] the longstanding traditional moral position that war may be engaged and conducted as a virtuous or righteous act, or at least as a 'lesser good' instead of a lesser or necessary evil."[6] In an ironic twist, Webster actually attributes the denial by Orthodoxy of its own justifiable war tradition to the "flurry of ecumenical contacts with Western Christians and an accelerated emigration of Orthodox Christians to Western Europe and North America."[7] Instead of blaming the West for poisoning the East with notions of just or justifiable war, the West gets blamed by Webster for influencing the Orthodox to forget its justifiable war tradition. One way or the other, the Orthodox always seem to find a way to blame the West.

The Orthodox, thus, agree that there is no just war "theory" in the Orthodox tradition in the form of distinctions between *jus in bello* and *jus ad bellum*, and their respective criteria; there is also consensus that within the tradition there is discussion about the need to go to war; the current debate, however, centers on how going to war is characterized: For Harakas, it is always a necessary evil; for Webster, under certain conditions, it is virtuous and of moral value. This difference, however, reveals another, more implicit, agreement between Harakas and Webster: although both agree there is no just war theory within the Orthodox tradition, both seem to operate within the moral categories and framework of the just war tradition. What the just war tradition attempts to discern is whether both the action to go to war and the conduct within war fall on the side of right or the side of wrong relative to the moral divide. Although Harakas and Webster distance themselves from a just war theory, they are still looking for the moral categories that would establish certain actions to go to war and conduct within war as belonging on either one side or the other of the right/wrong divide. To characterize war as either a necessary evil, lesser evil, lesser good, justifiable, or as a virtuous and righteous act is to attempt to do the same thing that a just war theory tries to do—establish the moral rightness or wrongness of an act, given the specific conditions. Even such distinctions as that between killing as murder and killing for defense reinforce this particular moral framework that centers on the rightness or wrongness of moral acts. From a Christian perspective, the concern with the rightness or wrongness of moral acts has to do with one's positioning in relation to God and, in the end, with one's positioning within the eschatological consummation, or heaven.

What is remarkable about the entire debate is that there is little attention to what is arguably the core and central axiom of the Orthodox tradition—the principle of divine-human communion. Webster speaks of war as "virtuous," and yet pays absolutely no attention to the tradition of thinking on virtue either in the ascetical writings or in such thinkers as Maximos the Confessor; in both cases, the understanding of virtue is inherently linked to one's struggle toward communion with God—theosis. How exactly is claiming to have fought in a virtuous war, or to have killed virtuously, consistent with this tradition of thinking on virtue in light of the principle of divine-human communion? Is it really the case that being virtuous in war means moving *toward* a deeper communion with God? Webster does not answer these questions. Although Harakas does argue for the patristic bias for peace, approaching the issue from an eschato-logical perspective, his emphasis is still on how to label the action to go to war, or the conduct during war, and pays no attention to war from the perspective of the Orthodox understanding of creation's destiny for com-munion with God.

THE VICE OF WAR

To affirm that creation is created for communion with the uncreated is simultaneously to affirm that all of creation is sacramental, which means that it is always already shot through with the divine presence. There is no "space" between the created and the uncreated (to spatialize God makes no sense); creation is not given the capacity to "jump over" an abyss to meet the divine presence; it is given the task to relate to itself and to God so as to tap the potential of a created "thing" to iconically mani-fest the divine presence that is already there. Sin is not so much a missing of the target as it is a blocking of the divine that is "in all things and every-where present." Whatever the motivation and whichever way it is di-rected, violence is a form of blocking of the divine presence both in a social sense, that is, in the space of relationships—human-to-human and human-to-nonhuman—and within oneself. War is a space saturated with violence, an engagement in a set of practices that are unsacramental in the sense that created reality is used to foster division, destruction, denigra-tion, desperation, destitution, and degeneration; put simply, it is a mani-festation of the demonic. This is not to say that there are not godly moments in the midst of war—loyalty, sacrifice, and even love. As a whole, however, war is the realm of the demonic.

Given this understanding of divine-human communion, one thing is certain: no matter what side one is on, to be complicit in violence of any kind is damaging to one's struggle for communion with God. Put an-other way, to be complicit with violence of any kind, even in self-defense, cannot but be damaging to one's soul. Violence does not discriminate—it does not affect only those who use it unjustly. Even if one were to en-gage in conduct with noble intentions, even if one were to exhibit mo-ments of sacrifice, affection, and love in the midst of war, violence works in the direction opposite to that toward which humans were created—divine-human communion. What discussions of labeling decisions to go to war and actions during war forget is that war is inevitably spiritually harmful. One result of understanding war from the principle of divine-human communion is attention to the effects of war on those who live through it, no matter what side one is on. Discussions of justifiable war may create the impression that as long as one is on the morally justified side of war, that should be enough to mitigate the existential effects of war and violence. There is plenty of evidence to indicate that the "side" one is on makes absolutely no difference to the nondiscriminatory effects of violence in war.

In recent memory, the only war on which there is little debate about the "right" side is World War II. Much has been said about this greatest generation of soldiers, who sacrificed themselves in the morally justified cause of fighting either German or Japanese aggression. In the standard American narrative, going to war against Germany and Japan was the morally right thing to do, and few Americans would dispute this claim. World War II veterans should, thus, feel proud of their blameless service, and have since received unequivocal praise and adulation from most Americans.[8] There is mounting evidence, however, that even given this unwavering support for their service in World War II, which would give the soldiers every reason to believe that they fought in a just war, many World War II veterans suffered from the effects of violence that was inflicted on them, violence inflicted on others near them, and violence they inflicted on the "enemy."

In *Our Fathers' War*, Tom Mathews narrates the effects of World War II on his own father, who, after visiting the ground in Italy where his division fought the Germans, and describing his role for his division, eventually broke down, saying, "'I killed a lot of people,' . . . in a strangled voice that turned to a sob. 'Jesus Christ . . . I killed so many people.'" Later at a restaurant, Mathews's father looked at him "as if he'd just come out of electroshock. 'What happened back there?' he said. 'I've *never* voiced that stuff. *Never.*'. . . 'Not to anyone. Not to myself.'"[9] The father continues the reflection: "'I hated the Germans. I did hate them. But it doesn't matter. You look and you see something you hate in yourself, something atavistic, something deep in the bottom of the cortex. You don't feel right. It doesn't make sense. You should feel victorious. You should feel triumph. You don't. Too much has happened. All you know is that you're a killing machine.'"[10] This confession of the effects of war on Mathews's father comes after a life marked by a strained relationship with his son, infidelity, and addiction. There are similar stories from other World War II veterans, but under the so-called code of silence, World War II veterans were not given the space to express the effects that war had on the soldiers who fought for the "right" side, or, as Webster would call it, the "virtuous" side.[11]

There is no shortage of stories of the traumatic effects of war from soldiers who fought in the Vietnam War, or the most recent wars in Iraq and Afghanistan.[12] One might argue that because the "morality" of these wars is ambiguous, the traumatic effects experienced by these veterans were more acute than was the case for World War II veterans. There are a few problems with this argument, not least of which is the assumption that trauma was not experienced by World War II veterans; the other unsupportable assumption is that the degree of trauma experienced in war correlates with the moral clarity on the justifiability of the war itself. Evidence indicates that the trauma experienced by war veterans has little to do with the justifiability of a war. The effects of the violence of war do not distinguish between sides.

What stories from veterans of war reveal is that violence becomes embodied—its insidiousness seeps into the physiological infrastructure of the human person. If creation is created for communion, and if humans are the center of this divine-human drama, then divine-human communion itself is the presencing of the good into the deep recesses of the body—it is an embodied experience. Violence opens up the body not to God, but to the inhabitation of the anti-God.

This absence of the divine is evident in the staggering statistic that at least "one-third of homeless males are [Vietnam] veterans, with 150,000–250,000 veterans homeless on a given night and at least twice that number homeless at some time in the course of a given year."[13] It is also apparent in the study that showed that "35.8 percent of male Vietnam combat veterans met the full American Psychiatric Association diagnostic criteria for PTSD [post-traumatic stress disorder] at the time of the study, in the late 1980s. . . . This is a thirty-two-fold increase in the prevalence of PTSD compared to the random sample of demographically similar civilians. More than 70 percent of combat veterans had experienced *at least one of the cardinal symptoms* ('partial PTSD') *at some time in their lives*, even if they did not receive the full syndrome diagnosis."[14] This high rate of the experience of PTSD symptoms among Vietnam veterans demonstrates that the effects of war linger in the body long after a soldier's tour of duty. This lingering is in the form of "(a) hostile or mistrustful attitude toward the world; (b) social withdrawal; (c) feelings of emptiness or hopelessness; (d) a chronic feeling of being 'on the edge,' as if constantly threatened; (e) estrangement."[15] Those who suffer from combat trauma often experience flashbacks to traumatic events, in which the primary image that is governing their emotional state is one of violence and impending threat to life.

One would hope that sleep would give respite to such suffering, but combat trauma often leads to recurring nightmares; and the lack of deep sleep leads to other inevitable emotional disturbances, such as increased irritability and tendency to anger. Beyond the recurring nightmares, combat veterans often simply cannot sleep because they trained themselves for the sake of survival to be hyperalert and to react to sounds that may, in combat situations, be life threatening; as any good ascetic would know, such training of the body is simply not undone by returning home.[16] Add to all this "random, unwarranted rage at family, sexual dysfunction, no capacity for intimacy, [s]omatic disturbances, loss of ability to experience pleasure, [p]eripheral vasoconstriction, autonomic hyperactivity, [s]ense of the dead being more real than the living."[17] What is most damaging to combat veterans who suffer from symptoms of PTSD is the destruction of their capacity to trust,[18] which inevitably renders impossible any forms of bonding with others that are meaningful. If Jesus' greatest commandment was to "love the Lord your God with all your heart, with all your soul, and with all your mind" and to "Love your neighbor as yourself" (Matt. 22:37–39), then experiencing PTSD symptoms simply makes that impossible. What is most demonic about the violence of war is its power to debilitate the capacity to experience love—both in the form of being loved and loving another.

Most frightening of the diverse forms in which PTSD is manifested in combat soldiers is that which is called the "berserk state." The state of being berserk also poses a formidable challenge to Christian conceptions of the spiritual life, and, in particular, the notion of deification. Berserk is an extreme state of PTSD that is triggered by such events as "betrayal, insult, or humiliation by a leader; death of a friend-in-arms, being wounded; being overrun, surrounded, or trapped; seeing dead comrades who have been mutilated by the enemy; and unexpected deliverance from certain death."[19] Shay elaborates, "I cannot say for certain that betrayal is a necessary precondition. However, I have yet to encounter a veteran who went berserk from grief alone."[20] The characteristics of the berserk state are "beastlike, godlike, socially disconnected, crazy, mad, insane, enraged, cruel, without restraint or discrimination, insatiable, devoid of fear, inattentive to own safety, distractible, reckless, feeling invulnerable, exalted, intoxicated, frenzied, cold, indifferent, insensible to pain, suspicious of friends."[21] Soldiers who go berserk in combat are often those who put themselves in the greatest danger and, if they survive, are deemed, ironically, the most heroic. There is growing research that indicates that the berserk state entails "changes in the parts of the brain that process incoming sensations for signs of danger and connect sensation with emotion."[22] Even after combat, a veteran can go berserk, and often have no recollection of it, as was the case with John, an Iraqi war veteran, who cut his fiancée and her mother with a knife after an argument over bus schedules, and after a long stretch in which John was showing progress through treatment.[23] After cutting his fiancée and her mother, John then cut himself, telling the police as they walked in, "see, it doesn't hurt."[24] John could not immediately recall the event; he had to be told what had happened; and, on being told, he was afraid that he had killed his daughter, which he had not.

What's most troubling about the berserk state is that violence can imprint itself on the body—and, thus, on the soul—in ways that could be permanent: "On the basis of my work with Vietnam veterans," Shay writes, "I conclude that the berserk state is ruinous, leading to the soldier's maiming or death in battle—which is the most frequent outcome—and to life-long psychological and physiological injury if he survives. I believe that once a person has entered the berserk state, he or she is changed *forever*."[25] He amplifies that "more than 40 percent of Vietnam combat veterans sampled in the late 1980s by the congressionally mandated

National Vietnam Veterans Readjustment Study reported engaging in violent acts three times or more in the previous year."[26] The spiritually challenging question is, What meaning could speaking about theosis possibly have for someone whose physiology has been permanently scarred by violence?

More recently, Shay has distinguished between simple PTSD and complex PTSD. In simple PTSD "injuries can be disabling in the same sense that physical injuries are. But they do not *necessarily* blight the whole life of the person that bears them. . . . Their life is changed, to be sure, and often limited in specific ways, but the possibility of it being a good human life is not destroyed."[27] There is hope, which is rooted in both the use of pharmaceuticals and an ascetics that undoes the undoing of character. More troubling from a spiritual perspective is complex PTSD, which "invades character, and the capacity for social trust is destroyed, all possibility of a flourishing life is lost. . . . When social trust is destroyed, it is not replaced by a vacuum, but rather by a perpetual mobilization to fend off attack, humiliation, or exploitation, and to figure out other people's trickery."[28] It's not that complex PTSD is untreatable per se, but that because of the way in which the world is perceived, those who suffer with PTSD cannot bring themselves to relate to the people who could help them with this injury. Again, what does theosis possibly mean to those who suffer from complex PTSD?

It is very disturbing to hear the stories of combat veterans, which include not sleeping with their spouses for fear that a nightmare may lead them to physically harm their spouse; not being able to sleep in the middle of the night because of hypervigilance; not wanting to be outdoors for fear that a sound, such as a bird chirping or water running, may trigger combat mode; not being able to enter public spaces, such as grocery stores or elevators; having dreams of mutilating one's children; alienating friends and families; not being able to hold a job, or even get a job for fear of public spaces.[29] These and many such similar stories reveal that there is an ascetics to war: either through the training received in the military, or through the practices that one performs in the midst of war to train the body for survival against constant threat of violence, war is the undoing of virtue in the sense that it impacts negatively a combat veteran's capacity for relationship with family, friends, and strangers. War does not simply cause "lifelong disabling psychiatric symptoms but can *ruin* good character."[30] From the perspective of the principle of divine-human communion, the ruin of good character is not limited to the "soul" of the combat veteran; "character" is a relational category, and the ruin of character is simultaneously the ruin of relationships.

WHAT DOES THEOSIS HAVE TO DO WITH WAR?

At this point, much like a person watching a Hollywood movie, one is expecting the happy ending—yes, there is tragedy in war, but there's a way to fix it and make everyone happy. If only it were so easy. The berserk state, as I mentioned, challenges easy happy endings. On the surface, it would seem that for those who suffer from PTSD as a result of combat, or any trauma, talk of theosis or divine-human communion seems like a luxury. To some extent, the Orthodox have contributed to this perception of the irrelevancy of theosis to those who are in the midst of perpetual suffering by predominantly linking deification to the monk in the monastery, in the desert, on a stylite, or in the forest; add to this the tendency to describe theosis in supernatural terms of being surrounded by divine light, battling demons, or eating with the bears. On my reading, one of the few places in the Orthodox tradition where one can hear stories of mundane theosis is the novels of Dostoyevsky, such as in the person of Sonya in *Crime and Punishment*, and, ironically, of Tolstoy, such as in the person of Pashenka, whom the reader encounters at the end of Tolstoy's short story "Fr. Sergius." In order to have any relevancy for the experience of trauma, theosis must expand the boundaries of the monastery and be made more worldly.

This more mundane form of theosis is rendered possible in the Greek patristic tradition in its linking of divine-human communion to virtue, which can illuminate what Shay means by the "undoing of character" that occurs as a result of war. In the writings of Maximos the Confessor (d. 662), communion with God, which is an embodied presencing of the divine, is simultaneous with the acquisition of virtue: virtue is embodied deification. To say that the human is created with the potential to be godlike should not conjure up images of Greek mythology; within the

Greek patristic texts, it simply means that if God is love, then the human was created to love, and this love is simultaneously a uniting oneself with God, since God is love. In Maximos the Confessor, deification is the acquisition of love, the virtue of virtues, and his *Centuries on Love* is a treatise in which Maximos discusses a trajectory of the acquisition of virtues toward the acquisition of the virtue of virtues—love. For Maximos, the human is created to learn how to love and is in constant battle against that which weakens the capacity to love.

Virtue, for Maximos, is not a building of character for character's sake; it is not a state of being where one displays one's virtues like badges of honor; it is not simply the basis for proper moral decision making. The acquisition of virtue is the precondition for enabling the human capacity to love: "Scripture calls the virtues ways, and the best of all the virtues is love" (4.74).[31] Virtues are necessary for the learning and acquisition of love: "All the virtues assist the mind in the pursuit of divine love" (1.11).[32] Maximos does not restrict himself to only the four cardinal virtues—prudence, courage, temperance, and justice—but, consistent with the Eastern Christian patristic tradition, gives a wider catalog of virtues and vices that correspond to the three parts of the soul: the sensible, the irascible, and the rational. Particular virtues correspond to particular vices, insofar as each virtue is meant to neutralize a particular vice. The hermeneutical key to Maximos's complicated detailing of the relation of virtues and vices to the inner life of the human person and to human agency is "progress in the love of God" (2.14), which is measured ultimately by how one relates to others, especially those to whom one feels hatred or anger (1.71).[33] This particular definition of virtue, then, illuminates the full force and terrifying implications of Shay's idea of war leading to the "undoing of character." What is being undone is the human capacity to love and to receive love. When something like the berserk state "destroys the capacity for virtue,"[34] this destruction is not simply an evacuation of a "sense of being valued and of valuing anything,"[35] as Shay defines it; according to the description of how combat veterans relate to their family, neighbors, friends, and strangers, what is impaired is the capacity for authentic relationships marked by intimacy, trust, depth—love.

If virtues are embodied deification, the precondition for the learning of the virtue of virtues, which is love, then vice impairs the capacity for love. Maximos explains that "the purpose of divine Providence is to unify by an upright faith and spiritual love those who have been separated in diverse ways by vice" (4.17).[36] He elaborates that the "vice that separates you from your brother" includes "envying and being envied, hurting or being hurt, insulting or being insulted, and suspicious thoughts" (4.18–19).[37] Maximos is also astute enough to know that vice breeds vice; that is, that it is not simply the doing of vice that harms the capacity for love, it is being "viced upon": "The things which destroy love are these: dishonor, damage, slander (either against faith or against conduct), beatings, blows, and so forth, whether these happen to oneself or to one's relatives or friends" (4.81).[38] Vices produce and *are* such affective emotions as anger, hatred, and fear. Throughout this treatise, Maximos is attempting both to advise and to exhort a form of training that can overcome what are ultimately corrosive emotions, no matter how justified.

Also relevant to illuminating the "undoing of character" that war and violence potentially effect on a combat veteran is Maximos's discussion of the relation of images to the cultivation of vices and virtues. According to Maximos, what often incites and reifies a vice is images or thoughts that present themselves to the human person. Maximos explains that "love and self-mastery keep the mind detached from things and from their representations. . . . The whole war of the monk against demons is to separate the passions from the representations" (3.39; 3.41).[39] He adds that the "virtues separate the mind from the passions" (3.44).[40] Maximos also warns, "[When] insulted by someone or offended in any matter, then beware of angry thoughts, lest by distress they sever you from charity and place you in the region of hatred" (1.29).[41] "Detachment," for Maximos, "is a peaceful state of the soul in which it becomes resistant to vice" (1.36).[42] In terms of images that incite vice, this resistance is not a removal of the image, but disabling of its power to evoke such feelings of anger or hatred. To be virtuous is to experience in the face of images the emotions and desires that cultivate authentic relationships.

The problem that veterans with PTSD often face is that the images they confront, whether real or imaginary, trigger the emotion of impending fear, which leads to other negative emotions, such as anger-turned-to-rage and hatred, which then lead to a withdrawal from the other. The relation between images of impending threat and certain emotions and desires is reminiscent of St. Anthony the Great's encounter with images of the demonic; Anthony's struggle was against those images and their potential impact on the passions.[43] In this sense, the acquisition of virtue has something to do with the affective response to certain images, either real or imaginary. Virtue is not the elimination of images—how could one forget a friend's head being blown off?—but, rather, an attenuation of the power of demonic images on the landscape of one's emotions and desires, a landscape that forms the basis for the shape of relationality. In combat trauma, the redoing of virtue does not mean forgetting one's friend's head being blown off; rather, healing is about acquiring a new kind of memory of the events.[44] The acquisition of virtue would be an affective response to the images of war and violence that does not destroy relationships but opens the path for a breakthrough of love.

If the ascetics of war is an undoing of good character, which is the destruction of the capacity for authentic relationships, then the challenge for combat veterans is to engage in the tasks that lead to a redoing of virtue, which would increase their capacity for such relationships and for the embodied presence of the divine—theosis. Maximos discusses the virtues in terms of the power to counter particular vices.[45] Insofar as virtue is related to love, virtues build relationships of intimacy, trust, compassion, empathy, friendship, sharing, caring, humility, and honesty: all that is apparently threatened by the experience of vice. Insofar as virtues build proper relationships while vices destroy such relationships, the ascetics of theosis must be relevant to those attempting to undo the ascetics of war. According to Maximos, the acquisition of virtue is a training realized in and through certain practices that forms both the body and the inner life (soul) of the human person; virtue is a wiring of the self as openness to love. Thinking about the healing of combat trauma along the lines of practices and virtues provides a way for intersecting the psychological literature on trauma and the ascetical/mystical tradition on the formation of virtue. The connecting category is that of practices, since the combat veteran must engage in a new kind of ascetics, one that replaces the ascetics of war in order to combat the demonic images impacting his relationships to self and others.

Although there are many practices that enable the acquisition of virtue and thus the capacity for relationships of trust, intimacy, depth, and love, I will restrict my focus to one that is key to any redoing of virtue in both the psychological and the ascetical/mystical literature—the practice of truth telling or confession. In the Christian tradition, truth telling is primarily associated with the sacrament of confession understood forensically as fulfilling a contractual obligation to tell a priest one's sins before forgiveness is granted, or with the moral obligation not to lie. When speaking about truth telling as a practice that enables the capacity for love through the acquisition of virtues, I am not referring strictly to either a forensic understanding of the sacrament of confession or the moral obligation to tell the truth. Speaking certain truths in the presence of another or other persons has the power both to reconfigure the relationships in which such a truth is spoken and to produce an affective effect on the landscape of one's emotions and desires. Truths spoken hover in the midst of a relationship with the power to affect both the speaker and the listener(s). It is not uncommon to think that one can protect oneself from a traumatic experience by simply attempting to forget it or by not verbalizing it to others. The irony is that only through a verbal acknowledgment or recognition, which cannot be revoked, can the power of the traumatic image be mitigated. It is also the case that the affective result of truth telling as an event depends on the listener, who can either use the spoken truth to iconically presence the divine toward mitigating the power of the effects of violence, or can image the demonic by adding violence to violence. In short, the event of truth telling to another is an iconically charged event, which can potentially presence either the divine or the demonic.[46]

Both Jonathan Shay and Judith Herman, from their experience with trauma victims, attest to the basic truth that healing cannot occur until the trauma victim can begin to speak about the traumatic events. Truth telling in and of itself is not sufficient for healing, but it is absolutely necessary. Also, truth telling of trauma cannot begin until a safe and secure environment is established for the trauma victim, what Herman refers to as stage one of recovery.[47] Once such a secure and safe environment is established, it is absolutely essential that the victim of combat trauma speak the truth about the traumatic event and reconstruct a narrative of the event itself.

To even speak the truth about the trauma of war can be interpreted as an embodiment of the virtue of humility, in the sense that making oneself vulnerable is requisite to opening the self to loving and being loved. The sixth-century Syriac Christian ascetic Dorotheos of Gaza analogizes the Christian life to building a house:

> The roof is charity, which is the completion of virtue as the roof completes the house. After the roof comes the crowning of the dwelling place . . . [i.e., railings around the flat roof]. . . . The crown is humility. For that is the crown and guardian of all virtues. As each virtue needs humility for its acquisition—and in that sense we said each stone is laid with the mortar of humility—so also the perfection of all the virtues is humility.[48]

As Shay declares, "The fact that these veterans can speak at all of their experience is a major sign of healing."[49] The reconstruction of the narrative must also be in the context of other persons, in the form of a community. Shay argues that the "healing of trauma depends upon the communalization of the trauma—being able to safely tell the story to someone who is listening and who can be trusted to retell it truthfully to others in the community."[50] The mitigation of the demonic, thus, depends on truth, even if such a truth has to do with the experience of the demonic; and this truth needs to be "communalized," told and *listened to* by others.

Over the years, Shay has discovered that such communalization is most effective when the community itself consists of those who know, either directly or indirectly, the effects of combat trauma. As in meetings of Alcoholics Anonymous, the healing power of truth telling depends not simply on telling the truth, but on *who* is listening.[51] The rebound effect of truth telling depends on the symbolic/iconic significance of the one listening. The healing power of this communalization of trauma is evident not simply in face-to-face encounter, but in a community-email conversation among Vietnam veterans.[52] The symbolic/iconic role of the listener is so important, it leads Shay to argue that

> restoration . . . of the capacity for social trust happens only in community. This simple and seemingly innocent statement is actually quite subversive, because it casts doubt upon a great deal of what mental health professionals do (following the cultural and economic model of medicine), how they find their value in the world, how the

mental health workplace is organized, and how power is used there. In fact, the overall effect of this simple statement is to push mental health professionals off of center stage in the drama of recovery from trauma, and to place them in the wings of stagehands.[53]

In the end, the veterans heal each other.[54] Theologically, the veterans are iconically charged to presence the divine to each other, even in the midst of, and because of, their shared suffering.

The affective effect of truth telling might also require a listener beyond a community of combat veterans. Shay reports: "[Our] clinical team has encouraged many of the veterans we work with to avail themselves of the sacrament of penance. When a veteran does not already know a priest he trusts to hear his confession, we have suggested priests who understand enough about combat neither to deny that he has anything to feel guilty about nor to recoil in revulsion and send him away without the sacrament."[55] What this need for a form of truth telling beyond the community of combat veterans reveals is that the experience of forgiveness needs another kind of listener other than the empathetic combat veteran. Although it is the same ascetical practice, truth telling to distinctive listeners does different kinds of work on the landscape of one's emotions and desires. The chances are very high that the ascetics of war will lead some to engage in practices in which there is a felt need for forgiveness. Tom Mathews's father felt this need, as did John the Iraqi war veteran mentioned above, who could barely speak about how combat in Iraq led to killing of kids who he realized "could be your kids."[56] On the cosmic scale, other combat veterans cannot iconically symbolize that forgiveness; cannot be a kind of listener that enables the realization of that forgiveness as an affective event in the combat veteran. Someone like a priest is iconically charged to perform that role.

The importance of truth telling in the redoing of virtue only highlights how the military culture of denial and repression of the combat experience is corrosive. When mistakes were made and innocent people were killed rather than the "enemy," the military thought it was helping by covering for the soldiers, who were told that it would be "all right." Shay relays one story in which the soldiers involved in such a mistake were actually given medals as a way of covering up for the mistake.[57]

When friends are lost, soldiers are told to "stuff those tears," or "to get even." Whereas in ancient cultures, dead bodies, including those of the enemy, were treated with respect, the US military had no mechanism in Vietnam for memorializing the dead. Ancient cultures also had rituals for reintegrating soldiers back into society after battle.[58] Such rituals did not depend on whether the battle was just or not. American soldiers return from war with little to no fanfare, trying to figure out what to do next.[59] What's especially egregious is how the US military has not provided sufficient resources for combat veterans showing symptoms of PTSD, often making difficult the availability of such resources because of budgetary constraints. Although improvements have been made, what pervades military culture, and American culture in general, is a Pelagian-like "suck it up" attitude, with no realization of how a combat veteran is ultimately in the grip of the demonic until engaging in ascetic practices that undo the effects of war and violence.

It is encouraging, ironic, and a little troubling to contemplate how an ascetics of virtue in the form of fostering a community of people who learn to trust each other, who form bonds of affection through telling personal stories, who become friends, has the power to mitigate the effects of the ascetics of war. Beyond the debates over whether Christians should think about criteria for judging decisions to go to war, which this essay has not necessarily dismissed as illegitimate, the formation of communities of virtue both before and after combat has the power to mitigate the effects of violence on any one of the members in the community itself, especially if that community of virtue presupposes an open space for truth telling.[60]

There is an even deeper theological significance to the necessity of truth telling as part of an ascetic of virtue that undoes the ascetic of war. First, it reveals that God meets someone in the truth of her concrete, historical situation. In the case of combat trauma, it is not a matter of first undoing the effects of war and then going off to the desert to achieve theosis; undoing the effects of violence is itself the desert in which combat veterans find themselves in their struggle to (re)experience the presence of the divine. The ascetical struggle toward divine-human communion is entrenched in a particular history and a particular body, which then demands the virtue of discernment on the part of the community of combat veterans, the mental health professional, the priest, even family and friends in order to extricate the combat veteran from the grip of the demonic. As Shay argues, "Modern combat is a condition of enslavement and torture."[61] The formation of communities of virtue, which presuppose truth telling, mitigates and breaks the cycle of violence. Second, sin committed and sin that is done to us cannot be forgotten, repressed, or denied. It is part of the fabric of the universe that the truth must be recognized; otherwise it will haunt us in other forms. It is only by the integration of the truth of sin into our narrative that it can then be neutralized in its effect. In the end, God is the God of truth, which includes the unique and particular truths of our narratives; if God is truth, then God is found in the verbal recognition of the truths of our narrative, no matter how horrific those truths may be. Although "neither death, nor life, nor angels, nor principalities, nor things present, nor things to come, nor powers, nor height, nor depth, nor anything else in all creation, will be able to separate us from the love of God in Christ Jesus our Lord" (Rom. 8:38–39 RSV), to love and be loved by God and neighbor depends ultimately on the practice and virtue of honesty, which includes the courage to acknowledge and accept the truths of our own narrative.

NOTES

1. George Dragas, "Justice and Peace in the Orthodox Tradition," in *Justice, Peace and the Integrity of Creation: Insights from Orthodoxy*, ed. Gennadios Limouris (Geneva: WCC Publications, 1990), 42.

2. "The Teaching on Peace in the Fathers," in *Wholeness of Faith and Life: Orthodox Christian Ethics*, part 1, *Patristic Ethics*, ed. Stanley S. Harakas (Brookline, MA: Holy Cross Orthodox Press, 1999), 154. The bracketed Latin phrases are in the source.

3. Ibid., 156–57.

4. For such examples of self-identification, see George Demacopoulos and Aristotle Papanikolaou, eds., *Orthodox Constructions of the West* (Bronx, NY: Fordham University Press, 2013).

5. Alexander F. C. Webster and Darrell Cole, *The Virtue of War: Reclaiming the Classic Christian Traditions East and West* (Salisbury, MA: Regina Orthodox Press, 2004).

6. Ibid., 118.

7. Ibid.

8. In terms of unequivocal support for a decision to go to war and for the soldiers who fought in a war, World War II is the exception. The only other war in which soldiers received such unequivocal support was the War of 1812. In no other war in American history, including the Revolutionary War, were American soldiers treated as they were after World War II. For details, see Jonathan Shay, *Odysseus in America: Combat Trauma and the Trials of Homecoming* (New York: Scribner, 2002), 154.

9. Tom Mathews, *Our Fathers' War: Growing Up in the Shadow of the Greatest Generation* (New York: Broadway Books, 2005), 268–69; emphasis added.

10. Ibid., 269.

11. See the HBO documentary *Wartorn*, directed by John Alpert, Ellen Godsenberg Kent, and Matthew O'Neil, aired November 11, 2011, produced by HBO Documentary Films in association with Attaboy Films.

12. For the Vietnam War, see especially Jonathan Shay, *Achilles in Vietnam: Combat Trauma and the Undoing of Character* (New York: Scribner, 1994); Shay, *Odysseus in America*. For the wars in Iraq and Afghanistan, as well as Vietnam, see Nancy Sherman, *The Untold War: Inside the Hearts, Minds, and Souls of Our Soldiers* (New York: W. W. Norton & Company, 2010). For the most recent war in Iraq, listen to the radio show *This American Life*, episode 359, "Life after Death," July 18, 2008, http://www.thisamericanlife.org/radio-archives/episode/359/life-after-death. For the existential effects of soldiering, see Lt. Col. Dave Grossman, *On Killing: The Psychological Cost of Learning to Kill in War and Society*, rev. ed. (New York: Back Bay Books, 2009).

13. Jonathan Shay, *Achilles in Vietnam*, 179.

14. Ibid., 168; emphasis added. In *Odysseus in America*, 166, Shay distinguishes between simple and complex PTSD. On trauma, see also Judith Herman's classic, *Trauma and Recovery: The Aftermath of Violence from Domestic Abuse to Political Terror* (New York: Basic Books, 1992).

15. Shay, *Achilles in Vietnam*, 169.

16. One day in August 2010 at 4:00 a.m., a rock was thrown through the window of my home randomly by teenagers (confirmed by a neighbor who heard them outside his window). A few days later, and probably unrelated, the doorbell was rung at my home at 9:00 p.m., and when I opened the door, no one was there. A few days after experiencing those two events, I was awoken during the night by a dream in which I heard the sound of a police radio, which was vividly clear, and by another dream in which I heard the sound of a crystal-clear doorbell. In addition to this, for at least a month, I was "jumpy"—I made sure that

all the lights around the house were turned on in the middle of the night, I added a timer to the light inside the house so it could turn on in the middle of the night so as to deter any would-be rock throwers, I would wake up frequently in the middle of the night and check outside the window, close all the shades in the evening, and obsessively check all the doors before going to sleep. I am absolutely in no way comparing my experience to combat; but if something like a rock being thrown through a window can cause one to be mildly symptomatic, I can only imagine the long-term effects of experiencing the incessant violence of guns and bombs. This point is relevant not simply to war, but to those living in violent urban environments.

17. Shay, *Achilles in Vietnam*, 165–66. For the American Psychiatric Association's official diagnostic criteria for PTSD, see 166–67.

18. Shay, *Odysseus in America*, 166.

19. Shay, *Achilles in Vietnam*, 80. In a brilliant analysis of the *Iliad*, Shay demonstrates how Achilles went berserk after the death of his friend, Patroklos.

20. Ibid., 96.

21. Ibid., 82.

22. Ibid., 93.

23. *This American Life*, "Life after Death."

24. Ibid.

25. Ibid., 98; emphasis original. See also Shay, *Odysseus in America*, 149.

26. Shay, *Achilles in Vietnam*, 98.

27. Shay, *Odysseus in America*, 150.

28. Ibid., 150–51.

29. For many such stories, see Shay, *Achilles in Vietnam*; Shay, *Odysseus in America*; Sherman, *Untold War*, especially 231. Also listen to *This American Life*, "Life after Death."

30. Shay, *Achilles at War*, xiii; emphasis original. See his discussion of the ruining of Achilles' character, 28–35. See also 169–87.

31. George C. Berthold, trans., *Maximos the Confessor: Selected Writings*, The Classics of Western Spirituality (Mahwah, NJ: Paulist Press, 1985), 83.

32. Ibid., 36.

33. Ibid., 48 and 42. See also 37 (1.15).

34. Shay, *Achilles in Vietnam*, 86.

35. Ibid., 85.

36. Berthold, *Maximos the Confessor*, 77. On the divisiveness of vice, see also 1.55; 1.58.

37. Ibid., 77.

38. Ibid., 84.

39. Ibid., 66. See also 41 (1.63), 57 (2.74), 58 (2.84), 63 (3.20), 74 (3.97).

40. Ibid., 67.

41. Ibid., 38.

42. Ibid., 39.

43. See Athanasius of Alexandria, *Life of Antony and the Letter to Marcellinus,* trans. Robert C. Gregg (New York: Paulist Press, 1980).

44. As John, from *This American Life*, "Life after Death," poignantly confesses, "You can't forget."

45. On linking virtues and vices, but in a much less coherent form, see also John Climacus's *The Ladder of Divine Ascent*, trans. Colm Luibheid and Norman Russell (New York: Paulist Press, 1982).

46. For a more detailed account of truth telling, see Aristotle Papanikolaou, "Liberating Eros: Confession and Desire," *Journal of the Society of Christian Ethics* 26, no. 1 (2006): 115–36; "Honest to God: Confession and Desire," in *Thinking through Faith: New Perspectives from Orthodox Scholars*, ed. Aristotle Papanikolaou and Elizabeth H. Prodromou (Crestwood, NY: St. Vladimir's Seminary Press, 2008), 219–46.

47. Shay, *Odysseus in America*, 168; Shay is drawing on Herman's *Trauma and Recovery*.

48. Dorotheos of Gaza, *Discourses and Sayings*, trans. Eric P. Wheeler (Kalamazoo, MI: Cistercian Publications, 1977), 203. Earlier, Dorotheos identifies humility as the mortar of the house of the soul, mortar that "is composed from the earth and lies under the feet of all. Any virtue existing without humility is no virtue at all" (203).

49. Shay, *Achilles in Vietnam*, xxii.

50. Ibid., 4.

51. On truth telling in Alcoholic Anonymous, see Papanikolaou, "Liberating Eros."

52. Shay, *Odysseus in America*, 180–81.

53. Ibid., 162.

54. Ibid., 166, 168.

55. Ibid., 153–54.

56. See *This American Life*, "Life after Death."

57. Shay, *Achilles in Vietnam*, 3–4.

58. Shay, *Odysseus in America*, 152.

59. See James Dao, "After Combat, the Unexpected Perils of Coming Home," *New York Times*, May 28, 2011, http://www.nytimes.com/2011/05/29/us/29soldiers.html?_r=1&emc=eta1.

60. On the question of prevention, Shay has argued that the effects of war could be mitigated if the military changed its way of training and deploying

soldiers. If soldiers were to train in groups, be deployed in the same groups, take leave with the same group of people, and return home as a group, such a communal support system would be effective both in preventing and treating combat trauma. Although there are not official statistics of World War II combat veterans who suffered from PTSD, one of the reasons why one hears less about the traumatic effects of war on World War II veterans, in addition to the code of silence, could be that soldiers were never separated from the men with whom they trained. In the Vietnam War, soldiers were deployed individually, often forced to integrate as the new guy, went on leave individually, and returned home alone. See Shay, *Achilles in Vietnam*, 195–204.

61. Ibid., 160.

CHAPTER 2

EXPOSING THE STATE
OF THE QUESTION

*A Case Study of American Orthodox
Responses to the 1999 War in Kosovo*

ANDREW WALSH

As American bombs fell on Belgrade and other Yugoslav cities, one thousand protesters marched down Pittsburgh's Liberty Avenue. The *Pittsburgh Post-Gazette* reported on March 29, 1999, that the marchers were softly singing an Orthodox hymn: "O Lord, save thy people and bless thine inheritance. Grant victories to the Orthodox Christians over their adversaries." Most marchers, the newspaper said, were Serbian Americans, and the line of the march moved from the downtown headquarters of the Serbian National Federation to Pittsburgh's federal building. But, considering the circumstances of the American-led NATO intervention to prevent the Yugoslav government's forced eviction of one million Albanians from Kosovo, which Orthodox Christians needed victories granted to them, and who were their adversaries?

In an effort to clarify what Orthodox Christians believe and teach about war and peace, it might prove valuable to examine a single case of war and Orthodox reactions to it. This chapter will, therefore, examine the reaction of Orthodox Christians in America to the 1999 intervention in Kosovo. The war included a fifty-eight-day bombing campaign against the Yugoslav government which killed about two thousand Serb civilians and caused major economic and infrastructure damage in Serbia. By means of strategic bombing, the Clinton administration eventually achieved its stated goal, forcing the Yugoslav government to abandon its efforts to drive Albanians out of Kosovo. The NATO bombings, however, were bitterly criticized throughout the Orthodox world. Patriarch Bartholomew of Constantinople issued a widely reported appeal "on bended knee" for a halt to the bombing. The Greek, Russian, and Romanian primates issued similar statements. The British magazine *The New Statesman* on May 31 carried a headline "In Cyprus, Even Pizza Is Pro-Serb."

The war for Kosovo crowned a decade of bloody war in the territory of Marshall Tito's Yugoslavia, which disintegrated into warring regions during the course of four pulses of warfare: a brief struggle in Slovenia in 1992; more serious and protracted warfare in Croatia from 1992 to 1995; a hellish, multicombatant civil war in Bosnia from 1992 to 1995; and Serbia's long struggle to hold on to Kosovo, which began with a crackdown on the Albanian majority in 1990 and ended with the collapse of Serb power in June 1999. By the close of the decade, it was clear that the greatest losers were the Serbs, hundreds of thousands of whom were forced from their homes by warfare in Croatia, Bosnia, and, lastly, Kosovo.

In the judgment of many, each of these debacles was initiated by aggressive actions by Slobodan Milosevic's rump Yugoslav government. Other assessments distribute blame more generally—including onto the United States and other NATO countries. But during the 1990s, in most journalistic accounts in the United States and Europe, the Serb name was besmirched, connected to authoritarian repression, death squads, massive ethnic cleansing, concentration camps, ritualized humiliations and violence against women and children, even large-scale massacres. Fairly or not, the Serbian Orthodox Church was frequently charged with providing a hypernationalist ideology that justified Serb oppression and atrocities, and many of its leaders seemed to consort openly with ruthless warlords. Beyond question, in the hands of many Serb combatants the symbols of the Orthodox faith were totems of war.

In March 1999, American newspapers and broadcast networks were full of reports of the efforts of Serbian Americans (and other Orthodox) to respond to the challenge of an American war against what was, at least ostensibly, an Orthodox people. Over the next few months an immense amount of information about the Serbian Church and about the ambivalence of Orthodox Americans (especially those of Serb descent) in the face of the US decision to smash Yugoslav power outside Serbia washed through the media. Some of this information worked to correct common mistaken assumptions about the Serbian Church's support for the Milosevic regime and for ethnic cleaning in Kosovo. For example, Steven Erlanger's June 14, 1999, article in the *New York Times* reported that monks from the Orthodox monastery at Decani, in western Kosovo, had systematically risked their lives to rescue Albanian neighbors, as retreating Serb paramilitaries and troops evicted Albanians and burned their homes. "They are the best people you can ever see," Venera Lokaj, an Albanian, told Erlanger. "They are people of God. They heard Decani was burning and they came to search for people. They found us in the open, with everything burning, and they told us, 'We are blessed to find you alive. Please be reasonable, and come with us. Please come to the monastery.'"

But in the United States, journalists, especially in the first days of the war, often observed scenes that focused pretty much exclusively on Serbian American grief and resentment about the American bombing. David Welna's March 29 report on National Public Radio's *Morning Edition* described a weeping congregation at Holy Resurrection Serbian Orthodox Cathedral on Chicago's Far Northwest Side. The cathedral's pastor, Father Dennis Pavicovic, was heard from his pulpit. "All of us who gather here come with heavy hearts, laden with sadness, with tragedy, with frustration, with anger, even with hostility." Welna then reported that "the third-generation Serbian American priest implores God to protect the Serbs, whether, as he puts it, they're in the foxholes or down in their basements during air strikes. Serbia, he warns, is being crucified. Not once during the two-hour service is there any mention of the atrocities reported to have been carried out against the mostly Muslim ethnic Albanians in Kosovo."

In many American cities, local Serbian Orthodox priests were giving lessons in history—usually history as perceived by Serbs—to journalists. "The Very Rev. Jovan Todorovich leaned forward in his chair and, through a thick accent of his homeland, lamented the slaughter of 77,000 Serbs in Kosovo at the hands of the Turks in 1389," Michael Zuckoff of the *Boston Globe* reported on April 8, in a story on the Serbian community in Merrillville, Indiana. "Todorovich told the story as though it had happened the night before, and if people only knew it, they would realize that NATO is bombing the wrong side." The priest said, "Why are we the enemy? Why are we the pariah of the Balkans? Kosovo was ours. Kosovo is ours, and Mr. Clinton better register this: Kosovo will remain ours one way or another." Zuckoff reported that Todorovich's church was "ringing its bells throughout daylight hours since the bombing began, in sadness and solidarity. "I'm trying to be forgiving, to have compassion for the Albanians, for everyone. But I think of Kosovo and it starts digging inside me."

Similar stories appeared in newspapers in Milwaukee, Cleveland, St. Louis, Philadelphia, Denver, Boston, Orlando, Houston, and Baltimore, with reporters stopping to check in with priests and congregants, almost all of whom were having trouble summoning compassion for the Albanians, too. Sudharsan Raghavan of the *Philadelphia Inquirer* had the savvy to check with both Albanian Orthodox and Serbian Orthodox churches in his city and found that both congregations were thinking about Christ's crucifixion and its meaning in Kosovo, but reported that the churches drew different conclusions about who was playing the metaphorical part of the Romans. For the Albanian Orthodox, it was the Serbs. For the Philadelphia Serbs, it was the Clinton administration.

In this first, and almost wholly reactive, phase of response, questions were coming to priests and others at the congregational level. The Orthodox hierarchy, intelligentsia, and policy leaders were not trying very hard to offer a distinctively Orthodox interpretation of the situation. At the end of March, that began to shift as Orthodox leaders began to intervene publicly in an attempt to shape American policy. The first sally was made by Archbishop Spyridon, the leader of the Greek Archdiocese of America, who wrote President Clinton, calling on both the US and Yugoslav governments to suspend both bombings and military action during a proposed two-week truce period that would cover both Western and Eastern Holy Weeks. The Greek Archdiocese also mobilized the National Council of Churches, whose president, Rev. Joan Brown Campbell, backed the idea of an Easter cease-fire and new negotiations. These appeals focused on the avoidance of violence and the vulnerability of civilians in Serbia, and did not take sides in the conflict between Serbs and Kosovar Albanians.

On March 31, a group of Serbian priests and Bishop Mitrofan of the church's Eastern Diocese issued their own appeal, emphasizing the justice of Serbian claims to Kosovo.

> We are in total solidarity with the suffering Serbian people under attack and oppose vigorously the aggressive actions of NATO. The bombing must stop and the Serbian people be permitted to pursue peace in the sacred land [Kosovo], which has always been and will always be theirs. . . . The blood of Serbian saints soaked the sacred ground of Kosovo centuries ago. The saints are intercessors before our Lord at this time. The justice and mercy of God will prevail in the end.

Writing in the April 3 *Hartford Courant* and quoting from the appeal, Gerald Renner noted that the clergy's statement

> made no reference to Milosevic's responsibility in provoking the crisis in Kosovo. His Serbian forces have killed an unknown number of people, including women and children, and forced tens of thousands of Albanian Muslims from their homes. It does say, however, that the church has denounced the bombing and atrocities which have occurred and prays around the clock for peace to come. Concern exists for the many thousands of people who have lost their homes, for those who have died, who have been injured, and live in fear every moment of the day.

Serge Schmemann of the *New York Times* entered the discussion on April 4, noting that the NATO bombing was widely condemned in Eastern Europe, where complaints of Western European and American "hypocrisy and condescension" were increasing. "Again and again the argument is heard that the West is not even aware of Albanian actions against Serbian Kosovars in the recent past, or that NATO did nothing to help the Kurds in Turkey, or the Tutsis in Rwanda. There is fury that in its simplistic faith in the efficacy of bombing, the West is only consolidating Mr. Milosevic's power and demonizing the entire Serbian nation."

"What irritates the Greeks is the unfairness of it, the disproportionality, that the other point of view is not heard," said the Reverend Robert Stephanopoulos, dean of Holy Trinity Greek Orthodox Cathedral in New York. "There is a sense that the Orthodox are quickly stereotyped and quickly demonized," said the Reverend Leonid Kishkovsky, ecumenical officer of the Orthodox Church in America. What was alarming, he added, was that the demonstrators in Moscow, Athens, or Belgrade included not only ultranationalists, but apparently average young people. Even among the most pro-Western Russians and Serbs, he said, there was a growing resentment against Washington's approach. "It worries me that this could be the beginning of a process that will lead to a new polarization," he said. "Once again, between East and West."[1]

The Clinton administration swept aside this advice to stop the bombing and condescend less. When Pope John Paul II issued his own Easter appeal for a cease-fire, President Clinton responded. "We are determined to stay united and to persist until we prevail. It is not enough for Mr. Milosevic to say that his forces will cease-fire in a Kosovo denied its freedom and devoid of its people."[2] NATO, in fact, brought in more war planes and increased its bombing in April.

The result in America was a lot of coverage of unhappy Serbs at worship on Easter. "Warfare in Yugoslavia Casts Cloud over Easter for Orthodox Christians," noted a headline in the *Buffalo News*. "Area Serbs Mark the Holiday with Sadness and Fear," headlined the *Cleveland Plain Dealer*. "Portland Serbs Struggle with 'Worst' Easter," commented the *Portland Oregonian*. The *Boston Globe*'s Orthodox Easter story on April 12 quoted Greek Orthodox Metropolitan Methodios's sermon in Worcester. "We are disillusioned by a failed American diplomacy, and an immoral foreign policy, bereft of ethical and moral standards," Methodios complained. "On his holy cross of pain and love, our Lord taught that violence cannot be fought with violence." The *Globe* then quoted the rebuttal of the pastor of St. Mary's Assumption Albanian Orthodox Church in Worcester: "Those are very beautiful sounding platitudes, but the fact remains that Serbians who are Orthodox . . . are not practicing the teachings of Christ. They are literally slaughtering, raping, and forcibly removing the Kosovars from their country."

At this stage of the crisis, American Orthodox leaders were making harsher statements about American foreign policy than they had ever uttered. And the seeming inability of Orthodox and Serbian American voices to address forthrightly the persecution of Albanians in Kosovo by Serbs was undercutting the credibility of the Orthodox defense of Serbs and Serbian Orthodoxy.

Two things changed this situation in April and May. The first was the emergence of a new spokesman for the Serbian Orthodox Church, a Cleveland priest named Irinej Dobrijevic, American by birth and education, but with ministerial experience in Belgrade during the 1990s.[3] Dobrijevic proved to be an effective speaker, especially in the give-and-take of cable television news talk shows, where he began to turn up frequently. On April 3, he appeared for the first time on a CNN evening program, where he defended the Serbian Church against the complaints of human rights activist Vanessa Redgrave. Calm and steady, Dobrijevic did something no Serb spokesman had yet done—he admitted that ethnic cleansing was taking place in Kosovo and he condemned it. He laid the entire blame on Slobodan Milosevic. He also vigorously defended the Serbian Church, and especially Patriarch Pavle and the Serb clergy in Kosovo.

> First of all, I must categorically state that the Serbian Orthodox Church, as any Orthodox Church, condemns any and all forms of violence, which includes the NATO bombing. It includes, also, the Milosevic government's enforcing these people to flee, and we are also joined by Archbishop Carey of the Anglican Church and his Holiness Pope John Paul II of the Catholic Church, who condemn any and all forms of violence, and both have joined the Orthodox primates in calling for a cease fire during Orthodox Christian holy days so that peace may be had.

After sparring with Redgrave, Dobrijevic explained that the NATO strikes followed on years of missed opportunities for Western democracies to support critics of the Milosevic regime, and in particular, he lamented the Western failure to support the Serbian Church's preferred solution to the Kosovo problem—cantonment that would leave the hundreds of ancient Serb churches and monasteries clustered in Kosovo surrounded by enough Serbs to prevent their abandonment or worse. Further, he argued that the NATO bombing didn't harm Milosevic; it harmed innocent Serb civilians. "I feel that the bombing is an equal evil to the human exodus that we are watching over our television screens. One cannot use violence and violent means to bring about a peaceful end and a peaceful solution. You see, if the bombs were meant to attack Milosevic and the military infrastructure, they're not doing that. They're attacking the civilian infrastructure and they're destroying many, many innocent lives."

Dobrijevic appeared on April 12 on Jesse Jackson's CNN program, where he pushed hard for diplomatic effort to end the fighting. That appearance may have led to the second major turn, Jesse Jackson's mission to Belgrade to persuade the Milosevic government to release three American POWs. Organized by Jackson and the National Council of Churches, a nineteen-member mission of Americans included Protestant, Catholic, Muslim, and Jewish clerics, but was weighted toward American Orthodox leaders, including Dobrijevic, Bishop Mitrofan, Bishop Dimitrios Couchell of the Greek Archdiocese, and Fr. Leonid Kishkovsky of the OCA. Through Bishop Mitrofan's mediation, the delegation met with Patriarch Pavle and other members of the Serbian Synod, and the church's disagreements with Milosevic and opposition to his violent policies were publicly discussed. A good measure of the rapid refinement of the defense of the Serbian case (say, in comparison with Serbian clergy statements of late March) came in an interview Mitrofan gave to the *Pittsburgh Post-Gazette* after his return from Belgrade on May 5.

Mitrofan told the *Post-Gazette*'s reporter Ann Rodgers-Melnick that ordinary Serbs on the street wanted to release the American POWs in order to encourage a negotiated settlement. "For his part, Mitrofan will continue to tell Americans that the Serbian Orthodox Church wants to respect the rights of Albanians in Kosovo and that the bombing is hurting only the ordinary people of Yugoslavia." Rodgers-Melnick then quoted Kishkovsky's account of the group's conversation with Slobodan Milosevic.

At one point, Milosevic complained bitterly about biased coverage by the Western media, particularly CNN, saying that the reports were full of anti-Serbian prejudice and propaganda. Kishkovsky replied that, while it was true that Americans were not hearing about the attacks on Serbs by the Kosovo Liberation Army, credible reports from other sources seemed to confirm the television accounts of official persecution of the Albanians. Furthermore, he said, his Serbian friends in Belgrade told him that Serbian television never showed images of the Albanian refugees.

The delegation's basic message to Milosevic was that "the situation was moving inexorably toward more bombing and military action. Releasing the three men might start a process [of negotiation], but . . . the process had to include early cessation of violence in Kosovo, commitment to a return by refugees, and a sign of accepting an international force," Kishkovsky said.

Writing on May 19 in the *Christian Century*, Kishkovsky and Joan Brown Campbell of the NCC returned to the theme of the Serbian Church's misunderstood role. "The witness for peace and justice given by Patriarch Pavel, a man of prayer, spiritual integrity, and moral vision, is a profile in spiritual courage. His witness against violence has been consistent from the beginning of the violent dissolution of Yugoslavia, through the war in Bosnia, and now, in conjunction with the conflict over Kosovo." Kishkovsky and Brown Campbell argued:

> It is not well known in the U.S. that the Serbian Orthodox bishop in Kosovo, Artemije, has for several years insisted that the conflict in Kosovo can be resolved only through free and honest dialogue between the ethnic communities in Yugoslavia. And this, he warned, has been impossible because the government in Belgrade, as a dictatorship, has blocked freedom and democracy in Yugoslavia, while in Kosovo acts of terrorism and a culture of violence have set the stage for escalating violence. Bishop Artemije is a man of Christian faith and ministry, not a man of political calculation.

The bombing ended on June 7, and the withdrawal of Serb forces—along with most of the Serb minority in Kosovo—began soon after. On June 16, the Serbian Synod of Bishops called for the replacement of the Milosevic government (which did not happen), and at the end of June

Patriarch Pavle traveled to Kosovo, largely abandoned by its Serb population, to give a speech on the tenth anniversary of Milosevic's "Field of Blackbirds" speech. Pavle was deeply agitated by the visible signs of destruction—dynamited mosques and the burned lintels of Albanian homes marked by crude painted crosses. At the Gracanica monastery Pavle uttered remarks subsequently held up by all defenders of the Serb Church's conduct in the 1990s. "If the only way to create a greater Serbia is by crime, then I do not accept that and let that Serbia disappear," Pavle said. "And also, if a lesser Serbia can only survive by crime, let it also disappear. And if all Serbs had to die and only I remained and I could survive only by crime, then I would not accept that—it would be better to die."[4]

Jim Forest, the leader of the Orthodox Peace Fellowship (OPF), jumped in to defend Pavle and the Serbian Church, penning a series of defenses in May, June, and July in publications ranging from *Touchstone* to *Sojourners* to the OPF's *In Communion*. Most carried a headline like "NOT the Church of Ethnic Cleansing: Serbian Orthodox Church Resisted Ultra-nationalism." In that *Sojourners* piece from the July–August 1999 issue, Forest argued that Tito's communist government had been "extraordinarily successful in its thirty-five-year struggle to marginalize the Orthodox Church" and that the church had to struggle to regain its footing in postcommunist Yugoslavia. "The art of enmity has for years given us a steady diet of images of evil Serbs, sometimes shown as cavemen, often dripping with blood, victimizing their neighbors," Forest wrote in the July 1999 *In Communion*. "Nor is it unusual to show the Serbian Orthodox Church playing the role of chaplain to the state and accomplice in Serbian war crimes, preacher of a nationalistic mythology which the faithful heard as a blessing to create, by any means necessary, a Greater Serbia."

This blizzard of protest produced a journalistic reaction—lengthy stories in the *Wall Street Journal* and the *New York Times* suggesting that the Serbian Church had a bigger problem with Milosevic than it was willing to admit in the wake of the Kosovo catastrophe. "When Mr. Milosevic rocketed to power 12 years ago, the then little-known Communist party official metamorphosed almost overnight into champion of the faithful and savior for a church seeking political redemption after more than 40 years of Communist rule," the *Journal*'s Andrew Higgins and Robert Block reported on June 24. "He vowed never to yield Kosovo,

90 percent ethnic Albanian and heavily Muslim, but the site of the Serbian church's most sacred shrines. Like many other priests, Bishop Amfilohje embraced Mr. Milosevic's nationalist policies. He cheered Serb wars for 'self-determination' first in Croatia, and later in Bosnia."

The *Journal* and the *Times* were not out so much to discredit Pavle or bishops like Artemije, but rather to point out that the church's hierarchy included many who supported Milosevic and his wars. Blane Harden of the *Times* noted on July 3 that many Serbian Church leaders did not want to trigger an extensive period of Serbian self-criticism. "Until the Patriarch began to speak out recently of the 'evil' he had seen in Kosovo, the focus of church criticism has not been that Mr. Milosevic's Government committed atrocities in trying to create a new Serbian empire but that it had not been successful in building that larger state." Bishop Atanasije, one of Pavle's assistants, told Harden, "We blame Milosevic not for trying to defend the nation, but for failing."

However, with memories of the eleven-week-long NATO bombing campaign fading, public discussion of the war faded, more or less at the same time that a continuing campaign of Albanian retaliatory attacks on Serb churches and monuments outside a few small Serb enclaves in Kosovo was carried on. With fewer friends than ever outside the Orthodox fold, the Serbian Church in America decided it had to summon the resources necessary to create a permanent advocate for Serbian causes. It assigned Fr. Irinej Dobrijevic to lead a newly created Office of External Affairs in Washington, DC. Within a few months, Dobrijevic was offering testimony to congressional committees, organizing political events, and delivering papers at international conferences and meetings. The chief focus of his efforts was the marshalling of Serbian American resources to attempt to block formal Kosovar independence, to call attention to the continuing Albanian attacks on Serb churches, monasteries, and monuments in Kosovo, and to defend the reputation and honor of the Serbian Church.

So, perhaps the most important direct consequence of American Orthodox discussion of the war for Kosovo was the decision to try to create a stronger political voice, at least for Serbian Orthodox interests. "Understanding Washington and our need for institutional presence is straightforward," Dobrijevic wrote in the Serbian Unity Congress's online newsletter *Communique* in July 2003. "In our Capital, meetings transpire on a daily basis among established institutions. We Serbs have a clear choice: either to interact and have our consistent, proactive voice heard, or merely react and suffer repercussions." He continued:

> The Office of External Affairs of the Serbian Orthodox Church in the USA and Canada (OEA) was opened in June 1999 in response to the overwhelming reaction of our Serbian faithful and secular organizations to the NATO bombing of Yugoslavia. In the absence of diplomatic representation, the Church was deemed a most credible witness for the silenced Serb voice. The Church, in traditional Orthodox nations, assumes representation of its people until political solutions are restored. . . . Over the span of four years, the OEA has carried out many functions: liaised with key Serbian organizations here and in the Fatherland and convened Serbian-American Leadership Conferences, putting a "face to a cause," interacted with human rights groups and institutions monitoring international religious freedom, affected [*sic*] vital changes in diplomatic language, secured funding for repatriation, humanitarian aid, and media assistance in Kosovo; and helped pass a resolution on post-NATO environmental degradation. By opening lines of communication with governments, think tanks, non-governmental and faith-based organizations, the OEA secured a solid and effective operational base in Washington.

Dobrijevic wrote the 2003 column to announce the realignment of Serb and Orthodox representation in Washington. He said he expected that the Standing Conference of Canonical Orthodox Bishops (SCOBA) would soon open its own Washington office. It would handle Orthodox matters, while the Serbian Unity Congress's new office would keep an eye on Serbian affairs. Although a search for a director was announced in 2003, SCOBA never opened a Washington office. In 2010, SCOBA was dissolved and replaced by the Assembly of Canonical Orthodox Bishops of North and Central America.[5] Neither before SCOBA's dissolution nor after the establishment of the Assembly of Bishops has a Washington office been opened.

During the brief 1999 war itself, strikingly little theological discussion took place among American Orthodox. Perhaps that is not surprising—theological reflection does not follow the daily news cycle. But there were soon signs of active reflection. As early as August 1999, Fr. Alexander Garklavs published a rather anguished analysis called "Orthodox Christianity and Nationality" on the Orthodox Church in America's Diocese of New York and New Jersey website. "This is a difficult topic! It is exceedingly complex and unpleasantly sensitive. The tragic events in Yugoslavia are horrible manifestations of inhuman evil and destructive political ambitions, in which all participating parties are guilty. In addition, for Orthodox Christians the Kosovo conflict brings out deep and conflicting emotions. Somewhat indifferent to the injustice going on in Kosovo before the bombing, we Orthodox became acutely concerned when NATO began its immoral bombing campaign," Garklavs wrote.

Garklavs's argument teetered back and forth, offering abundant evidence both for the importance and sacredness of the nation in Orthodox eyes, on the one hand, and for Orthodox reverence for universal and irenic human values, on the other. (Orthodoxy venerates both soldier saints and passion bearers—those who accept death rather than react violently to threats, Garklavs observed.) But he finally found the courage to admit, "We cannot deny that among Orthodox Christian people there are strong nationalistic feelings. Often this nationalism is a blind wormhole leading to folly, fanaticism, and destruction. Orthodox Christians, like Christians in general, need to remember the Gospel-inspired attitudes of the early Church regarding the kingdoms of this world and the 'Kingdom not of this world'; there is simply no other pattern for a life that is simple, good, and pure."

The problem was not that the church was hopelessly conflicted about nationalism and its ambitions, Garklavs argued. It was, rather, that too many nominal Christians spoke and acted in the name of Christ. "The present crisis in Yugoslavia is not due to anything that is, properly speaking, Orthodox Christianity. It is due, in part, to the sinful actions of some people who pretend they are Orthodox." As he closed his analysis he suggested that there was nothing that prevented Americans from making the sorts of mistakes that Yugoslavs had made in the name of their country. It was this new skepticism about American intentions and claims to act as an agent of peace that struck a new note in post-Kosovo among American Orthodox intellectuals.

The clearest manifestation of this skepticism was "The Iraq Appeal: A Plea for Peace from the Orthodox Peace Fellowship in North America," a letter from the OPF to President George W. Bush which was signed in the run-up to the 2003 Iraq War by dozens of Orthodox leaders, including four American bishops and the leadership and most of the faculty of the leading American Orthodox seminaries—St. Vladimir's, Holy Cross, and St. Tikhon—as well as by many other Orthodox academics.[6] The appeal suggested how deeply doubts about aggressive American foreign policy and American claims to act altruistically in the world had penetrated among American Orthodox since the 1990s. "The United States is ready to overthrow [Saddam Hussein] by any means," the appeal stated, "including an attack which would kill thousands of civilians and maim many more, justifying such an attack on the possibility that Hussein's regime is producing weapons of mass destruction and preparing to use them against America, and Israel and their allies." Because, the appeal continued,

> we seek the reconciliation of enemies, a conversion which grows from striving to be faithful to the Gospel, the Orthodox Church has never regarded any war as just or good, and fighting an elusive enemy by means which cause the death of innocent people can be regarded as murder. Individual murderers are treated by psychiatrists and priests and isolated from society. But who heals the national psyche, the wounded soul of the nation, when it is troubled by the slaughter of non-combatant civilians?

The appeal's key claim—that there is no Orthodox just war theory— reflected a trend of American Orthodox ethical thinking that surfaced in the 1990s. Father Stanley Harakas of Holy Cross, for example, published an essay, "No Just War in the Fathers," in an Orthodox Peace Fellowship occasional paper in 1992. In it, he rebutted Lawrence Uzell's "view that in Orthodoxy there is an imprecise acceptance of a 'just war' theory," an assumption that Harakas said he had shared until he carefully reviewed patristic evidence in 1986. "In light of the patristic evidence," Harakas wrote,

> My conclusion was and still is: The East did not seek to answer questions concerning the correct conditions for entering war and the cor-

rect conduct of war on the basis of the possibility of a "just war," precisely because it did not hold to such a view. Its view of war, unlike that of the West, was that it is a necessary evil. The peace ideal continued to remain normative, and no theoretical efforts were made to make conduct of war into a positive norm. In short, no case can be made for the existence of an Orthodox just war theory.

Harakas's rejection of an Orthodox just war theory was seconded in the early 1990s by another Holy Cross scholar, Fr. George Dragas, and in the early work of Fr. Alexander F. C. Webster, a priest of the Ukrainian metropolitanate, who looked hard at pacifism as a preferred option.[7] In recent years, a number of Orthodox academic theologians have continued to develop this argument, including many of authors in this volume. Their emphasis tends toward rejecting the idea that war can ever be considered a positive good. Most derive this position chiefly from the work of fourth-century theologians, the Cappadocian Fathers and St. Basil above all. Along with Basil, they tend to argue that war and violence are sometimes unavoidable in order to avoid even greater evil. In the shorthand of moral theology and ethics, this position is often described as the "lesser evil" view.[8]

But in the wake of Kosovo, the flat rejection of a just war theory, especially as packaged by academic theologians and the Orthodox Peace Fellowship, generated opposition in a new quarter. These objections came chiefly from a group of writers who had converted to Orthodoxy in recent decades, many of whom aligned themselves with conservative political and social positions and were, especially in the wake of the September 11, 2001, bombings, anxious to defend both the American right of self-defense and an aggressive, perhaps even militant, foreign policy, especially where Muslim terrorists were concerned.

Frank Schaeffer, a member of the Greek Archdiocese, published an especially bitter op-ed article complaining about the impact of the OPF in the April 6, 2003, *Washington Post*. "Some Orthodox Christians . . . have circulated an antiwar declaration harshly condemning the U.S. government's policies in Iraq. In this 'peace statement' the authors call all soldiers who kill in battle murderers, no matter what the cause. They accuse our country of using 'any means' to overthrow Saddam Hussein." Schaeffer said he believed the OPF had "simplistically misrepresented the teachings of [his] church," but he saved his harshest words for the clergy who signed the appeal. "I am saddened because so many of my bishops and priests have signed this antiwar statement in the name of my church and my God. They have dragged not only my church but Jesus into their stand against our government and the war in Iraq."

Fr. Patrick Henry Reardon, a priest of the Antiochian Archdiocese, weighed in on Schaeffer's behalf in a long column entitled "Not So Quiet on the Eastern Front: Orthodox Christians & the Iraq War," in the November 2003 *Touchstone Magazine*. After outlining differences in Eastern and Western Christian approaches to the moral evaluation of war, Reardon noted that many American Orthodox Christians supported the Iraq war

> for much the same reasons that most other Americans favored it. Indeed, they used the same categories to describe it: self-defense against a threatening aggressor, the liberation of an oppressed people from a horrible tyrant, the overthrow of a rogue regime that was fostering terrorism elsewhere in the Middle East, the extension of free government and its economic prosperity to another nation, and so on. That is to say, the Orthodox who favored going to war did so for the same reasons as other American citizens.

Reardon continued, "These Orthodox Christians, faced with a prudential decision regarding a matter of geopolitics, preferred to trust their government rather than their bishops. In Orthodox churches all over the country, prayers were offered daily, not only for peace but also for victory." Yet,

> on the other hand, the widespread Orthodox opposition to the Iraqi war, particularly by the bishops, was a source of discouragement, even dilemma, for some Orthodox Christians, especially when that opposition was accompanied, as it frequently was by the comment that "the Orthodox Church does not accept or espouse a just-war theory; all wars are evil, and participation in them is necessarily and intrinsically evil." This judgment, voiced by some of the names most respected in Orthodox moral theology, was a cause of bewilderment because, if true, it appeared to guarantee that the Orthodox Church, committed to an ethics of pacifism, would remain forever on the

fringes of American life. . . . Many Orthodox Christians began to wonder, therefore, if their own church, thus committed to a pacifist ethic so out of step with American history (if not incompatible with American patriotism), could ever hope to be more than a fringe religion in this country.

Reardon then advanced his own counterargument, one that emphasized the American nation's divine mission. From his point of view, a negative evaluation of American behavior rooted in transnational "non-Western" Orthodox experience or shared ethnic identification (say, Serbian) was most unwelcome. "A good number of American citizens, including not a few who are neither committed globalists nor disciples of Leo Strauss, believe that the Lord of history has laid on the United States of America, now and for the foreseeable future, a unique charge with respect to the preservation of world stability and the well-being of mankind."

In 2003, Fr. Alexander Webster repudiated his earlier argument that there was no legitimate, binding Orthodox just war theory in an article published in *St. Vladimir's Theological Quarterly* called "Justifiable War as a 'Lesser Good' in Eastern Orthodox Moral Tradition." Fr. Webster "disavowed" his earlier "lesser evil" stance in a brief footnote. War, under certain limited and controlled circumstances, may be just, and a just war may also be virtuous and hence morally good.

> This is the ineluctable conclusion to which the scores of texts adduced above give rise. Whenever the Holy Scriptures, Church Fathers, canons, lives of the saints, liturgical and hymnographic texts, and modern theologians and literary authors speak of military activity in terms of right or righteousness or nobility or valor or heroism, their individual and collective impact alike is the same: a justification for such activity as a moral good and of the soldiers who serve as its agents as virtuous warriors.

By 2003, Webster's moral priority was to defend the virtue of American soldiers committed to the war on terror. In retrospect, he attributed the "no just war" argument to "modern revisionism in Orthodox thinking" that is "external to the Orthodox tradition" and which "infiltrated

Orthodoxy as a result of a flurry of ecumenical contacts with Western Christians and accelerated immigration of Orthodox Christians to Western Europe and North America." It was, in short, a bad, Western thing.[9]

The following year, Webster's *The Virtue of War: Reclaiming the Classic Christian Traditions East and West* (cowritten with Darrell Cole) was published by Frank Schaeffer's Regina Orthodox Press. *Touchstone* reviewer David B. Hart greeted the book with a slashing attack on Orthodox pacifism. "It strikes me as a singular sort of delusion to imagine that the Eastern Orthodox tradition is any more hospitable to pacifism than the Western Catholic tradition, given the utter absence of pacifist tenets from Orthodoxy's teaching, liturgy, or history. And yet, it is a delusion shared by a not inconsiderable number of (Western) Eastern Christians at present."[10]

Under Schaeffer's editorship, Regina Press has also published Serge Trifkovic's *The Sword of the Prophet: The Politically Incorrect Guide to Islam; History, Theology and Impact on the World.* Its promotional copy reads: "We hear it said: 'September 11 changed America forever.' Less often do we hear a coherent explanation of what, exactly, changed. What changed, in fact, was that for the first time in American history we have been forced to confront Islamic militancy as it has assaulted the rest of the world for almost 14 centuries."

By projecting American force against an Orthodox population for the first time, the 1999 NATO bombing of Serbia created a discussion about the morality of war among American Orthodox, a discussion that intensified during the American wars in Iraq and Afghanistan. The Orthodox Peace Fellowship labored to create a forum for discussion in the early 1990s, particularly by providing a forum in its publication *In Communion*. This growing discussion, however, revealed diversity of opinion among American Orthodox, rather than consensus.

Several discernible clusters of opinion, however, emerged, with each emphasizing different elements of Orthodox thought, sources, or history to support its views. Pacifists, clustering around the Orthodox Peace Fellowship, had a long head start and tended to base their views about pacifism on the early church. The "lesser evil" school, mostly composed of academic theologians and including Stanley Harakas, Philip LeMasters, and John McGuckin, emphasized patristic theology and canon law. In context, their position emphasized universal aspects of Orthodox teaching and identity, rather than specific national ones. Hierarchs, many still in close touch with ethnic identities or belonging to jurisdictions based in Eastern Europe or the Middle East, tended to make public statements condemning violence, but often reacted more urgently to violence or potential violence against Orthodox peoples.[11] Reacting against most of these positions were defenders of Orthodox "justifiable war" theories, many of whom were converts interested in aligning Orthodox values with patriotic American ones.[12] They often cited the very large body of liturgical and hymnological evidence (Like the hymn "O Lord, Save Thy People," which began the chapter) to emphasize that there was a long Orthodox record of support for the military struggles of Orthodox states, beginning with the Byzantine state and extending to the contemporary era.

It seems likely to me that the future discussion will be dominated by the "lesser evil" and "justifiable war" approaches. The more detached, lesser evil school presents authentic Orthodox teaching as quite distinctive, hewing a middle path between pacifists and the just war theorists. From this position, the celebration of American virtue looks unlikely. On the other hand, those taking the justifiable-war approach see Orthodox teaching both as sharing more with well-understood Catholic and Protestant views of war and as more compatible with mainstream American identity and values. They seem to be hoping for the development of a "Holy America," aligned historically with earlier Orthodox celebrations of the Byzantine Empire and of Holy Russia, Holy Serbia, and so on. It will be hard to hold these two visions in one house.

NOTES

1. Quotations from Serge Schmemann, "The World: Storm Front: A New Collision of East and West," *New York Times*, Week in Review, April 4, 1999.

2. William J. Clinton, "Remarks to the United States Institute of Peace," April 7, 1999. Available online by Gerhard Peters and John T. Woolley, *The American Presidency Project*. http://www.presidency.ucsb.edu/ws/?pid=57368.

3. Today, Rev. Irinej Dobrijevic serves as bishop of the Metropolitanate of Australia and New Zealand of the Serbian Orthodox Church.

4. Joan Brown Campbell and Leonid Kishkovsky, "Journey to Belgrade: Religious Partnership," *Christian Century* 116, no. 20, May 19, 1999, 14–21.

5. In April 2014, a further reorganization occurred that established separate assemblies for Canadian and US bishops and that attached the Central American bishops to other Orthodox bishops in Latin America.

6. See "OPF's Iraq Appeal: A Letter to President Bush," In Communion [website of the Orthodox Peace Fellowship], October 19, 2004, http://incommunion.org/2004/10/19/iraq-appeal/.

7. See Alexander F. C. Webster, "Just War and Holy War: Two Case Studies in Comparative Christian Ethics," *Christian Scholar's Review* 15, no. 4 (1986): 343–71; Webster, *The Pacifist Option: The Moral Argument against War in Eastern Orthodox Theology* (Lanham, MD: International Scholars Publications, 1998).

8. See, for example, the Antiochian ethicist Fr. Philip LeMasters, "Orthodox Perspectives on Peace, War and Violence," *Ecumenical Review* 63 (March 2011): 54–61. LeMasters and other scholars also cite the statement of the 2009 Inter-Orthodox Consultation Towards the International Ecumenical Peace Convention, which took place in Leros, Greece, from September 15 to 22, as evidence of Orthodox teaching. It asserts flatly that there is no developed just war doctrine in Orthodox theology. Paragraph 19 states: "The Church may tolerate the limited use of force as a tragic necessity for the defense of justice and the preservation of the imperfect, yet still imperative, peace that is possible among the nations and peoples of the world in given situations."

9. Alexander F. C. Webster, "Justifiable War as a Lesser Good in Eastern Orthodox Moral Tradition," *St. Vladimir's Theological Quarterly* 47, no. 1 (2003): 53, 54.

10. David B. Hart, "Ecumenical Councils of War," review of *The Virtue of War: Reclaiming the Classic Christian Traditions East and West*, by Alexander F. C. Webster and Darrell Cole, *Touchstone*, November 2004, http://www.touchstonemag.com/archives/issue.php?id=103.

11. Metropolitan Philip Saliba (d. 2014) of the Antiochian Christian Archdiocese of North America, a constituent diocese of the Greek Orthodox Patriarchate of Antioch based in Damascus, Syria, offers an instructive example. His public statements on the American bombing of Serbia tracked closely with those of other Orthodox hierarchs (opposition to the bombing), but his statements on American involvement in Iraq and the Middle East reflected a special concern that any war waged by the United States against Saddam Hussein might have a profoundly destabilizing impact on Middle Eastern societies, where Orthodox Christians were a vulnerable minority. Metropolitan Philip, who died in the fall of 2014, ended his life as an open supporter of the Assad regime in the Syrian

Civil War that began in 2011, despite that government's record of massive violence against civilians. If Assad's regime lost the war, the result would be catastrophic for Syrian Christians, he said, as the Iraq War had been for Iraqi Christians. For a few helpful discussions of the effects of the Iraq War upon Christians in Iraq, see Suha Rassam, "The Plight of Iraqi Christians," *One in Christ* 42, no. 2 (2008): 286–301; Bill Bowring, "Minority Rights in Post-war Iraq: An Impending Catastrophe?," *International Journal of Contemporary Iraqi Studies* 5, no. 3 (February 2012): 319–35.

12. Some prominent Orthodox writers on the "lesser evil" and pacifist sides of the discussion are also converts, e.g., John McGuckin and Philip LeMasters, among the academic theologians, and Jim Forest and Frederica Mathewes-Green, among the pacifist-leaning. In addition, some of the "justifiable war" writers—Alexander F. C. Webster and David B. Hart—are well-qualified academic theologians. The key distinguishing characteristic seems to be insistence on shaping an American Orthodox identity that "fits" America and supports their view that the American role in the world is honorable and necessary.

PART TWO

REENGAGING ORTHODOXY'S
HISTORY AND TRADITION

CHAPTER 3

CHARIOTS OF FIRE, UNASSAILABLE CITIES, AND THE ONE TRUE KING

A Prophetically Influenced Scribal Perspective on War and Peace

NICOLAE RODDY

One thing upon which urbanized peoples of the ancient Near East in the Middle Bronze through Persian periods (ca. 2000 BCE–539 BCE)[1] would have agreed was that iron-plated, horse-drawn chariots offered the highest and best line of defense beyond their own fortified city walls, ensuring levels of security commensurate with the size of their kings' arsenals and fleets. Trembling under the threat of Mesopotamian imperial incursions into the Levant during the Iron Age II period (1000 BCE–550 BCE), the petty monarchies of Israel and Judah were no exceptions. Squeezed precariously along the narrow rift separating the Mediterranean Sea from the Arabian desert in the shifting buffer zone between meddlesome Egypt and the relentless kingdoms of Mesopotamia, these tiny kingdoms regarded their respective kings' fortified cities and chariots of iron as sources of pride and assurance in times of peace and stability and as desperate last chances for survival in times of insecurity and war.

The historical/prophetic corpus of the Bible has a great deal to say concerning these human-wrought means of self-defense—speaking even louder in the things its writers and editors chose to ignore—all of which is at odds with the sort of descriptions one would expect to issue forth from that perilous Age of Empires.[2] With an eye toward the material remains of Iron Age Israel,[3] this study examines the perspective of biblical writers and editors who witnessed firsthand the extremes of both the *Pax Iosiana* (ca. 622–609 BCE)[4] and the Babylonian destruction of Jerusalem (586 BCE), in order to understand more clearly what for most readers would have seemed the stark absurdity of these scribes' collective position on war and peace. Moreover it will suggest that even though all of Israel's iron chariots, fortified cities, and mortal kings were wiped out millennia ago—and perhaps *because* they were—the prophetic tradition's seemingly absurd view may prove no less relevant for the world today. Adrift and forlorn beside the "waters of Babylon" (Ps. 137), the exiles had experienced firsthand the futile consequences of placing their trust in human achievement and the ability of their institutions to save them.

Because this chapter is part of an edited volume produced by Orthodox Christian scholars, perhaps addressing a few anticipated methodological considerations would be in order. First, the Orthodox reader will note a general lack of reference to patristic sources, the reason for which is that patristic commentary, with only a few exceptions, largely ignores the historical material of the Former Prophets.[5] When the fathers have occasion to use these books, they usually focus only upon certain key names or events, which they then interpret allegorically and typologically for homiletic purposes.[6] Modern critical methodologies were simply not available to patristic writers, leaving the critical exegetical enterprise open for modern Orthodox biblical scholars who would have something of value to offer not only to the church but also to the field of biblical studies at large—as an antidote to the failures of modern historical-critical scholarship on the part of their Protestant and Catholic colleagues. As a result, it will be up to the discerning reader to judge the veracity of this writer's assertion that the Older Testament exegesis that follows meets the Orthodox criterion of standing up under the discerning lens of the gospel, serving the "two-edged sword" of God's Word (Heb. 4:12).

This contribution arises from the writer's larger, ongoing scholarly and pedagogical project that seeks to examine the stage at which the Bible came together as "Bible," by which is meant the emergence into history of a collection of Hebrew scrolls produced on the basis of selected edited oral and textual materials, replete with dissonant voices expressed through a variety of genres and generally cohering into a grand narrative of a people's past.[7] Intertextual analysis aided by external evidence from archaeology and other historical sources suggests that the implied editors of this literary enterprise most likely belonged to a late sixth- and early fifth-century BCE community of prophetically influenced priestly scribes, responding to what was, at least from their perspective, the end of their national history. It was at that time that formerly divergent priestly and royal traditions, both oral and written, came to be woven together in response to ultimate questions provoked by the sudden end of their nation's history, which for some had been thought to be eternal and divinely protected.

The comprehensive prophetic enterprise that sought to answer the question "What went wrong?" comprises several related aspects of an overall critique of certain Israelite institutions, which the prophetically influenced scribes set over and against a corresponding ideal parallel universe. This negative assessment of the mundane world targets the following Israelite institutions in which Israel had erroneously placed its trust: (1) the monarchy, which had supplanted the notion of God as king;[8] (2) fortified cities, instead of the prophetic word as the only inviolable city of refuge;[9] and (3) the erroneous understanding of what it means to be a human being created in the image of God, augmented by the flipside of Exodus 3's "I Am," which can only be a resounding, "You're not!"[10] To this we will add the misplaced trust in Israel's military defenses, which replaced Israel's only impenetrable defense: the line of true biblical prophets stretching from Moses through Elijah-Elisha and culminating in Jeremiah, symbolized by chariots and horses of fire.

This topic is situated within the larger context of divine warfare, which cannot be addressed here in its entirety; however, significant for our purposes is the fact that "holy war" as described in the Bible is not something that Israelites themselves were called upon to instigate, but that Israel's God in fact undertook as warrior.[11] Yahweh fought Israel's earlier battles, but as a fearsome and just divine warrior the Deity can turn against his own people as well.[12] Other works, especially those that attempt to bring the Older Testament into the broader, modern discussion of war and peace, often fail to distinguish critically among the various textual strata accumulated and edited during the formation of the Bible, positing some sweeping pseudohistorical portrait of biblical Israel's development from "primitive barbarism" through a "progressive moral tightening" to a "more complex ethical civilization in the Maccabean period . . . and on to the perfect holiness revealed by Jesus Christ in the New Testament Gospels," in the words of Fr. Alexander F. C. Webster, an Orthodox chaplain who has written extensively on Orthodox responses to war.[13] However, lack of sensitivity to literary responses arising in the face of historical realities obscures the fact that at a critical stage in the formation of the Bible—its defining impetus, no less—the attitude toward war in both its execution and defense was that in light of the shattered terms of the covenant, all military involvements are ultimately futile. The prophetically influenced priestly scribes who produced the Bible recycled their romanticized descriptions of higher-order covenantal existence, contrasted by the lapses of Achan (Josh. 7) and King Saul (1 Sam. 15), for the purpose of illustrating Judah's abandonment of God through misplaced trust in its own institutions.

CHARIOTS OF FIRE VERSUS CHARIOTS OF IRON

The material record of the Levantine Iron Age II period (1000 BCE–550 BCE), the historical context that the prophetically influenced priestly writers and editors of the Former Prophets (the so-called Deuteronomistic History, or DH) seek to address, indicates that iron-plated chariots were primarily used for military purposes, in contrast to the use of simple carts for transporting goods. The most common chariot design comprised a two-wheeled, horse-drawn platform large enough to support two or three men,[14] one of whom steered, the others armed with bows and arrows or spears. Chariot wheels usually had six spokes, which offered adequate durability over rugged terrain, and a platform with a curved iron plate that protected the driver at the front and sides. Although the biblical term for this military conveyance is רכב ברזל (*rekeb barzel*, or "iron chariot"), these war machines would not have been constructed entirely of iron, but were simply plated with iron in strategic places.

Little can be known about actual numbers of chariots possessed by the various kingdoms of the ancient Near East. Accounts of the Battle of Qadesh, fought along the banks of the Orontes River in Syria around 1274 BCE, describe one of the largest military engagements on record in the ancient Near East, in which Egyptian forces, commanded by Rameses II, clashed with Hittite armies led by Muwatalli II, with each ruler touting final victory. Although numbers from ancient sources should never be trusted, the Battle of Qadesh may have involved as many as six thousand chariots.[15] The sight of even a mere hundred iron chariots and horsemen swarming over the land would have been enough to strike fear in the hearts of average village dwellers, especially if their defending king lacked the means to fend them off.

It is all but certain that Israel and Judah possessed horses and chariots, although it is not possible to determine their numbers. Horses are attested in Palestine from the beginning of the second millennium BCE, but do not appear to have been used for agriculture or the transport of goods; instead, donkeys, mules, and oxen served these purposes, as depicted in reliefs and mentioned in the Bible and in other ancient texts. Horses, it appears, were primarily associated with warfare, supporting riders and pulling chariots in battle as early as the middle of the second millennium BCE, thus available to the monarchies of Israel and Judah from their inception late in the tenth century BCE.

One might then look for Iron Age structures that would serve as stables for large numbers of horses, but here again the evidence is sparse; what little exists has been the subject of vigorous debate. Large tripartite buildings uncovered at major sites throughout Israel (e.g., Hazor, Megiddo, Jezreel, Lachish, Beersheba, Tell Qasile, Tell Abu Hawam, Tell el-Hesi, and others) may have served such purposes, but the material remains recovered from them suggest a variety of possible uses for this common structural design.[16] Pillared, tripartite buildings at Megiddo, Jezreel, and Lachish—cities which served as important administrative centers during this time—appear most likely to have served as stables and/or barracks. Megiddo Stratum IV A (ninth century BCE), for example, yields the most compelling evidence for the presence of one, possibly two stables, with related assemblages that seem likely to have served as tethering pillars and feeding troughs. If these structures are rightly interpreted as stables—and it is now almost certain that they are—then Megiddo would have sheltered hundreds of horses at a time.[17]

The discovery of ostraca from an Aram victory stele found at Tel Dan during the 1993–94 seasons suggests that the kings of Israel and Judah commanded a significantly large number of horses and chariots. The inscription claims that King Hazael of Aram (or perhaps his son, Bar Hadad) killed a number of marauding kings, including Jehoram, son of Ahab, King of Israel, and Ahaziayahu, son of Jehoram, "King of the House of David," who had invaded Aram with thousands of chariots and horses.[18] Thus the presence of iron chariots in Israel and Judah is fairly well attested in the material record; however, references to this technology are oddly missing from the prophetic narrative of Israel's past.

As a point of transition from the material record to the biblical perspective on the significance of chariots, we turn to one last artifact, the Kurkh monolith, which bears an Assyrian inscription that refers to the infamous King Ahab of Israel (reigned ca. 870–853 BCE). The stele witnesses to the first six years of Shalmaneser III's Assyrian military campaign in the region. It reports that a twelve-nation coalition[19] led by King Hadad-Ezer of Damascus and supported by Egypt engaged the armies of Shalmaneser III along the Orontes River in 853 BCE in a bloody confrontation known as the Battle of Qarqar. The Assyrian monolith understandably does not admit defeat, but the fact that Shalmaneser III was unable to make any significant advances for the next four years attests to the relative success of the coalition's campaign against him.[20] Important for our purposes is the Assyrian claim that King Ahab of Israel had contributed no less than two thousand chariots of iron and ten thousand infantrymen to the opposing coalition and that the Israelite chariots numbered more than half the total of all allied fleets combined and numbered 40 percent more than Hadad-Ezer's contingent. Although these numbers may not be historically accurate, the fact that the coalition succeeded in halting the Assyrian advance strongly supports the assertion that Israel and its allies possessed a well-equipped fighting force. The Bible, however, is strangely silent on the matter.

The Deuteronomistic writer devotes several chapters to King Ahab and his Phoenician wife Jezebel, but avoids mentioning this monumental victory. The writer seems interested only in assessing their moral character and religious preferences and states that any further information, which would doubtless include descriptions of his victories, palaces, and fortified cities, may readily be gathered from the Annals of the Kings of Israel (1 Kings 22:39).[21] He does attribute a military victory to Ahab in a campaign against the Arameans, but interprets the occasion in a way that only provides further evidence of the king's disregard for Yahweh's prophets. The fact that Ahab obstinately refuses to acknowledge Yahweh's sovereignty in light of his successes supports the writer's assertion that Ahab "did more to provoke the anger of the LORD, the God of Israel, than had all the kings of Israel who were before him" (16:33 NRSV).

In contrast to the DH's dismissive cloaking of Israel's military might, the compiler of the books of Chronicles is less reticent. For example, he boasts that King Solomon had fourteen hundred chariots and twelve thousand horsemen at his disposal (2 Chron. 1:14), this in striking contrast to the DH's warning that a king of Israel "must not acquire many horses for himself, or return the people to Egypt in order to acquire more horses, since the LORD has said to you, 'You must never return that way again.'"[22] However, it should be remembered that the Chronicles scrolls are numbered among the Writings (*Ketuvim*) and are postexilic, likely produced during the Persian period under Ezra and marking the second major phase of the Bible's formation. The Chronicles offer a somewhat romanticized version of Israel's past that attempts to restore the tarnished glory of the monarchy, retelling Israel's national story in a didactic way and whitewashing all of the DH's royal dirty laundry. Thus it stands that an important aspect of the DH is its refusal to acknowledge that Israel's iron chariots were of any real military value, no matter how many their kings possessed.

By contrast, biblical editors of the exile period were willing to acknowledge the military might of Israel's enemies, retaining older references to that effect. The book of Judges records that even though the LORD was with Judah, the tribe was unable to wrest possession of the plain from the Canaanites because the latter had iron chariots (Judg. 1:19); King Jabin of Hazor was able to oppress the Israelites for twenty years because he controlled nine hundred chariots (Judg. 4:3); and Israel's perennial enemies, the formidable Philistines, are accorded no less than thirty thousand chariots (1 Sam. 13:5), a ludicrously wild exaggeration, but, in the face of overwhelming enemy forces, no less fantastic than Isaiah's oracular observation that the land of the Assyrians "is filled with horses, and there is no end to their chariots" (Isa. 2:7). Enemy chariots could be presented as innumerable, especially in light of the conviction that Israel's God commands them for historical purposes.

In sum, despite the material remains of monumental architecture at places like Megiddo, Hazor, and Jezreel, which strongly support the likelihood of a powerful Israelite military presence in the mid-ninth century BCE, the perspective of the editors of the Former Prophets, shaped largely by the vantage point of 20/20 hindsight in the aftermath of the destruction of Jerusalem and its palace-temple complex, weighs in against those who trusted in the efficacy of iron chariots for defense.

This view is rooted in the oracles of the prophets themselves; for what is almost certainly a somewhat later Judahite interpolation into Hosea's prophecy of Samaria's destruction declares (1:7):

> I will have pity on the house of Judah, and I will save them by the Lord their God; I will not save them by bow, or by sword, or by war, or by horses, or by horsemen.

A Psalmist perhaps from around this period seems to agree:

> A king is not delivered by his great army;
>   a warrior is not delivered by his great strength.
> The war horse is a vain hope for victory,
>   and by its great might it cannot save.[23]

Similarly,

> Some take pride in chariots, and some in horses,
>   but our pride is in the name of the Lord our God.
> They will collapse and fall,
>   but we shall rise and stand upright.[24]

If the highest and best line of military defense known to the inhabitants of the Iron Age was of no avail, then what could possibly have delivered Samaria and Jerusalem from destruction? Of course, the biblical writers had an answer, found in part within the Elijah/Elisha cycle.

Following Elijah's humiliating defeat of the prophets of Ba'al on Mt. Carmel (1 Kings 18) and his subsequent but non-sequitur flight to the wilderness in despair, Yahweh assigns the defeated and discouraged prophet three tasks: (1) go to Damascus to effect a coup d'état, replacing Ben Hadad with Hazael; (2) go to Samaria to overthrow Ahab in favor of Jehu; and (3) call Elisha to be his disciple. Elijah sets out immediately, but oddly begins tackling his tasks in reverse order when he happens upon Elisha plowing his family's fields.

At this time Elijah does not explicitly call Elisha to follow him; nevertheless the young farmer responds to the beleaguered prophet's unspoken call and demonstrates his worthiness by shadowing his master faithfully as Yahweh drives them from city to city. As Elijah's career draws to a close, Elisha requests "a double portion" of his master's spirit (2 Kings 2:9), the biblical proportion of a firstborn son's inheritance, which attests to the special nature of their master/disciple relationship. The elder prophet admonishes Elisha that he has asked for a difficult thing, but says that the request will be granted if the disciple *sees* him as he is being taken up (v. 10).[25]

Whatever it is Elisha stands to gain by seeing Elijah as he is taken up has something to do with Moses, given the striking parallels between them, including such things as representing Yahweh in confronting a powerful ruler, encountering Yahweh on Mt. Sinai/Horeb, parting waters and crossing over "on dry ground," and obscurity surrounding a final resting place. The writer indicates that Elisha is successful in fulfilling the necessary obligation to "see," for when fiery chariots and horses suddenly pass between them, Elisha exclaims, "Father, Father! The chariots of Israel and its horsemen!" as his master is taken up in a whirlwind (v. 12). With respect to traditional interpretations of this story, the text does not state that the chariot serves as Elijah's conveyance to the skies; rather the chariots of fire and horses of fire serve another, more important purpose.

In order to understand the literary role of the fiery chariots and horsemen, it would first be helpful to think of them as something that connects Elisha and Elijah in the narrative world, not something separating them, much the same way the iconostasis in an Orthodox Church mystically serves to unite the faithful with the Holy Mystery being enacted on the other side. It is also helpful to examine other appearances of fiery chariots in the Former Prophets.

In 2 Kings 6, the king of Aram (Syria) is launching repeated raids against Israel's towns and villages, only to be intercepted by a readied Israelite army that seems to anticipate his every move. Frustrated by the fact that he is unable to take these cities by surprise, the Aramean king begins to suspect that he has a spy among his ranks. When one of his advisers informs him that the reason for his military failures is that Israel's prophet Elisha is able to tell the king of Israel every word the warring king speaks even in the privacy of his own bedchamber (v. 12), the king then redirects his energies toward finding Elisha. Learning that the prophet has been located at Dothan, he sends "horses and chariots there and a great army," coming by night and surrounding the city (v. 14). The following morning, Elisha's servant looks out and sees the vast enemy army. Trembling with fear, he implores Elisha to tell him what to do, to which the prophet calmly replies, "Do not be afraid, for we outnumber them." Elisha then prays that the eyes of the servant be opened (v. 17): "So the LORD opened the eyes of the servant, and he saw; the mountain was full of horses and chariots of fire all around Elisha." As the Arameans begin to attack, Elisha prays to the LORD that they be struck blind. Elisha rounds up the confused, blinded warriors and delivers them to the king of Israel, who acknowledges Elisha's power and authority by calling him "father" and seeking his advice concerning what should be done with the captives (vv. 21–22).

In 2 Kings 13:14, the fiery chariot motif appears yet again: "Now when Elisha had fallen sick with the illness of which he was to die, Joash king of Israel went down to him, and wept before him, crying, 'My father, my father! The chariots of Israel and its horsemen!'" Here the king's words call to mind Elisha's exclamation upon inheriting his master's spirit. With the repetition of these words in this new context—spoken now by no less than a king—it should be apparent that the Bible's fiery chariot motif serves as a literary motif, symbolizing the divine power at work through the spiritual lineage of true biblical prophets. What passes between Elijah and Elisha is represented by fiery chariots, uniting them in a pedigree that originates with Moses, continuing all the way through the unnamed "prophet like me [i.e., Moses]" foretold ex eventu (after the fact) in Deuteronomy 18:15: "The LORD your God will raise up for you a prophet like me from among your own people; you shall heed such a prophet." Given that the words were almost certainly written at the end of the seventh century (or the beginning of the sixth century) BCE and expressed in the language and viewpoint of the book of Jeremiah, it is almost certain that the author had Jeremiah in mind, lending him credibility in his own time by connecting him through Elijah and Elisha directly back to Moses.[26]

Thus it appears that what originally may have been separate legends about two Israelite prophets were artfully combined into a narrative cycle that stresses the succession of prophetic power and authority through a particular prophetic lineage as a kind of Israelite "apostolic" succession. This assertion is supported by the fact that the two coups d'état assigned to Elijah in 1 Kings 18:15–16 are executed by Elisha (2 Kings 9:1–11; 10:1–11)! The prophetic perspective asserts that history is shaped by the Word of the LORD carried out in the line of true biblical prophets, represented in chariots of fire.

In sum, hindsight was 20/20 for the prophetically influenced scribal community of the exile, which remained faithful to Yahweh even though David's eternal city and its temple lay in ruins. Israel's iron chariots did not—could not—deliver the Israelites from destruction, so the second of its two national histories had come to a tragic end. The demands of the divine warrior motif of Deuteronomy carried out in the conquests of Moses' successor, Joshua, continue throughout the "authentic" prophetic line, namely that obedience to God's law would lead to victory, but disobedience only to defeat. The conviction of the sixth-century BCE Deuteronomistic school, that if Jerusalem and its temple lay in ruins, then only the LORD could have brought it about, was supported in part by the assertion that Israel's faith in its own military might had been sorely misplaced. From the prophetic perspective from the exile, the word of God issuing through the lips of the true biblical prophets was always Israel's highest and best line of defense; had it been heeded, Jerusalem would have been saved.

CITIES OF THE WORD VERSUS FORTIFIED CITIES OF STONE

The monumental remains of Late Bronze and Iron Age cities in the Levant are impressive by the standards of any era. Enclosed within massive stone walls laid with engineered precision by slaves in widths of more than twenty-five feet and standing upwards of two stories in height, and accessed through chambered gate complexes flanked by even higher towers, these fortified cities lured masses of fearful and insecure people to settle near the cities' promise of relative protection in unstable times. However, the biblical writers express an altogether different point of view regarding the advantages of fortified city walls.[27] According to them, the first earthly city was founded by Cain, that notorious fratricide-in-exile (Gen. 4:17), whose seed lives on in subsequent urban society in that his descendants, not his brother Seth's, engage in occupations largely associated with urban life, including artisans, musicians, toolmakers, builders, and so on.

In Genesis 10, Ham is cursed because he "saw the nakedness of his father" (Gen. 9:20–22),[28] but the curse falls upon Ham's son, Canaan, eponymous ancestor of the land of great cities, including Sidon, the infamously wicked cities of Sodom and Gomorrah (Gen. 10:15–19), and the thirty-one royal cities of Canaan later vanquished by Joshua and the Israelites (Josh. 12:23). Cush, another son of the accursed Ham, is associated with the formidable cities of Mesopotamia, most notably Babylon and Nineveh: "Cush became the father of Nimrod. . . . The beginning of his kingdom was Babel, Erech, and Akkad, all of them in the land of Shinar. From that land he went into Assyria and built Nineveh, Rehoboth-ir, Calah and Resen between Nineveh and Calah; that is the great city."[29]

In the final episode of the primeval narrative, the apex of human achievement is reached with the founding of the fortified city of Babel, an imposing monumental city with a tower reaching high into the sky (Gen. 11:4).[30] Although popularly known as the "Tower of Babel" story, the narrative refers only to a city and its tower, (עיר ומגדל), or just "the city" (העיר). When Yahweh looks down and beholds the tower and fortified city that human beings, unified in purpose by language, have constructed, he expresses concern that there will now be no limit to human ambition. Reassigning human beings to their rightful place in creation, Yahweh scatters them abroad and confounds their language with the result that they leave off building the city (v. 8). Thus the greatest of all ancient construction projects remains empty and incomplete, a testament to humankind's proud and foolish ambitions.

The Bible's negative critique of cities continues throughout the rest of the Pentateuch and Former Prophets. In its final formulation, the pro- phetically influenced priestly perspective rests upon the fact that fortified cities, including especially Samaria and Jerusalem, were not able to deliver upon the promises of protection for which they were built. This perspec- tive may be rooted in popular movements during the Omride-dynasty Israel (ninth century BCE), which may have viewed major cities as places where advocacy and justice no longer obtained, a social context giving rise to eighth-century BCE anti-establishment prophetic figures like Amos and Hosea, whose rhetoric influenced later Judahite prophets, including Jeremiah, Ezekiel, and the Deutero-Isaianic school.

Amos, for example, challenges the arrogant confidence that Israel misplaces in its citadels, proclaiming, "I abhor the pride of Jacob and hate his strongholds; and I will deliver up the city and all that is in it" (6:8). He assures Israel that its cities will see their protecting armies com- pletely overrun (5:3) and that anyone seeking refuge in Samaria will be dragged away with grappling hooks through breaches in the city wall (4:2–3). Cities such as Bethel and Gilgal, where Jeroboam's established, state-supporting cultic shrines continue to rubber-stamp unchecked royal policies, will not be divinely protected, nor will they save anyone seeking refuge there (5:4–5).

The prophet Hosea, Amos's somewhat later contemporary, decries the fact that Israel has "forgotten his Maker and built palaces" (Hosea 8:14a), establishing a correlation between these two activities. Hosea ex- claims that Judah, too, has proudly and foolishly "multiplied his fortified cities" (v. 14b), for which Yahweh will send a fire upon these cities and devour all Judah's strongholds (v. 14c). In short, fortified cities offer the unjust and idolatrous wicked no place to hide.

Isaiah ben Amoz, court prophet and priest of the Aaronid-Zadokite line, in service to kings Ahaz and Hezekiah, also rails against the pride of Judah's cities and the false promises of security they offer. Ironically, the fact that Isaiah is an official representative of the monarchy makes his case as a critical insider all the more extraordinary. Perhaps the still-smoldering destruction of Samaria by the Assyrians helped shape his conviction that Israel's fortified cities represented repositories of misplaced trust in the promise of deliverance, which could only come from Yahweh; for, Isaiah proclaims, "their strong cities will be like the deserted places of the Hivites and the Amorites . . . and there will be desolation; for you have forgotten the God of your salvation" (Isa. 17:9–10). Again, as with Hosea, the life and death of fortified cities depends upon remembering the LORD.

Later Judahite prophets and their schools would continue building on the prophetical convictions of the mid- to late eighth century BCE, which they came to apply full-force to their own social and political situations. The so-called Isaiah apocalypse (chs. 24–27), likely a reworked oracle against Israel, now becomes an anti-establishment diatribe against Judah's reckless leaders, proclaiming a powerful and enigmatic judgment against the city, expressed in rural metaphor:

> The city of chaos is broken down,
>> every house is shut up so that no one can enter.
> There is an outcry in the streets for lack of wine;
>> all joy has reached its eventide;
>> the gladness of the earth is banished.
> Desolation is left in the city,
> the gates are battered into ruins.
> For thus it shall be on the earth and among the nations,
>> as when an olive tree is beaten,
>> as at the gleaning when the grape harvest is ended.[31]

In the end, the unnamed city serves as a symbol for any and every city that fails to offer true justice and refuge, principles established by the God of Moses for the welfare of the poor and the needy; therefore God is the only true city of refuge:

> For you [LORD] have made the city a heap,
>> the fortified city a ruin;
> the palace of aliens is a city no more,
>> it will never be rebuilt.
> Therefore strong peoples will glorify you;
>> cities of ruthless nations will fear you.
> For you [LORD] have been a refuge to the poor,
>> a refuge to the needy in their distress,
>> a shelter from the rainstorm and a shade from the heat.[32]

In 597 BCE, roughly a century after Isaiah's support of King Hezekiah during the Assyrian siege of Jerusalem, King Nebuchadnezzar of Babylon attacked Jerusalem and carried off young King Jehoiachin, the queen mother, and several other members of Jerusalem's elite society, including an Aaronid-Zadokite priest named Ezekiel. According to the book of Ezekiel, in the third year of his deportation (ca. 594 BCE), as the displaced priest without an altar sat along a tributary of the Euphrates River in Babylon, the heavens opened and Ezekiel saw visions of God, inaugurating his career as a prophet. As Babylon continued to administer the affairs of Jerusalem under the puppet-king Zedekiah, Ezekiel foretold the city's inevitable destruction and warned against the insidious dangers of prophetic rivals who would "whitewash the truth" with their erroneous assertions that Jerusalem would be spared its destruction and that refuge could be taken there (Ezek. 13:1–16).

Indeed, nowhere is the prophetic indictment against cities more forcefully delivered than in Ezekiel's indictment against Jerusalem, which he calls a "whore" (16:35–52) and a "city of blood" (22:2; 24:6). Ezekiel asserts that Jerusalem's sins are far more grievous than those of Sodom and Gomorrah in that she has learned nothing from the example of their destruction, nor from the destruction of her sister, Samaria.

Although different from Ezekiel in terms of priestly lineage and outlook, the prophet Jeremiah agrees with his exiled contemporary that Jerusalem's destruction is inevitable and that the city can no longer offer any refuge (Jer. 23:17; 27:9–10). In Isaiah, Yahweh himself serves as the only true city of refuge (Isa. 25:2–4a), but for Jeremiah, the word of the LORD dwells in him just as it once did in the now forsaken Jerusalem, so that the prophet himself represents the new city: "And I for my part have made you today a fortified city, an iron pillar, and a bronze wall, against the whole land—against the kings of Judah, its princes, its priests, and the people of the land. They will fight against you; but they shall not prevail against you, for I am with you, says the LORD, to deliver you."[33]

The juxtaposition of the books of Ezekiel and Jeremiah at the center of the Tanach could not have been random. Together they form a kind of diptych, symbolically representing a crucial moment in history during which disparate roles (priestly and prophetical), traditions (Priestly and Deuteronomistic), and perspectives (past and future) came together, providing the defining and refractive orientation for the overall structure of the Hebrew Bible. From these two influences the prophetical priestly critique of the fortified city is retrojected into Israel's past, running like a crimson thread from the bleak etiology of its institution by Cain, throughout the Law and the Prophets, to Jerusalem in ruins.

KINGS OF ISRAEL VERSUS THE KING OF HEAVEN

The prophets' critique of Israel's earthly leadership, especially its kings, is a third aspect of war and peace reflected in the prophetically influenced priestly perspective from the exile, for the same misplaced trust invested in Israel's chariots of iron and fortified cities was also foolishly wasted on the kings, whose responsibility it was to command them. In fact, one can see in the biblical narrative the institutionalization of military self-reliance in the very establishment of the monarchy. Having approached the priest/prophet/judge Samuel with demands for a king, the elders of Israel are warned: "He [Samuel] said, 'These will be the ways of the king who will reign over you: he will take your sons and appoint them to his chariots; and he will appoint for himself commanders of thousands and commanders of fifties, some to plow his ground and to reap his harvest, and to make his implements of war and the equipment of his chariots.'"[34] It seems the prophetic tradition had known all along the futility of relying upon kings, for Hosea's proclamation that Yahweh will send a fire upon Israel's cities "that shall devour its strongholds" (Hosea 8:14) is followed up by the acerbic taunt, "Where now is your king that he may save you? Where in all your cities are your rulers?" (13:10).

Throughout the entire DH, no king is spared from criticism. Even David, the greatest of kings, stands convicted of committing a host of transgressions. The David and Uriah the Hittite story[35] begins with the ironic statement, "In the spring of the year, at the time when kings [of other nations] go out to battle," David sent Joab, his cousin and commander, off to war, but David remained in Jerusalem (2 Sam. 1:1). David's responsibilities as Israel's king obligate him to know and carry out whatever it takes to uphold the laws of Israel and its God—one set of laws, really; not two. However, the expectations that one would have of

Israel's greatest king are not fulfilled, for even though as king he is an adopted son of God (Ps. 2),[36] he sets about breaking several commandments in the span of two days, doing whatever he wants because he can, calling to mind Mel Brooks's portrayal of the hedonistic Louis XVI in his 1981 film *History of the World, Part I*, for which he observes, "It's good to be the king!"

By contrast, David's valiant infantryman, who bears a Yahwistic theophoric name (Ur-i-[y]*ah*) modified by a Hittite ethnic identity marker, demonstrates the highest loyalty to his fellow soldiers on the field of battle by rejecting two urgent royal invitations to go home and sleep with his wife: "The ark and Israel and Judah remain in booths, and my lord Joab and the servants of my lord [i.e., the king] are camping in the open field; shall I then go to my house, to eat and to drink, and to lie with my wife?"[37] Imagine a soldier today, summoned by his president from some far-off field of battle to enjoy some time at home. Who would not take advantage of this offer? After all, what difference would it make to one's fellow combatants whether the soldier went home or not? However, the undeserved privilege made a difference to Uriah, who seems to be answering to a higher king, demonstrating the kind of loyalty to Israel and its God that was expected of David.[38] Although Nathan later restores David to proper humility, the despicable results of his actions were irreversible.

If King David represents so fallible a leader, what must the rest be like? According to the prophetically influenced scribal perspective from the exile, the very idea of the monarchy was a bad one from the start. The reason the Bible offers for the institution of the monarchy is that the people wanted to "be like other nations" (1 Sam. 8:5), a naïve reason to be sure, but telling in light of the fact that being like other nations is precisely what they were called *not* to be. That historically Israel *had* a monarchy could not be ignored by the writer, so its inception is portrayed as an act of supreme condescension, even though the real-world process of centralizing a government among warrior chieftains is not so easily achieved (as can be seen today throughout central Asia). The biblical writer's assessment of the monarchy is summed up in Yahweh's consoling words to Samuel, "For they have not rejected you, but they have rejected me as king over them" (v. 7).

Indeed, from the perspective of the Deuteronomistic writer the subsequent history of the monarchy is a devastating one. Saul, the first anointed king, is described as tall and handsome, an effective military leader; but following an act of pride he is informed by Samuel that the LORD regrets that he had made him king (1 Sam. 15:10). From there the king spirals downward in paranoia and despair, tragically taking his own life on Mt. Gilboa in a battle with the Philistines (1 Sam. 31:1–7). After that, every Judahite king from David to the sons of Josiah, as well as every king of the northern kingdom of Israel, falls far short of the standard expected by the biblical writer.[39] Solomon, for example, takes many wives for himself, and his heart is turned to idolatry, just as the Deuteronomistic prophecy warns after the fact (v. 17). Even Josiah, in whom the biblical writer's expectation appears to have been fulfilled, is shown to have previously fallen short of the Deuteronomistic standard when he rends his clothes in anguish at the finding of the lost scroll.[40] Thus Josiah is regarded as good only insofar as he realizes that he has not been good and redeems himself only by setting about to fulfill the demands of the lost scroll, which includes reading the Law of Moses "all the days of his life" (v. 19). Still, having to deal with the historical fact of Jerusalem's destruction roughly two decades after Josiah's death, the biblical writer asserts that Josiah's devotion to Yahweh was not enough to atone for the sins of his grandfather, King Manasseh:

> Still the LORD did not turn from the fierceness of his great wrath, by which his anger was kindled against Judah because of all the provocations with which Manasseh had provoked him. The LORD said, "I will remove Judah also out of my sight, as I have removed Israel; and I will reject this city that I have chosen, Jerusalem, and the house of which I said, My name shall be there."[41]

Similarly, the fall of Samaria was also attributed to the actions of a king, one that reigned roughly two centuries before the event occurred:

> Jeroboam drove Israel from following the LORD and made them commit great sin. The people of Israel continued in all the sins that

Jeroboam committed; they did not depart from them until the LORD removed Israel out of his sight, as he had foretold through all his servants the prophets. So Israel was exiled from their own land to Assyria until this day.[42]

Thus, the two greatest disasters to fall upon the Israelites are blamed upon the actions of their kings.

The scathing critique of Israel's leadership is not limited to kings, but extends to all who occupy positions of responsibility and leadership. For example, Zephaniah's condemnation of Jerusalem, reminiscent of the major prophets above, is followed by accusations against its leaders, leaving no civil or religious office exempt from judgment:

Ah, soiled, defiled,
    oppressing city!
It has listened to no voice;
    it has accepted no correction.
It has not trusted in the LORD;
    it has not drawn near to its God.
The officials within it
    are roaring lions;
its judges are evening wolves
    that leave nothing until the morning.
Its prophets are reckless,
    faithless persons;
its priests have profaned what is sacred,
    they have done violence to the law.[43]

Hosea, from the eighth century BCE, will have the last word on this:

Hear this, O priests!
    Give heed, O house of Israel!
Listen, O house of the king!
    For the judgment pertains to you;
for you have been a snare at Mizpah,
    and a net spread upon Tabor,

and a pit dug deep in Shittim;
    but I will punish all of them.[44]

MISPLACED TRUST IN ANY AGE

Standing at the end of their own national history in a strange and far-off land among bewildered fellow exiles dazed by the fact that Jerusalem's once-inviolable palace-temple complex now lay in ruins, a handful of faithful visionaries responded to the challenge of ultimate times with agonizing self-honesty, daring to assert that as a nation and a people, Israel had sinned so grievously against their God that destruction was the only fair and imaginable recompense.

Collecting their various oral and written stories and other surviving documents, these prophetically influenced priestly scribes set about to write a comprehensive answer to the question of what had gone so terribly wrong. It was not to be an actual, factual account of history as modern readers have come to understand and expect of the term; rather, it would be what one might call *ultimate history* in taking into account convictions about divine forces at work behind human events. Had the biblical writers been writing mere history, they would have recorded that King Nebuchadnezzar of Babylonia destroyed Jerusalem, and that would have been sufficient; but as evidenced by biblical references to lost books, such as the Annals of the Kings of Israel and Judah, ordinary history simply does not survive—unless, of course, it happens to be resurrected by the archaeologist's spade. Apparently the boasts of kings die with kings.

From the perspective of the exiled faithful it was ultimately God who had awakened the fearsome empires for the purpose of chastising a people who had forsaken him as their divine King. No earthly king, no fortified city, no number of iron chariots, could deliver Israel from Yahweh's fearsome wrath. Only the word of Israel's true King remains an inviolable city of refuge, and the Prophets, his chariots of fire, the highest and best line of defense. In this dangerous age of nuclear proliferation, unstoppable armored tanks, and fifth-generation fighter jets, it may serve well to keep humbly in mind that the only true repository for one's trust transcends the works of human hands.

NOTES

1. Warfare is no more impervious to changes over time than anything else, so while the dates I have chosen are somewhat arbitrary, they mark the era of significant use for iron chariots.

2. This body of literature, known collectively in the Hebrew Bible as the *Nevi'im*, or Prophets, includes what traditionally has been called the Former Prophets (Joshua through 2 Kings) plus the fifteen books of the Latter, or Writing Prophets. Although modern scholarship refers to the Former Prophets as the Deuteronomistic History, its outlook is far less historical (in the modern sense of the word) than prophetic.

3. Unless otherwise noted, "Israel" will refer to both kingdoms of the divided monarchy in the Iron Age II period, namely Israel and Judah.

4. Although characterized by bloody religious reforms, Josiah's reign is celebrated by the Deuteronomistic historian for centralizing religion in Jerusalem and expanding Judah's territorial control, a feat made possible by the waning of Assyrian power in the immediate region. See 2 Kings 23:4–25.

5. For a good introduction to patristic exegesis for the generally educated reader, see C. Hall, *Reading Scripture with the Church Fathers* (Downers Grove, IL: InterVarsity Press Academic, 1998); for a more thorough and highly specialized resource, see Charles Kannengiesser, *Handbook of Patristic Exegesis: The Bible in Ancient Christianity*, 2 vols. (Leiden: Brill Academic, 2006).

6. See Kannengiesser, *Handbook of Patristic Exegesis*, 1:290–95.

7. The literary assemblage envisioned here presupposes the Enneateuch, most of the Latter Prophets, and some of the Writings (*Ketuvim*), especially the Psalms. On the Enneateuch, see C. Levin, "On the Cohesion and Separation of Books within the Enneateuch," in *Pentateuch, Hexateuch, or Enneateuch? Identifying Literary Works in Genesis through Kings*, ed. T. Dozeman, T. Römer, and K. Schmid (Leiden: Brill, 2011), 127–54.

8. Steven McKenzie, *The Trouble with Kings: The Composition of the Book of Kings in the Deuteronomistic History* (Leiden: Brill, 1991).

9. Nicolae Roddy, "Landscape of Shadows: The Image of City in the Hebrew Bible," in *Cities through the Looking Glass*, ed. R. Arav (Winona Lake, IN: Eisenbrauns, 2008), 11–21.

10. Nicolae Roddy, "În căutarea unei antropologii scripturistice autentice: două studii de caz" [In search of a genuine biblical anthropology: Two case studies], in *Biserica Ortodoxă și Drepturile Omului: Paradigme, fundamente, implicații*

[The Orthodox Church and the rights of man: Paradigms, foundations, and implications], ed. and trans. N. Răzvan Stan (Bucharest: S.C. Universul Juridic, S.R.L., 2010), 180–92.

11. See Patrick D. Miller, *The Divine Warrior in Early Israel* (Cambridge, MA: Harvard University Press, 1973); Paul C. Craigie, *The Problem of War in the Old Testament* (Grand Rapids: Eerdmans, 1978).

12. See Millard C. Lind, *Yahweh Is a Warrior: The Theology of Warfare in Ancient Israel* (Scottdale, PA: Herald Press, 1980). Writing from a Mennonite peace church perspective, Lind anticipates the prophetically influenced scribal perspective by calling attention to the postexilic view of the divine warrior turned against Israel, in which case holy war is the domain of the prophet, not the soldier (see especially 109–68).

13. A. Webster and D. Cole, *The Virtue of War: Reclaiming the Classic Christian Traditions East and West* (Salisbury, MA: Regina Orthodox Press, 2004), 55. This book followed upon a publication based upon Webster's doctoral dissertation, *The Pacifist Option: The Moral Argument against War in Eastern Orthodox Theology* (Lanham, MD: International Scholars Publications, 1998). I will leave the critique of Webster's notion of "justifiable war" to other contributors to this volume.

14. Egyptian chariots appear to have been swifter and lighter than their northern counterparts and usually supported two men as opposed to three.

15. See M. Healy, *Qadesh 1300 BC: Clash of the Warrior Kings* (New York: Osprey Publishing, 1993).

16. See L. G. Herr, "Tripartite Pillared Buildings and the Market Place in Iron Age Palestine," *Bulletin of the American Schools of Oriental Research* 272 (1988): 43–58; Zeev Herzog, "Administrative Structures in the Iron Age," in *The Architecture of Ancient Israel: From the Prehistoric to the Persian Periods*, ed. Immanuel Dunayevsky, Aharon Kempinsky, Ronny Reich, and Hannah Katzenstein (Jerusalem: Israel Exploration Society, 1992), 223–30.

17. Although some objections to the interpretation remain, a recent Ph.D. dissertation by equine specialist D. O'Daniel Cantrell effectively deflates their arguments, restoring horses and chariots to the landscape of Iron Age Israel; see *The Horsemen of Israel: Horses and Chariotry in Monarchic Israel (Ninth–Eighth Centuries BCE)* (Winona Lake, IN: Eisenbrauns, 2011).

18. Aviram Biran and Joseph Naveh, "The Tel Dan Inscription: A New Fragment," *Israel Exploration Journal* 45 (1995): 1–18.

19. Apparently a round number, as only eleven kings are listed.

20. Shalmaneser III was eventually successful in establishing Assyrian dominance in the Levant, as shown on the famous Black Obelisk, on display in the

British Museum, in which King Jehu of Israel is depicted in bas-relief bearing tribute to the Assyrian king, ca. 840 BCE.

21. The DH recounts that Ahab was occupied with hostilities against Aram (Syria) for much of his reign. Even though a treaty eventually results (1 Kings 20:26–34), it is difficult to reconcile this account with the Kurkh monolith, which states that under Ahab, Israel and Aram are allied. Without blunting the point of the present argument, it is possible that the Assyrians misidentified the Israelite king, who may have been one of Ahab's Omride dynastic successors, Jehoram perhaps. See M. Coogan, *A Brief Introduction to the Old Testament* (Oxford: Oxford University Press, 2009), 237.

22. Deut. 17:16. Unless otherwise indicated, all biblical quotations follow the NRSV.

23. Ps. 33:16–17.

24. Ps. 20:7–8.

25. Elisha's obligation to "see" is an admonition to the reader to pay close attention. Unfortunately, the traditional understanding of what happens next seems to indicate most readers have not.

26. Isaac Abravanel (also, Abarbanel), a fifteenth-century Portuguese Jewish sage, seems to be the first scholar on record to have expressed this view. If R. Friedman is correct in suggesting that the author is Jeremiah's scribe, Baruch ben Neriah, then the identification becomes even more likely. See Richard E. Friedman, *Who Wrote the Bible?* (San Francisco: HarperCollins, 1997), 147–48.

27. See also Roddy, "Landscape of Shadows," 11–21.

28. Probably the sin imputed to Ham involved more than simply seeing his father in the nude.

29. Gen. 10:8–12.

30. The name Babel plays on the Akkadian word for gate (*bab*; *bab-ilani* = gate of the gods) and the Hebrew word for confusion (*babel*, originally *balal*).

31. Isa. 24:10–13.

32. Isa. 25:2–4a.

33. Jer. 1:18–19.

34. 1 Sam. 8:11–12.

35. This episode, commonly called the David and Bathsheba story, is primarily about the contrast between David and his soldier. Bathsheba is a "flat" character in the story, a mere literary prop whose character and motivations are not revealed.

36. In contrast to the kings of Egypt, who were affirmed to become semidivine upon assuming the throne, the kings of Mesopotamia were believed to remain human, but become adopted sons of the foremost god of their pantheon.

37. 2 Sam. 11:11.

38. It is also possible to suppose that Uriah knew what the king was doing all along, even though exposing him would have still resulted in tragic consequences.

39. This standard is outlined in Deut. 17:14–20.

40. Scholars have long held this lost scroll essentially to be the law code at the core of the book of Deuteronomy.

41. 2 Kings 23:26–27.

42. 2 Kings 17:21–23.

43. Zeph. 3:1–4.

44. Hosea 5:1–2.

CHAPTER 4

HERODIAN-ROMAN DOMINATION, VIOLENT JEWISH PEASANT RESISTANCE, AND JESUS OF NAZARETH

JOHN FOTOPOULOS

Give us today our much-needed bread, and release our debts in the same way that we have released our debtors.

—Matt. 6:11–12 (translation mine)[1]

Jesus said to them, "Have you come out with swords and clubs to arrest me as though I were a bandit?"

—Mark 14:48

The inscription of the charge against him read, "The King of the Jews." And with him they crucified two bandits, one on his right and one on his left.

—Mark 15:26–27

Jesus of Nazareth was born in about 4 BCE in a world filled with oppression, strife, and violence. Roman imperial rule over Palestine in the first centuries BCE and CE together with the Herodian royal dynasty which reigned over some of Palestine's Roman provinces as client rulers made life extremely difficult for Jewish peasants, who constituted the majority of the population. It is estimated that approximately five hundred thousand Jewish peasants occupied the rural villages of Judea, Galilee, and Samaria in the first century CE,[2] constituting about 90 percent of the total population. The harsh socioeconomic policies and severe taxation imposed on these peasants by both Roman imperial officials and the Herodian client rulers together with the substantial tithes expected of the peasants by the Jewish high priestly aristocracy who controlled the temple in Jerusalem made survival at subsistence levels extremely difficult.

Of course, not all of the Jewish people were willing to live with the dire socioeconomic, political, and religious situation of their land—a land which they believed God had given to them as part of the Abrahamic covenant (Gen. 17). Indeed, some of the earliest precepts in Israelite tradition which were kept alive both in the Hebrew Bible and among the Jewish peasantry were the Deuteronomic commands for justice and equality, especially on behalf of the poor and the powerless (cf. Deut. 10:18; 24:17; 27:19). From the time of Herod the Great's death in 4 BCE, there arose from among the Jewish peasantry numerous popular leaders who tried to oppose the hegemonic policies of the Roman imperial government, the Herodian dynasty, and the Jewish high priestly aristocracy. Sometimes these Jewish popular leaders and their followers took up arms in revolt, while other such leaders proclaimed the imminence of God's violent judgment against those in power. Josephus, the renowned Jewish historian, records the names and details of numerous bandits, prophets, rebels, and messiah-type popular kings in Palestine who arose from among the Jewish peasantry and took action throughout the period of 4 BCE to the First Jewish War against Rome (66–73 CE). Such leaders were often inspired by Jewish apocalyptic beliefs as they stirred up a popular following among the Jewish peasantry in their efforts to resist the oppressive status quo. These popular Jewish leaders and their followers regularly faced a similar end as Roman and/or Herodian military units of infantry and cavalry moved swiftly and violently to destroy all vestiges of their movements, while also frequently making an example of those leaders by way of public execution.

This was the world that Jesus of Nazareth was born into and the context in which he pursued his public ministry among Jewish peasants, proclaiming to them the good news of the βασιλεία τοῦ θεοῦ (the kingdom of God)—that is, a vision of the world as it will be when it is ruled immediately and directly by God.[3] It should not come as a surprise, then, that those in the highest positions of power and privilege, such as Roman imperial officials, Herodian rulers, and Jewish high priestly aristocrats, collaborated in order to bring Jesus and his particular Jewish peasant movement to an end by sending out an armed security detail which captured him and then crucified him after dispersing his closest followers—followers who then initially went into hiding because of their fear that they might also be put to death in similar fashion to Jesus (cf. John 20:19). Although Jesus' resistance to the status quo was perceived by those in power as a threat similar to the many Jewish bandits, prophets, rebels, and messiah-type popular kings of his time that were also captured and killed, Jesus' message and methods of resistance were quite different. Simply stated, Jesus of Nazareth was opposed to war as a means of problem solving or establishing lasting peace and justice in the world despite the popularity of military action among Jewish popular leaders and their movements at that time. Rather, Jesus spread the good news of the kingdom of God to the poor and the powerless (cf. Luke 4:16–21) and to anyone else who would listen,[4] while enacting this alternative society by healing the infirm (cf. Mark 1:34), casting out demons (cf. Luke 11:19–20), and eating with the "nuisances and nobodies" of his day (cf. Luke 7:34).[5]

A METHODOLOGY FOR DETERMINING JESUS OF NAZARETH'S VIEWS ON WAR AND PEACE

Josephus, our primary source of information on Jewish history for the first centuries BCE and CE, is not without bias. Even so, when Josephus's background and agenda are considered, the information that he provides on Jewish peasant movements and their leaders is all the more significant.

Josephus was a Jewish aristocratic priest who also became a Pharisee, later serving as a leader of Jewish rebel forces who fought in the First Jewish War against Rome. Josephus is well known for his subsequent defection to the side of the Romans in order to deliver to the Roman general, Vespasian, a prophetic message that he claimed to have received from God. This message rightly conveyed that Vespasian would soon become the world's king, that is, the Roman emperor. After Vespasian returned to Rome to become emperor, Josephus served alongside Vespasian's son, Titus, for the remainder of the war as his interpreter and eventually became a part of Emperor Vespasian's imperial court in Rome.

Josephus's writings about Jewish history were aimed at a Roman audience as they conveyed his apologetic interests and put the best face possible on the Jewish people after the First Jewish War against Rome, squarely blaming the Jewish peasantry, Jewish bandit leaders, and a few inept Roman officials for the recent conflict. From Josephus's perspective, those Jewish bandit leaders who were acclaimed popular kings by the peasantry were simply messianic pretenders, especially since Josephus believed that Vespasian himself was the true messiah. Despite Josephus's background and apologetic concerns, his writings are considered one of the best sources of information on Jewish history in the first centuries BCE and CE.[6] The critical use of information found in Josephus, together with available archaeological evidence, the findings of contemporary biblical and sociological scholarship, and postcolonial theory, allows for a fairly clear picture to emerge of the socioeconomic, political, and religious realities of Jewish Palestine under the hegemony of Roman imperial rule in the first centuries BCE and CE. The dire socioeconomic and political situation of the Jewish peasantry in Palestine under Roman imperial rule in the first centuries BCE and CE, coupled with popular Jewish religious beliefs, led the Jewish peasantry to numerous acts of resistance and rebellion, ultimately climaxing in full-scale war. By seriously considering that historical situation and various Jewish peasant leaders who struggled against the status quo, we can better understand Jesus of Nazareth's views on resistance, violence, war, and peace.

The present study finds inadequate those investigations which seek to ascertain Jesus' attitudes on war simply by quoting particular Gospel sayings of Jesus that have been removed from their historical context (e.g., sayings on "violence/force," "sword(s)," "peace," "love"). To be sure, any use of such logia of Jesus must consider their pre-Gospel *Sitz im Leben*, not simply in the sense of their presupposed use in the life of early Christians (*Sitz im Leben der Kirche*), but foremost in the way that such sayings may have functioned in the life of Jesus of Nazareth (*Sitz im Leben Jesu*) and among his peasant followers living under the dire socioeconomic and political realities of Roman and Herodian rule.[7] Even so, it needs to be clearly emphasized here that a consideration of Jesus' sayings alone may not be sufficient to settle questions of Jesus' attitudes toward violence and war—especially when Jesus' sayings have been divorced from their particular historical and/or literary contexts. Indeed, a survey of all the relevant sayings of Jesus regarding violence and war produces very meager results and does not resolve questions about Jesus' attitude toward those issues. For example, although Jesus' sayings on loving one's enemies and turning the other cheek are commonly raised in order to assess Jesus' attitudes toward violence and war, "there is no indication in the Gospels that loving one's enemies had any reference to the Romans or that turning the other cheek pertained to nonresistance to foreign political domination."[8] Indeed, attempts to apply such sayings of Jesus to questions of war and peace were rejected back in 1625 by Hugo Grotius in his *The Law of War and Peace* as interpretations that were being done out of context.[9] This is not to say, on the other hand, that such sayings of Jesus support the untenable thesis that Jesus was a pro-violence Zealot who "stormed" the city of Jerusalem before being captured and crucified by the Romans, as promoted by Reza Aslan in his deeply flawed book *Zealot: The Life and Times of Jesus of Nazareth*.[10]

Moreover, contemporary approaches which seek to isolate sayings of Jesus that seem relevant to questions of war and violence often read such sayings as though they are aimed at the Western individual rather than to a community of people living in an ancient rural, peasant, collectivist society that was very different from the Western, individualistic, imperialistic culture that shapes most citizens of the United States today.[11] Such readings tend to forget that Jesus of Nazareth spoke primarily to rural communities of Jewish peasants from the villages of Galilee and Judea that were dominated by the hegemonic policies of the Roman imperial government, their Herodian client rulers, and the Jewish high priestly aristocracy—the latter two groups both being appointed by the Romans during that time.[12] Stated simply, by better understanding the socioeconomic, political, and religious realities of Jewish peasants living in first-century CE Palestine and responses to those realities led by their peasant leaders, it is possible to better appreciate Jesus' words *and* actions in relation to questions of war and peace.

HERODIAN-ROMAN DOMINATION

In the year 63 BCE the Roman general Pompey took control of Jerusalem and effectively began the period of Roman rule over Jewish Palestine. This change of power brought an end to a nearly one-hundred-year period of Jewish independence under the Hasmonean Dynasty that had been brought to power by the Maccabean/Hasmonean Rebellion (163–63 BCE). Although the Maccabean Rebellion had been fought in part as a response to the increased Hellenization of the Jewish high priestly aristocracy, after the rebellion and subsequent change in priesthood from Zadokite to Hasmonean, the Hellenization continued and began creating a religious and cultural chasm between the high priestly aristocracy and the Jewish peasantry.[13] Moreover, many individuals from the Hasmonean dynasty ruled over the people of Israel in the capacity of both high priest and king, effectively controlling the Jewish peasantry through a system of tithes and taxes. Richard A. Horsley sums up the arrangement of the temple-state succinctly: "The temple-state had been set up in Jerusalem in the sixth century B.C.E. by the Persian imperial regime as an instrument of imperial control. The temple provided a religious-political-economic formation in which the Judean people could serve their own 'God who is in Jerusalem' (Ezra 1:3) while providing economic support for a priestly aristocracy who both controlled the area and rendered tribute to the Persian court."[14]

Such a system continued during the periods of Hasmonean and Roman rule. Indeed, the Hasmonean high priestly aristocrats were quite useful to the Romans since Roman government policy for its eastern provinces was to rule and maintain order through the oversight of native client aristocrats. However, through a series of astute political and military maneuvers by a non-Hasmonean leader, Herod the Great, the Hasmonean reign over Israel came to an end.

Herod the Great was the son of a savvy and powerful political leader, Antipater (an Idumean convert to Judaism), and a Nabatean woman named Cypros. While Herod served as the governor of Galilee at the beginning of his political career, his violent campaign against the Jewish bandit-chief Hezekiah and his men caused Herod to gain the support of Hellenized citizens of Syria while being despised by the Jewish peasantry for his repressive policies.[15] Herod, who desired one day to replace John Hyrcanus as king of the Jews, attempted to better his own position through a politically expedient marriage to an important Hasmonean heir, Mariamne I.[16] Herod's rise to the position of king of the Jews occurred through further military and political maneuvers against a rival claimant to the Kingdom of Judea, Antigonus, a Hasmonean who had the military support of the Parthians.[17] Herod, however, received his title as king of the Jews by a vote of the Roman senate through the intervention of his patron, Marc Antony, who supported Herod in order to gain his assistance against the Parthians.[18] Although Herod was ultimately victorious against Antigonus, Herod had chosen the wrong side in the Roman civil wars by siding with Marc Antony, who was defeated at Actium. Herod made amends with the victorious Octavian Augustus by promptly sailing to him in Rhodes and swearing his loyalty to him. Augustus in turn recognized Herod as βασιλεὺς Ἰουδαίων—king of the Jews.[19] Herod consolidated his power by commonly resorting to violence: assassinating his political rivals and hiring the best mercenary soldiers from Syria, Thrace, Gaul, and Germania for his royal army,[20] including a highly skilled, specialized unit of five hundred horse-mounted archers from Trachonitis to whom he gave free plots of land and the privilege of tax immunity.[21] He also used a network of spies to enforce his rule.[22] To ensure his own personal safety, Herod had a large force of bodyguards including a unit of four hundred soldiers from Gaul that had formerly served as the bodyguards of Cleopatra but after her death were given to Herod as a gift from Octavian.[23]

Because Herod had survived as a client king of the Romans after the downfall of Marc Antony only due to Octavian's benevolence, Herod felt it necessary to flatter his new Roman patron, Octavian/Augustus, with a massive building program.[24] Herod had numerous buildings constructed all over Palestine in Greek style, such as an amphitheater, theater, and new royal palace in Jerusalem, while also renovating and expanding the Jewish temple; he also built palace-fortresses all over his land. But his most ambitious project was the construction of a new port city on the west coast of Palestine, built in honor of Augustus and named Caesarea Maritima.

To pay for this extravagant building program and for the annual monetary tribute that Herod was expected to give to the Romans, he heavily taxed the Jewish peasantry which made up roughly 90 percent of the population. The already existing taxes and tithes that the Jewish peasantry was paying to support the Jewish temple-state, at least 40 percent of their harvest, together with this additional taxation created a situation where the Jewish peasantry lived at barely subsistence levels. The Jewish peasantry also loathed Herod's construction of Hellenistic buildings and pagan temples throughout the land as a violation of the laws of Torah prohibiting idols and images, and his explanation that such edifices were built to honor their Roman patrons only exacerbated popular resentment.[25] Moreover, the landed gentry further exploited the Jewish peasantry by charging them high rents to work the gentry's land as tenant farmers and by charging them illegal interest on loans necessary to pay off their sizable debts.[26] Hunger and debt were real day-to-day concerns among the peasantry, something succinctly illustrated by the Lord's Prayer, taught by Jesus: "Give us today our much-needed bread, and release our debts in the same way that we have released our debtors" (Matt. 6:11–12; my translation). The problems of not having enough bread for today while having too much debt from yesterday are squarely addressed by Jesus' prayer. If the hungry Jewish peasantry were to acquire enough bread just for today, it would be a most welcome gift from God. Likewise, God is petitioned as the ultimate social superior to release the poor Jewish peasantry from their debts in like measure to the action that each petitioner takes in releasing social inferiors from debt—a clever yet biting rebuke of the landed gentry's economic exploitation of desperate Jewish tenant farmers. The problems of not enough bread and too much debt seem to have forced some Galilean Jewish peasants and their families to resort to banditry while taking refuge in remote caves—but they were killed in a commando-style raid by Herod the Great's special forces.[27]

It was upon the death of Herod the Great in 4 BCE that widespread peasant revolts broke out throughout Palestine. After the seven-day mourning period for Herod was completed, his son, Archelaus, took power over Judea—and hence the important city of Jerusalem—with the expectation that Herod's will naming him king of the Jews would soon be ratified by Augustus. Archelaus entered into the temple complex in a white garment—probably a sign of his presumed kingship and/or purity—in order to be hailed by the higher-status citizens of Jerusalem. Archelaus also had the support of Herod the Great's army, which attempted to place a diadem on Archelaus's head earlier at Jericho.[28] However, Archelaus was aware that he could only be legitimately named king and receive the diadem from the Roman emperor, Augustus.

At Jerusalem crowds of Jewish peasants came to Archelaus seeking improvements to the dire living conditions that had been caused by Herod the Great. The crowds made enormous demands (μεγάλοις αἰτήμασιν) on Archelaus, asking for economic relief through a reduction in general taxation (ἐπικουφίζειν τὰς εἰσφοράς) and a cessation of the taxes on sales and purchases (ἀναιρεῖν τὰ τέλη), while also seeking the release of some captives who had been imprisoned by Herod the Great.[29] The crowds also demanded that those who were responsible for the death of the Jewish sages Judas, Matthias, and their disciples be punished. The sages had been burned alive by Herod the Great after they had encouraged their disciples to remove and destroy the golden eagle that Herod had erected at the entrance of the temple sanctuary.[30]

Soon after all of these demands were made, multitudes of Jewish pilgrims gathered in the Jerusalem temple for the Festivals of Passover and Unleavened Bread while some protesters began clamoring again about the death of the Jewish sages.[31] Archelaus, probably fearing that any disturbances caused by the peasantry before his fragile reign had even officially begun would be perceived by Augustus as a sign of weakness, took swift and violent action.[32] While the pilgrims and protestors were offering their Passover sacrifices, Archelaus sent a tribune with a double cohort of soldiers (probably one thousand men) to the temple complex to silence the protestors, but the soldiers were met by a stoning and many of them were killed.[33] The tribune barely escaped with his life, while the pilgrims returned to their religious sacrifices. Archelaus, realizing that this would not play well in Rome, responded even more violently later in the day by sending his entire military force against the pilgrims. The infantry slaughtered Jewish peasants within the temple who were still holding their sacrificial animals, while the cavalry killed many pilgrims who were camping in tents outside the city in the nearby plains.[34] Those who were able to escape the massacre fled into the nearby Judean mountains and eventually dispersed to their homes. In total, three thousand Jewish pilgrims were killed on that day.[35]

JEWISH POPULAR KINGSHIP AND PEASANT REVOLTS

After Archelaus's slaughter of the peasant pilgrims at Passover in 4 BCE in Jerusalem, he sailed to Rome with his entourage in the hopes of having Augustus ratify Herod the Great's will, which named Archelaus the next king of the Jews. However, just fifty days after Passover, at the Festival of Pentecost, peasant revolts began to break out all over Palestine. Josephus writes: "At this time there were great disturbances throughout the land and in many areas; and the opportunity that now offered itself induced a great many to aspire to kingship" (*Jewish War* 2.4.1). He conveys that numerous peasant movements led by popular kings took violent military action against the Romans and those forces loyal to the Herodians.

Popular kingship is a concept that goes back at least as far as David in the eleventh century BCE. However, it should be remembered that the Israelites originally resisted any notions of kingship, probably in reaction against the unjust monarchical rule of Canaanite city-states, and the Israelites originally seemed to have viewed only Yahweh as their king. Nevertheless, even with some traditional suspicion of Israelite kingship, the idea of a popular king did come to be generally accepted by the Israelites. The notion of popular kingship in Israelite tradition in some cases blurred the line with social banditry. Eric Hobsbawm, who wrote the foundational work on social bandits, has argued that social banditry is a universal phenomenon arising in agrarian societies where oppressive socioeconomic conditions created by those in power lead peasants to aggressive resistance.[36] Graham Seal sums up the phenomenon of social banditry nicely:

Outlaw heroes arise in historical circumstances in which one or more social, cultural, ethnic, or religious groups believe themselves to be oppressed and unjustly treated by one or more other groups who wield greater power. These power differentials cause continual underlying tension that can flare into open conflict. There is also an important cultural dimension to these socio-political and economic differences. The oppressed group often has a fear—not necessarily made explicit—that its sense of identity, as coded into its traditions, customs, and worldview, is being outraged, ignored or otherwise threatened. While the specifics of time, place, and situation are conditioned by current socio-political and economic forces, the hero's actions and words accord remarkably consistently with the social bandit tradition across cultures. This similarity is the basis of Hobsbawm's seminal insight and formulation of the social bandit concept.[37]

David, who would one day be regarded as the most celebrated king of Israel, initially started his popular movement as a bandit who appealed to rural peasants over against the oppressive sociopolitical and economic realities created by King Saul and the Philistines. First Samuel 22:2 states that when David had taken refuge from King Saul, "Everyone who was in distress, and everyone who was in debt, and everyone who was discontented gathered to him; and he became captain over them. Those who were with him numbered about four hundred." In this way a peasant leader such as David could go from being a bandit leader who fought against the powerful Philistines and was pursued in the wilderness by King Saul's forces to becoming the king of Judah.

Kings were generally elected in ancient Israel from the eleventh century to the seventh century BCE in times of revolution against foreign enemies. Such popular election became synonymous with anointing: "Then the people of Judah came, and there they anointed David king over the house of Judah" (2 Sam. 2:4).[38] The word *messiah* is derived from the Hebrew term *masiah* (anointed one), a term which came to refer to an Israelite king (cf. 2 Sam. 3:39; 5:3; 1 Sam. 24:6; 26:9). As Horsley rightly notes, "The rise of David, in particular, shows that, although a king might begin as a bandit-chief, popular kingship was a distinct sociopolitical form."[39]

Although the official ideology of kingship in Israelite tradition after the seventh century BCE became identified with the royal house of David and with the temple-state in Jerusalem, the idea of popular kingship and election by the peasantry seems to have remained alive among the common Jewish people into the first century CE in their folk traditions ("little traditions"). The renewed reflections on a coming anointed king in the Pharisaic and Qumran Essene movements in the face of unpopular Hasmonean high priest–kings together with the subsequent brutal reign of Herod the Great also probably helped to reignite peasant traditions about a popular anointed king elected by the Jewish peasantry that would lead the people in revolt against foreign oppression.[40] Indeed, traditions among the peasantry of a coming popularly anointed king would be revived during the annual Passover Festival celebrations and the annual Festival of Tabernacles, both of which commemorated the Exodus event and for which 300,000–500,000 Jewish pilgrims would gather in Jerusalem, the city of David, celebrating Israel's liberation from foreign oppression in former times.

Josephus describes tens of thousands of Jewish peasants streaming into Jerusalem in 4 BCE for the Feast of Weeks (Pentecost), just fifty days after Archelaus's slaughter of the pilgrims who sought tax relief at Passover. These peasants were indignant about the slaughter of the Passover pilgrims and the ensuing plundering of Herod the Great's considerable wealth by Sabinus, Roman procurator of Syria; the peasantry most likely viewed this wealth as having been unjustly taken from them by Herod's exploitative tax policies.[41] Josephus writes that "there were a great many crowds of Galileans, Idumeans, and people from Jericho, as well as those living beyond the Jordan River who had crossed over."[42] The Jewish pilgrims took up positions in strategic parts of Jerusalem and attacked Sabinus and his Roman soldiers. Josephus states that the Jewish peasants believed that they, "after a long time, were restoring their ancestral self-rule" (διὰ χρόνου πολλοῦ κομιζομένοις τὴν πάτριον αὐτονομίαν).[43] Many of the Jewish peasants who poured into the temple from all quarters of Palestine hoped to achieve an independent Jewish kingdom once again. However, because of the skillful tactics of the Roman forces in Jerusalem together with some of Herod's fiercest royal forces, including three thousand troops from Sebaste under the command of Rufus and Gratus that had remained loyal to the Romans, these Jewish peasants would not achieve the freedom that they sought.[44]

Nevertheless, revolts broke out all over Jewish Palestine—in Galilee, Perea, and Judea. Many of these revolts were led by Jewish popular kings whom Josephus, as a method of character assassination, associates with the violence of banditry. Even so, the fact that Josephus is willing to refer to *any* Jewish popular kings while associating them with social banditry is especially remarkable when considering his aristocratic, priestly, pro-Roman background and apologetic purposes in writing. He writes: "But Judea was full of banditry [ληστηρίων] and whenever some of the insurgents [οἳ συστασιάσοιεν] happened upon someone to lead them, he was made king [βασιλεὺς], thereby leading the masses to ruin."[45]

For example, in 4 BCE at Sepphoris of Galilee, the bandit leader Judas son of Hezekiah led a peasant revolt which attacked the royal palace, plundering the weapons and further arming his men, and carrying off the money that had been stored there.[46] Judas then proceeded to attack other Jewish popular kings who were vying with him for sovereign power over Israel (τοῖς τὴν δυναστείαν ζηλοῦσιν ἐπεχείρει).[47] In the Israelite tradition of bandit leaders like David being elected popular king by the peasantry, Judas son of Hezekiah seems to have been regarded by his followers as the rightful Jewish king or messiah. Josephus writes clearly that Judas took such actions out of "a desire for better circumstances and a zeal for royal dignity" (ἐπιθυμίᾳ μειζόνων πραγμάτων καὶ ζηλώσει βασιλείου τιμῆς).[48]

Another bandit leader at this time who was elected by his peasant followers as a popular Jewish king or messiah was Simon of Perea. Although he had been a slave of Herod the Great, his handsome appearance and strong physique contributed to his leadership of a group that gathered around him, described by Josephus as λησταί (bandits). Josephus writes that Simon "dared to place a diadem on his head, while a crowd [πλήθους] gathered around him and he was proclaimed to be king [καὶ αὐτὸς βασιλεὺς ἀναγγελθείς]."[49] Simon and his followers plundered and burned several of Herod's royal palaces, while also attacking many villas of the rich.[50]

One final popular king or messiah who arose after the death of Herod the Great in 4 BCE was Athronges. Athronges was a shepherd—as was

David before becoming a popular king—who gathered his four brothers around him as commanders within his messianic movement. Josephus writes that Athronges "placed a diadem on his head and led a council regarding what things should be done, while all matters were decided by his judgments. This man retained his power for a great while and was called king" (ὁ δὲ διάδημα περιθέμενος βουλευτήριόν τε ἦγεν ἐπὶ τοῖς ποιητέοις καὶ τὰ πάντα γνώμῃ ἀνακείμενα εἶχεν τῇ αὐτοῦ διέμενέ τε ἐπὶ πολὺ τῷδε τῷ ἀνδρὶ ἡ ἰσχὺς βασιλεῖ τε κεκλημένῳ).[51] Josephus conveys not only that Athronges was elected a popular king/messiah in the mold of King David, but also that Athronges was likely attempting to fulfill various messianic expectations about the messiah leading a more egalitarian community while deciding important matters according to his wise judgment.[52] Athronges and his followers attacked Herod's royal military forces as well as Roman army units and were successful for quite some time, on one occasion attacking a Roman military supply train carrying wheat and weapons to the army.

Although Josephus does not provide information on what finally happened to Judas son of Hezekiah, he does convey that Simon of Perea, Athronges (or his brothers), and their respective followers were all captured or killed by skilled royal forces who, under the leadership of Gratus, engaged these leaders and their followers.[53] Varus, the Roman imperial legate (governor) of Syria, also traveled into Jewish Palestine with two legions of Roman soldiers and four troops of cavalry, together with auxiliary units provided by other native client kings in the region, and snuffed out the remaining rebels throughout the land, in at least one case crucifying two thousand peasant insurgents in the Judean countryside, while also burning down the towns of Sepphoris and Emmaus.[54]

While these things were taking place in Israel, Augustus in Rome divided up Herod the Great's former kingdom among three of Herod's sons: Archelaus became the ethnarch over Judaea, Samaria, Idumea, and several subject cities (4 BCE–6 CE); Herod Antipas became tetrarch over Galilee and Perea (4 BCE–39 CE); and Herod Philip became tetrarch over Batanea, Trachonitis, and Auranitis (4 BCE–34 CE).[55] This arrangement would ensure that Roman authorities would not have to worry about so much power being consolidated again in a single Jewish client king. Although Archelaus was then able to return to Jerusalem and to rule over

Judea as ethnarch with the hope that he would soon be elevated to king, he was deposed in 6 CE after his continued mistreatment of his subjects and was banished to Vienna. As a result, the Romans hoped to control the situation in Judea more closely by making it a Roman province placed under the direct oversight of a Roman prefect. Coponius was named the first prefect of Judea, while at the same time Quirinius was named imperial legate of Syria. However, because of a Roman tax census proposed by Quirinius, Judas the Galilean and a Pharisee named Zadok together incited the Jewish peasantry to revolt. "Both asserted that this taxation was outright slavery and entreated the nation to seize its liberty."[56] From a Roman perspective, any refusal to pay taxes was interpreted as an act of war, while Judas and Zadok themselves sought freedom from Roman rule by means of violent revolution.[57] The added financial strain that would be created by a new tax census, coupled with the misery caused by direct Roman rule, created a desperate situation. Josephus asserts that the resistance of Judas and Zadok inspired acts of sedition throughout Israel that would lead to the destruction of Jewish cities and to the eventual destruction of the Jewish temple by fire during the Roman siege of Jerusalem in 70 CE. [58] Although Josephus is silent about the end of Judas the Galilean, Acts 5:37 notes that "Judas the Galilean revolted at the time of the census and people revolted behind him; he was also killed, and all who followed him were scattered." Once again the Jewish peasantry was led to revolt and to shed their blood before their movement came to a violent end.

Because the Romans began directly administering Judea, and hence Jerusalem, in 6 CE, after Archelaus's exile, the Jewish high priest was no longer appointed by a Jewish king but by the Roman prefect of Judea. Nevertheless, the Jewish high priestly aristocracy increased their power significantly because there was no longer a Herodian king ruling over Judea. Horsley writes that "when the Romans ostensibly imposed direct rule by a Roman governor, the four high priestly families appointed by Herod were placed in charge of Judean society. The incumbent high priest was appointed by the Roman governor from among those four families, and, in effect, served at his pleasure. . . . The temple-state, as much or more than Herodian kingship and Roman governors and garrisons, constituted the face of Roman imperial rule in Judea."[59]

Josephus writes that in Judea from 6 CE "the form of government was an aristocracy, and the high priests were entrusted with leadership over the nation" (ἀριστοκρατία μὲν ἦν ἡ πολιτεία, τὴν δὲ προστασίαν τοῦ ἔθνους οἱ ἀρχιερεῖς ἐπεπίστευντο).[60] Thus, the high priests were given the important duty of collecting Roman taxes and tithes from the Judean peasantry, while also being responsible for the people's irenic behavior. In this way, the oppressive social, economic, and political conditions in Judea persisted for the peasantry, as well as for Jewish peasants living under the direct Herodian rule of Herod Antipas in Galilee.[61]

JESUS OF NAZARETH, KING OF THE JEWS

This is the world into which Jesus of Nazareth was born. According to the Gospel of Matthew, Jesus was born just prior to the death of Herod the Great (Matt. 2:15) in about 4 BCE; soon after that, Joseph, Mary, and the infant Jesus moved out of Judea to Nazareth in Galilee because of the dangers presented by the rule of Herod's son, Archelaus (Matt. 2:22–23). By contrast, the Gospel of Luke records Jesus' birth as occurring at the time of the Roman tax census by Quirinius (Luke 2:1–7) in about 6 CE.[62] Despite the contradictions in the date of Jesus' birth, details from those two birth narratives are relevant to Jesus, his movement, and questions of war and peace in that Jesus was raised in the tumultuous period after the death of Herod the Great, while the Jewish peasantry (90 percent of the population) also faced severe problems paying the high rate of Roman taxation. In any case, all four Gospels are consistent that Jesus later began his public ministry as an adult in Galilee, probably in about 26 or 27 CE, after having first been a disciple of John the Baptist.

Although there is very little evidence in Josephus of widespread banditry or rebellions from 7 to 44 CE, possibly due to a lack of available sources on the period, there is evidence of various protests by Jews and Samaritans after some provocative actions taken by Pontius Pilate, Roman prefect of Judea (26–36 CE) during the time of Jesus' public ministry.[63] A few occasions worthy of memory recorded by Josephus are when Pilate brought Roman military standards into Jerusalem, when he took monies from the temple treasury to fund an aqueduct and had the Jewish pilgrims who subsequently protested beaten to death, and when he sent to Mt. Gerizim a sizable military force of cavalry and infantry against the Samaritan prophet and the unarmed peasants who followed him and slaughtered many of them.[64] Pilate's demeanor as recorded by Josephus is considerably different from the vacillating man portrayed in the Gospels, who considers Jesus to be innocent and attempts to release him. Philo of Alexandria describes Pilate's rule as characterized by "briberies, insults, robberies, outrages, wanton injustices, constantly repeated executions without trial, and ceaseless and grievous cruelty."[65] To be sure, Pilate was an exceptionally brutal Roman official who did not hesitate to use deadly force on his subjects, ultimately being removed from his position as Roman prefect and recalled to Rome as a consequence of his unnecessary slaughter of the Samaritan peasants.[66] In one regard, however, the portraits of Pilate in the Gospels are consistent with reality: Pilate had Jesus executed as a potential threat to Roman and Herodian rule and to the interests of the Jewish high priestly aristocracy (Mark 15:15b, 26).[67]

Although there is little evidence in Josephus for banditry or revolts from 7 to 44 CE, the Gospels of Mark and John do provide such evidence.[68] Mark records at least one insurrection during the time of Jesus' public ministry: "Now a man called Barabbas was in prison with the rebels [στασιαστῶν] who had committed murder during the insurrection [στάσει]" (Mark 15:7). This piece of information seems to be historical since it is supported by multiple attestation (a basic scholarly criterion establishing historical authenticity for traditions about Jesus), being corroborated by the Gospel of John: "They shouted in reply, 'Not this man, but Barabbas!' Now Barabbas was a bandit [λῃστής]" (John 18:40). As was discussed earlier in reference to social banditry, the lines between bandits, insurrectionists, and popular kings were often blurred in Israelite history (e.g., King David) and throughout Palestine in the first centuries BCE and CE. "Bandit" (λῃστής) was a term commonly used by Josephus and other social elites in the Greco-Roman world to impugn the character and social origins of peasant leaders. Bandits, as Josephus frequently referred to them, were those who often led popular rebellions against Herodian and Roman rule.

Barabbas is not the only character in the Gospels to be associated with banditry. So, too, Jesus of Nazareth seems to have been branded as a bandit by those in power during his lifetime. When the Jewish high priestly authorities and temple guards come out to arrest Jesus (Mark 14:48), he says to them, "Have you come out with swords and clubs to arrest me as though I were a bandit [λῃστήν]?" So, too, in the Gospel of John, Jesus states, "Very truly, I tell you, anyone who does not enter the sheepfold by the gate but climbs in by another way is a thief and a bandit [λῃστήν]" (John 10:1). Jesus goes on to say, "All who came before me are thieves and bandits [λῃσταί]; but the sheep did not listen to them. I am the gate. Whoever enters by me will be saved, and will come in and go out and find pasture" (John 10:8–9). All previous thieves and bandits who came before him to lead the Jewish peasantry are not like Jesus, the good shepherd who enters by the gate (10:2) and is himself the gate (10:9). Thus Jesus clearly conveys that he is not a bandit.

There also seems to be a case of cultural hybridity—"creative re-workings and adaptations of the dominant culture"[69]—in the words of Jesus regarding his alleged association with banditry when he says to those buying, selling, and changing money in the temple, "Is it not written, 'My house shall be called a house of prayer for all the nations'? But *you* have made it a den of bandits [σπήλαιον λῃστῶν]" (Mark 11:17; emphasis added). Jesus seems to be saying that *he* is not a bandit; rather, it is those who work as part of the sanctuary's corporate infrastructure facilitating the temple-state's exploitation of the peasantry with oppressive taxes and tithes who are the *true* bandits! The sharp implications of Jesus' words were loud and clear: "And when the chief priests and the scribes heard it, they kept looking for a way to kill him" (Mark 11:18). One more example of Jesus' identification with banditry occurs at the time of his crucifixion: "And with him they crucified two bandits [λῃστάς], one on his right and one on his left" (Mark 15:27). The fact that Jesus was crucified together with two bandits, while Barabbas, who was in prison with the rebels (στασιαστῶν) who had committed murder during the insurrection (στάσει; Mark 15:7), was released is interesting enough. However, these details, considered in conjunction with the reason for Jesus' execution, help to better clarify Jesus' attitudes toward questions of war and peace. The reason for Jesus' death is recorded clearly in the Gospels: "The inscription of the charge against him read, 'The King of the Jews'" (Mark 15:26). In other words, Jesus was crucified for the crime of sedition as the Jewish peasantry's popularly elected king—the messiah. Thus, the Roman soldiers who abused Jesus before his crucifixion derisively placed a crown of thorns on his head as his diadem—a royal symbol of kingship, authority, and power—thus mocking Jesus' election by the peasantry as their popular king/messiah.

The numerous associations of Jesus with banditry in the Gospels reflect ways that Jesus of Nazareth was perceived and vilified during his lifetime by the Roman hegemony, the Jewish high priestly aristocracy, other powerful Jewish religious authorities, and Herod Antipas. From the perspective of the powerful, Jesus was nothing more than a dangerous, seditious, peasant bandit who had been elected by the Jewish peasantry as their popular king—the messiah. To be sure, these powerful groups had reasons which seemed valid to them for identifying Jesus as a bandit and revolutionary leader who sought to overthrow those in power in order to become king of the Jews. Jesus had organized a large movement of peasant resistance to the socioeconomic oppression and political domination that those powerful groups had created, while also speaking out against wealthy, exploitive landowners on behalf of hungry, debt-ridden Jewish peasants; he also cleverly encouraged the refusal of tax payments to Rome (Mark 12:13–17; Matt. 22:17–21; Luke 20:22–25).[70] Jesus had cast out demons such as "Legion" that shackled Jewish peasants and forced them to live among the dead (Mark 5:2–13; Luke 8:26–33), "Legion" being a clear metaphor for the demonic and militaristic Roman hegemony over the Jewish people. Moreover, Jesus had flipped over the tables of those buying, selling, and changing money in the temple—a prophetic act symbolizing the destruction of the oppressive temple-state which engaged in socioeconomic and political collaboration with the Herodian and Roman imperial rulers over the Jewish peasantry. Thus, when Jesus was brought by the council of high priests and scribes to Pilate for his trial, they made the following accusations against him: "We found this man leading our nation to revolution, forbidding us to pay taxes to the emperor, and saying that he himself is the Messiah—the king" (Luke 23:2).[71] In fact, these accusations were not entirely false. Jesus' reply to the question about the propriety of paying taxes to the emperor (Mark 12:17) does seem to have been understood by some as a prohibition of paying Roman taxes. Any refusal by the Roman Empire's subjects to pay their taxes was interpreted by Roman leaders as an act of revolution, while even client kings who did not have their kingship bestowed by the emperor were seen as royal usurpers. To be sure, a peasant popular king/messiah elected by crowds of Jewish peasants would be interpreted by those in power as a bandit engaged in a revolt.[72]

It should come as no surprise to find that the Jewish high priestly aristocracy, other powerful Jewish religious authorities, and those loyal to Herod Antipas (Mark 3:6; 12:13; Matt. 22:16) all desired to do away with Jesus.[73] In addition to Jesus' symbolic destruction of the temple, he had also been healing numerous people of their infirmities and was thus acting as an alternative locus of Yahweh's mercy from that of the temple cult controlled by the high priestly aristocracy in Jerusalem, such as when Jesus healed a leper (Mark 1:40–45) and instructed him, "Go, show yourself to the priest."[74] Such actions of Jesus, his proclamation of the kingdom of God, his advocacy of the poor, and the Jewish peasants' declaration of Jesus as the Messiah as he entered into Jerusalem had created a situation where the Jewish high priestly aristocracy and other Jewish religious authorities sought Jesus' death. Mark 14:1–2 states, "It was two days before the Passover and the festival of Unleavened Bread. The chief priests and the scribes were looking for a way to arrest Jesus by stealth and kill him; for they said, 'Not during the festival, or there may be a riot among the people.'" The Jewish high priestly aristocracy and the other Jewish religious authorities plotted to execute Jesus, but because of their fear of the crowds of Jewish peasants following Jesus (cf. also Mark 3:6; 11:18) and the potential for an uprising, they had difficulty in doing so. This forced them to seek an opportunity to capture Jesus privately, something which happened when Jesus was arrested during the middle of the night on the Mount of Olives when even the disciples were asleep.[75]

It should also come as no surprise to find that Herod Antipas was also seeking to kill Jesus. Herod Antipas had been greatly concerned that John the Baptist's movement could end up in revolt, so Antipas made a preemptive strike by having John arrested and beheaded.[76] Jesus, however, was of even greater concern to Antipas since rumors of the Galilean Jewish peasantry's desire to elect Jesus as their popular king/messiah (John 6:15) would have certainly reached his ears. Luke writes that some Pharisees came and warned Jesus that Antipas was seeking his life, saying, "'Get away from here, for Herod wants to kill you.' He said to them, 'Go and tell that fox for me, "Listen, I am casting out demons and performing cures today and tomorrow, and on the third day I finish my work""" (Luke 13:31–32). By casting out demons, performing healings, and eating with "nuisances and nobodies," Jesus was responding to the broken condition of the peasantry and enacting the kingdom of God.[77]

Although Jesus was perceived by the powerful as a bandit and by the Jewish peasantry as a popular king/messiah, Jesus' methods of resistance and leadership were quite different from those of other Jewish bandit leaders, popular kings, and messianic claimants of his day. Jesus did not engage in any overt acts of violent resistance,[78] preferring to ride into Jerusalem on a humble donkey while being acclaimed as the victorious messiah by the peasantry greeting him with palm fronds rather than riding in on a military chariot or on a horse as a leader of the cavalry.[79] Jesus' entrance into Jerusalem on a village donkey served to fulfill Jewish peasant ideas of popular kingship by conveying the image of the messiah as being a member of the peasantry (a hope recorded in Zech. 9:9 and cited in Matt. 21:5). As Matthew 21:5 reads, "Tell the daughter of Zion, Look, your king is coming to you, humble, and mounted on a donkey, and on a colt, the foal of a donkey." Jesus had also warned his disciples not to exercise leadership in the despotic fashion of client kings and their Roman patrons, but to imitate his model of humble service (Luke 22:25–27).

Moreover, Jesus carried out his public ministry unarmed. Even so, the Jewish peasantry's access to weapons was quite limited, and those weapons that were available were relatively simple, such as farming tools, knives, clubs, slings, stones, and possibly some swords. Those weapons were certainly not like the advanced weaponry available to the well-trained, specialized Roman military and the royal forces of client kings: helmets, shields, armor, swords, spears, bows and arrows, catapults, incendiary missiles, siege towers, horses, and fortresses.[80] The Romans and their allied royal forces were quite simply the most advanced and highly skilled military in the world.

Although Jesus told the disciples to carry a sword just before going to the Mount of Olives where he would be arrested, when they acquired two swords the disciples obviously misunderstood that the reason for Jesus' instructions was that of prophetic fulfillment (Luke 22:35–38). Two swords would clearly not be enough to fight the temple guards and would especially not be enough to bring about a violent end to the military might of the Herodian and Roman forces, although that seems to be how several of the disciples understood the purpose of those swords when Jesus was arrested, asking him, "'Lord, should we strike with the sword?'" (Luke 22:49). Certainly they had misunderstood Jesus' instructions, but had they also reverted to their latent peasant aspirations of violent revolution in order to acquire political independence for the Jewish people, or had they simply reacted without thinking in order to attempt to defend their beloved Jesus? In any case, during the arrest, when one of Jesus' disciples struck the ear of the high priest's slave, Jesus responded by demanding, "'No more of this!' And he touched his ear and healed him" (Luke 22:51).[81] Jesus then said, "All who take the sword will perish by the sword" (Matt. 26:52b), clearly rejecting violence or warfare as a means of problem solving or establishing the kingdom of God. Rather than engaging in social banditry or starting a violent insurrection by engaging in a military conflict within Jerusalem, Jesus had proclaimed the kingdom of God while enacting it through his works of healing, casting out demons, and eating with the poor and powerless as a means of restoring the peasantry to wholeness, also reflecting within his ministry those traditions from past Israelite history where the peasantry was to be a society of equals.

IMPLICATIONS FOR CONTEMPORARY THINKING ON WAR

For modern Americans who have been shaped by Western imperialist culture to read the Gospels without a serious consideration of the harsh socioeconomic policies and political domination imposed on Jewish peasants by Roman imperial officials, Herodian client rulers, and Jewish high priestly aristocrats in the first centuries BCE and CE, conclusions about the morality of war are untenable. Simply stated, the Gospels do not directly address our modern Western social location, perspectives, or questions regarding war. However, it would behoove us to recognize that Jesus and those around him were not part of an imperialist power: they were not the colonizers, but the colonized and the oppressed. Jesus spoke and acted against the Roman imperialist and Herodian client aggressors and the high priestly aristocracy who oppressed the poor and the powerless.

Nevertheless, it is untenable to take the teachings or actions of Jesus and twist them to justify acts of imperialist expansion, oppression, or war, as is done in certain forms of just war theory, liberation theology, and hypernationalist Orthodox Christian theological reflection and in certain Christian circles (across denominations) within the United States today where armed conflicts involving the United States military are simplistically equated with the freedom and defense of Christianity, the church, or the American "Christian" nation.[82]

Indeed, the present study has shown that those Christian theologies or theories seeking to justify war on theological grounds do so without any solid evangelical foundation in the words and deeds of Jesus. This is likely the reason that the main scriptural arguments used in Fr. Alexander Webster's attempt to develop an Orthodox just war theory (or justifiable war, which he has positively lauded as "the virtue of war") are culled from the Old Testament/Hebrew Bible.[83] So, too, arguments used by others which point out Jesus' tolerance of soldiers as conveyed in several New Testament narratives do not provide a solid evangelical foundation for any just war theory. For example, soldiers coming to Jesus for miraculous healing (Matt. 8:5–13; Luke 7:1–10), soldiers declaring the crucified Jesus to be the Son of God (Mark 15:39; Matt. 27:54) or innocent (Luke 23:47), and the soldier, Cornelius, coming to the faith and being baptized by Peter (Acts 10:1–48) without the Scripture saying that it was necessary for these soldiers to leave the military do not imply that Jesus or the authors of the New Testament accepted violence, war, or Christian participation in the armed forces as normative.

Similarly, those New Testament texts which use military language or metaphors as part of their spiritual/theological reflection (e.g., Phil. 2:25; Philem. 2; 2 Tim. 2:3; 1 Thess. 5:8; 2 Cor. 10:3–6; Eph. 6:17; Rev. 19:11–16) do not give New Testament support for any just war theory. Rather, these verses simply reflect that soldiers and warfare were a common part of the New Testament world within which these early Christian traditions developed and spread. Moreover, early Christians were part of a subjugated, minority community with Jewish origins struggling for the survival of their faith and movement after the execution of their leader within the overwhelmingly pagan, Hellenized, Roman Empire. The New Testament writings reflect this reality in their own ways. Thus, the Gospels and other writings of the New Testament do not engage in extensive theological reflection on issues of Christian participation in soldiering and war.[84] Indeed, many radical Christian pacifists today tolerate soldiers in their discussions with them, while also being capable of using military metaphors to convey their ideas. This should not be confused with an endorsement or justification of war.[85]

Finally, the New Testament text probably cited most often in favor of Christian just war theories is that of soldiers coming to John the Baptist (Luke 3:1–14) and his advising them regarding good conduct without any demand made that they abandon military service. Indeed, even Thomas Aquinas's just war theory appeals to this text by quoting Augustine's interpretation of the verses.[86] John the Baptist's instructions, however, were given in the context of excoriating those who fled to him in the desert for baptism in order to join his movement. He said to them, "You brood of vipers! Who warned you to flee from the wrath to come? Bear fruits worthy of repentance. Do not begin to say to yourselves, 'We have Abraham as our ancestor'; for I tell you, God is able from these stones to raise up children to Abraham. Even now the ax is lying at the root of the trees; every tree therefore that does not bear good fruit is cut down and thrown into the fire" (Luke 3:7–9). As a result of John's rebuke that his followers were not to flee the coming wrath by staying out with John in the desert but that they should go back to where they came from and immediately bear good fruit since the time is short, different parts of the crowd began to ask John what good in particular they should return and do.[87] John replied, "Whoever has two coats must share with anyone who has none; and whoever has food must do likewise." The text goes on to say, "Even tax collectors came to be baptized, and they asked him, 'Teacher, what should we do?' He said to them, 'Collect no more than the amount prescribed for you'" (Luke 3:11–13).

This, then, is the context in which John gave his instructions for the good that those soldiers who came to him should do upon their return from the desert before the coming wrath of God: "Do not extort money from anyone by threats or false accusation, and be satisfied with your provisions" (Luke 3:14). John's instructions to soldiers should not be interpreted as a Christian acceptance or endorsement of the propriety of war. First, it is not certain that combatants are in view here. It is possible that these στρατευόμενοι could be police who protected the tax collectors just mentioned in Luke 3:12–13. However, even if they were soldier combatants, the movement led by John the Baptist was a separate movement within Israel from the movement that was led by Jesus of Nazareth. John the Baptist was an apocalyptic prophet leading a Jewish renewal movement reenacting the Exodus event by baptism in the Jordan River while calling fellow Jews to rededicate themselves to the covenant with a life of purity and holiness upon their return home from the desert as they eagerly awaited the imminent judgment of God against Israel's enemies.[88] In this way, John's followers functioned like sleeper cells of apocalyptic expectation secretly planted all over Israel, anticipating God's swift and violent judgment. Therefore, in the way that John's movement was structured and functioned, there was no need for soldiers to abandon military service and to join him in the desert. Rather, John's method strategically planted Jewish members of his movement who were already soldiers back within the military of Herod Antipas—a military that was being used to control Herod's territory and oppress the Jewish peasantry.[89] Second, although Jesus began as a member of John the Baptist's movement,[90] Jesus' own movement, public ministry, and methods were quite different from those of the Baptist. Rather than instructing his followers to wait for God to solve the problem of evil in the world (apocalyptic eschatology), Jesus asked his followers to work together with God in solving the problem of evil by the way that they lived (ethical eschatology). All of these points considered together make clear that a use of John the Baptist's words to soldiers as a New Testament argument in favor of any just war theory is untenable and an example of interpreting Scripture out of context.

Certainly Jesus' vision of the kingdom of God demands that his followers treat all people with dignity, respect, and love. No less is demanded of those Christians who are theologically or philosophically opposed to war in their treatment of soldiers employed in military service. Nevertheless, we must also clearly understand and admit that Jesus was not on the side of dominating empire and that Jesus did not advocate war as a means of problem solving or righting societal wrongs, no matter how unjust, even though the option of military action was available to Jesus and indeed expected by many Jewish peasants of their popular king/messiah in first-century CE Palestine. I, for one, as a citizen of the United States, must continually strive to remember this. Indeed, Jesus promoted an egalitarian society of socioeconomic justice primarily among the poor and oppressed, where healing and wholeness were basic priorities. Jesus the Messiah advocated the kingdom of God and was executed by the military superpower of his day—rather than fighting—for peacefully working to make his vision a reality.

NOTES

1. Unless otherwise indicated, all translations of the Bible are from the New Revised Standard Version.

2. Richard A. Horsley, "Jesus and Empire," *Union Seminary Quarterly Review* 59, no. 3–4 (2005): 47–48.

3. Cf. Mark 1:15; 4:10; 10:14; 14:25. See also John Dominic Crossan, *Jesus: A Revolutionary Biography* (New York: Harper, 1994), 55.

4. Although Jesus himself came from among the peasantry, was raised in the simple village of Nazareth, and likely worked for some time as an artisan (a low-social-status laborer who works with their hands), the evidence of several higher-status Jews among Jesus' followers, such as Joseph of Arimathea (Matt. 27:57) and Nicodemus (John 19:38–39), indicates that Jesus did not restrict his message only to the peasantry.

5. Crossan entitled the third chapter of his *Jesus: A Revolutionary Biography* "A Kingdom of Nuisances and Nobodies" without using this most appropriate catchphrase again in the chapter.

6. Magen Broshi, "The Credibility of Josephus," *Journal of Jewish Studies* 33, no. 1–2 (1982): 379–84; Steve Mason, "Will the Real Josephus Please Stand Up?," *Biblical Archaeology Review* 23, no. 5 (1997): 58–65, 67–68; Mason, "Contradictions or Counterpoint? Josephus and Historical Method," *Review of Rabbinic Judaism* 6, no. 2–3 (2003): 145–88.

7. For example, a biblical study done by an Orthodox Christian on the topic of war where the social, economic, and political realities of first-century CE Jewish Palestine are not treated is an article written by John Breck, "'Justifiable War': Lesser Good or Lesser Evil?," *St. Vladimir's Theological Quarterly* 47, no. 1 (2003): 97–109. Breck surveys various scriptural verses on violence and pacifism in response to a study by Alexander Webster in the same volume of the *St. Vladimir's Theological Quarterly* in order to address questions related to war and peace. Although I am in general agreement with Breck's perspective that war is

inherently evil, his brief survey of some relevant words and deeds of Jesus (among other scriptural texts) does not consider the political, social, and economic realities necessary for understanding such verses. Rather, Breck attempts to settle the apparent contradiction between Gospel texts which seem to make Jesus a "pacifist" and those which seem to make him a "militant" by taking refuge in their *eschatological* setting" (108; emphasis original). The result of such an approach is to create a kind of artificial, spiritualized, otherworldly meaning for such texts while divorcing them from their historical contexts. Thus, Breck's study gives the impression that, by attempting to take refuge in eschatology, one can somehow ignore that Jesus' ministry was primarily aimed at subjugated rural Jewish peasants struggling to survive under the hegemonic policies of Roman and Herodian rule and the high priestly aristocracy in the first century CE, thereby forgetting that eschatology addresses historical reality with the "'in-breaking' of the Kingdom of God" (106; emphasis original). Attempts to ascertain Jesus' views on war and peace without considering the entire gestalt of socioeconomic, political, and religious realities of first-century CE Jewish Palestine, as well as the way that the Gospels were composed and the communities for which they were composed, can result in debates on war and peace that are reduced to a contest between selective scriptural verses taken out of context. Finally, Breck's concluding assessment that "Scripture never condones violence as a means to pursue social or political goals" (109) is untenable. Although there are indeed numerous texts in the Old Testament/Hebrew Bible which reject violence and war as legitimate means for pursuing social, political, and religious objectives, certain texts of the Old Testament/Hebrew Bible view violence and war as acceptable. For example, some Old Testament/Hebrew Bible texts advocate *herem* (Hebrew, "the ban"), which is tantamount to mass murder or genocide commanded by God or done for God by the Israelites in pursuit of political, social, and religious goals (e.g., Deut. 20; Josh. 6; 1 Sam. 15). Such kinds of troublesome texts are one reason among many that some of the fathers resorted to allegory in their interpretation of Scripture. One more example of a biblical study pertaining to war done by an Orthodox Christian where the political, social, and economic contexts of the relevant verses are not treated is an essay done by a St. Vladimir's Orthodox Theological Seminary student (at the time of composition), Ray Fulmer, "Sword and War Metaphors in the New Testament," website of the Mystagogy Resource Center, http://www.johnsanidopoulos.com/2012/12/sword-and-war-metaphors-in-new-testament.html.

    8. Richard A. Horsley, "Ethics and Exegesis: 'Love Your Enemies' and the Doctrine of Non-Violence," *Journal of the American Academy of Religion* 54 (1986): 3–31.

9. Hugo Grotius, *De Jure Belli ac Pacis* 1.2.9. Many of the scriptural passages used to justify or to reject war by Christian thinkers are considered in Grotius's work.

10. Reza Aslan, *Zealot: The Life and Times of Jesus of Nazareth* (New York: Random House, 2013).

11. Postcolonial studies on the Bible in general and on Jesus in particular are abundant in the field of biblical studies and often seek to highlight how Western readings of the Bible result in interpretations that are very different from those who read the sacred writings from other (collectivist) cultural perspectives. See, e.g., R. S. Sugirtharajah, *Postcolonial Criticism and Biblical Interpretation* (Oxford: Oxford University Press, 2002); Brian K. Blount, *Cultural Interpretation: Reorienting New Testament Criticism* (Minneapolis: Fortress, 1995); Priscilla Pope-Levison and John R. Levison, *Jesus in Global Contexts* (Louisville: Westminster/John Knox, 1992).

12. It is a matter of scholarly debate whether Jesus of Nazareth focused his public ministry only in Galilee for a period of about one year and then traveled to Jerusalem for only one Passover, when he was arrested and crucified (as conveyed by the Gospel of Mark and utilized by the Gospels of Matthew and Luke), or whether Jesus engaged in his public ministry within several provinces in Palestine, traveling back and forth from Galilee to Jerusalem on multiple occasions for a period of more than three years, being arrested and crucified at the last of several Passover festivals he had attended (as conveyed in the Gospel of John). It seems that the Johannine tradition contains more accurate traditions of Jesus' travels and the chronology of his public ministry, especially because the Torah commanded that all Jewish men of age who lived within the boundaries of the land of Israel were required to attend the three annual pilgrimage festivals in Jerusalem (Deut. 16:16). Unless there were extenuating circumstances, most Jewish men tried to attend all three pilgrimage festivals each year. Moreover, a one-year period does not seem long enough to account for Jesus' active public ministry and popular following.

One should also note that, when the Romans began directly administering Judea, and hence Jerusalem, in 6 CE after the exile of Archelaus, Herod the Great's son, the Jewish high priest was no longer appointed by the Jewish king but by the ruling Roman prefect until 41 CE. So, too, in 6 CE did the Roman prefect take charge of the high priest's vestments until 37 CE, giving them to the high priest for service in the Jewish temple four times a year during the four great festivals and subsequently receiving them back again each time for storage. The high priests' appointment by the Roman prefect, Pilate, and Pilate's control of the high priestly vestments during the time of Jesus' public ministry should help us understand the relationship and collaboration between Roman prefects and high priests in Judea.

13. Although a change in the Jewish priesthood from Zadokite to Hasmonean is still widely accepted among scholars, a few have challenged this position. See, e.g., Alison Schofield and James C. VanderKam, "Were the Hasmoneans Zadokites?" *Journal of Biblical Literature* 124, no. 1 (2005): 73–87.

14. Horsley, "Jesus and Empire," 55.

15. Josephus, *Jewish War* 1.10.5–6.

16. Ibid., 1.12.3. Although Herod was already married to his first wife, Doris, who was an Idumean not of royal blood, he was happy to replace her with Mariamne, whose grandfather was John Hyrcanus on her mother's side, and whose other grandfather was Antigonus on her father's side. Mariamne thus had double claims on Hasmonean royalty.

17. Ibid., 1.13.9.

18. Ibid., 1.14.4.

19. Ibid., 1.20.1–3. Herod minted coins during his reign, and the only legend appearing on them conveyed his name and title: ΒΑΣΙΛΕΩΣ ΗΡΩΔΟΥ.

20. Ibid., 1.33.9. Client kings (*amici*) of the Romans regularly had their own royal forces that were used to secure such client kingdoms and to support Roman interests by fighting alongside Roman legions in their military campaigns. Mason writes, "Augustus generally allowed eastern client kings to maintain their own, independent armed forces; when their territories were later incorporated as provinces those units would become the foundation of 'auxiliary' units—cavalry wings, infantry cohorts, and other specialty groups that supported the legions in campaigns (Webster 1985: 35)." See Steve Mason, ed., *Flavius Josephus: Translation and Commentary; Judean War 2*, vol. 1b (Leiden and Boston: Brill, 2008), 35n316.

21. Josephus, *Antiquities* 17.2.1–3.

22. Ibid., 15.8.5.

23. Josephus, *Jewish War* 1.20.3; *Antiquities* 15.7.3. To describe Herod's bodyguards, Josephus uses the word Γαλάται, which could be translated "Gauls" or "Galatians." However, it seems best to view these soldiers as Gauls since it is well known that the Roman armies of Marc Antony and Octavian both used auxiliaries from Gaul.

24. Josephus, *Jewish War* 1.21.4, remarks, "One can mention no suitable site within his kingdom which he left bare of some mark of honor to Caesar" (καθόλου δὲ οὐκ ἔστιν εἰπεῖν ὅντινα τῆς βασιλείας ἐπιτήδειον τόπον τῆς πρὸς Καίσαρα τιμῆς γυμνὸν εἴασεν).

25. Josephus, *Antiquities* 15.9.5.

26. Richard A. Horsley, *Bandits, Prophets, Messiahs: Popular Movements in the Time of Jesus* (Harrisburg, PA: Trinity Press International, 1985, 1999), 60.

27. Josephus, *Jewish War* 1.16.2–5.

28. Ibid., 2.1.1. A diadem (διάδημα) is a decorative band of cloth fastened around the head which symbolizes that person's kingship, authority, and power.

29. Ibid., 2.1.2.

30. The crowd was not only angry about the death of the two sages, but charged that the high priest, Ioazar (the brother of Herod's third wife, Mariamne II), was not sufficiently pure and pious, having been appointed by Herod the Great as an act of patronage.

The reasons for Herod's erection of the golden eagle, as well as its removal and destruction by the sages' disciples, are not entirely clear. Its erection by Herod may have been a sign of Herodian-Roman domination. Its removal and destruction may have been an overt act of popular resistance to Herodian-Roman rule or an expression of popular piety and devotion to the Torah, since such an animal representation may have been interpreted as a violation of the second commandment, which prohibits idolatrous images (Exod. 20:4–6). For Josephus's accounts of the sages and the golden eagle, see *Jewish War* 1.648–55 and *Antiquities* 17.6. For a scholarly discussion of the possible interpretations of the golden eagle as well as its removal and destruction, see Jan Willem van Henten, "Ruler or God? The Demolition of Herod's Eagle," in *The New Testament and Early Christian Literature in Greco-Roman Context: Studies in Honor of David E. Aune*, ed. John Fotopoulos, Supplements to Novum Testamentum 122 (Leiden: Brill, 2006), 256–86.

31. Josephus, *Jewish War* 2.1.3. Josephus refers to the pilgrims of this festival as a λαὸς ἄπειρος (an immeasurable crowd). Elsewhere he conveys that over two million people attended the Passover Festival (*Jewish War* 6.9.3), but Josephus's estimations of numbers are generally inflated in his writings. E. P. Sanders, *Judaism: Practice and Belief, 63 BCE–66 CE* (London: SCM, 1992), 126, has calculated based on the dimensions of the temple complex that 300,000–500,000 pilgrims could be accommodated. Additionally, in early Judaism, Passover and Unleavened Bread were two distinct festivals celebrated successively. Passover was a one-day festival (the fourteenth day of the lunar month Nisan), while Unleavened Bread was a seven-day festival (fifteenth to twenty-first of Nisan). Together they constituted, for those Jews who were ritually pure, eight days of celebration in Jerusalem that commemorated the Exodus event and Israel's liberation from Egypt by Yahweh.

32. Josephus, *Antiquities* 17.9.1.

33. Ibid., 2.1.3. These soldiers seem to have been members of the armed forces that Archelaus inherited from his father, Herod the Great, rather than

being part of the Roman military. Client kings loyal to the Romans commonly imitated the organization of the Roman army with their own forces. Cohorts (σπεῖρα) in Herod the Great's military are thought to have consisted of about five hundred soldiers, but in this case Archelaus's cohort is led by a tribune (χιλίαρχος) which seems to indicate that this was a double cohort of a χιλιαρχία (a one-thousand-man force). See Steve Mason's translation of *Jewish War* 2.1.3.11 in *Judean War 2*, vol. 1b, 13nn78, 79.

34. Josephus, *Jewish War* 2.1.3.

35. Ibid., 2.1.3.

36. Eric Hobsbawm, *Bandits* (New York: Delacorte, 1969).

37. Graham Seal, "The Robin Hood Principle: Folklore, History, and the Social Bandit," *Journal of Folklore Research* 46, no. 1 (2009): 70.

38. Anointing is a ritual act whereby persons or objects have olive oil poured out over or rubbed on them as a way of setting them apart or dedicating them for God's special service or use. Anointing of the face or feet with olive oil was also done as an expression of love and joy.

39. Richard A. Horsley, "Popular Messianic Movements around the Time of Jesus," *Catholic Biblical Quarterly* 46 (1984): 475.

40. 4Q169 (Nahum Commentary of the Dead Sea Scrolls) refers to the Hasmonean king-priest, Alexander Jannaeus, as the "furious young lion." He, together with five other candidates, may also meet the description of "the wicked priest" referred to in 1QpHab (Habbakuk Commentary) and 4QpPs[a] (Commentary on Ps. 37).

41. Josephus, *Jewish War* 2.3.1.

42. Josephus, *Antiquities* 17.10.2. Translations of Josephus are my own unless otherwise indicated.

43. Josephus, *Jewish War* 2.3.4. In *Antiquities* 17.10.3, Josephus writes that the Jewish peasants claimed that they would "recover for themselves at the present time their ancestral liberty" (τοῦ ἀποληψομένου χρόνῳ παροῦσαν αὐτοῖς ἐλευθερίαν τὴν πάτριον).

44. Josephus, *Jewish War* 2.3.2. The troops from Sebaste were Hellenized residents of Samaria who were not sympathetic to the Jewish people, but rather shared interests with the Romans. The royal/auxiliary forces of client kings were typically led by Italians or Romans, or by native aristocrats who had been granted Roman citizenship as a result of their families' military service to the Romans.

45. Josephus, *Antiquities* 17.10.8.

46. Judas's father, Hezekiah, is referred to by Josephus as an ἀρχιληστής (chief bandit), and he is the bandit leader that had fought against and was killed by Herod the Great when Herod was the governor of Galilee. Cf. Josephus, *Jewish War* 1.10.5.

47. Josephus, *Jewish War* 2.4.1.

48. Josephus, *Antiquities* 17.10.5.

49. Ibid., 17.10.6.

50. Ibid.; Josephus, *Jewish War* 2.4.2.

51. Josephus, *Antiquities* 17.10.7.

52. In this way Athronges' symbolic egalitarian leadership structure is similar to the one that Jesus of Nazareth would create a few decades later. Jesus was surrounded by twelve disciples who were free to debate matters among themselves, while Jesus decided important matters himself as leader of the movement. The number of the disciples, twelve, represented the restoration and fullness of Israel being realized in the Jesus movement.

53. Josephus, *Jewish War* 2.4.2–3.

54. Ibid., 2.5.1–2.

55. *Ethnarch* is a Hellenistic term used to describe a leader of a nation or an ethnic group. In the case of Archelaus, being named ethnarch by Augustus was a step just below Archelaus's desire to be recognized as king of the Jews, but it was a step above the title of tetrarch, which was given to his two brothers. A lost passage of Strabo quoted by Josephus (*Antiquities* 14.7.2) describes the role of the ethnarch for the Jewish community in Alexandria, Egypt: "He both manages the nation [ἔθνος] and administers justice and takes charge of contracts and ordinances, as if he were head of a self-governing political entity [ὡς ἂν πολιτείας ἄρχων αὐτοτελοῦς]." Translation is that of Mason, *Judean War 2*, vol. 1b, 62n560.

Tetrarch designates a ruler over a quarter of the land. Herod Antipas and Herod Philip were each respectively given roughly a quarter of Herod the Great's former kingdom, while their brother, Archelaus, was given about one-half of the kingdom.

56. Josephus, *Antiquities* 18.1.1.

57. An example of how seriously the Romans viewed the failure to pay taxes is when the residents of several towns in Palestine (Emmaus, Gophna, Lydda, and Thamna) were sold into slavery for not raising their tax payment quickly enough. Cicero writes that Roman taxes and tributes are "a reward for victory and a penalty for having made war" (*In Verrem* 2.3.12).

58. Josephus, *Antiquities* 18.1.1.

59. Horsley, "Jesus and Empire," 56.

60. Josephus, *Antiquities* 20.10.5. Helen Bond writes: "Annas was the first high priest appointed by Rome when Judaea was made a province in 6 CE; he himself occupied the high priesthood for nine years and was followed at various points prior to 70 CE by five of his sons, one grandson, and, of course, his son-

in-law, Caiaphas." See Helen Bond, "Joseph Caiaphas: In Search of a Shadow," http://www.bibleinterp.com/articles/Bond_Joseph_Caiaphas.shtml.

61. For an overview of the conditions in Galilee during the reign of Herod Antipas which may have encouraged the Jesus movement, see Sean Freyne, "A Galilean Messiah?," *Studia Theologica* 55, no. 2 (2001): 198–218.

62. Most scholars hold that Matthew's dating of Jesus' birth is more accurate and that Jesus was born in 4 BCE just before the death of Herod the Great.

63. The problem of lack of sufficient sources is raised by Horsley, *Bandits, Prophets, Messiahs*, 66. Pilate's primary responsibilities as prefect were to manage Rome's interests in Judea, Samaria, and Idumea by commanding the Roman military and using it to maintain peace and security, while also overseeing the collection of Roman taxes and adjudicating judicial matters.

64. Josephus, *Jewish War* 2.9.2–3 and 2.9.4, and *Antiquities* 18.4.1, respectively. The introduction of Roman military standards into Jerusalem was a severe violation of Jewish religious sensibilities since the standards had pagan religious symbols on them and were thus seen as a violation of the Torah's second commandment, prohibiting idolatrous images (Exod. 20:4–6). The appropriation of temple funds was seen as another violation of Jewish religious sensibilities in that funds from the temple treasury were being inappropriately used by a pagan, Roman official.

65. Philo of Alexandria, *On the Embassy to Gaius* 302.

66. Josephus, *Antiquities* 18.4.2. Josephus does not state how many Samaritan peasants were slaughtered, but he previously described the group as a "great multitude" (ὡς μεγάλῳ πλήθει).

67. Pilate and the high priest, Caiaphas, obviously had a good working relationship since Caiaphas was the sole high priest during Pilate's tenure as prefect (26–36 CE). Caiaphas served as high priest for eighteen years (19–37 CE) and was deposed, possibly because he had become too powerful, just after Pilate's recall to Rome.

68. It is generally assumed that Josephus simply lacked sources with detailed information on banditry and rebellions in Israel during this period. Evidence for parallel material in Matthew and Luke is not useful for establishing historical authenticity of traditions if such material is taken from Mark, since scholars generally presume that Matthew and Luke have both used Mark as a primary source for their Gospels. However, Matthew's and Luke's traditions are of value for establishing historical authenticity if such traditions stem from Q, Special M, or Special L. Parallel material in Mark and John (and also in Q, Special M, or Special L) is referred to by scholars as multiple attestation, a basic criterion for historical authenticity.

69. Paul Spilsbury, "Reading the Bible in Rome: Josephus and the Constraints of Empire," in *Josephus and Jewish History in Flavian Rome and Beyond*, ed. J. S. Sievers and G. Lembi, Supplements to the Journal for the Study of Judaism 104 (Leiden: Brill, 2005), 210.

70. Mark 12:13–17 reads:

> Then they sent to him some Pharisees and some Herodians to trap him in what he said. And they came and said to him, "Teacher, we know that you are sincere, and show deference to no one; for you do not regard people with partiality, but teach the way of God in accordance with truth. Is it lawful to pay taxes [κῆνσον] to the emperor, or not? Should we pay them, or should we not?" But knowing their hypocrisy, he said to them, "Why are you putting me to the test? Bring me a denarius and let me see it." And they brought one. Then he said to them, "Whose head is this, and whose title?" They answered, "The emperor's." Jesus said to them, "Give to the emperor the things that are the emperor's, and to God the things that are God's." And they were utterly amazed at him.

This text is commonly interpreted as Jesus' endorsement of paying taxes to the Romans. However, further consideration of Jesus' clever words "Give to the emperor the things that are the emperor's, and to God the things that are God's" generates the opposite conclusion. From an Israelite/Jewish perspective all things belong to the God of Israel, while the emperor has no rightful claim on the land of Israel—the land that God gave to Abraham and his descendants in the covenant. Thus, even a coin with the emperor's image and title on it belongs to God (such a coin also being a violation of Torah's commandment against idolatrous imagery [Exod. 20:4–6], especially since the emperor was worshiped as a pagan god throughout the empire). It also does not seem to be coincidental that those who posed this question to Jesus were some Herodians, that is, those with a vested interest in the status quo who had a collaborative relationship with the Romans. Indeed, why would they ask Jesus an entrapping question about the lawfulness of paying taxes to Rome if they did not have good reason to expect a negative answer? Finally, the question about payment of Roman taxes should not be confused with the disciples' question to Jesus about the propriety of paying the "temple tax" (Matt. 17:24–27)—a very different matter because during Jesus' lifetime this was a voluntary tithe that some Jews paid to support the priesthood and the religious rituals of the temple in Jerusalem. Even so, Jesus' main point that Yahweh is king and "the children are free" (i.e., Israel) conveys that Jews are not obliged to pay tax to the temple-state and high priestly aristocracy, a position further supported by Jesus and Peter's remittance with a lost didrachma recovered from a fish's mouth, rather than from personal resources.

71. Τοῦτον εὕραμεν διαστρέφοντα τὸ ἔθνος ἡμῶν καὶ κωλύοντα φόρους Καίσαρι διδόναι καὶ λέγοντα αὐτὸν χριστὸν βασιλέα εἶναι. The phase τοῦτον εὕραμεν διαστρέφοντα τὸ ἔθνος ἡμῶν could also be translated as "we found this man misleading our nation." However, διαστρέφοντα in this case more likely means "turning aside," hence, that Jesus was leading the Jewish people to revolution. Josephus uses many such euphemisms for revolution or sedition in his writings.

72. Josephus's numerous references in *Jewish War* and *Antiquities* to popular leaders followed by large groups of the Jewish peasantry whom he labels as bandits make this point abundantly clear.

73. Several of Jesus' parables give some indication of how he had spoken out against wealthy landowners who exploited the peasantry, such as Mark 12:1–9; Matt. 18:23–35; Luke 15:11–32; and Luke 16:1–6. Certainly these wealthy landowners would have complained to Herod Antipas and to the religious authorities about some of Jesus' words and deeds.

74. The Torah's ritual instructions for healing and cleansing of leprosy are quite detailed (cf. Lev. 14:1–57). The Torah clearly states that a person who is thought to have been healed of leprosy is to be inspected by a priest, and several sacrificial offerings are also to be made. Once these have occurred and several days have passed, the priest can then declare the former leper to be ritually clean. For lepers who are poor, less-costly sacrificial offerings are prescribed, which take into account their lesser financial means. Even so, the Torah mandates inspection by a priest and sacrificial offerings from all lepers thought to have been healed before they can be declared clean. However, while Jesus instructs the leper to see a priest, presumably so he can offer the mandated sacrifice and officially be declared clean (in compliance with Lev. 14), Jesus tells the leper to do so "as a testimony to them."

75. Jesus' selection of the Mount of Olives, a tree-lined ridge located directly across from nearby Jerusalem (about 1.2 km away), as the location for his camp (Luke 21:37; John 8:1–2; cf. Luke 19:37) would reinforce ideas about Jesus' messianic identity and movement among his followers. The Mount of Olives had taken on messianic associations in the first century CE, and according to Zech. 14:1–9 it was the place in Jewish tradition where the Lord was to stand on the final day of battle against Israel's enemies, resulting in Yahweh's recognition as king over the entire earth. The Mount of Olives would provide a tactical advantage to any armed force in that it provides elevated terrain with a clear view of the Kidron Valley below and onward to the city of Jerusalem. It does not seem to be coincidental that Luke's Gospel records Jesus beginning his triumphal entrance into Jerusalem by riding down a path from the Mount of Olives, at which point he is greeted by crowds of followers proclaiming him to be the

messiah (Luke 19:37–40). In a similar vein, the Mount of Olives was the place where the popular Jewish messianic leader known as the Egyptian prophet had brought his followers and from where he was to command the walls of Jerusalem to collapse (as did the walls of Jericho for Joshua). After this was to occur, the Egyptian prophet and his forces were to descend from the Mount of Olives and forcibly enter Jerusalem, where they were to conquer the Romans so that the Egyptian prophet could rule Israel as God's messianic king (cf. Josephus, *Jewish War* 2.13.5; *Antiquities* 20.8.6).

76. Josephus, *Antiquities* 18.5.2.

77. F. F. Bruce, "Herod Antipas, Tetrarch of Galilee and Peraea," *The Annual of Leeds University Oriental Society* 5 (1963–65): 14–15, writes:

> Nevertheless, that Antipas should threaten Jesus' life is not surprising. If John the Baptist's activity had caused him disquiet, the proclamation of a new kingdom by Jesus and his disciples must have been more disturbing. "I beheaded John," said Antipas, "but who is this?" He had solid ground for being disturbed and wishing to see this new prophet, for when Jesus sent the twelve apostles two by two through the towns and villages of Galilee, they apparently acted with more zeal than discretion as they announced the advent of the divine kingdom; and when they came back to Jesus to report on their mission, he immediately took them across to the east side of the Lake of Galilee, out of Antipas's jurisdiction. But they were followed there by crowds of excited Galilaeans in militant mood who tried to compel Jesus to become their king and lead them against Rome and Rome's allies. It was with much ado that Jesus convinced them that he was not minded to be the kind of king they wanted; but more than enough had been done to excite Antipas's suspicions against him. Nor is it surprising to find the "Herodians" pursuing a hostile policy towards Jesus both in Galilee and in Jerusalem.

78. Although the Johannine version of Jesus' prophetic-symbolic destruction of the temple (John 2:15) records Jesus using a whip of cords, it was for the purpose of driving out the animals from the temple complex and was not used against any person.

79. Palm fronds were widely used by Jewish royalty in their coinage as a sign of their kingship and power—such as by John Hyrcanus, Herod the Great, Herod Archelaus, and Herod Antipas—as well as being used in the coinage of various Roman prefects who later ruled Judea.

80. Well-stocked fortresses were strategically located all over Israel, with Herod Antipas having at his fortress in Tiberius alone enough armor for seventy thousand soldiers (cf. Josephus, *Antiquities* 18.7.2). Such information can help

us better understand why popular kings who revolted often attacked royal palace fortresses.

81. Clearly, the disciple in question was not aiming for the slave's ear, but for his head. As the sword was swung, the slave probably reacted instinctively in self-defense by attempting to move his head away from the impending blow and was instead struck on the ear. The disciple is unnamed in Mark 14:47, Matt. 26:51, and Luke 22:50, but is identified as Peter in John 18:10.

82. One such example is a recent article in the Greek Orthodox Archdiocese of America newspaper, *The Orthodox Observer*, in which an American soldier stationed in Iraq who is an Orthodox Christian wrote that he was fighting there for the freedom and defense of the Orthodox Church in the U.S.A. Such a statement is problematic for a number of reasons, one of them being that many Iraqis are Orthodox Christians who have far less freedom and safety since the US-led 2003 invasion of their country.

83. Alexander Webster and Darrell Cole, *The Virtue of War: Reclaiming the Classic Christian Traditions East and West* (Salisbury, MA: Regina Orthodox Press, 2004). Webster is clearly interested in more than simply developing an Orthodox just war theory or theory of justifiable war, but also in defending the Bush administration's preemptive military attack on Iraq.

84. Attempts to cherry-pick verses from the Gospels so as to create or defend any just war theory fail to recognize that the process of Gospel composition in the first century CE was much more complicated than is often assumed by many Orthodox Christians. The Gospels were not written from scratch by four eyewitnesses to the life and death of Jesus (even in popular Orthodox Christian piety only two of the four evangelists are said to be eyewitnesses to Jesus' life—Matthew and John). Rather than the four evangelists writing their Gospels like journalists who were each objective eyewitnesses to the same historical events from different perspectives, each of the four canonical Gospels is the result of a long process of interpretation and reinterpretation of available traditions concerned with Jesus that were redacted and layered one upon the other while addressing the needs of particular Christian communities. This process of Gospel composition for the Synoptic Gospels of Mark, Matthew, and Luke occurred roughly as follows: (layer 1) the life and death of the historical Jesus of Nazareth was witnessed by, and belief in his resurrection from the dead occurred among, his disciples; (layer 2) traditions containing words and deeds attributed to Jesus were spread orally (oral tradition), including proclamations of his death and resurrection; (layer 3) traditions of Jesus' words and deeds, as well as of Jesus' death and resurrection, were written down (Jesus material); (layer 4) the Gospel of Mark was composed using available Jesus material and some oral tradition;

and (layer 5) the Gospels of Matthew and Luke were each composed independently of one another, using the Gospel of Mark as their primary source, as well as other Jesus material that was available to each evangelist (e.g., Q [a source consisting mostly of Jesus' sayings that was used independently by Matthew and Luke]; Special M [a variety of Jesus material unique to Matthew]; Special L [a variety of Jesus material unique to Luke]). This process of Gospel composition is known in New Testament scholarship as the Two-Source Theory. The Gospel of John is the result of a similar process of interpretation and reinterpretation of traditions concerned with Jesus that were redacted and layered one upon the other while addressing the needs of a particular Christian community, but in this case stemming from a variant stream of tradition—that of the Beloved Disciple and the Johannine Community—that was not based on the apostolic teaching of the twelve disciples. In any case, without a serious consideration of the way that the Gospels were composed, as well as the socioeconomic, political, and religious realities of Jewish Palestine under the hegemony of Roman imperial and Herodian rule, debates on Jesus' attitudes toward war and peace can result in a battle between selective Bible verses taken out of context and subjectively interpreted.

85. For example, I heard one Christian pacifist say that he became so upset at his interlocutor's argument that he "went ballistic." This hardly stands as a Christian pacifist endorsement of the use of intercontinental missiles.

86. Thomas Aquinas, *Summa Theologica* II-II, q. 40 a. 1 (New York: Benziger Bros., 1947), answer to objection 4. Aquinas writes, "Augustine says in a sermon on the son of the centurion [Ep. ad Marcel. cxxxviii]: 'If the Christian Religion forbade war altogether, those who sought salutary advice in the Gospel would rather have been counseled to cast aside their arms, and to give up soldiering altogether. On the contrary, they were told: "Do violence to no man . . . and be content with your pay" [Lk. 3:14]. If he commanded them to be content with their pay, he did not forbid soldiering.'" Augustine's words endorsed by Aquinas do not explain to the reader that the "salutary advice in the Gospel" was spoken by John the Baptist, and not by Jesus himself, giving the false impression that such a view was normative for the Gospels, for Jesus, and for the "Christian religion," and, thus, that a war can somehow be just and acceptable. It seems that these words of John the Baptist are so frequently appealed to because there are so few words of Jesus that can be used to justify war.

87. "Wrath" is a common term in the Old Testament/Hebrew Bible and is used to describe the Day of the Lord (the *Yom Yahweh*), when God's final, violent, apocalyptic judgment will be inflicted upon Israel's enemies.

88. By being baptized in the Jordan River, these followers of John the Baptist were engaging in an act of ritual purification while also reenacting the journey

of the Israelites entering through the river into the promised land, thus engaging in an act of expectant liberation by God since God had acted similarly for their ancestors. See, e.g., John Meier, *A Marginal Jew*, vol. 2/3, 100–116.

89. Forces of Herod Antipas were eventually the ones that captured John the Baptist, threw him in prison at the palace fortress of Machaerus, and finally beheaded him. John had been previously active up and down the banks of the Jordan River primarily within the territory ruled by Herod Antipas (Perea and possibly Galilee), but also farther south within the territory of Judea administered by a Roman prefect since the time of Archelaus's exile in 6 CE. It is possible that some of these Jewish soldiers who were members of John's movement could have also been planted within the Roman forces, but this is very unlikely since soldiers in the Roman legions were usually Roman citizens and pagans, rather than being devout, Torah-observant Jews with apocalyptic expectations. Indeed, Jewish men were generally exempt from military service in the Roman army (cf. Josephus, *Antiquities* 14.10.223–30). In any case, very few soldiers from the Roman legions were permanently stationed in Judea. Rather, several Roman legions were strategically located north in Syria and could be summoned when needed. The vast majority of soldiers in Israel were Herodian royal forces. Client kings (*amici*) allied with the Romans were commonly allowed to maintain their own royal military forces, which served as auxiliary troops fighting alongside or in place of the Roman legions. Such royal forces of client kings or auxiliaries were noncitizen soldiers recruited from various peoples typically living within the Roman Empire and who volunteered to join the military for a variety of reasons (expertise in fighting; political sympathies; and a desire to gain Roman citizenship along with their immediate family after twenty-five years of military service). Royal/auxiliary forces in a given area of the Roman Empire did not usually consist of large numbers of natives, for fear that they might join their compatriots in popular revolt. However, some Herodian royal troops/auxiliaries were indeed Jews since some soldiers did join the Jewish peasantry in various revolts arising upon the death of Herod the Great. Even so, the great majority of the Herodian royal forces were gentiles, such as Hellenized noncitizens of the cities of Sebaste and Caesarea Maritima sympathetic to the aristocracy, as well as Syrians, Thracians, Germans, and Gauls—groups that were well known for their expertise in war and for providing large numbers of recruits for Rome's auxiliary forces. The commanders of royal/auxiliary forces of client kings were typically Italians, Romans (such as Rufus and Gratus, who fought for Herod the Great and Archelaus), or native aristocrats who had been granted Roman citizenship (such as some of Herod the Great's relatives). Moreover, we know that most of the men serving in Herod the Great's army were gentiles because on one occasion, when he was planning to enter Jerusalem with his army at the Festival of Pentecost

(*Jewish War* 1.11.6), Herod was commanded by the king–high priest of the time, John Hyrcanus, not to enter the city under the pretext that foreigners were forbidden from entering the city since the Jewish people were purifying themselves (ἐκώλυεν τοὺς ἀλλοφύλους εἰσαγαγεῖν ἐφ᾽ ἁγνεύοντας τοὺς ἐπιχωρίους). Finally, the historicity of Luke's account of soldiers coming to John the Baptist and being counseled by him is questionable since (1) this tradition appears only in the Gospel of Luke and (2) it accords only too well with Luke's overall gospel agenda. A major theme in Luke's Gospel is Jesus' innocence of fostering sedition, together with an explanation of the phenomenon of gentile conversion to Christianity throughout the Roman Empire as the result of God's divine plan. Thus, Luke has redacted many traditions he has inherited from Mark and Q in order to make Jesus and his movement seem nonthreatening. In this way the Romans should have nothing to fear from gentile conversion to Christianity—a perceived Jewish sect growing in numbers even after the recent First Jewish War against Rome (66–73 CE). Thus, having soldiers counseled by John the Baptist to be more conscientious and responsible would be quite amiable to Roman ears and fits very well with Luke's Gospel agenda.

90. All four Gospels verify this fact and struggle in their own way to explain why Jesus, if superior to John, would have been baptized by him. As Meier, *Marginal Jew*, 2:105, writes, "We may thus take the baptism of Jesus by John as the firm historical starting point for any treatment of Jesus' public ministry."

CHAPTER 5

"THEIR HANDS ARE NOT CLEAN"

Origen and the Cappadocians on War and Military Service

VALERIE A. KARRAS

To those who ask about our origin and our founder we reply that we have come in response to Jesus' commands to beat into plowshares the rational swords of conflict and arrogance and to change into pruning hooks those spears that we used to fight with. For we no longer take up the sword against any nation, nor do we learn the art of war any more. Instead of following the traditions that made us 'strangers to the covenants' (Ephes. [2:12]), we have become sons of peace through Jesus our founder.

—Origen, *Against Celsus*[1]

Our Fathers did not reckon killings in war as murders, but granted pardon, it seems to me, to those fighting in defense of virtue and piety. Perhaps, however, it is well to advise them that, since their hands are not clean, they should abstain from communion alone for a period of three years.

—St. Basil the Great, *Epistle 188* ("canon 13")[2]

125

Although some Orthodox Christians are relatively unconcerned with what the early church may have taught and practiced since, they believe, we live in an entirely different society today and must "change with the times," for most Orthodox the practices and theological views of the early church have a normative value extending to the present day. This can present tensions within Orthodoxy, as some treat those views and practices in a dogmatic, noncontextualized manner akin to the interpretive style of biblical fundamentalists, while others examine the various contextual aspects of early Christian faith and practice and seek to discern, from within the faith tradition, which ones resonate within our own contemporary social, cultural, and political contexts or perhaps may have a more universal and normative value which may then be adapted and applied to our own contemporary situation. The articles in this historical section of the present volume make clear that there was no single view on war and military service in early and Byzantine Christianity. We may discern, however, a certain congruency of perspective that extends among most, if not all, of these historical studies—a theological, pastoral, and pragmatic approach which is distinctively Eastern Christian or Orthodox, and which may help inform contemporary discussions of the morality of war and of various military strategies pursued in armed conflict.

The literature on early Christian views of war and military service is plenteous, much of it coming from a Catholic or Protestant confessional perspective, and this article cannot hope to encompass its breadth.[3] It will, however, illuminate several aspects of this complicated issue by analyzing selected writings of several early Christian writers, with a focus on the Alexandrians and Cappadocians, particularly on the brilliant and theologically daring third-century Alexandrian theologian Origen and the bishop, monastic founder, and theologian Basil of Caesarea—known even in his own lifetime as Basil the Great—who was one of the fourth-century Cappadocians strongly influenced by Origen's theology and spirituality.[4]

Origen and Basil provide an interesting comparison on this topic both for their differing political contexts and for their differing personalities. Origen, an emotionally high-strung, speculative, creative, soulful, and intensely intellectual scholar, was born in the late second century in Alexandria and died, after having been tortured for his faith in his last years, sometime around 254 in Palestinian Caesarea, having lived his entire life while Christianity was still a marginalized and sporadically persecuted religion within the Roman Empire. By contrast, Basil (330–79)—intelligent, devout, and pastoral, but also supremely pragmatic and politically astute—and his younger brother, Gregory of Nyssa, lived during the post-Constantinian era of the mid-fourth century, when Christianity was not only legal but favored, enjoying the not-always-desirable patronage and attentions of the sons of Constantine, one of whom (Constans) supported Arianism.[5] The church did briefly lose its position of religious privilege after the death of the last of those sons, when Constantine's nephew, Julian, ruled as emperor (361–63). Julian had been raised as a Christian and counted among his former schoolmates at the Academy in Athens the young Basil and Basil's friend, the future fellow Cappadocian bishop and theologian, Gregory of Nazianzus. Nevertheless, Julian later renounced Christianity and became a pagan, at least in part out of disgust with ecclesiastical politics. Christianity returned to favored status, however, with Valens's accession to the imperial throne, even if his Arian leanings put him at odds with Basil.

In such circumstances, the basic question of whether military service was moral was no longer a theoretical question concerned with the abstract ethics of violence against others per se and debated from the relatively safe position of a religious minority who could leave the responsibility for protecting the empire to the majority pagan population. Rather, the rapid change in religious demographics following Constantine's conversion and consolidation of the imperium as sole Roman emperor introduced further moral complexity as the military became responsible for protecting what was quickly becoming a predominantly Christian empire.[6]

Moreover, in addition to noting the effect of the changed religious dynamics of the empire between the pre- and post-Constantinian periods, it is important to observe other, nonchronological distinctions. Some of these are (1) the distinction between soldiers who became Christians and Christians who became soldiers; (2) the related distinction between the passive continuation of a soldier in a noncombat position and his active participation in battle or other acts of violence or injustice, especially the persecution and capture of Christians; (3) the military activity of a non-Christian, invasively conquering empire (or emperor) versus the military activity of a Christian, self-defensive empire; and (4) the question of literal versus metaphorical or allegorical scriptural hermeneutics, particularly for the Old Testament.

Sensitivity to these distinctions is necessary if contemporary conversations on this important topic are to avoid anachronistic projections of modern arguments and issues into the early Christian period, and, conversely, if retrieval of still-valuable patristic insights is to be done in a nuanced, contextualized, and intellectually honest manner. Ultimately, I hope to show that, for both Origen and Basil—as well as for Basil's brother Gregory of Nyssa and his friend Gregory of Nazianzus—one can discern a common thread, plaited from several interwoven strands, underlying their individualized situations and temperaments as they treat these and other questions of war and military service in a manner that balances their positions on a tripod of ethical, pastoral, and pragmatic considerations. Those complex and remarkably nuanced strands include (1) an utter rejection of war for anything but self-defense; (2) a rejection of moral justice, much less holiness, even in wars of self-defense; (3) an allegorization, if not outright silence, regarding divine commands to violent action in Old Testament texts; (4) an acquiescence to Christian military service for those already serving at the time of their conversion to Christianity or, later, for those serving under Christian emperors; and (5) a simultaneous recognition of the immorality of certain actions required of those in military service which, depending on the action, must either be refused or dealt with penitentially afterward.

METAPHORS AND MODELS

Adolf von Harnack observed more than a century ago the numerous positive references to the military in terms of metaphorical language and model behavior found in the New Testament and other early Christian writings.[7] The genuine Pauline and deutero-Pauline corpora are both filled with military imagery applied to spiritual warfare.[8] Paul several times refers to fellow Christians as "soldiers," that is, in spiritual battles against the enemies of Jesus Christ and his church, and in 1 Thessalonians (5:8) he provides a particularly notable military metaphor: "But since we belong to the day, let us be sober, and put on the breastplate of faith and love, and for a helmet the hope of salvation" (NRSV).[9]

In responding to the second-century pagan philosopher Celsus's attack on Christians' refusal to defend the empire by serving in the Roman army,[10] Origen quoted Ephesians 6:11, arguing that "we may reply to this that at appropriate times we render to emperors divine help, if I may so say, by taking up even the whole armour of God."[11] Gregory of Nazianzus also employed military terminology when, in his farewell address upon abdicating his episcopal see of Constantinople, he compared himself to a soldier receiving his discharge papers from the emperor[12] or when, in his first invective against the emperor Julian, he prayed that God would give grace to God's "soldiers," who are Gregory and his fellow Christians, that they be sacrificed to Christ and ruled only by him.[13] Gregory of Nyssa, too, called his fellow bishop, Ablabius, a "courageous soldier of Christ."[14] In the *Paedagogus* (Educator), Clement of Alexandria, who was Origen's teacher, likened Jesus Christ himself to a general who "directs the phalanx, taking care to protect his soldiers."[15]

Beyond the frequent use of military metaphors and allusions, early Christian authors recommended that their flock or audience follow the exemplary conduct of soldiers in certain ways. For example, just as Clement of Rome, in his epistle written toward the end of the first century, exhorted the Christian community to behave in the same orderly fashion as an army would,[16] so too, in a similar vein, Gregory of Nazianzus, in *Oration 32* on limiting who should engage in theological discourse, questioned why his listeners would "try to play the general" when they had been "assigned to the ranks."[17] In addition to advocating the order and discipline of the military, he also compared the faithful of Constantinople, diverse in class and station, to soldiers united in their zeal and warrior spirit: "All are soldiers of God—gentle in other respects, but warlike on behalf of the Spirit."[18]

At issue here is how much weight should be given to (1) the use of military metaphors and (2) the praise of certain types of military conduct and what can legitimately be inferred from that praise about participation in the military more generally. With respect to the former, it is clear that the Roman military was a visible presence in most urban centers. The Balkan Peninsula (modern-day Greece, Albania, Bulgaria, etc.), Asia Minor, the Middle East, and North Africa were, after all, occupied territories. Furthermore, in addition to the troops permanently stationed in these locales, additional troops traveled through many of the regions periodically on their way to the frontier to fight off various would-be invaders. Finally, Christians such as the apostle Paul and Ignatius of Antioch had close-up experiences of the Roman military in their arrests, jailings, and transport to Rome.[19] So, it is not surprising that Origen and the Cappadocians, just as other early Christian writers from the apostle Paul on, chose to use analogies and metaphors based on the Roman army, something with which both they and their readers were quite familiar, and that military metaphors would continue to remain popular even after the empire became Christianized. Nevertheless, the use of such metaphors should not be understood to imply approval of the military. For example, despite Clement of Alexandria's use of the metaphor of Jesus Christ as a general, noted above, he vigorously opposed Christians' engaging in military service.[20]

With respect to the latter issue enumerated above, that of Christian praise for military conduct, the types of military activities and conduct which Gregory of Nazianzus and others encouraged their audiences to emulate were not violent except in a spiritualized or allegorized sense. Discipline and order in church organization and activity was a common theme; the only fighting early church fathers commended to their flocks was a zealous and ferocious "combating" of evil and following Christ's "commands." The types of military activities and conduct which Christians were to imitate, in other words, were invariably virtuous and were applicable well beyond the military milieu. For example, Clement of Rome, in the passage cited above, opined that Christians should emulate the obedience and orderliness of an army, with each person carrying out the duties of his (or her) "rank," that is, position within the church, inviting a hierarchical comparison between military officers and the orders of clergy in the church. Gregory of Nazianzus's admonition in *Oration 32* against acting as a general when one is a soldier is similar.

Louis Swift, while admitting that "the text [in Clement's epistle] does not endorse Christian participation in war," claims that "one would nonetheless have difficulty in reconciling it with a pacifist stance. The fact that the author is not at all embarrassed by such imagery very likely indicates that the problem of Christians' serving in the army was not an issue for him."[21] It is difficult to see on what basis Swift makes this claim, however. As mentioned above, most people in the empire—especially urban residents—would be familiar with the Roman army and would therefore understand military imagery. But assuming that the use of positive metaphorical language regarding army structure and discipline implies endorsement of military service and warfare for Christians is an unwarranted inferential leap and is contradicted by what we know of both Christian demographics and the qualifications for military enlistment at that time.[22] Soldiers had to be Roman citizens and, originally, property owners; most Christians at the end of the first century were neither. The lack of references, either positive or negative, regarding Christians' enlistment in the Roman army prior to the late second century is most likely because there were few who were qualified, quite aside from any possible moral qualms about military service in general and, particularly, military service in an army which was periodically responsible for arresting and executing Christians. Even later, there is no suggestion in the writings of Nazianzen or the other Cappadocians that their allusions to positive aspects of military culture such as order, courage, and commitment imply a broader approval of Christians in military service.

ORIGEN AND THE "PATRIOTISM" OF CHRISTIAN PACIFISM

In fact, far from showing support for or approval of the Roman military, it is clear from pre-Constantinian Christian and pagan writings that Christians were often considered "unpatriotic" and traitorous to the Roman Empire both because of their refusal to sacrifice to the cult of the emperor during the empire-wide persecutions initiated under the emperors Decius in 250 and Diocletian in 303 (such refusal provoked most of the martyrdoms suffered before Constantine's Edict of Toleration in 313) and because of their general refusal to enlist in the military. Both imperial sacrifices and military service were seen as important to the defense and health of the empire, yet both created ethical and spiritual dilemmas for Christians.

In stark contrast to the ideal (if not always the reality) of the modern nation-state—united by language, culture, and, often, religion—the Roman Empire encompassed an amazing number of cultures, tongues, and faiths or philosophies. In fact, it was, proportionately, a far more diverse, multiethnic, and multireligious society than is the present-day United States. How, then, was unity created? On one level, the imposition of Roman law, political institutions, civic structures and activities, plus the infrastructure—such as roads—accompanying military occupation, coupled with the earlier imposition (in the eastern half of the empire) of Greek language and culture created a semiuniform civic and cultural overlay facilitating communication, commerce, and travel from one part of the Mediterranean to another. Roman citizenship, extended to non-Italians such as the apostle Paul, was another means of uniting diverse peoples and inculcating in them a "patriotic" commitment to the welfare of the empire.

But, some type of consistency or uniformity in the religious realm was also important to forging bonds of loyalty to the empire. Despite the diversity of local and regional religions of the vast Roman Empire, they almost all shared one trait that made it relatively easy to find common ground: they were polytheistic. Adding one more god or goddess to the list of local or regional deities was innocuous for most pagans, so the cult of the emperor as a minor divinity, a cult imported to Rome from the Middle East, became a practical way to provide religious coherence and simultaneously ensure the loyalty and patriotism of subjugated populations across Rome's far-flung empire. Only the "troublesome Jews" were granted dispensation from sacrificing to the emperor, after it became clear that the whole population would revolt if compelled to betray their strict monotheism. In the early days of Christianity, the dispensation provided to the Jews gave cover to Christians as well since the Christian movement began as a Jewish sect.

However, (Jewish) Christians' expulsion from the synagogues before the end of the first century CE removed that protection from Christians and led many Roman authorities to view Christianity as a brand-new and superstitious cult with no ties or commitment to the empire or its populace. We can see a similar set of doubts and prejudices today in those Americans who refuse to accept Muslims as truly American, even if born and raised in the United States, much less if they are immigrants. Christians' refusal to worship the Roman pantheon, and in particular to sacrifice to the cult of the emperor, thus engendered the view among much of the empire's populace at large that Christianity was a superstitious and, ironically, atheist religion because of its rejection of the Roman gods and the emperor's cult—hence, the sporadic persecutions of Christians, including the two systematic and empire-wide persecutions conducted under the emperors Decius and Diocletian, persecutions often conducted by military personnel.[23] And, as John Helgeland and other scholars have pointed out over the past few decades, the particular expectation of soldiers' participation in pagan religious ceremonies appears to have been as central to early Christians' discomfort with and outright rejection of military service as was their moral repugnance at the killing of prisoners or battlefield enemies.[24] (This issue will be treated in greater detail below.)

In any case, the combination of refusal to sacrifice to the emperor and refusal to serve in the military led the Roman public to deem Christians not only superstitious and atheistic but downright unpatriotic and even traitorous, endangering the very stability of the empire. One of the strongest and most explicit condemnations in this regard came from the brilliant but caustic pagan philosopher Celsus. Although he wrote his anti-Christian work, *The True Word* (Ὁ Ἀληθὴς Λόγος) around the time of Origen's birth, Celsus's reputation and the quality of his arguments still had such force decades later that Origen spent considerable energy responding to them in his monumental work *Against Celsus* (*Contra Celsum*). In particular, Origen argued that Christians were indeed as patriotic as anyone else and that they contributed as much to the defense and stability of the empire as did the military engaged in the physical fighting, but the Christians fought on the spiritual plane through their prayers, fighting the root cause of violence, namely, evil. He even linked the exemption he requested for Christians to the exemption given to pagan priests:

> Celsus goes on to encourage us "to assist the emperor with all our strength, to work with him on just undertakings, to fight for him and to serve in his army, if he requires it, either as a soldier or a general." To this we should reply that when the occasion arises, we provide the emperors with divine assistance, as it were, by putting on the "armor of God" (*Ephesians* 6.11). We do so in obedience to the voice of the Apostle who says "My advice is that first and foremost you offer

prayers, supplications, petitions and thanksgiving for all men, especially for the emperors, and all those in authority" (I *Timothy* 2.1–2). To be sure, the more pious a man is the more effectively does he assist the emperors—more so than the troops that go out and kill as many of the enemy as possible on the battleline. This would be our answer to those who are strangers to our faith and who ask us to take up arms and to kill men for the common good. Even in your religion priests attached to certain images and guardians of temples which are dedicated to what you believe are gods should keep their right hand undefiled for sacrifice so as to make their usual offerings to beings that you consider deities with hands that are free of blood and murder. And, of course, in war time you do not enlist your priests. If this is a reasonable procedure, how much more so is it for Christians to fight as priests and worshippers of God while others fight as soldiers. Though they keep their right hands clean, the Christians fight through their prayers to God on behalf of those doing battle in a just cause and on behalf of an emperor who is ruling justly in order that all opposition and hostility toward those who are acting rightly may be eliminated. What is more, by overcoming with our prayers all the demons who incite wars, who violate oaths and who disturb the peace we help emperors more than those who are supposedly doing the fighting. . . . We do not go out on the campaign with him [i.e., the emperor] even if he insists, but we do battle on his behalf by raising a special army of piety through our petitions to God. (*Against Celsus* 8.73)[25]

CHRISTIANS IN A PAGAN ARMY

Second- and third-century Christian writings regarding the question of whether Christians should, or even can, engage in military service are uniformly negative in both the Latin West and the Greek East. Ronald J. Sider is unequivocal on this point: "Up until the time of Constantine, there is not a single Christian writer known to us who says it is legitimate for Christians to kill or to join the military."[26] Given that we have no written evidence of Christian soldiers at all before the second half of the second century, it may well be that it was not an existential issue for the Christian community until then. Even after that time, there is almost no explicit evidence of baptized Christians entering military service, as opposed to (pagan) soldiers becoming Christian. Given the generally high moral standards required of those seeking Christian baptism and the severity of penances for lapses, leading to regular delays of baptism even in Christian households until well into adulthood, it is not surprising that all the contemporaneous references we have from the pre-Constantinian period about Christians either enlisting in or returning to military service are negative and uphold a high moral standard.

Nevertheless, we have both implicit and explicit written evidence, as well as archaeological evidence from a few epitaphs, that, from the late second century on, some Christians *did* indeed serve in the Roman army, if with mixed results (the occasional refusal of Christian soldiers to sacrifice or to engage in violent actions, especially against other Christians, resulted in even greater suspicion by the public and civil authorities of Christians' commitment to the Roman state and its people . . . and in martyrdom for the defiant soldiers).[27]

Strong Christian pacifist writings at the end of the second century and into the third century may indicate that Christians were then present in the military in noticeable numbers for the first time in Christian (and Roman) history. As the requirement of Roman citizenship for enrollment in the army was relaxed in the second century, more Christians qualified for military service.[28] Nevertheless, "noticeable numbers" is a relative and vague term. As Sider has astutely noted, Origen could easily have refuted Celsus's assertion that Christians refused to serve in the army simply by pointing out that substantial numbers were indeed serving . . . if that were the case. Yet Origen's arguments are all based on his agreement with Celsus's statement regarding Christians' refusal to serve in the army while simultaneously contending that Christians *do* support the empire's defense through their prayers.[29] That he did not challenge Celsus's remarks about the absence of Christian soldiers, although elsewhere in the treatise he mocked the attempt by some Christian soldiers to downplay their participation in pagan military religious rites, indicates that Origen was aware that at least *some* Christians were serving in the military but that their numbers were negligible.[30]

By the end of the third century and beginning of the fourth, it is clear that there were more Christians serving in the Roman army; we can see this in part because of the accounts of military martyrs arising particularly out of the Decian and Diocletian persecutions.[31] However, we still have absolutely no idea, in either sheer numbers or ratios, how many soldiers were already Christian at the time of their enlistment rather than becoming Christian *after* entering the military.[32] The existence of prohibitions against enlistment for catechumens and baptized Christians, with the punishment of expulsion from the church, shows the seriousness of the offense in the eyes of at least some church officials but also indicates that the practice must have occurred at least occasionally, thus prompting the ban in the first place.[33]

Nevertheless, we should be cautious in assuming that increasing numbers of Christians in the military—which is documented—necessarily implies equally increasing numbers of *already-baptized* Christians *entering* the military. It may be, at least in part, that the commonly held view of Christians as soft and unmanly because of their pacifism was gradually being replaced by a more admiring assessment of Christian courage and valor in the face of persecution and martyrdom, leading to higher rates of conversion to Christianity within the existing Roman military ranks. Certainly, as James C. Skedros has detailed in his article in this volume, all of the military martyrs venerated by the early and Byzantine church were valorized in their *vitae* or *passiones* not for any military prowess (as Skedros points out, the early evidence of military participation for many of them is dubious at best) but for their courage in maintaining their Christian faith and their refusal to sacrifice to the emperor or other Roman gods even to the point of death. In fact, it is not clear *when* exactly most of them converted to Christianity. For the few for whom we do have that information, they converted *after* their enlistment in the army, typically after seeing the faith and fortitude of Christians being martyred (e.g., the soldier who replaces the apostasizing Christian to become one of the 40 Martyrs of Amorion). This is, in fact, one of two recurring themes in the accounts of soldier martyrs of the third and early fourth centuries, the other being that the soldier declares his Christianity and is martyred when he is conscripted, expected to make a pagan sacrifice, or ordered to persecute or execute other Christians himself.[34]

If the cult of the emperor was an important element in unifying the general populace of the empire, it (along with the imported Persian mystery cult of the warrior-hunter god Mithras) played that role in spades within the military, where recruits from all over the empire and from numerous religious backgrounds marched and fought side by side. The negative public sentiment engendered by Christians' widespread refusal to enter the military was only deepened in the case of some soldiers who, having converted to Christianity after entering military service, refused not only to carry out orders requiring them to kill, especially those orders involving the arrest and execution of Christians, but even to participate in cultic rites that were important to the cohesion and morale of combat units.

Thus, in addition to the moral questions concerning Christians' engaging in violence and killing as part of their military responsibilities, Christian soldiers in the pre-Constantinian period faced a unique theological dilemma because military service plunged them into an entire pagan religious culture filled with holidays, sacrificial rites, and other obligations.[35] In his treatise *On Idolatry*, written around 211 although perhaps as early as 202,[36] the North African Christian theologian Tertullian argues that the pagan religious culture inherent in military service presents an insurmountable roadblock to Christians, while acknowledging that true participation in morally and theologically offensive activities such as cultic sacrifices and capital punishment cases are not required of non-officers.[37]

David Hunter credits John Helgeland for bringing proper attention to this important component of pre-Constantinian Christian opposition to participation in military, but criticizes him for "neglect[ing] other dimensions of the early Christian objection to military service."[38] For example, Tertullian mentioned capital punishment together with cultic sacrifices as activities that were unacceptable for Christians.[39] Likewise, Sider remarks that the poorly grounded overcorrective bias of Helgeland, Daly, and Leithart, who argue that opposition to idolatrous rites was a more important basis than moral pacifism for pre-Constantinian patristic negativity toward Christians in the military, "is not only sheer speculation, but also runs counter to the evidence that we do have."[40] Indeed, Sider notes, "The rejection of killing is comprehensive."[41] The spurning of military service in early church treatises and apologies should therefore be understood as part of a broader rejection of violence on the part of Christians and should not be undervalued simply because early Christian opposition to military service was multidimensional.

MILITARY SERVICE IN A CHRISTIAN STATE

Another argument that could dilute a strong pacifist stand is self-defense, and some scholars have sought to make just such an argument—and even to see in it the roots of a just war theory—in the passage quoted above from Origen's *Against Celsus*. Robert Daly, a well-known Origen scholar, contends that, in this passage, "we can also find the roots of the medieval two-sword theory, and . . . Origen himself also concedes some points that, in a changed context, were foundational for the later Christian just-war theory."[42] David Hunter, however, expresses surprise and sharp disagreement with Daly, noting that "the whole point of Origen's discussion is to insist that Christians may not participate in warfare, *even for a just cause.*"[43] In fact, Origen argued, much as did his contemporary Tertullian in Latin-speaking North Africa, against military service primarily on the basis of the violence inherent in the position, despite the "just cause" of defense against invaders.

Nevertheless, as the empire became predominantly Christian in the decades following Constantine's promulgation of the Edict of Milan, the church's insistence on Christians' avoidance of military service became more and more untenable since Origen's assumption that Christians could serve the empire by praying while pagans served it by fighting no longer worked demographically: by the late fourth century, Christians probably constituted well over half the empire's population, so there simply weren't enough pagans to fill the military ranks without sharply increasing the proportion of the pagan population in the army relative to the general populace. The issue of the "justness" of Roman military encounters was also seen as less morally problematic since Christian emperors appeared to internalize the limitation of warfare to self-defense, no longer seeking to expand the empire's borders beyond the shape it had taken. In fact, the notion that one had to belong to the faith of the empire in order to be "patriotic" and to serve as a soldier—the very principle which had made Christians suspect for the preceding three centuries—was turned on its head only a century after Christianity's legalization, when Theodosius II in 439 demanded that *only* Christians serve in the military.

Given these changes in circumstance from the early to the late fourth century, what is perhaps most notable about Basil and the other Cappadocians is how *little* any of them discusses the twin issues of Christians in military service and a Christian nation engaging in warfare. Claudia Rapp observes, for example, that Basil corresponded with "praetorian prefects, the masters of offices, military generals, and provincial governors" for various types of waivers and privileges.[44] In none of this correspondence, however, does he either chastise or laud these officers for their choice of career, nor does he address to them disparaging remarks or moral condemnations of war and military service from his perspective as a bishop and theologian.

Gregory of Nazianzus is similarly silent on this subject even though his sister, Gorgonia, was married to a high-ranking military officer from Iconium named Alypius. John McGuckin argues that Gregory's *Epistle 86*, in which the bishop responded to someone who had written him about his desire to join Gregory for an impending church festival, is addressed to Alypius. McGuckin therefore interprets Gregory's remarks about the recipient's changing clothes or causing a commotion with his attire as a reference to the inappropriate nature of Alypius's attending a church service in uniform (although Gregory himself claims to be more sanguine about it).[45] If true, this letter could provide an important insight into Gregory's views of military service vis-à-vis the church.

However, the identity of the recipient is far from clear.[46] Even assuming that it is Alypius, the question about clothing could have had to do with the assumption that Gregory's brother-in-law would have insufficient time to change out of his soiled traveling clothes (whether a uniform or civilian togs) before attending the service rather than concern over his attending church in military attire. Moreover, if this letter (and two others) are not assumed to be addressed to Alypius, then we have little indeed to go on regarding either Gregory's personal relationship with his brother-in-law or his feelings about Alypius's military career.

Raymond Van Dam, in fact, theorizes that "it is possible that Gregory of Nazianzus had never met Gorgonia's husband."[47] That notion seems overblown since it is based on Van Dam's misinterpretation of a remark Gregory made in his funeral oration for his sister: Gregory described Alypius simply as Gorgonia's husband, opining, "For I know not what further *need* be added" (emphasis added).[48] Van Dam misconstrues this as Gregory not actually *knowing* anything more about Alypius: "All he knew of Gorgonia's husband was . . . that he was her husband!"[49] That level of ignorance seems quite implausible given the amount of time Gregory spent in Nazianzus (not that far from Iconium) and the warm sentiments he displayed toward his niece Alypiana, whom he could scarcely have come to know only from afar.[50]

However, while Van Dam has undoubtedly exaggerated Gregory's remoteness from his brother-in-law, it is certainly true that the Cappadocian bishop says very little about Alypius in the funeral oration, and, in fact, the most positive statement he makes about him is actually praise for Gorgonia and a very backhanded compliment for Alypius when Gregory applauds Gorgonia for having "won over her husband and gained, instead of an unreasonable master, a good fellow servant."[51] Gregory's silence about Alypius's military profession does not necessarily indicate disapproval, but it may at least suggest a lack of approval for a military career. Moreover, Alypius's conversion to Christianity came at his wife's behest when she was on her deathbed and so occurred long after he had entered the army, thus following the pattern seen with almost all of the early Christians in the military about whom we have specific information on their time of conversion.

Ultimately, the silence of the Cappadocians regarding the morality of military service per se may be, as with the apparent acquiescence of pre-Constantinian Christians toward their military brethren's continued service after conversion, due to the nonviolent nature of much of military life. Much of soldiering had to do with providing a deterrent presence against banditry and potential threats along the border, and with providing security in many urban areas, which lacked a modern-style police force. As long as soldiers were not actually engaged in combat on the field of battle, it was possible for them to avoid the moral dilemmas military service typically presents in terms of the taking of human life, and the conversion of emperor and empire to Christianity meant that the earlier fears of Christians about participating in pagan rituals had become moot.

THE PROMULGATION OF WAR BY A CHRISTIAN STATE

If Christians' individual entry into military service in the early church was thus seldom praised *or* condemned by fourth-century Christian writers, much more complex were the related questions of a Christian soldier and, more broadly, of a Christian *state* actually making war. Pre-Constantinian antimilitary arguments regarding the pagan rituals endemic in the army became moot, and the *Pax Romana* which Christians had formerly assessed positively, mainly for its ability to secure safe passage for missionaries and evangelists spreading throughout the empire, was now seen by some as a divine peace protecting and promoting Christianity more generally, and, as such, worthy of protection, even if the idea of protecting peace through war was admittedly oxymoronic.

Although the New Testament and pre-Constantinian Christians had little to say about such a situation since the empire was decidedly *non*-Christian in their time period, there was one group of writings accepted by the church that provided unambiguous approval of a faithful state waging war: the Old Testament. The book of Joshua, in particular, championed God-ordained wars of conquest by the Israelites on the indigenous Canaanite people, and even the wisdom literature poetically gave its due to war: "a time to kill, and a time to heal, . . . a time for war, and a time for peace" (Eccl. 3:3, 8).

How, then, were such texts interpreted by the Cappadocians and by their exegetical predecessors, Origen and Gregory Thaumaturgus? Did they agree that the nation of Israel, because of its status as God's chosen people, was therefore "righteous" in its wars, and extrapolate from the "old" Israel to the "new"? That is, had the still-Christianizing Roman Empire become Israel's successor in both its divinely appointed status and therefore the justice and morality of its wars?

Origen's student, Gregory Thaumaturgus (who would become mentor to Basil's grandmother, Macrina the Elder), interpreted Ecclesiastes 3:8 not as acceptance of the inevitable and even seasonal nature of war, but rather as evidence that God's hand does not guide humanity in war. War is an evil which represents humanity's changeable, sinful nature and which Gregory contrasted with the true joy and fulfillment which comes from God alone:

> For the affairs of men are at one time in a condition of war, and at another in a condition of peace; while their fortunes are so inconstant, that from bearing the semblance of good, they change quickly into acknowledged ills. Let us have done, therefore, with vain labours. For all these things, as appears to me, are set to madden men, as it were, with their poisoned stings. And the ungodly observer of the times and seasons is agape for this world, exerting himself above measure to destroy the image of God, as one who has chosen to contend against it from the beginning onward to the end. I am persuaded, therefore, that the greatest good for man is cheerfulness and well-doing, and that this short-lived enjoyment, which alone is possible to us, comes from God only, if righteousness direct our doings. But as to those everlasting and incorruptible things which God has firmly established, it is not possible either to take anything from them or to add anything to them.[52]

Origen himself, in his defense of Christians' attitudes toward war against the attacks of Celsus, limited and qualified any notion of actual war in terms of self-defense and justice while continuing to maintain a pacifist model, and allegorized away any literal sense of God's approval of or command for war in his exegeses of several Old Testament passages concerning war. So, in his *Against Celsus*, while proclaiming Christians' patriotism and commitment to the empire and its emperor, Origen brilliantly inserted a note of subtle ambiguity when he averred that Christians "fight," through their prayers, "for those who fight in a *righteous cause* and for the *emperor who reigns righteously*, in order that everything which is opposed and hostile to *those who act rightly* may be destroyed" (emphasis added).[53]

Of course, Origen was writing a century before Constantine's Edict of Milan and Christianity's rise to dominant imperial religion. Nevertheless, Origen spiritualized Old Testament passages involving war out of an explicit discomfort with the notion that God would order killings and warfare.[54] Thus, when considering the divinely authorized violence in the book of Joshua, Origen outright rejected the literal sense of such texts and argued that their scriptural importance lies rather in the spiritual meaning to be recovered by allegorizing such texts:

> Unless those carnal wars [i.e., of the Old Testament] were a symbol of spiritual wars, I do not think that the Jewish historical books would ever have been passed down by the Apostles to be read by Christ's followers in their churches. . . . Thus, the Apostle, being aware that physical wars are no longer to be waged by us but that our struggles are to be only battles of the soul against spiritual adversaries, gives orders to the soldiers of Christ like a military commander when he says, "Put on the armor of God so as to be able to hold your ground against the wiles of the devil [Eph. 6.11]."[55]

In only one passage did Origen consider the situation of ancient Israel in a way that evokes a strong correspondence with the Roman state in the late fourth century, as Christianity found itself the favored and increasingly dominant religion of the empire:

> Again, if you took away from the Jews of that time, who had their own political life and country, the power to go against their enemies and to fight for their traditional customs, and to take life, . . . the inevitable consequence would have been their complete and utter destruction when their enemies attacked the nation, because by their own law they would have been deprived of strength and prevented from resisting their enemies.[56]

However, there was an important theological difference beyond that of a Christian Roman Empire versus the earlier nation of Israel. Origen's acquiescence in this one passage to the wars of the ancient Israelites was based on a progressive view of God's economy, on the unfolding of salvation history with its supplanting of the old covenant, old law, and "old Israel" by the new—that is, the church—and with consequently higher moral demands:

But the providence which long ago gave the law, but now has given the gospel of Jesus Christ, did not wish that the practices of the Jews should continue, and so destroyed their city and temple and the service of God in the temple offered by means of sacrifices and the prescribed worship.[57]

Gregory of Nyssa, in his *Homilies on Ecclesiastes*, followed Origen's method of interpretation, summing up an extensive allegory on the deeper meaning of "a time for war, and a time for peace" in this manner:

What is the good army, with which I am to join forces through peace? Who is the king of such an army? It is clear, from what we are taught by the inspired scriptures, that it is the array of the angels of the host of heaven.[58]

Nyssen similarly allegorized the plague of death to the Egyptians' firstborn in his *Life of Moses*, opining that, by the death of the firstborn in Egypt, Moses "laid down for us the principle that it is necessary to destroy utterly the first birth of evil."[59] Of course, the entire work is meant to be a manual of spiritual progress with Moses as the model. Nevertheless, Gregory was well aware that accepting at a literal level the plague against the firstborn in Exodus required one to believe that God would unjustly inflict punishment on the helpless innocent, and so proposed an alternative:

The Egyptian acts unjustly, and in his place is punished his newborn child, who in his infancy cannot discern what is good and what is not. His life has no experience of evil, for infancy is not capable of passion. . . . If such a one now pays the penalty of his father's wickedness, where is justice? Where is piety? Where is holiness? Where is Ezekiel, who cries: *The man who has sinned is the man who must die* and *a son is not to suffer for the sins of his father*? How can the history so contradict reason? (92) Therefore, as we look for the true spiritual meaning, seeking to determine whether the events took place typologically, we should be prepared to believe that the lawgiver has taught through the things said. The teaching is this: When through virtue one comes to grips with any evil, he must completely destroy the first beginnings of evil.[60]

The overriding tendency, clearly, in both the Cappadocians and the theological predecessors who most influenced them, was to allegorize difficult passages in the Old Testament in which God sanctioned or even ordered violence. If they did notice correspondences between ancient Israel and a newly Christianized Roman Empire, they did not choose to make use of them in order to justify Christian participation in the army or military actions by a Christian state.

In fact, only one of the three Cappadocian bishops, Basil, dealt straightforwardly with the question of the morality of war and of Christians killing in war, and even then only because of a specific question put to him by the young bishop of Iconium, Amphilochius (who happened to be Gregory of Nazianzus's cousin). Basil was, without a doubt, the least "countercultural" of the Cappadocians. For instance, unlike the renowned Greek and Latin bishops and theologians of the next generation, John Chrysostom and Augustine, who forcefully argued that extramarital relations by married men should be considered adultery regardless of imperial law and social custom, Basil acceded (if somewhat reluctantly) to the legal and canonical double standard which considered a married woman to be guilty of adultery for extramarital sexual relations, but defined a married man as guilty only of fornication for his extramarital relations, explicitly citing custom.[61] Basil was also the most politically astute, combining the genuine compassion underlying his monumental *Basileias* charitable complex with a savvy pragmatism. His ease at navigating political waters may be why he appears to be the only one of these three Cappadocian bishops who actually desired the episcopacy.[62]

It is therefore all the more remarkable that Basil, given his political pragmatism, his voluminous correspondence with high-ranking military officers, and the sheer fact of Cappadocia's proximity to the eastern borders of the empire, did not give soldiers a moral or ecclesiastical "pass" for their service in defense of the empire. In *Epistle 188* to Amphilochius, in which he responded to questions on various moral matters, Basil asserted in a section which has become known as canon 13: "Our Fathers did not reckon killings in war as murders, but granted pardon, it seems to me, to those fighting in defense of virtue and piety. Perhaps, however, it is well to advise them that, since their hands are not clean, they should abstain from communion alone for a period of three years."[63]

John McGuckin believes that the "Fathers" to whom Basil refers in his canon 13 are simply Athanasius of Alexandria in his (in)famous *Letter to Amun*[64] (McGuckin argues that Basil used the plural form to blunt any direct criticism of the Alexandrian church father).[65] He may be correct, or perhaps Basil was thinking of both Athanasius and Eusebius, bishop of Caesarea, court historian to Constantine, and perhaps the only early Christian author to write in positively glowing terms about military exploits and conquests as God-ordained acts of violence.[66] Basil frequently used the phrase "our fathers" in the context of theological polemics to refer to previous generations of theologians and church leaders, particularly bishops. In any case, laudatory rhetoric for Christians engaging in bloody battle was not widespread, at least among generations earlier than Basil's, so it is difficult to imagine whom Basil might have had in mind beyond Athanasius and Eusebius.

There are two important words and phrases in this short "canon" that illuminate Basil's feelings on this subject. The first is the Greek word φόνος, "murder." Contrary to most translations of canon 13, including the one above, Basil did not use different words to distinguish between killings on the battlefield and other types of killing, although he certainly could have, given the massive number of Greek terms meaning "to kill."[67] Rather, he used the term φόνος—murder—for both. The first sentence of the canon should more accurately read, then: "Our Fathers did not reckon *murders* in war as murders, but granted pardon, it seems to me, to those fighting in defense of virtue and piety."[68] This is echoed in canon 43 of another canonical letter of Basil to Amphilochius, *Epistle 199*, where he asserted that anyone who strikes his neighbor and kills him is a murderer (φονεύς), "whether he gave the first blow or was retaliating."[69]

Basil's use of the word φόνος for battlefield slayings, then, is enormously significant since, together with the second half of the sentence, it shows clearly that Basil did not consider violent acts in war to be qualitatively different, but, rather, that pardon or forgiveness (συγγνώμην) was extended to soldiers because they murdered "in defense of virtue and piety."[70] Basil's reasoning here is consistent not only with his passing statement in a homily on theodicy that war is evil,[71] but with what he expressed several paragraphs earlier, in his canon 8, where he distinguished among categories of killing that we would today define as involuntary manslaughter, voluntary manslaughter, second-degree murder, and first-degree or premeditated murder. For Basil, all are forms of killing and will require some penance, but they must be treated differently from one another because of the intent of the witting or unwitting perpetrator.[72] Basil's younger brother, Gregory of Nyssa, articulated a very similar set of distinctions, offering varying lengths of penance in accordance with the degree to which a slaying was voluntary or involuntary (ἐκουσίου τε καὶ ἀκουσίου) in a canonical letter, in a chapter known as canon 5.[73]

Basil's classification of all forms of killing as murder is the interpretive key, then, with respect to the second significant phrase, that the hands of a soldier returning from war are "not clean." Fighting and endangering oneself to preserve the lives of others is noble, but taking one life to preserve others is still the taking of a human life;[74] thus, the hands of a soldier returning from war are "not clean." Nevertheless, following the philosophy of differing intent he enunciated in canon 8, Basil's recommendation of three years' penance (as excommunication) treated the soldier returning from war much differently from a murderer who acted out of rage or premeditation, and who would thus normally suffer excommunication for thirty years.[75]

At the same time, the period of penance, in spite of its relative lightness, recognized the moral ambiguity of taking one life to save others, and—what was no doubt also in Basil's mind—the effect that the taking of human life was bound to have on the soldier himself, no matter how "just" or "righteous" the reason for the war might be deemed.[76] Basil's response to Amphilochius is, in fact, despite its brevity a very thoughtful and well-considered pastoral response that recognizes not only military violence's deviation from the absolute standard of not taking human life, but also the deep moral and spiritual conflict which warfare brings upon those in the military, whom society sends out to kill for its own protection.[77] John McGuckin is thus quite correct in his overall assessment of Basil's advice to Amphilochius:

> What this Basilian canon does most effectively is to hold up a No Entry sign in front of any potential theory of just war within Christian theology and should establish a decided refusal of postwar

church-sponsored self-congratulations for victory. All violence, local, individual, or nationally sanctioned, is here stated to be an expression of hubris that is inconsistent with the values of the Kingdom of God. Although in many circumstances that violence may be considered necessary or unavoidable—Basil states the only legitimate reasons as the defense of the weak and innocent—it is never justifiable. Even for the best motives in the world, the shedding of blood remains a defilement such that the true Christian afterward would wish to undergo the cathartic experience of temporary return to the lifestyle of penance, that is, be penitent.[78]

IN CONCLUSION, we can discern areas of both difference and congruence between pre- and post-Constantinian Eastern Christian theologians on the question of Christian involvement in military service and war. Perhaps the most important difference was that between a non-Christian empire, emperor, and army in the pre-Constantinian period, on the one hand, and (at least ostensibly) Christian versions of those from Constantine's reign onward (excepting the short reign of his nephew Julian, of course), on the other. The expectations of a polytheistic military culture both to participate in pagan rites and perhaps even to apprehend and kill fellow Christians created insurmountable ethical conflicts for Christian soldiers. Moreover, Christians such as Origen, marginalized in the pre-Constantinian empire, had the "luxury" of maintaining their pacifist ideals precisely because they were a religious minority who benefited from the safety provided by the legions of pagan soldiers defending the borders of the empire.

Despite this admittedly major difference, the Cappadocians, living in a very different political and demographic context, did not develop any theological reflection wholeheartedly supporting a Christian army in defense of a Christian state, nor did they extol the virtue of a Christian soldier killing presumably non-Christian enemies, even invaders, out of self-defense, to keep church and society peaceable and free. Like the earlier generations of theologians on whose backs they stood, they allegorized those Old Testament passages which could most conveniently have provided biblical and theological support for a theory of God's people waging war in God's name. To the contrary, they explicitly rejected such literal interpretations, operating from an eschatological perspective and so choosing instead to interpret the violence in such passages as references to the ongoing spiritual war against evil.[79] Every Christian is a soldier in such battles.

The Cappadocians certainly evince a pragmatic acceptance of the reality, and even the necessity, of Christian soldiers serving in a Christian army in defense of a Christian state: the luxury of a pure pacifism is no longer practicable in a world where Christians dominate. Nevertheless, even within the limits of defensive action, the common thread of a moral abhorrence of war so forcefully argued by Origen and other pre-Constantinian Christian writers continues to underlie the more nuanced and pragmatic approach of the Cappadocians. As Basil's *Epistle 188* makes abundantly clear, that pragmatism does not negate the piercing moral evil of one human being, created in the image of God, ending the life of another human being, who bears that same image.

NOTES

1. *Contra Celsum* 5.33; English translation in Louis Swift, *The Early Fathers on War and Military Service*, Message of the Fathers of the Church 19, ed. Thomas Halton (Wilmington, DE: Michael Glazier, 1983), 57. See also George Kalantzis, *Caesar and the Lamb: Early Christian Attitudes on War and Military Service* (Eugene, OR: Wipf & Stock, 2012), 136.

2. Saint Basile, *Lettres*, text establ. and trans. Y. Courtonne (Paris: Les Belles Lettres, 1961), 2:130; English translation in Saint Basil, *Letters, Vol. II (186–368)*, trans. Sister Agnes Clare Way, C.D.P., FC 28 (1955), 23. This disciplinary suggestion and those in much of the rest of the letter, as well as in two other letters responding to the various questions posed to him by Amphilochius of Iconium, became, over time, unofficial canons of the Eastern church (with Basil's responses in *Ep. 188* being divided into sixteen canons). They later were included as part of about two hundred such, derived from episcopal letters and other sources, which were formally adopted as canons in the Byzantine church through canon 2 of the so-called Quinisext Council or Council *in trullo* in 691–92, with this particular one known as canon 13.

3. A number of scholarly works treat the issue of early Christian views on war and military service. Among those treating Eastern (Greek) early church writers are Rob Arner, *Consistently Pro-Life: The Ethics of Bloodshed in Ancient*

Christianity (Eugene, OR: Pickwick Publications, 2010); C. J. Cadoux, *The Early Christian Attitude toward War* (London: Headley Brothers, 1919); James F. Childress, "Moral Discourse about War in the Early Church," *Journal of Religious Ethics* 12 (Spring 1984): 2–18; John Helgeland, "Christians and the Roman Army: A.D. 173–337," *Church History* 43 (1974): 149–63; Robert M. Grant, "War—Just, Holy, Unjust—in Hellenistic and Early Christian Thought," *Augustinianum* 20 (1980): 173–89; John Helgeland, Robert J. Daly, and J. Patout Burns, *Christians and the Military: The Early Experience* (Philadelphia: Fortress Press, 1985); Kalantzis, *Caesar and the Lamb*; J. A. McGuckin, "A Conflicted Heritage: The Byzantine Religious Establishment of a War Ethic," *Dumbarton Oaks Papers* 65/66 (2011–12): 29–44; McGuckin, "Nonviolence and Peace Traditions in Early and Eastern Christianity," in *Religion, Terrorism and Globalization: Nonviolence; A New Agenda*, ed. K. K. Kuriakose (New York: Nova Science Publishers, 2006), 189–202, repr. in Jeremy P. Ruther, ed., *Foundations of Religion*, Religion and Spirituality (New York: Nova Publishers, 2012), 21–40; Ronald J. Sider, ed., *The Early Church on Killing: A Comprehensive Sourcebook on War, Abortion, and Capital Punishment* (Grand Rapids: Baker Academic, 2012); Swift, *Early Fathers on War*. For a discussion of the confessional nature of some of the (particularly earlier) literature, see, e.g., Helgeland, "Christians and the Roman Army"; McGuckin, "Conflicted Heritage," 32–34.

4. Cappadocia is a geographically stunning region of central Asia Minor (modern-day Turkey). Christianity developed strongly in that region from at least the early fourth century, and numerous monastic churches and cells were carved into its soft volcanic rock "chimneys" during the middle Byzantine period, many of them surviving to the present day.

5. While Christianity had become legal following Constantine the Great's rise as sole Roman emperor and his legalization of Christianity across the empire with his Edict of Milan in 313, exactly *which* form of Christianity was favored varied during much of the fourth century according to time and place, as Nicene Christianity—based on the Trinitarian and christological elements of the creedal statement adopted by the First Ecumenical Council, which met in the Asia Minor town of Nicaea in 325—locked horns with several other lines of Trinitarian and christological thought based more or less on the theology of an early fourth-century Alexandrian priest, Arius, and thus known collectively as "Arianism." The Cappadocians supported Nicaea and so were not always in good graces with the imperial government, e.g., when a pro-Arian emperor such as Valens (364–78) sat on the throne. For an excellent analysis of the Cappadocians' Trinitarian theology vis-à-vis Arianism, see Lewis Ayres, *Nicaea and Its Legacy: An Approach to Fourth-Century Trinitarian Theology* (Oxford: Oxford University Press, 2004).

6. For some recent scholarship dealing with the ways in which Christianity historically has influenced its imperial oppressors and, conversely, how it has internalized and manifested imperial ideology and political pragmatism through its various national and imperial manifestations both ancient and contemporary, see, e.g., Joerg Rieger, *Christ & Empire: From Paul to Postcolonial Times* (Minneapolis: Fortress Press, 2007); Kwok Pui-Lan, Don H. Compier, and Joerg Rieger, eds., *Empire and the Christian Tradition: New Readings of Classical Theologians* (Minneapolis: Fortress Press, 2007).

7. Helgeland, Daly, and Burns, *Christians and the Military*, 16, citing Adolf von Harnack, *Militia Christi: The Christian Religion and the Military in the First Three Centuries*, trans. D. Gracie (Philadelphia: Fortress Press, 1981; first published in German, 1905), 27–64. For a more recent discussion of early Christian use of military images and metaphors, see McGuckin, "Conflicted Heritage," 34.

8. E.g., Eph. 6:12; 2 Cor. 6:7; Phil. 2:25; Philem. 2; 2 Tim. 2:3. See Swift, *Early Fathers on War*, 21; Helgeland, Daly, and Burns, *Christians and the Military*, 16–17.

9. Unless otherwise noted, the English translations of all biblical quotations are from the New Revised Standard Version (NRSV).

10. *The True Word* (Ὁ ἀληθὴς λόγος), Celsus's scathing and multipronged attack on Christianity from sixty years earlier, in 178, has been lost, but Origen quoted parts of it in his response.

11. Origen, *Contra Celsum* 8, 73; English translation in Henry Chadwick, *Origen: Contra Celsum* (London: Cambridge University Press, 1953), 509. Also see Kalantzis, *Caesar and the Lamb*, 143.

12. Gregory of Nazianzus, *Or. 42*, 25 (PG 36:488).

13. "Δὸς χάριν τοῖς σοῖς στρατιώταις· Χριστῷ σφαγίασον ἡμᾶς, ᾧ μόνῳ βασιλευόμεθα." Gregory of Nazianzus, *Or. 4* (*Contra Julianum imperatum 1*) (PG 35:612).

14. *Ad Ablabium quod non sint tres dei*, in F. Mueller, *Gregorii Nysseni opera*, vol. 3, pt. 1 (Leiden: Brill, 1958), 37.

15. Clement of Alexandria, *Paedagogus* 1.7.54.2; English translation in Kalantzis, *Caesar and the Lamb*, 95.

16. "Let us, therefore, serve as soldiers, brothers, with all earnestness under his faultless orders. Let us consider the soldiers who serve under our commanders, how precisely, how readily, how obediently they execute orders. Not all are prefects or tribunes or centurions or captains of fifty and so forth, but each in his own rank executes the orders given by the emperor and the commanders." Clement of Rome, *First Letter to the Corinthians* 37.1–3; English translation in J. B. Lightfoot and J. R. Harmer, *The Apostolic Fathers*, ed. Michael W. Holmes

(Grand Rapids: Baker, 1989), 48–49. Also see Helgeland, Daly, and Burns, *Christians and the Military*, 17–18.

17. Gregory of Nazianzus, *Or. 32*, 13 (PG 36:188); translation in St. Gregory of Nazianzus, *Select Orations*, trans. Martha Vinson, FC 107 (2003), 200.

18. "πᾶσι Θεοῦ στρατιώταις, ἡμέροις τἄλλα, πολεμικοῖς ὑπὲρ Πνεύματ." Gregory of Nazianzus, *Or. 42*, 11 (PG 36:472); translation in Brian E. Daley, S.J., *Gregory of Nazianzus*, The Early Church Fathers (London: Routledge, 2006), 145.

19. Adolf von Harnack, *Militia Christi*, 41, observed that Ignatius adopted the vocabulary of his captors.

20. Clement of Alexandria, *Stromateis* 5.126.5 (PG 9:81–88).

21. Swift, *Early Fathers*, 33. Alexander F. C. Webster and Darrell Cole, *The Virtue of War: Reclaiming the Classic Christian Traditions East and West* (Salisbury, MA: Regina Orthodox Press, 2004), 63–65, argue similarly in their exegesis of several New Testament passages, e.g., Luke 3:14 and 2 Tim. 2:3–6.

22. Certainly the coenobitic monastic founder Pachomius, a former military officer who organized his Egyptian desert monasteries with the kind of strict regimen that he had learned in the Roman army, would have been surprised by such an assumption.

23. For more on the issue of Roman persecution of Christians, see, e.g., T. D. Barnes, "Legislation against the Christians," *Journal of Roman Studies* 35, no. 1–2 (1968): 32–50; G. E. M. de Ste. Croix, *Christian Persecution, Martyrdom, and Orthodoxy*, ed. Michael Whitby and Joseph Streeter (New York: Oxford University Press, 2006); L. F. Janssen, "'Superstitio' and the Persecution of the Christians," *Vigiliae Christianae* 33, no. 2 (1979): 131–59.

24. The second-century North African theologian Tertullian is perhaps most explicit on this point in his *De corona militis* (On the military crown), the only full treatise on this subject penned by an early Christian writer. For more on the question of religious military rites and the quandary they posed for Christian soldiers, see Hunter, "A Decade of Research on Early Christians and Military Service," *Religious Studies Review* 18, no. 2 (1992): 87–94, especially his discussion (87–88) of the writings and thesis of John Helgeland on this topic.

25. Origen, *Contra Celsum* 8.73; translation in Swift, *Early Fathers*, 55. Also see Kalantzis, *Caesar and the Lamb*, 143–44. Note, however, Origen's qualifications regarding a "just cause" and an emperor "ruling justly," which implicitly undercut the unfettered nature of his defense of Christian patriotism toward the empire. These qualifications will be discussed later in this article.

26. Sider, *Early Church on Killing*, 190.

27. See ibid., 145–51, especially the discussion citing the very small number (six) of epitaphs with military references that can definitively be placed in the pre-Constantinian era.

28. The continued exclusion of slaves probably affected the Christian population disproportionately, however.

29. Sider, *Early Church on Killing*, 185–90.

30. Origen, *On 1 Corinthians 9.11*; cited in Sider, *Early Church on Killing*, 70–71.

31. See Hippolyte Delehaye, *Les legends grecques des saints militaires* (Paris: A. Picard, 1909); James C. Skedros, "Lessons from Military Saints in the Byzantine Tradition," ch. 7 in this volume; Christopher Walter, *The Warrior Saints in Byzantine Art and Tradition* (Aldershot: Ashgate, 2003); Alexander Webster, "Varieties of Christian Military Saints: From Martyrs under Caesar to Warrior Princes," *St. Vladimir's Theological Quarterly* 24 (1980): 3–35.

32. See Sider, *Early Church on Killing*, 185–90; Swift, *Early Fathers on War*, 71–79. In addition to these sources, as well as the rest of the extensive bibliography listed above in note 3, two useful short articles which provide some review of the literature and state of the question as well as furthering the discussion are Hunter, "Decade of Research"; James J. Megivern, "Early Christianity and Military Service," *Perspectives in Religious Studies* 12, no. 3 (Fall 1985): 175–84.

33. In ch. 16.9, the author (traditionally, Hippolytus) of the *Apostolic Tradition*, a third-century church manual, admonishes churches not to admit to the catechumenate any military officers or enlisted men who order or carry out executions, who take military oaths, or who serve as military governors (presumably, the oath taking would refer to any oaths taken after beginning the process of becoming a Christian). See McGuckin, "Conflicted Heritage," 37. A later church manual, the *Testament of the Lord* (Testamentum Domini), which is believed to date from the fourth or fifth century but clearly incorporates earlier material, calls for the expulsion of any catechumen or baptized Christian who desires to enter the military. Skedros, "Lessons from Military Saints," notes that (1) all of the early Christian soldiers honored as saints became Christian *after* having entered the military, according to their *vitae*; and (2) all of these "military saints" died as martyrs for their faith, not as soldiers in battle.

34. Swift, 71–79.

35. Helgeland, Daly, and Burns, *Christians and the Military*, ch. 8, "Roman Army Religion," 48–55; Helgeland, "Christians and the Roman Army."

36. Swift, *Early Fathers on War*, 40, suggests that it may be contemporaneous with Tertullian's *Apology*.

37. Tertullian, *On Idolatry* 19.1.

38. Hunter, "Decade of Research," 88.

39. Capital punishment continued to be regarded by some as morally problematic centuries after the Christianization of the empire, e.g., the early ninth-century iconophile abbot Theodore of Stoudios regarding the execution of heretics; Anna Komnena, who felt it necessary in her *Alexiad* to justify her father's imposition of the death penalty for a leader of the heterodox Bogomils in her history of the reign of her father, the eleventh-century emperor Alexios I Komnenos; and, outside the boundaries of the empire itself, the first Christian prince of the Rus', Vladimir, who abolished the death penalty precisely because it was at odds with the ethics of his newly adopted religion . . . ironically, to the dismay of a Greek bishop from Constantinople.

40. Sider, *Early Church on Killing*, 191.

41. Ibid.

42. Helgeland, Daly, and Burns, *Christians and the Military*, 40.

43. Hunter, "Decade of Research," 88.

44. Claudia Rapp, *Holy Bishops in Late Antiquity* (Berkeley: University of California Press, 2005), 265.

45. Gregory of Nazianzus, *Ep. 86*, in Saint Gregory of Nazianzus, *Lettres*, ed. and trans. Paul Gallay (Paris: Les Belles Lettres, 1964), 1:107. See John A. McGuckin, *Saint Gregory of Nazianzus: An Intellectual Biography* (Crestwood, NY: St. Vladimir's Seminary Press, 2001), 26–27.

46. McGuckin, *Saint Gregory of Nazianzus*, argues that the relationship between Gregory and Gorgonia was distant and that this accounts for his odd reference in *Ep. 86* to "the sister" with no possessive modifier in either the first or second person. Given that McGuckin himself, however, points out (p. 27, main text, and n. 102) that "sister" was also sometimes used by Gregory to refer to someone's wife (he cites *Ep. 197* [PG 37:321] and the *Epitaph for Theosevia*), there is no need to imagine a double entendre; the recipient's ἀδελφή could have been his wife (or sister) without requiring us to infer a reference to Gregory's own sister.

47. Van Dam, *Families and Friends in Late Roman Cappadocia* (Philadelphia: University of Pennsylvania Press, 2003), 94. See also Virginia Burrus, "Life after Death: The Martyrdom of Gorgonia and the Birth of Female Hagiography," in *Gregory of Nazianzus: Images and Reflections*, ed. Jostein Bortnes and Tomas Hagg (Copenhagen: Museum Tusculanum, 2006), 160n13.

48. "καὶ οὐκ οἶδ' ὅ τι χρὴ πλέον εἰπεῖν" (note the word χρὴ); *In laudem sororis Gorgoniae* 20 (PG 35:813).

49. Van Dam, *Families and Friends*, 94.

50. McGuckin, *Saint Gregory of Nazianzus*, 6 and 395.

51. *In laudem sororis Gorgoniae* 8 (PG 35:797); English translation in *Funeral Orations by Saint Gregory Nazianzen and Saint Ambrose*, trans. Leo McCauley et al., FC 22 (1953), 105–6.

52. Gregory Thaumaturgus, *A Metaphrase of Ecclesiastes* 3; English in *ANF* 6:11.

53. Origen, *Contra Celsum* 8.73; English translation in Chadwick, 509. Also see Kalantzis, *Caesar and the Lamb*, 143–44.

54. For a brief discussion of early Christian allegorization of divine commands to kill in the Old Testament, see McGuckin, "Conflicted Heritage," 29–30, text and n. 3.

55. Origen, *Homilies on Joshua*, Hom. 15.1 (SC 71:330); English translation in Swift, *Early Fathers on War*, 59. See also the introduction to and translation of this passage in Kalantzis, *Caesar and the Lamb*, 146–47. Swift gives other examples as well (*Contra Celsum* 7.19 and 22) of Origen's refusal to accept literally any divinely ordered violence in the Old Testament.

56. Origen, *Contra Celsum* 7, 26; English translation in Chadwick, 415–16.

57. Ibid.; English in Chadwick, 416.

58. Gregory of Nyssa, *Homily 8 on Ecclesiastes*; in P. J. Alexander, *Gregorii Nysseni opera* (Leiden: Brill, 1962), 5:435, lines 1–7; English translation in Gregory of Nyssa, *Homilies on Ecclesiastes: An English Version with Supporting Studies*, ed. Stuart George Hall (Berlin: de Gruyter, 1993), 139.

59. Gregory of Nyssa, *De vita Moysii* 2.89; English translation in Gregory of Nyssa, *The Life of Moses*, trans., intro., and notes Abraham J. Malherbe and Everett Ferguson (New York: Paulist Press, 1978), 75.

60. Gregory of Nyssa, *De vita Moysii* 2.91–92; English in Gregory of Nyssa, *Life of Moses*, 75–76; emphasis original.

61. Judith Evans Grubbs, *Law and Family in Late Antiquity: The Emperor Constantine's Marriage Legislation* (Oxford: Clarendon Press, 1995), 225. Grubbs wryly observes: "Basil admitted being a little puzzled by the double standard, but accepted it because there were no earlier canons penalizing a husband's affairs as *moicheia* [adultery] and because custom (*sunetheia*) so dictated." See also Anna Silvas, *Macrina the Younger, Philosopher of God* (Turnhout: Brepols, 2008), 70.

62. In fact, he feigned to his friend Gregory a mortal illness in order to persuade him to come to Caesarea, thereby being present to lobby for and vote on Basil's behalf in the impending election for a new bishop for the metropolitan see (Basil having suddenly recovered upon Gregory's arrival). Basil's manipulation of Gregory angered his friend enough to put their friendship on shaky ground. A complete rupture developed when Basil, now metropolitan bishop of Caesarea

and in a power dispute with fellow bishop Anthimos after the province of Cappadocia was split into two (with Anthimos the bishop of the new Cappadocia Secunda), persuaded Gregory to become one of Basil's suffragans as bishop of the town of Sasima. Gregory finally arrived in the small town after procrastinating for several months following his consecration as its bishop. He took one look at the chickens in the road and the small, unimpressive houses and public buildings, and promptly left again. The rift in their friendship was healed only shortly before Basil's death, although Basil's multiple manipulations of Gregory left the latter with a residual resentment. See McGuckin, *Saint Gregory of Nazianzus*, 372.

63. "Τοὺς ἐν πολέμοις φόνους οἱ πατέρες ἡμῶν ἐν τοῖς φόνοις οὐκ ἐλογίσαντο, ἐμοὶ δοκεῖν, συγγνώμην δόντες τοῖς ὑπὲρ σωφροσύνης καὶ εὐσεβείας ἀμυνομένοις. Τάχα δὲ καλῶς ἔχει συμβουλεύειν, ὡς τὰς χεῖρας μὴ καθαρούς, τριῶν ἐτῶν τῆς κοινωνίας μόνης ἀπέχεσθαι." *Ep. 188*, 13 (PG 32:681); English translation in Saint Basil, *Letters*, 23.

64. Athanasius, *Ep. 48*; P.-P. Joannou, *Fonti. Fasciolo ix. Discipline générale antique (ii–ix s.). Les canons des pères grecs* (Rome: Tipographia Italo-Orientale "S. Nilo," 1963), 2:63–71.

65. McGuckin, "Nonviolence and Peace Traditions," 196–97; McGuckin, "Conflicted Heritage," 37–38. McGuckin's argument in the former article that Athanasius was being sardonic is unconvincing, though, since, although McGuckin is correct that the Alexandrian bishop ultimately is concerned with ascetic struggle rather than actual military violence, his distinction between battlefield and other types of killings parallels his distinction between licit, marital sex and sinful, extramarital sexual relations. In the latter article, McGuckin points out that Athanasius drew such a big distinction between murder and killing in war as an analogy to emphasize his point that context is crucial in determining the morality or immorality of an action.

66. Swift, *Early Fathers on War*, 82–89. Also see the essay by George E. Demacopoulos, ch. 6 in this volume.

67. The Perseus Digital Library provided ninety-three Greek entries for "kill"; Basil could easily have used any one of at least two dozen of those to provide the meaning of "kill" without implying "murder."

68. Note that George Kalantzis, in *Caesar and the Lamb*, 200, correctly translates this passage.

69. Basil, *Ep. 199*, 43 (PG 32:729). English translation in Saint Basil, *Letters*, 59. See Alexander F. C. Webster, *The Pacifist Option: The Moral Argument against War in Eastern Orthodox Theology* (San Francisco: International Scholars Publications, 1998), 306n21.

70. For an in-depth discussion of this, also see McGuckin, "Conflicted Heritage," 38.

71. PG 31:332; English in St. Basil the Great, *Homily Explaining That God Is Not the Cause of Evil* 2, in *On the Human Condition*, trans. and intro. Nonna Verna Harrison (Crestwood, NY: St. Vladimir's Seminary Press, 2005), 67.

72. Basil, canon 8 of *Ep. 188*, 8 (PG 32:676–77).

73. Gregory of Nyssa, *Epistula canonica ad Letoium* (PG 45:232); G. A. Rhalles and M. Potles, Σύνταγμα τῶν θείων καὶ ἱερῶν κανόνων, 6 vols. (Athens: G. Chartophylax, 1852–59; reprint Athens, 1966), 4:316. See a discussion of this canon in Webster, *Pacifist Option*, 170. Gregory, however, unlike Basil, only classified as murder (φόνος) those killings which are voluntary.

74. Webster refers to this high moral position as "maximalist morality" grounded in Christology in Webster, ibid., 26. This maximalist morality may be seen particularly in the unanimous canonical witness against clerical participation in any type of bloodshed, including military battles; see Webster, ibid., ch. 7, "The Canonical 'Dual Standard,'" 165–81.

75. Basil, canon 7 of *Ep. 188*, 7 (PG 32:673–76).

76. See the discussion of war's impact on soldiers from an Orthodox perspective in ch. 1 of this volume, by Aristotle Papanikolaou: "The Ascetics of War: The Undoing and Redoing of Virtue."

77. For a thoughtful discussion of the moral and penitential aspects of Basil's canon 13, see John McGuckin, "St. Basil's Guidance on War and Repentance," *In Communion*, www.incommunion.org. (This article is extracted from McGuckin's "Non-violence and Peace Traditions.") Some of the more recent work on the morality of war by Orthodox military chaplain Fr. Alexander F. C. Webster is surprisingly lacking in this respect. See his "Justifiable War as a 'Lesser Good' in Eastern Orthodox Moral Tradition," *St. Vladimir's Theological Quarterly* 47, no. 1 (2003): 3–57; and Webster and Cole, *Virtue of War*, whose ch. 9, "Penance, Just War, and Recent Conflicts," 194–216, includes a sterile discussion of knighthood and a lengthy polemic on just war, but no compassionate pastoral exploration of the role of penance in helping soldiers work through the psychological and spiritual wounds wrought by their own violent actions. For a more pastoral and compelling account of the traumatic effect of war on soldiers' spiritual lives, see Papanikolaou, "Ascetics of War."

78. McGuckin, "Conflicted Heritage," 39 (cf. McGuckin, "Nonviolence and Peace Traditions," 197–98, and "St. Basil's Guidance"). A bit earlier in "Nonviolence and Peace Traditions," McGuckin similarly observes that Basil's canon 13 is "an 'economic' reflection on the ancient canons that forbade the shedding of blood in blanket terms . . . [but which] nevertheless makes it abundantly clear

that the absolute standard of Christian morality turns away from war as an unmitigated evil." Note that McGuckin uses the term "economic" here not in the sense of God's activity in creation or salvation history, but in the sense of the Orthodox approach to adjusting the implementation of canon law more or less harshly depending on the circumstances of an individual case, the practice known as *economia* (also spelled *oikonomia*).

79. For more discussion of the eschatological focus underlying patristic views on war, see McGuckin, "Conflicted Heritage," esp. 39.

CHAPTER 6

CONSTANTINE, AMBROSE, AND THE MORALITY OF WAR

*How Ambrose of Milan Challenged the
Imperial Discourse on War and Violence*

GEORGE E. DEMACOPOULOS

In his essay "The Teaching on Peace in the Fathers," Rev. Stanley Harakas, seeking to differentiate the Orthodox Christian attitude toward peace from that of the Roman West, argued that Ambrose and Augustine were guilty of transforming the Christian priority for peace into a view of the Christian soldier that ultimately led to the valorization of violence as a positive virtue.[1] While it is certainly true that Ambrose and Augustine employed the language of "just war" (*iustum bellum*) in a way that Eastern authors of their age typically did not, the patristic record, both East and West, is more complicated than the usually careful Harakas makes it out to be.

And it is not just Harakas and Orthodox interpreters who have failed to grasp the ingenuity and complexity of Ambrose's position. Indeed, it seems that all previous scholarly assessments of Ambrose's reflections on war have made one of the following three mistakes: (1) they anachronistically compare his ideas to those of the scholastic discussions of just war, (2) they argue for a radical break between pre-Constantinian and post-Constantinian authors and do so with an assortment of straw-man arguments, or (3) they compare (as does Harakas) Ambrose to an empty-handed list of post-Constantinian Greek authors who never asked or answered the war question in the same way.[2] In short, previous scholarly investigations have failed to assess Ambrose's thinking on war in its proper Greco-Roman and Christian context. A broader consideration of these contextual elements, however, leads to an interpretation that shows Ambrose's view on war and capital punishment as one that limited, rather than sanctioned, the violence that many other Christian bishops of the post-Constantinian age were willing to ignore altogether.

This essay intends to nuance the question of "just war" in the fourth century not by asking whether a particular late-ancient Christian author believed that war could be just in the scholastic sense (which is an ahistorical question), but by seeing the extent to which the Constantinian revolution spawned new, and multiple, Christian hermeneutics of war.[3] From this wider perspective, we see that Ambrose of Milan, unlike most of his contemporaries, including those in the East, challenged the increasingly hegemonic control that the imperial court sought to wield over the Christian moral discourse. In short, Ambrose offered an alternative to the imperialist propaganda promoted by other Christian bishops (Eusebius, first among them), which granted the emperor the right to determine life and death (both the right to wage war and the exercise of capital punishment). Seeing Ambrose as part of a broader moral debate stretching back to Roman antiquity shows that he remained more consistent with pre-Constantinian theologians than is generally acknowledged and that he was more willing to challenge the imperial prerogative over life and death than any of his episcopal contemporaries.

Throughout the following essay, I offer three overlapping arguments: (1) I submit that although there is a real difference in the way that pre-Constantinian and post-Constantinian Christian authors typically engaged the issues of war and violence, the distinctions between these groups of authors are not as neat or as sharp as many modern scholars suggest; (2) I critique the thesis, shared by many Orthodox commentators, that Ambrose was more militant than his Greek contemporaries; and (3) I affirm that Ambrose is best understood as a Christian moralist who sought to limit, rather than valorize, violence by Christians.

THE LEGACY OF CICERO

As is well known, the writings of the Roman orator Cicero (106–43 BCE) were among the most important non-Christian influences on both Ambrose and Augustine. Among his many other important intellectual legacies, Cicero's writings on war offer the most substantial examination of the subject from the ancient world. Indeed, his treatment is so important that most modern studies of war and peace attribute the concept of "just war" to him.[4] Perhaps the most significant aspect of Cicero's discussion of war was the extent to which he disparaged it. Indeed, he argues in book 1 of his *De officiis* (On the office) that there are two ways in which we contest things with others: (1) through a legal procedure (*disputationem*) employing reason and oratory and (2) through violence. One of these, he argues, belongs to humans (*hominis*), the other to beasts (*beluarum*).[5] So long as humans continue to act like humans, there is no role for violence; but when one party abandons the use of reason and resorts to violence, the other party must necessarily do so as an act of self-preservation.[6] As a corollary, Cicero believed that it was morally imperative that victorious armies spare their conquered enemies (so long as the conquered have not been barbarous in their tactics) and that the victors grant citizenship and protection to former enemies.[7]

Cicero also famously differentiates between wars of survival and wars for supremacy (*imperio*). But Cicero's position is curiously ambiguous. While he seems to deem wars of supremacy legitimate, he argues paradoxically that they "should not fail to start from the same motives as a war of [self-defense]."[8] Cicero's ambivalence, in this respect, may reflect a subtle attempt to critique the increasingly militant and imperialist actions of the current Roman regime.

But perhaps the most overt condemnation of militancy, one that would have been quite provocative for his contemporaries, emerges during his comparison of the public magistrate and the field general (*De officiis* 1.72–78). "Most people," he writes, "believe that the achievements of war are more important than those of peace, but this opinion needs to be corrected. This is because many have sought the occasion for war from the mere ambition for fame."[9] But it is peace, not war, he argues, that is superior.[10] A military victory is a one-time event; but the establishment of a body of laws that guarantees peace and justice will last forever.[11] Even more startling is Cicero's claim that the public magistrate who pursues the moral high ground against the forces of public opinion is more courageous than the soldier in the field.[12] This was a direct challenge to the long-held Greco-Roman concept of courage. The Christian martyrs, of course, developed yet another model of courage, which was an even greater challenge to Greco-Roman sensibilities.

CHRISTIAN AUTHORS PRIOR TO CONSTANTINE

The subject of war and Christian participation in the army provided a consistent, albeit muted, subject of interest in the period prior to Constantine's conversion. Although one could argue that both the Old and New Testaments offer an ambivalent attitude toward military service, Christian authors between the second and early fourth centuries (whose works survive) consistently disapproved of Christians engaging in violence and/or participating in the Roman army.[13] Justin Martyr, Athenagoras, Irenaeus of Lyons, and the ever-influential Egyptian theologian, Origen, all implied (contrary to the surviving historical evidence) that Christians did not serve in the army and that they did not resist the Roman soldiers sent to arrest them but, instead, willingly gave themselves over to martyrdom.[14] Of these authors, Origen was the only one to acknowledge the need for the Roman state, as an act of self-preservation, to engage in war; but Origen argued that Christians could not take part in combat because the Christian scriptures forbade it.[15] From Origen's perspective, both pagans and Jews were able to bear arms in combat but Christians served the state by offering their prayers—their training was in the realm of spiritual, not physical, warfare.[16] Subsequent authors condemned military service even more strongly. For example, Cyprian of Carthage (d. 258) suggested that there was little difference between a soldier who killed in battle and a murderer.[17] And the Latin rhetorician Lactantius (260–330) defined any form of killing (whether warfare, capital punishment, or gladiatorial spectacle) to be the sinful destruction of God's sacred creation.[18]

Writing in the late second and early third centuries, the North African Christian author Tertullian, however, begrudgingly acknowledged that there were Christians in the Roman army.[19] Tertullian is, in fact, the only author of the pre-Constantinian period to have a surviving treatise (*De corona militis*; Concerning the military crown) about Christian involvement with the army. In an earlier apology, Tertullian, like Origen, acknowledged the need for the Roman state to maintain an army and affirmed that Christians prayed both for brave armies and for the protection of the empire.[20] In *De corona militis*, however, Tertullian begins with a story of the martyrdom of a Christian soldier who refused to wear a pagan headdress during a victory celebration.[21] Tertullian uses the example of the martyred soldier to discourage other Christians from enlisting in the army on the grounds that Roman soldiers are expected to participate in certain pagan rituals that Tertullian believes to be in violation of their belief in Christ.[22] It is perhaps surprising that in his lengthy critique of military service, Tertullian only briefly includes a concern about violence (in the form of a pair of rhetorical questions) in his argument against military service.[23] Indeed, his objection throughout the treatise emphasizes the idolatry associated with Roman military practice; he never actually identifies the violence of combat as a specific reason that a Christian should not join the army.[24]

Archaeological evidence from the same period, and a small collection of Roman authors, confirm Tertullian's acknowledgment that there were Christian soldiers among the Roman legions.[25] In general, the empire did not prohibit Christians from serving in the army.[26] Further confirmation of Christian involvement in the Roman legions stems from the pre-Constantinian accounts of the soldier-martyrs.[27] Of course, the earliest surviving descriptions of these military saints all suggest that their heroes left the army upon conversion to Christianity and that their martyrdoms were a consequence of that defection.[28] Only later, during the retelling of their stories in the Byzantine period, were the military saints described as having remained in the army.[29]

The discrepancy between the majority of theological writers who suggested that Christians did not (or at least should not) serve in the army and the large number of other sources from the same period that suggest otherwise has caused modern readers great consternation. In not a few cases, scholars have too easily dismissed or ignored one group of evidence in favor of another, arguing that pre-Constantinian Christians either were decidedly pacifist (as in the case of Hershberger and Hauerwas) or were only rarely concerned about Christian involvement in the Roman army (e.g., Helgeland). It seems more likely, however, that there was a mixture of opinions about the subject among Christians in this period.

One way to understand the competing data (without simply dismissing a large part of it) would be to recognize that some of the proscriptions against joining the army would have been initially directed to a Christian civilian audience, whereas many of the Christian soldiers likely converted to the faith after they had already enlisted, at which point leaving the army would have been difficult. This theory is evinced, at least in part, by the fact that the third-century martyr accounts of soldiers that survive describe men who converted to Christianity after their enlistment.[30] An alternative explanation rests on the idea that a Christian's self-identity was not entirely informed by his religious practice.[31] Tertullian, Origen, and others like them spent enormous mental energy attempting to understand the place of a Christian within a non-Christian empire.[32] Scripture, not Roman law or Greek philosophy, provided the primary source for moral reflection for these authors, and their faith in Christ was the dominant feature of their self-identity. But it is unlikely that most Christians, whether in the army or not, would have labored these questions to the same degree or with the same result.[33] Indeed, we should not presume that all (or even most) Christians of the pre-Constantinian era saw their religious faith and their political identity as mutually exclusive affiliations.[34] In other words, it is quite plausible that there were thousands of Christian soldiers among the Roman legions in the years prior to Constantine's conversion, despite the theological protests of Tertullian, Origen, and others like them.

THE CONSEQUENCES OF CONSTANTINE'S CONVERSION

Of course the prevailing Christian attitude toward the empire changed with the conversion of Constantine to Christianity. While it is certainly true that the church benefited greatly from the patronage of Constantine and subsequent Christian emperors,[35] the immediate and unexpected fusion of church and empire proved to be a challenge as well. Indeed, the Constantinian revolution had done far more than end the persecutions— it spawned a new class of Christian public officials who were expected to retain order, punish criminals, and keep the barbarians at bay. These responsibilities necessarily challenged some pre-Constantinian ideas about the possibility of a Christian working for the state or serving in the army. Moreover, the combination of church and state necessarily put bishops into the business of civic responsibility and, as a consequence, made them subject to imperial appointment and reproach.[36] This, of course, complicated the way that Christian leaders understood the role of the state in relation to the moral policies of the church.[37]

One of the most dramatic examples of this is reflected in the ways in which Christian historians (such as Eusebius, Orosius, Socrates, Sozomen, Procopius, etc.) began to describe the military exploits of their rulers. Whereas no Christian author of the pre-Constantinian period is known to have praised the military talents of Roman generals, Eusebius and like-minded imperial propagandists could hardly contain their praise of Constantine's exploits in the field. For Eusebius (the father of church history and bishop of Caesarea), Constantine was the perfect general.[38] He was fearless, decisive, and ever victorious. He knew when to attack and what tactics to employ. His troops were responsive, dedicated, and disciplined.[39]

Eusebius's praise for Constantine stemmed primarily from the bishop's understanding that the emperor was responsible for bringing an end to the persecutions. As such, Constantine had enabled an age of peace, which brought the empire into alignment with the cosmic peace initiated by Christ through the incarnation. Although wars continued (both on the frontier and between Roman generals), these wars were, for Eusebius, of a different sort because they stood in the way of the Constantinian peace. Thus, for Eusebius, Constantine engaged in war for the pursuit of peace, and, as a consequence, his efforts were in service to the church and endorsed by God.

In fact, Eusebius describes the conflicts Constantine wins as "holy wars" in which there exists a symbiotic relationship between Constantine's martial talent and God's direct intervention.[40] He describes Constantine's soldiers as members of God's army, and the emperor's opponents as the enemies of God. And at times, Eusebius chronicles Constantine's military victories as being directly linked to God's favor.[41] The story of Constantine's conversion, his creation of a new, cross-shaped military standard, the placing of the *chi rho* on the shields of his soldiers, and the holy war against Maxentius culminating at the battle of the Milvian bridge are all well known and need not detain us.[42] Often overlooked, however, are some of the details concerning Constantine's second civil war, the war with Licinius, in 323.[43] For example, during the final battle, Eusebius describes Constantine as using the *Labarum* as a powerful talisman that he shifts from one part of the field to another in order to alter the course of the battle.[44] Furthermore, unlike Maxentius, who drowned at the Milvian bridge, Licinius and many of his top lieutenants were captured by Constantine's forces in 323. According to Eusebius, Constantine then had them all summarily executed:

> He then proceeded to deal with this enemy of God [θεομισῆ] and his followers according to the law of war, and consign them to a fitting punishment [πρεπούσῃ παρεδίδου τιμωρίᾳ]. Accordingly, the tyrant and all who had advised him in his impiety were together subjected to the just punishment of death [τὴν προσήκουσαν ὑπέχοντες δίκην]. After this, those who until recently had been deceived by their vain confidence in false deities, acknowledged with unfeigned sincerity the God of Constantine, and openly professed their belief in him as the true and only God.[45]

The decision to kill Licinius, who was married to Constantine's sister at the time, may have contravened Cicero's dictum concerning defeated enemies.[46] And while it should not surprise us that Constantine acted as he did (most Roman emperors would have done the same), what is surprising is that Eusebius, a Christian bishop, would not only describe these executions as a "righteous punishment" but that he would attribute the conversion of countless others to the "God of Constantine" as something that could happen only after the execution of the emperor's chief rival.

Although the Eusebian material is critical to our assessment of the transformation of the Christian discourse about war, other important aspects of the Constantinian story are not included in the works of Eusebius. For example, as early as 314, Constantine was able to persuade a group of bishops meeting in a local council in Gaul to excommunicate any soldier who deserted his post during peacetime.[47] There is also evidence that one of Constantine's armies massacred a Donatist congregation in their church at Avioccala (Northern Algeria) in 317.[48] Evincing the gradual replacement of pagan religion by Christianity within the army, the fifth-century church historian Sozomen informs us that Constantine was responsible for placing Christian chaplains in every regiment of the army (corroborating a passage in Eusebius, which says that bishops accompanied Constantine on his final campaign against the Persians).[49] Eventually, Byzantine soldiers would be expected to attend religious services daily, confess their sins routinely, and receive the Eucharist before going into battle.[50] And as early as the sixth century, Byzantine soldiers would be used to enforce Orthodoxy among non-Chalcedonian populations.[51]

Equally instructive is Constantine's attitude toward capital punishment. Like all Roman emperors before him, Constantine was quite willing to impose capital punishment on those who had committed (ordinarily) noncapital crimes, including tax cheats, corrupt tax officials, shoddy builders, creditors who seized agricultural implements of their debtors, Jews who threw stones at Jews who had become Christians, slaves who had sex with free women, rapists, and maidservants who assisted in the abduction of their mistresses, to name only a few.[52]

Of course the most notorious case of capital punishment from Constantine's reign is that of his eldest son, Crispus, whose execution the emperor ordered in 326.[53] The entire affair is shrouded in mystery, and it is unlikely that we will ever know Constantine's actual motives.[54] Equally perplexing is the execution of Fausta (Constantine's second wife, the stepmother of Crispus, and the mother of Constantine's three sons who would divide the empire upon their father's death).[55] She was killed the year after Crispus, and although there are several salacious theories about the reasons, nothing is certain. Interestingly, Eusebius makes no mention of these or any other executions, apart from those related to the civil war in 323. Is this because he shared Lactantius's distaste for capital punishment, or because he deemed it unfitting to include these stories in works of imperial encomium?[56]

There is little denying that Constantine's reign transformed the way that Christians came to view the empire and their place in it. Eusebius was not the first to see the consolidation of the (known) world under the Roman Empire as a divinely inspired precondition for the eventual supersession of paganism by the Christian faith. Origen, for example, had argued similarly in *Contra Celsum*.[57] And it would be an exaggeration of the historical record to suggest (as all too many have) that Eusebius betrayed a uniformly pacifist Christian tradition prior to the fourth century.[58] But unlike Origen or the other apologists, Eusebius was able to point to a specific emperor, Constantine, as the instrument of God's activity who would do more than any other human to enable the spread of the faith. Eusebius, knowing that Constantine was able to achieve this only by asserting himself over his rivals through acts of war, embraced Constantine's wars as a vehicle of God's action in history, and he compared this divine-human cooperation in war to the assistance that God had provided the ancient Jews. By authoring the *Vita Constantini* shortly after the emperor's death in 337, Eusebius clearly sought to influence the actions of subsequent emperors, and by endorsing Constantine's wars as both divinely sanctioned and divinely assisted, Eusebius effectively authorized Christian violence in a way that it had never been previously articulated.[59] Although this necessarily challenged many pre-Constantinian Christian objections to Christian participation in war, for Eusebius and many others of his generation this was a divinely inspired transition to a new political and theological reality, one that came to view the Christian soldier as a valuable and necessary agent who protected the Christian empire from both internal and external threats.[60] The partial subjugation of the church to the state, which Eusebius also willingly accepted as a consequence of Constantine's ascendancy, however, would not go unchallenged. And for at least one Christian theologian of the later fourth century, the imperial prerogative over life and death became the subject of frequent theological scrutiny.

AMBROSE AND THE CHALLENGE TO IMPERIAL AUTHORITY

The history of fourth-century Christianity is often characterized as one of conflict: between orthodox and heterodox, between Christian and pagan, and between church and state. Of course, these disputes were often overlapping as imperial officials tried to persuade Christian bishops to adopt specific resolutions to dogmatic questions or sought specific policies (both irenic and hostile) toward pagan communities. Athanasius of Alexandria and Basil of Caesarea perhaps serve as the two most famous examples of bishops who challenged imperial authority on doctrinal matters. Indeed, the battle between Athanasius and the imperial court is the stuff of legends, but there is nothing in either Athanasius's or Basil's surviving works that substantially challenged the imperial prerogative to wage war or execute criminals.[61] It is within this context that St. Ambrose of Milan (ca. 337–97) serves as one of the most important moral writers of the early Christian tradition because he, more than any other theologian of the fourth century, wrote frequently about these issues. And like Athanasius and Basil, Ambrose was unabashed in his willingness to challenge imperial authority.[62]

Perhaps his confidence stemmed from previous experience—prior to his election as bishop, Ambrose had served as the consular prefect (i.e., governor) for Liguria and Emilia, headquartered in Milan. His father, also, had been a high-ranking imperial official (praetorian prefect of Gaul). As such, Ambrose had been steeped in the Roman traditions of politics and public service, and his involvement in the political affairs of Italy did not end with his episcopal election. Indeed, one might characterize his political theology as an attempt to fuse Christian moral principles with a Ciceronian conception of leadership. It is little wonder, therefore, that he borrowed Cicero's language of just war when he sought to balance the Christian principles of peace and the maintenance of public order in the wake of the Gothic invasions.

Note, however, that Ambrose did not author a systematic analysis of the morality of war, nor did he produce an elaborate formula for evaluating whether a specific war was just. Indeed, the vast majority of his comments about war originate as analogies in the service of a greater exegetical, instructional, or pastoral point. The realities of war, which would have weighed heavily upon the inhabitants of Milan in the late fourth century, no doubt made such analogies poignant, but because Ambrose's treatment of the subject was ancillary and not primary, the bishop's statements about war and violence are not always consistent.[63] Despite this lack of absolute consistency, however, we can identify eight points that appear without contravention within his corpus:[64] (1) war must be defensive in nature,[65] (2) agreements between enemies should be honored,[66] (3) an army may not take an unfair advantage over its enemy,[67] (4) mercy should be shown to those defeated,[68] (5) clerics may not participate in hostilities,[69] (6) the institutional church does not get involved in war,[70] (7) necessity can demand that one use force in the defense of the innocent,[71] and (8) the courage of the soldier in the field pales in comparison to that of the martyr who willingly goes to his or her death without recourse to violence.[72]

While it is true that Ambrose can rightly be identified as the first Christian author to employ the category of *iustum bellum*, we must use caution before anachronistically characterizing Ambrose as an advocate of just war in the scholastic or modern sense. As we will see, Ambrose was far more restrictive than Cicero in establishing just cause, he never advanced the Eusebian notion that a Christian emperor waged war on God's behalf, he consistently sought to limit capital punishment, and he encouraged spiritual healing for all whose station in life had led to the death of another.

Ambrose and Cicero

Like Cicero, Ambrose lived at a time of great disruption to the Roman way of life. Situated at the foot of the Alps in Northern Italy, Milan was under constant threat of Gothic invasion during Ambrose's tenure as bishop. It also centered prominently in a series of civil wars between competing claimants to the imperial throne in the West.[73] When Emperor Valens was killed by the Goths at the battle of Adrianople in 378, Milan was beset by waves of refugees, prompting one of the greatest pastoral challenges of its bishop's tenure.[74] Although Ambrose discusses certain questions concerning war in every genre of his writing, his most detailed comments appear in his *De officiis*, which, modeled after Cicero's book of the same title, sought to recast the responsibilities of the public magistrate in the form of the duties of the Christian bishop.[75]

Ambrose, like most Roman intellectuals, was openly hostile to civil wars because they undermined the stability and laws of a just society.[76] What is more, several passages in Ambrose's works similarly reflect a Greco-Roman cultural bias against non-Romans (i.e., the barbarians).[77]

Indeed, for Ambrose, the categories of "Roman" and "Christian" were always operative against those of "pagan" and "barbarian" when he discussed the possibility of war. From Ambrose's perspective, a just war was nothing other than the defense of Christian lands against barbarian (either pagan or Arian) invasion.[78] All other wars were to be avoided.[79] This, of course, marks a striking difference between Ambrose and the scholastic authors of the medieval West for whom the debates about just war were debates about the legitimacy of war between Christians.[80] That perspective also serves as an obvious, but significant, difference between Ambrose and Cicero, for whom the categories of Christian and pagan would have had no meaning. And yet despite Ambrose's frequent disparagement of the barbarians in various forms, his theological vision included the Christian concept that all humans were creations of God in a way that Cicero and other Greco-Roman thinkers would not have shared.[81]

The most significant difference between Ambrose and Cicero, however, concerns the bishop's reformulation of the necessity of defensive violence. Whereas Cicero (following both Plato and Aristotle) believed that the defense of self was the most reasonable occasion for violence, Ambrose held that to kill in self-defense was an act of selfishness and contrary to Christian teaching. In book 3 of *De officiis*, he rebukes Cicero directly when he writes:

> Some ask [cf. Cicero *De officiis* 3.23.89] whether a wise man who is shipwrecked should take away a plank from an unknowing sailor. Although it might appear better for the common good for the wise man rather than the fool to survive, I do not think that a Christian, a just and a wise man, should save his own life by the death of another; just as when he meets with an armed assailant he cannot return his blows, because in defending his own life he would compromise his love for his neighbor.[82]

In short, the Christian who kills another to save his own life necessarily destroys the piety that constitutes the proper relationship between humans as mandated by the scriptures.

Admittedly, this passage appears difficult to align with other statements in the bishop's corpus that show little reservation about the possibility of Christian participation in war or the defense of the Christian/

Roman empire. It is only when we consider that Ambrose tolerates the violence of war when it is directed for the protection of others, and not the self, that we understand his position. Indeed, earlier in book 3 Ambrose condemns killing in self-defense but praises the virtue of defending one's country in sequential sentences.[83] In other words, for Ambrose, one cannot kill for one's own survival, but one can employ violence in the act of protecting another. In another example, Ambrose notes:

> He who does not keep harm off a friend, if he can, is as much in fault as the one who causes it. This is why St. Moses gave this as a primary proof of his fortitude in war. For when he saw a Hebrew being beaten at the hands of an Egyptian, he defended him and buried the [dead] Egyptian in the sand [cf. Exod. 2.11].[84]

While I would not interpret Ambrose's position as decisively as Swift (who takes Ambrose to be saying that it is the same love of God that compels a martyr to go his death as it is that compels a Christian soldier to kill in the name of the innocent), it is clear that Ambrose commends the Christian who necessarily uses violence in the protection of the innocent.[85] And from this position, we can surmise that Ambrose extrapolates from the individual to the collective. In other words, Ambrose likely understood the goal of the imperial army to be the protection of the innocent from violent pagan incursions.

Ambrose further restricts Cicero's war ethic when he argues that the emotional rage that is necessary for violence must be directed at the wrong being done, rather than the wrongdoer (there is no similar distinction within Cicero's corpus). The fullest examination of this point appears in Ambrose's fifteenth homily on Psalm 118 (119).[86] Specifically, Ambrose asks the rhetorical question of how one balances the Old Testament injunction to hate our enemies (cf. Ps. 118:113) with Christ's instruction to love our enemies (cf. Matt. 5:44). Ambrose's solution to this exegetical conundrum is to interpret Psalm 118:113 allegorically in such a way as to redefine hate as a self-discipline that extricates any impulse that would restrict our affection for God or his law.[87] Although later authors would develop Ambrose's distinction between hating the act and hating the actor in order to condone multiple forms of violence, we must not conflate those later developments with Ambrose's desire to reconcile the Psalms and the Gospels.[88] For Ambrose, the impulse was always to limit, not validate, violence.[89]

Like Cicero's discussion of war, that of Ambrose reflects a series of predetermined bifurcations that separate the inhabitants of the world into distinct categories. For Cicero, the distinctions were between Roman and non-Roman or between patriot and traitor. For Ambrose, although the categories of Roman and non-Roman remain important, they are at least partially superseded by those of Christian and non-Christian (which in Ambrose's theological understanding placed Arians among the non-Christians). Thus, whereas Cicero could conceive of any threat to the Roman republic as a just cause for war (and, indeed, he validated some wars of expansion as well), Ambrose's view was more narrow. For him, just war was limited to a defense of the Christian (i.e., Roman) commonwealth against non-Christian barbarians who attacked it.

Ambrose, Eusebius, and Imperial Authority

Moving from a comparison of Ambrose and Cicero to one of Ambrose and Eusebius, we must consider several things.[90] First, like Eusebius, Ambrose extolled the military victories of past heroes and interpreted their victories as having been divinely assisted. But whereas Eusebius praised the exploits of Constantine and his fellow Christian rulers (including Licinius prior to the second civil war and Crispus prior to his execution),[91] Ambrose restricted his examples to the Old Testament saints (primarily Moses, Joshua, and David).[92] Indeed, nearly all of Ambrose's comments about war in *De officiis* derive from his tangential analysis of specific Old Testament passages that he employs in the service of other arguments that have little to do with war or violence. Ambrose never turns to the military conquests of Roman leaders (either past or present) as a direct example of divine intervention in human affairs. And while Eusebius too, of course, chronicled the victories of the ancient Jews as evidence of God's activity in history,[93] his emphasis in the *Life of Constantine* was with the newly Christianized empire and its leaders.

In contrast, Ambrose seems to believe that Christian rulers were more likely to be evidence against, rather than for, the possibility that God was actively working through the imperial court. The multiple altercations between Ambrose and civil authorities have been documented by others and need not detain us, apart from two quick observations.[94] First, for the early years of Ambrose's tenure as bishop, imperial leaders largely supported the *homoian* and not the Nicene Trinitarian position. That fact, no doubt, eclipsed any possibility that Ambrose might share a Eusebian-like euphoria for post-Constantinian rulers. Second, even after the Councils of Aquileia and Constantinople in 381, which effectively cemented the Nicene victory within the empire, Ambrose remained skeptical that the imperial court could be trusted to pursue the moral policies mandated by the Christian scriptures. One need look no further than his outrage when Theodosius I ordered the slaughter of the citizens of Thessalonica in 388.

Another important distinction between Ambrose's and Eusebius's understandings of justice in war is found in the treatment of the defeated.[95] Recall that Eusebius portrayed Constantine's execution of his defeated rival Licinius as a "just punishment." In contrast, Ambrose consistently argued that Christians must show mercy to those defeated.[96] For example, in the opening lines of a letter to Emperor Theodosius, dated to December of 388 (following the massacre in Thessalonica), Ambrose distinguished between good and evil emperors by employing as a single criterion of differentiation an examination of how an emperor dealt with defeated enemies: "There is no quality of an emperor more popular or loved than that he cherishes liberty even for those whom he has conquered on the battlefield. Indeed, it reveals the difference between good and bad emperors."[97] While it is clear that Ambrose was willing to accept the use of force, he believed that such force could only be employed in the protection of the innocent and it could not be exercised against those already captured.[98]

To ascertain more fully Ambrose's attitude concerning the role of the Christian emperor as the protector of peace, we must attend to two specific treatises in Ambrose's corpus. The first is his *De fide* (On the faith), written in 378 in response to a request from the Western emperor Gratian, who was preparing to march his armies east against the Goths. Gratian had asked Ambrose to provide him with a concise explication of the Nicene faith, so that he might be able to use it as he encountered Eastern officials who remained tied to the *homoian* position. In response, Ambrose composed the first two books of what today constitutes his *De fide*. In two passages (in the prologue and the final chapter respectively) Ambrose addresses the impending conflict directly. In the prologue, he writes: "You ask me for a book about the faith, holy emperor, as you set out for battle; indeed, you know that a victory is more often obtained by the faith of the commander than by the might of his soldiers."[99] Not surprisingly, Ambrose offers the example of a former commander who "overcame the might of five kings and their armies by the sign of the cross and the name of the Lord."[100] But Ambrose's example was not Constantine or another Roman general, as Gratian might have expected; it was the Hebrew Patriarch Abraham, who achieved such a great victory with only 318 men (cf. Gen. 14:14). Ambrose instructs Gratian to imitate the faith of Abraham. Like Abraham, he should trust that 318 would be sufficient—not 318 soldiers but the 318 bishops who had affirmed the coequality of Father and Son at the Council of Nicaea.[101]

At the conclusion of book 2, Ambrose turns once again to the impending battle and instructs the emperor that the war against the Goths has been foretold by the prophet Ezekiel, who warned (cf. Ezek. 38:14–39:10) that warriors from the north riding on horses would lay siege to Israel, but that they would ultimately be defeated and that Israel would be victorious.[102] Ambrose interprets the prophecy and its relevance for the present crisis through a specific theological filter. He tells Gratian that God is punishing the Romans, like the Jews of old, with foreign invaders because the empire has failed to adhere to the true faith.[103] But Ambrose emboldens the emperor that the Roman cause will be aided (*auxilium*)—note, not guaranteed—by the fact that he has personally embraced Orthodoxy. The passage ends with a prayer, offered by Ambrose, that the Italian peninsula, which has already suffered greatly at the hands of the Arians, will be spared from further turmoil of war.[104] Interestingly, the prayer includes no call for "victory."

Equally noteworthy is the funeral oration that Ambrose offered after the death of Emperor Theodosius.[105] The emperor had died in Milan in the winter of 394/395, and Ambrose offered the oration in presence of Theodosius's successor in the West, a minor, Honorius, as well as many leaders of the Western legions who Ambrose feared might seek to promote their own leader. Early in the oration Ambrose addresses this concern directly when he rhetorically commends the army for having embraced Honorius as Theodosius's rightful successor. He reminds those present how, in the midst of an uphill battle against enemies, Theodosius had roused his army to courage by imploring them to place their faith in God.[106] He then adds, "The faith of Theodosius, then, was your victory. Let your faith be the strength of his sons [i.e., Theodosius's successors]."[107] But rather than explore the relationship the emperor's faith and his conquests, Ambrose quickly shifts the discussion of warfare into a metaphor for the battle for correct faith. And here, as elsewhere in his corpus, he turns to the saints of the Old Testament, rather than Roman emperors, as his examples.[108] Near the end of the oration Ambrose does recount the pious deeds of recent Christian emperors, including those of Constantine, but when it comes to Constantine's bravery in the field, the bishop rather stealthily says only that Constantine "remained safe on the battlefield" due to the prayers of his saintly mother.[109]

Like Eusebius, Ambrose clearly believes that there are times when God intervenes in war on behalf of those who place their faith in him. Like Eusebius, Ambrose assumes that the Christian empire is favored by God among the people of the world, similar to the way that the Jews of the Old Testament were privileged. But whereas Eusebius extended this favored status to the rulers of the Roman Empire (e.g., presenting Constantine as a new Moses and his conquests as divinely sanctioned), Ambrose does not depict Christian emperors as divine agents, he does not understand them to wage war on God's behalf, and he does not believe that their political decisions embody the moral teachings of the scriptures. On the contrary, his experience was that the rulers of the Christian empire were deeply flawed individuals, often susceptible to heresy and violence, and, quite unlike the saintly Jews of old, were in desperate need of moral formation. Ambrose prays that Christians rulers will be victorious in their contests against enemy forces (because in doing so they can protect innocent Christians living peacefully within the border), but he never guarantees that God will assist their cause, nor does he claim that an emperor wages war on God's behalf. On the contrary, Ambrose characterizes the sins of the Roman people as the source of their suffering (which was enacted through foreign invaders). Although Ambrose rejoices that Gratian and Theodosius have embraced the Nicene faith, and he believes that this could (in the case of Gratian) enhance the emperor's chances for victory (as it did in the case of Theodosius), there is nothing in Ambrose's writing to suggest that he believed that a Christian emperor was necessarily the agent of God similar to the way that Eusebius had portrayed Constantine and Crispus.

Ambrose and Capital Punishment

Ambrose further challenged the government's right to employ violence by condemning the practice of capital punishment. Like Lactantius and other pre-Constantinian Christian authors, Ambrose understood capital punishment to be a form of violence against God's creation, one that cut short a criminal's opportunity for repentance. In fact, Ambrose offers the strongest condemnation of capital punishment of any post-Constantinian patristic author. The bishop's boldest critique survives in his *On Cain and Abel*, which, dated to 375, was one of his first biblical commentaries.[110] Assessing Genesis 4:15 ("If anyone kills Cain, vengeance will be taken on him sevenfold"), Ambrose asks why God would spare Cain, rather than exact an equal punishment for the murder of Abel. The bishop's answer is filtered through his reading of the prophet Ezekiel (cf. 33:11), who claims that God prefers the repentance of a sinner rather than his death.[111] According to Ambrose, God forbade retribution against Cain so as to offer him the possibility of future repentance. "A guilty man," Ambrose asserts, "provided that he is not deprived of his own life by a premature punishment, can obtain forgiveness through repentance, no matter how late he comes to it."[112] As a consequence, the man who deprives a sinner of the opportunity to repent must, himself, answer for the initial crime because he has prevented the sinner from seeking future forgiveness: "Therefore, the one who has not spared the life of a sinner has removed the possibility for the remission of his sins and at the same time stolen from him all hope for salvation. Such a one will, in fact, be subject in equal measure to divine vengeance."[113]

The implication is that both the judge who sentences a convict to die and the executioner who performs the act are liable for the unrepented sins of the criminal. This is an extraordinary claim. Not only did this directly challenge the imperial prerogative to prosecute capital cases; it asserted an ethical position, based upon the scriptures, that was in contradistinction to the highly developed Roman system of justice.[114] As a former governor himself, Ambrose would have known well the responsibility of a judge to punish criminals. But Ambrose sees in Genesis 4 a cautionary tale for all public magistrates. "God in his providence gives this type of verdict [i.e., that Cain is to be spared] so that judges might be taught the importance of magnanimity and patience and might not be carried away by a zeal to punish."[115] In the final lines of the homily, he adds once more, "And so, from the indulgence of the mystery [of our faith], no one ought to slay another who in the course of nature would still have an opportunity for repentance up to the very moment of his death."[116]

As we have seen in our assessment of Ambrose's statements about war, however, there exists in the bishop's corpus a not insignificant distinction between a nonviolent ideal that he hopes to promote in general and his willingness to accept the reality of necessity to which he gives consent in specific cases. The same seems true (albeit to a lesser extent) of his treatment of capital punishment. The strongest evidence of moderation from his initial position stems from his correspondence with a public magistrate, Studius, who sometime between 385 and 387 wrote to the bishop asking whether it was necessary for a public official to abstain from the Eucharist if he had sentenced a criminal to death.[117] Ambrose acknowledges that some, "outside of the church," would refuse the Eucharist to a man in Studius's situation. And while the bishop would not mandate that position, he commends any magistrate who, of his own account, would self-impose a temporary excommunication for sentencing another to death. Even more commendable, however, are those magistrates who refrain from executing criminals. Indeed, most of the letter is devoted to promoting mercy rather than punishment, through a careful examination of John 8:3–11 (the woman caught in adultery). Ambrose encourages Studius to exercise his authority in ways that will not cut short the possibility of repentance: he should neither order the execution of a criminal nor confine the prisoner to such a harsh existence that he languishes indefinitely in a decrepit prison.

Another letter, *Epistle 68*, takes up the same question and discourages capital punishment.[118] Here too, Ambrose devotes most of his epistle to examining John 8, hoping to show that mercy, not punishment, leads a sinner to repentance. Near the end of the letter he argues that "when a guilty man is put to death, the man and not his sin is punished; but if the sin is forsaken, the forgiveness of the person is itself a punishment of the sin."[119] He then concludes by examining the meaning of Christ's words "go and see that you sin no more." What does this mean, he asks rhetorically? For Ambrose, it means that "Since Christ has redeemed you, let grace correct you; for a penalty will not reform you but only punish you further."[120] While the force of Ambrose's conviction might not be as strong in these two letters as it was in his *On Cain and Abel* (neither letter, for example, warns its reader that a magistrate who sentences a criminal to death will have to account for the dead man's sins), Ambrose's resistance to capital punishment appears intact. And any assessment of Ambrose's attitude toward war, just like any comparison between Ambrose and the East, should account for this important aspect of his thought.

Ambrose and Spiritual Therapy

As we have seen, Ambrose's primary argument against capital punishment was that it cut short the possibility of repentance. As the author of one of the earliest pastoral treatises in Christian history, Ambrose was instrumental in developing two foundational aspects of the early Christian understanding of spiritual direction: (1) that everyone retained the possibility of forgiveness until the moment of death, and (2) that it was the cleric's responsibility to lead sinners to repentance.[121] In other words, Ambrose believed that Christ and his church offered salvation to all who sought it; but only those who were willing to dedicate themselves to progress in the Christian life could take advantage of Christ's sacrifice. From his perspective, the more grievous the sin was, the more important it was for the sinner to seek forgiveness.

Moving from the general to the specific, we see that these principles are very much in play in Ambrose's approach toward those who are responsible for the death of others. For example, although he does not insist that a magistrate who orders the execution of a criminal abstain from the Eucharist, he commends the piety that would lead a man such as Studius to pursue self-imposed penance. Examining the case of Studius more carefully, we see that Ambrose never suggests that he should abandon his role as public magistrate—indeed, he affirms the importance of Christian participation in government. Instead, the bishop encourages Studius to be guided in his profession by the moral principles of his faith. In other words, Studius is to retain his role as a public magistrate, even though doing so puts him into the position of judging capital cases. As often as possible, however, Studius is to show mercy. And if he cannot, then he is encouraged to seek spiritual healing.

The most famous example of Ambrose's handling of a penitent, of course, is his repudiation of Emperor Theodosius following the massacre of thousands of citizens in Thessalonica in 388. When Theodosius proved unwilling to self-impose spiritual discipline, Ambrose exerted the maximum pressure a bishop could by denying the emperor the Eucharist. Ambrose's *Epistle 11** records a direct attempt by the bishop to force the emperor to understand the gravity of taking the life of others (both the guilty and the innocent).[122] But he follows the chastisement with the promise of spiritual healing. Comparing Theodosius to King David, Ambrose affirms that the emperor's actions were horrible, but not beyond the mercy of God. Such mercy, however, requires both contrition and penance. So Ambrose forbids the emperor to receive the Eucharist until he has performed suitable penance.[123] Years later, Ambrose described Theodosius as having performed penance worthy of imitation by others.[124]

The examples of Studius and Theodosius confirm Ambrose's belief that although the preservation of the empire and its laws were important, those who were charged with preserving them were not exempt from the moral principles of the Christian faith. In an earlier letter to Emperor Theodosius, Ambrose had asked rhetorically "Which is more important: a demonstration of order or the cause of religion? Indeed, the maintenance of civil law should be a secondary concern to religion."[125] Whenever a Christian is forced, either by necessity or moral failure, to privilege the concerns of the state over those of his faith, the Christian is bound to seek spiritual healing.

Just a few years before Ambrose wrote to Studius and Theodosius, Basil of Caesarea famously argued that a soldier who killed in battle was required to abstain from communion for three years. That position is usually taken to mean that the soldier who kills in battle necessarily undergoes a form of spiritual trauma, thus requiring a period of penance in order to regain the proper spiritual perspective before receiving the Eucharist once again. There is a fascinating parallel between Basil's injunction and a short passage in Ambrose's funeral oration for Emperor Theodosius. After praising the emperor's willingness to humble himself and accept public penance when ordered, Ambrose adds that the emperor had piously abstained from the Eucharist following a military victory, "owing to the fact that his enemy lay fallen in battle."[126] In other words, according to Ambrose, Theodosius had also self-imposed excommunication because of an act of war.

While there is no evidence in Ambrose's corpus to suggest that the bishop of Milan imposed Basil's injunction on soldiers, he clearly understands Theodosius's self-imposed excommunication as a pious act, worthy of emulation. Thus, I believe that it would be a great mistake to argue that Ambrose's frequent discussions about war (and his appropriation of the phrase *iustum bellum*) necessarily situate him in a different theological or pastoral camp from Basil or any Greek theologian of the post-Constantinian era. In contrast to scholars who see in Ambrose a Eusebian-like capitulation to imperial authority or the seeds of a Christian valorization of violence that led to the scholastic justification of warfare, I have argued in this essay that, if assessed in the proper historical context, Ambrose is best understood as a moral voice that sought to limit rather than validate Christian violence. While it may be true that Ambrose chose to speak about the necessity of violence for the protection of the innocent in a way that many bishops of his era did not, he also went much further than his contemporaries to try to restrain the imperial prerogative over life and death, and he extolled the possibility of forgiveness, through repentance, for those whose station in life could lead to the death of another.

NOTES

In addition to acknowledging the many comments that members of LOGOS offered during the preparation of this essay, I thank Maureen Tilley, Nicholas Paul, and Charles Camosy, whose insights were invaluable in the final stages of writing. I dedicate this essay to Peter Kaufman, my dissertation mentor, who first encouraged me to look to authors such as Ambrose as a way to problematize the bifurcation of the Eastern and Western Christian traditions.

Unless otherwise noted, all translations in this essay are mine.

1. "These two seminal writers led the Western church not only to an acceptance of the military role by Christians, but to its enhancement into a positive virtue through the development of criteria by which a war could be distinguished from an unjust war and be called 'just.'" Stanley Harakas, "The Teaching on Peace in the Fathers," in *Wholeness of Faith and Life: Orthodox Christian Ethics, Part I* (Brookline, MA: Holy Cross Orthodox Press, 1999), 153–54.

2. The attempt to differentiate East from West in diametrically oppositional categories is an all-too-frequent and decidedly flawed enterprise. This is especially true of the pre-Carolingian period.

3. Harakas, like others who apply the category of "just war" to prescholastic authors, does not fully consider the anachronisms of this language. Ambrose, especially, did not establish a scholastic-like formula for evaluating whether a particular war is "just" in a legal sense. Similar anachronistic readings of the patristic record dominate modern ethical evaluations of war. See, for example, Guy Hershberger, *War, Peace, and Non-Resistance*, 3rd ed. (Scottsdale, AZ: Herald Press, 1969), esp. 43–77.

4. Cicero never actually uses the phrase *iustum bellum*; instead he speaks of the *iura belli*, literally "the laws of war," by which he means the ethical rules with which the state was bound to conduct war. What most of these commentaries fail to acknowledge, however, is that Cicero was writing at a critical juncture in Roman history (during the transition from republic to empire) and that his ideas very much derive from his personal stake in that transition. Cicero was highly critical of any consolidation of power into the hands of a few (e.g., whether it was the conspiracy of Catiline, the dictatorship of Julius Caesar, or the imperialist moves of the second Triumvirate), and his moral bifurcation between wars of self-defense (which are just) and wars for supremacy (which are less so) reflects the great orator's subjective reading of Roman history. In other words, Cicero believed that Rome, during the Republic, had almost always waged war as self-defense, but he also believed that ambition for supremacy was driving the current military machine. As a consequence, Rome had lost (or at least was losing) its moral supremacy.

5. Cicero, *De officiis* 1.34.

6. Ibid.

7. Ibid., 1.35.

8. Ibid., 1.38. Rather that state overtly that all wars for supremacy are wrong, the ever-astute and -subtle Cicero may simply have been attempting to protect himself, through ambiguity, from a possible charge of treason because his enemies might have interpreted *De officiis* to be critiquing the Roman expansion that so well characterized the era. Not surprisingly, scholars have debated the

extent to which Cicero endorsed Roman expansion. See, for example, Cary Nederman, "War, Peace, and Republican Virtue in Cicero," in *Instilling Ethics*, ed. Norma Thompson (New York: Rowman and Littlefield, 2000), 17–29; Alex Bellamy, *Just Wars: From Cicero to Iraq* (Cambridge: Polity, 2006), 18–20.

9. Cicero, *De officiis* 1.74: "Sed cum plerique arbitrentur res bellicas maiores esse quam urbanas, minuenda est haec opinio."

10. "War should be undertaken in such a way as to make it evident that it has no other object than to secure peace" (Bellum autem ita suscipiatur, ut nihil aliud nis pax quaesita videatur). Ibid., 1.80.

11. Ibid., 1.75. Cicero, of course, was himself a magistrate and was ultimately put to death by soldiers of Mark Antony (a general).

12. Ibid., 1.78. Specifically, Cicero boasts of his contributions during the attempted coup of Cataline in 63 BCE. In contrast to what Ambrose will later say about capital punishment, Cicero was responsible for having Cataline and his coconspirators executed for their crimes, without the benefit of an official trial.

13. The scholarly literature concerning war and scripture is overwhelming and remains beyond the scope of this essay. Concerning the early Christians, the arguments of Hershberger, C. J. Cadoux, and Stanley Hauerwas are certainly overstated with respect to uniform early Christian pacifist tradition. Nevertheless, the period between the New Testament and the conversion of Constantine saw the least literary support for Christian involvement in the army. As Bellamy summarizes, a number of factors likely contributed to this, not least that the Roman army was used to persecute Christians. See Hershberger, *War, Peace, and Non-Resistance*, 65–70; C. J. Cadoux, *The Early Christian Attitude toward War* (London: Headley Brothers, 1919), 122–51; Bellamy, *Just Wars*, 21–22. For Hauerwas's attitude, see his *Against the Nations: War and Survival in a Liberal Society* (Minneapolis: Winston Press, 1985), and *The Peaceable Kingdom: A Primer in Christian Ethics* (Notre Dame, IN: University of Notre Dame Press, 1983).

14. See Justin Martyr, *First Apology* 39 and *Dialogue with Trypho* 110; Athenagoras, *Plea Concerning Christians* 1; Irenaeus, *Against Heresies* 4.34.4.

15. Origen, *Contra Celsum* 2.30.

16. Ibid., 3.7: "For [the Jews] were permitted to take up arms in order to defend their families and to slay their enemies. But Christ nowhere teaches that it is right for his own disciples to be violent against anyone, no matter how wicked they are. For he did not consider it to be lawful to kill anyone." For his acknowledgment of the legitimacy of pagans engaging in war, see *Contra Celsum* 2.30 and 8.74. See J. T. Johnson, *The Quest for Peace: Three Moral Traditions in Western Culture* (Princeton: Princeton University Press, 1987), 25–29. By a

similar rationale, Origen argues that Christians do not take part in Roman civic life because they are focused on the life of the church, and those called to be leaders take administrative roles in the church, not the state. Origen, *Contra Celsum* 8.75.

17. Cyprian, *Ep. ad Donatum* 6. In another treatise, *On the Goodness of Patience* (14), Cyprian notes, "After the reception of the Eucharist, the hand is not to be stained with the sword and bloodshed." The second statement, however, was offered in the context of murder and says nothing directly about soldiers or war.

18. Lactantius, *Divine Institutes* 6.20.

19. Hippolytus of Rome, like Tertullian, acknowledged that there were Christians in the army, when he proffered that Christian soldiers should not kill their enemies, even if they were instructed to do so by their superiors.

20. Tertullian, *Apologia* 30.4.

21. For an excellent summary of the ways in which the Roman army had incorporated a series of religious practices into military life, see Robert Daly, "Military Service and Early Christianity: A Methodological Approach," in *Studia Patristica* 18, no. 1 (1985): 1–8, esp. 5. Daly draws from John Helgeland, "Roman Army Religion," in *Aufstieg und Niedergang der Romischen Welt*, ed. W. Haase (Berlin: Walter de Gruyter, 1979), 2.16.2:1470–1505.

22. Tertullian, *De corona militis* 10–11, offers a summary of many of the rituals involved in military service, all of which Tertullian deems to be idolatrous. In the same section, he acknowledges that many soldiers convert to Christianity during their service. Those converts, however, must leave the army, he argues, if they wish to become full members of the church.

23. Tertullian, *De corona militis* 11: "Is it lawful to make an occupation of the sword when the Lord proclaims that he who lives by the sword will perish by the sword? And should a son of peace take part in battle when it does not even become him to issue a civil lawsuit?"

24. Scholarship on this point seems to suffer from gross predetermination. Whereas John Helgeland, "Christians and the Roman Army, A.D. 173–337," *Church History* 43 (1974): 152, does not acknowledge any pacifist strain in Tertullian's argument, Hershberger, *War, Peace, and Non-Resistance*, 66–67; Louis J. Swift, *The Early Fathers on War and Military Service* (Wilmington, DE: Michael Glazier, 1983), 38; Bellamy, *Just Wars*, 22; and Harakas, "Teaching on Peace in the Fathers," 148, overstate the importance of nonviolence to Tertullian's rejection of army life. It also seems as though scholars (such as Helgeland) who wish to dismiss the pacifist sentiments of the pre-Constantinian authors empha-

size Tertullian's objection to the pagan rituals of army life and extrapolate from this single text a similar motive for all other early Christians who rejected military service.

25. Archaeological evidence at Dura-Europos evinces the presence of Greek-speaking Christian soldiers among the Roman legions in the 220s and 230s. See Robin Lane Fox, *Pagans and Christians* (San Francisco: HarperSanFrancisco, 1986), 277. Moreover, the memorial constructed by the Christian soldier Aurelius Gaius for his wife in Asia Minor ca. 303 offers an epigraphical record. See *L'Année épigraphique: Revue des publications épigraphiques relatives à l'antiquité romaine* (1981), 777. For textual evidence, see the example of Cassius Dio, the *proconsul Africae*, who observed that Christians were serving in the ranks of each of the tetrarchs at the close of the third century. *Acta Maximiliani* 2.9, ed. and trans. Herbert Musurillo, *The Acts of the Christian Martyrs*, Oxford Early Christian Texts (Oxford: Oxford University Press, 1972), 246. For an overview, see John Helgeland, "Christians and the Roman Army, A.D. 173–337," *Church History* 43 (1974): 149–63.

26. See Hugh Elton, "Warfare and the Military," in *The Cambridge Companion to the Age of Constantine* (Cambridge: Cambridge University Press, 2006), 335.

27. For example, the centurion Marcellus of Tingis was martyred in 298 because he refused to take a military oath at an imperial birthday parade. See the various accounts of his *vita* as prepared by H. Delehaye, "Les actes de S. Marcel le centurion," *Analecta Bollandiana* 42 (1923): 257–87 [Bibliographica hagiographica latina 5253 and 5254], and G. Lanata, "Gli atti del processo contro il centurione Marcello," *Byzantion* 42 (1972): 509–22 [Bibliographica hagiographica latina 5255a].

28. According to Daly, there are only five accounts whose authenticity and pre-Constantinian dating is considered solid. See Daly, "Military Service and Early Christianity," 4. The martyr accounts for four of these soldiers are included in Musurillo, *Acts of the Christian Martyrs*.

29. See the essay by James C. Skedros, ch. 7 in this volume. See also Hippolyte Delehaye, *Des légendes grecques des saints militaires* (Paris: A. Picard, 1909); Alexander Webster, "Varieties of Christian Military Saints: From Martyrs under Caesar to Warrior Princes," *St. Vladimir's Theological Quarterly* 24 (1980): 3–35; Leopold Kretzenbacher, *Griechische Reiterheilige als Gefangenenretter* (Vienna: Österreichische Akademie der Wissenschaften, 1983).

30. Typically these same men suffered martyrdom because their faith was exposed to their superiors by others, or because they were unwilling to continue in the pagan rituals that were part of military life. For this group of Christians,

the proscriptions against enlistment by Tertullian and Origen would have had little influence. See the essay by Valerie A. Karras, ch. 5 in this volume.

31. Daly offers yet another provocative theory, which emphasizes the possibility that many early adopters of Christianity among the Roman army would have simply added the Christian God to a pantheon of religious beliefs and, therefore, would not have adhered to the Christian expectation of religious exclusivity. See Daly, "Military Service and Early Christianity," 5.

32. Concerning the way in which early Christians employed the category of "resident alien" as being a compelling doubleness, simultaneously marginal and potent in their understanding of both themselves and others, see Benjamin Dunning, *Aliens and Sojourners: Self as Other in Early Christianity* (Philadelphia: University of Pennsylvania Press, 2009).

33. Daly rightly cautions that we should not allow our picture of early Christian practice, in this regard, to be formed entirely by the writings of the church fathers. Daly, "Military Service and Early Christianity," 7.

34. See Jeremy Schott, *Christianity, Empire, and the Making of Religion in Late Antiquity* (Philadelphia: University of Pennsylvania Press, 2008), 1–14.

35. For some of the details of Constantine's benefactions to the church, see Eusebius, *Vita Constantini* 1.41–44; 2.21, 24–45; *Church History* 10.5–7. See also Michael Grant, *Constantine the Great* (New York: Scribners, 1994), 160.

36. For a thorough account of the civic responsibilities performed by Christian bishops, see Claudia Rapp, *Holy Bishops in Late Antiquity: The Nature of Christian Leadership in an Age of Transition* (Berkeley: University of California Press, 2005), especially 279–89.

37. No doubt, it is for this reason primarily that modern commentators like Hauerwas and Hershberger are so critical of Constantine and what they see as the capitulation of Christian leaders to the empire. For an assessment of Eusebius's understanding of Constantine as the "universal bishop," see Claudia Rapp, "Imperial Ideology in the Making: Eusebius of Caesarea on Constantine as 'Bishop,'" *Journal of Theological Studies*, n.s., 49 (1998): 685–95.

38. For our purposes, it matters not whether Eusebius's portrayal of Constantine is historically accurate. What is significant is that the bishop chose to portray the emperor as he does. For a fine assessment of the scholarly debate concerning whether the *Vita Constantini* is rightly understood as history, biography, or hagiography, see Averil Cameron, "Eusebius' *Vita Constantini* and the Construction of Constantine," in *Portraits: Biographical Representation in the Greek and Latin Literature of the Roman Empire*, ed. M. J. Edwards and S. Swain (Oxford: Clarendon Press, 1997), 145–74.

39. Pauline Allen has rightly identified a marked shift in the way that Eusebius and other early Greek church historians chronicled war in comparison to

their pagan predecessors. Eusebius's *Church History*, although it carefully inter-weaves Roman and Christian history going back to the age of Augustus, deliber-ately supplants the narrative emphasis on war and conquest. According to Allen, Eusebius's motive is a Christian apologetic that sees the birth of Christ as the beginning of cosmic peace. Whatever wars remain are prompted by those who war against Christ. Thus, pagans and heretics are cast as the enemies of God. Although Allen is correct in her assessment of Eusebius's *Church History*, she does not account for the *Vita Constantini*, which, quite unlike the *Church History*, emphasizes Constantine's success in the field. Allen, "War and the Early Greek Church Historians," *Studia Patristica* 19 (1989): 3–7.

40. Eusebius, *Vita Constantini* 1.5–6. For more on Eusebius's view of Constantine's wars as acts of divine violence, see Demacopoulos, "The Eusebian Valorization of Violence and Constantine's Wars for God," in A. Edward Sie-cienski, ed., *Constantine: Religious Faith and Imperial Policy* (London: Ashgate, 2017), 115–28.

41. Eusebius, *Vita Constantini* 1.6.

42. Not only does Eusebius cast Constantine as God's agent righting a cos-mic wrong and Maxentius as the manifestation of evil and perversity; he even describes God as puppeteering Maxentius in a way that will lead directly to his death. Indeed, Eusebius compares God's manipulation of Maxentius in the battle with Constantine to God's hardening of Pharaoh's heart against Moses, which ultimately led to the liberation of the Jews. So too, Constantine's victories against Maxentius and Licinius enable the liberation of Christianity. See Eusebius, *Vita Constantini* 1.27–39 and *Church History* 9.9. Concerning Eusebius's direct com-parisons between Constantine and Moses, see Cameron, "Eusebius' *Vita Constan-tini* and the Construction of Constantine," 158–61. See also her *Christianity and the Rhetoric of Empire: The Development of Christian Discourse* (Berkeley: Univer-sity of California Press, 1991), 53–56. Concerning Eusebius's construction of Maxentius, see Jan Willem Drijvers, "Eusebius' *Vita Constantini* and the Con-struction of the Image of Maxentius," in *From Rome to Constantinople: Essays in Honor of Averil Cameron*, ed. Hagit Amirav and Bas ter Harr Romeny (Leuven: Peeters, 2007), 11–27.

43. It was through the victory over Licinius that Constantine was able to consolidate his power over the entire empire, an event that Eusebius presents not only as the most important of Constantine's career but as the culmination of God's victory over evil.

44. Eusebius, *Vita Constantini* 2.7.

45. Ibid., 2.18.

46. For Cicero, the question would center on whether Licinius was guilty of treason (the worst imaginable crime and one worthy of execution).

47. See Elton, "Warfare and the Military," 335. Recorded in Optatus of Milan, *S. Optati Milevitani libri VII* (CSEL 26), ed. C. Ziwsa (Vienna, 1893), which chronicles the Council of Arles 314. See appendix 4, canon 3. During the sixth century, the number of soldiers who deserted their posts to enter the monastic life was sufficient to prompt Emperor Maurice to pass a law forbidding it.

48. See Maureen Tilley, trans., *Sermon on the Passion of Saints Donatus and Advocatus* 2, in *Donatist Martyr Stories* (Liverpool: Liverpool University Press, 1996).

49. Sozomen, *Church History* 1.8.11–13. See Elton, "Warfare and the Military," 336, who follows Jones in suspecting that chaplains were not really present throughout the army until the fifth century. See A. H. M. Jones, "Military Chaplains in the Roman Army," *Harvard Theological Review* 46 (1953): 249–50. For Eusebius's account of the bishops who accompanied Constantine, see *Vita Constantini* 4.56.

50. According to a tenth-century military document, *Presentation and Composition on Warfare*, by Emperor Nikephoros Phokas, soldiers were expected to attend Matins and Vespers daily; failure to do so would result in strict punishment. Moreover, on the day before an anticipated battle, soldiers were encouraged to forgive one another, fast, confess their sins, and receive the Eucharist. Other prebattle rituals included the blessing of weapons and military standards. See J. R. Vieillefond, "Les pratiques religieuses dans l'armée byzantine d'après les traités militaires," *Revue des études anciennes* 37 (1935): 322–30.

51. The evidence for this is especially strong in Egypt during the reign of Justinian. See "'When Justinian Was Upsetting the World': A Note on Soldiers and Religious Coercion in Sixth-Century Egypt," in *Peace and War in Byzantium: Essays in Honor of George T. Dennis, SJ*, ed. T. Miller and J. Nesbitt (Washington, DC: Catholic University of America Press, 1995), 106–13.

52. See Michael Grant's summary of Constantine's legislative measures in his *Constantine the Great*, 101–2.

53. Orosius, *Historiae adversum paganos* 28.

54. In his *Church History*, which was completed before the execution, Eusebius presents Crispus alongside Constantine throughout the war with Licinius; but Eusebius never mentions him in the *Vita Constantini*, which was written after his execution.

55. When Constantine died in 337, the second of his three sons, Constantius II, led the massacre of his relatives descended from the second marriage of their grandfather, Constantius I (Constantine's father). This enabled the three sons of Fausta, Constantine II, Constantius II, and Constans, to divide the empire between them, according to Constantine's will. Their rule was marked by

in-fighting and civil war. Constans's army defeated that of his eldest brother, Constantine II, killing him in 340. Constans, in turn, was murdered by assassins of another Roman general, Magnentius, in 350. Constantius II died of fever while on campaign against his ultimate successor, Julian, in 361.

56. Although there is no record of a Christian bishop publicly criticizing Constantine's actions, Michael Grant has suggested that the emperor's closest theological adviser, Ossius, left the court in protest over the murder of Crispus. Grant, *Constantine the Great*, 113. See also Barnes, *Constantine and Eusebius* (Cambridge, MA: Harvard University Press, 1981), 384n10.

57. Origen, *Contra Celsum* 2.30.

58. Perhaps the best examples of this type of anachronistic and apologetic reading are those of Hershberger and Hauerwas.

59. See Cameron, "Eusebius' *Vita Constantini* and the Construction of Constantine." On the use of saints' lives as a vehicle for disseminating Christian ideology, see Cameron, *Christianity and the Rhetoric of Empire*, 141–54, including 144–45, which treats Eusebius's *Vita Constantini*.

60. As Averil Cameron has masterfully argued, the Christian bishops and chroniclers during the fourth and fifth centuries transformed the pre-Constantinian Christian narrative in a way that appropriated and exploited Roman political discourse.

61. While Basil did suggest in one of his letters (later restyled as a canon of the church) that soldiers who killed in battle should abstain from communion for three years, nothing in our sources suggests that he or anyone else in the latter part of the fourth century believed that Christians could not serve in the army or that the empire was not within its rights to wage war as the emperor deemed necessary. Rather, it seems Basil's admonition was entirely pastoral, dealing with the spiritual therapy needed as a consequence of a soldier's participation in war. Moreover, although Athanasius's reference in his *Letter to Amun* to the "glory of vanquishing an enemy in combat" (as distinct from the sin of murder) should not be taken as an endorsement of war, the passage clearly indicates the Alexandrian's comfort with the reality of Christian soldiers.

62. More than any other bishop in the fourth century, Ambrose challenged the authority of imperial officials. In 385/386, Ambrose refused to grant a church in Milan to the coemperor, Valentinian II, and his mother, Juliana, who remained Arian sympathizers. See Ambrose, *Ep. 76*.20 (60) to his sister, Marcellina, which recounts the affair. In 390, he excommunicated Emperor Theodosius I for executing seven thousand citizens in Thessalonica (a mob had killed the local governor, prompting Theodosius's heavy hand). On this, see Ambrose, *Ep. 11**(40) and Theodoret, *Ecclesiastical History* 5.17–18. I have relied upon M. Zelzer's

critical edition (CSEL 82.1–3) for the text and numbering of Ambrose's letters. The "*" indicates a letter in the "extra collection" as identified by Zelzer. For readers who rely upon the English translation of Ambrose's letters provided in vol. 26 of the Fathers of the Church series, I have included that sequencing of the letters (which is quite different) in parentheses.

63. The most significant study to date of Ambrose's attitude toward war is Louis Swift, "St. Ambrose on Violence and War," *Transactions and Proceedings of the American Philological Association* 101 (1970): 533–43.

64. Swift points to four elements in Ambrose's thought that are consistent with previous Roman thinkers. See Swift, "St. Ambrose on Violence and War," 534.

65. For example, from Ambrose's *De officiis*, see 1.27.129, which characterizes courage as a willingness to defend one's country against barbarians in a time of war, or 1.35.176–77, which characterizes King David's militarism as both defensive and divinely sanctioned.

66. Ambrose, *De officiis* 2.7.33, similarly employs the example of David's action in times of war and peace to characterize the proper way that a righteous leader responds to his enemies. *De officiis* 3.14.86–87 praises Elisha, who, contrary to the wishes of the king of Israel, advised that Syrian soldiers, who had previously imprisoned him, should not be murdered.

67. Ibid., 1.29.139.

68. Ibid., 3.14.87; *In Luc* 5.76; *In Ps. 38* 11.

69. Ambrose, *De officiis* 1.35.175. Roland Bainton identifies this as one of Ambrose's two contributions to the development of the Christian theory about war. See Bainton, *Christian Attitudes toward War and Peace* (Nashville: Abingdon Press, 1960), 91.

70. Ambrose, *De viduis* ("On Widows") 8.49. The similarities to Origen's position are obvious.

71. Ambrose, *De officiis* 1.36.179; 3.3.23.

72. Ibid., 1.41.211–13.

73. Perhaps one reason that Ambrose, unlike his contemporaries in the East, offers so many comments about the realities of war is that his congregations experienced the reality of war in a way that the churches of his Eastern contemporaries never did.

74. As the leading representative of the empire on the north-central frontier, Ambrose had to raise the money to ransom prisoners and to provide for those refugees who flowed into Milan.

75. Ambrose's *De officiis* is primarily a study of how the Christian leader should balance what is good with what is useful and how to reconcile the two when they come into conflict. Ambrose's *De officiis* is the oldest surviving treatise

of pastoral care—although Gregory Nazianzen's second oration, commonly known as *De Fuga*, is also a study of the priesthood. Predating Ambrose's *De officiis*, it was styled as a public oration, not a dogmatic treatise.

76. Ambrose, *Apologia prophetæ David ad Theodosium Augustum* 6.27. See also his *De obitu Theodosii oratio* (39). Both Cicero (cf. the Cataline affair) and Ambrose (cf. *Ep. 30* [10]) distinguish between civil wars, which are bad, and the government's right to prosecute a would-be usurper.

77. See, for example, a passage in his commentary *De Tobia* (15.51), which permits both usury and war against barbarians but not between Christians. See also *De officiis* 1.27.129, which defines the Roman virtue of courage in terms of a willingness to defend one's homeland against barbarians, and 1.27.135, which describes Moses as having been fearless against the savagery of barbarians.

78. For the complexity of understanding whether Ambrose views the Goths as Arian or pagan, see Peter Heather, "The Crossing of the Danube and the Gothic Conversion," *Greek, Roman, and Byzantine Studies* 27 (1986): 314.

79. Ambrose, *De Tobia* 15.51. Ambrose's objection to civil wars went beyond that of Cicero, because, for Ambrose, it was not just a patriotic objection but a religious one.

80. See, for example, Thomas Aquinas's position in his *Summa Theologica* II-II.40.

81. Ambrose, *De Noe* 26.94. See J. R. Palanque, *Saint Ambrose et l'empire romain* (Paris: E. de Boccard, 1933), 326n6, who argues that Ambrose follows standard Christian understandings of a church with a universal outlook, seeing no distinction between nations. Louis Swift aptly identifies the ambivalence in Ambrose's attitude toward the barbarians. See Swift, "St. Ambrose on Violence and War," 535.

82. Ambrose, *De officiis* 3.4.27. For similar statements, see his *In Luc* 5.77; *In Ps. 118* 18.45; *In Ps. 36* 37.

83. Ambrose, *De officiis* 3.3.23.

84. Ibid., 1.36.179.

85. Swift, "St. Ambrose on Violence and War," 540. As evidence, Swift cites *Ep. 48*, 1 (87) to Romulus—which he numbers as *Ep. 66*, following the Benedictine numeration. I would counter that Ambrose develops a specific pastoral message for Romulus and that we should not extrapolate an Ambrosian theology of the relationship between love and violence from this single example. There is also the evidence of *De officiis* 1.41.211–13, which suggests that the courage of the martyr is far superior to that of the soldier.

86. Ambrose briefly mentions the same point in an earlier homily, *In Ps. 118* 12.51, and in his examination of the "turn the other cheek" passage in his commentary on Luke. *In Luc.* 5.73.

87. Ambrose, *In Ps. 118* 15.15–22.

88. For example, Jonathan Riley Smith has employed the phrase "crusading as an act of love." See his essay by the same title in *History* 65 (1980): 177–92.

89. It is for this reason that Hershberger is mistaken. Hershberger, *War, Peace, and Non-Resistance*, 72–73.

90. Eusebius, unlike Ambrose, lived and suffered during the Diocletian persecution of Christians, prior to Constantine's conversion. His unbridled enthusiasm for the Constantinian regime was, no doubt, informed by his experience of the persecutions. In contrast, Ambrose's father had been a high-ranking member of imperial government, and he himself had served as a Roman governor, more than a generation after Constantine's death. His experience of the imperial government's promotion of Christianity was altogether different.

91. Eusebius, *Church History* 9.9.

92. Some examples include *De officiis* 1.28.135; 1.29.139; 1.35.175–77; 1.36.179; 1.41.211–13.

93. Eusebius, *Church History* 1.4.

94. For recent examinations, see Neil McLynn, *Ambrose of Milan: Church and Court in a Christian Capital* (Berkeley: University of California Press, 1994), especially 158–219, 291–360; Daniel Williams, *Ambrose of Milan and the End of the Arian-Nicene Conflicts* (Oxford: Oxford University Press, 1995).

95. For an excellent contemporary discussion of the treatment of the defeated, see Tobias Winright, "Jus Post Bellum: Extending the Just War Theory" (with Dr. Mark Allman), in *Faith in Public Life*, ed. William J. Collinge, College Theology Society Annual 53 (Maryknoll, NY: Orbis Books, 2008), 241–64.

96. Ambrose, *De officiis* 3.14.87; *In Luc* 5.76; *In Ps. 38* 11.

97. Ambrose, *Ep. 1a** (2). Similarly, two years earlier, Ambrose had condemned the usurper Maximus for having executed his prisoners. See Ambrose, *Ep. 30*, 10 (10).

98. Following Theodosius's defeat of the usurper Eugenius in 394 (a war that had forced Ambrose to flee Milan), Ambrose praised the emperor for pardoning the innocent. Ambrose, *Ep. 2** (5).

99. Ambrose, *De fide* prol.3.

100. Ibid.

101. Ibid., prol.5.

102. Ibid., 2.16.136–38.

103. Ambrose, *De fide* 2.16.139.

104. Ambrose, *De officiis* 2.16.141–43.

105. The oration was actually offered during the memorial service forty days after the death of the emperor.

106. Ambrose, *De obitu Theodosii* 7.

107. Ibid., 8.

108. Ibid., 9–10.

109. Ibid., 41.

110. *On Cain and Abel* was designed as a sequel to *On Paradise*. The critical edition is provided by C. Schenkl (CSEL 32.1 339–409), who includes in his notes an extensive list of parallels to Philo's *De sacrificiis Abelis et Caini*.

111. Ambrose, *On Cain and Abel* 2.38.

112. Ibid., 2.38.

113. Ibid., 2.34.

114. In his funeral oration for Theodosius I, Ambrose embellishes the emperor's record to suggest to those in attendance that Theodosius always granted clemency to any criminal who acknowledged his guilt. In so doing, Ambrose sought to influence the handling of future capital cases. Ambrose, *De obitu Theodosii* 13, 52.

115. Ambrose, *On Cain and Abel* 2.38.

116. Ibid.

117. Ambrose, *Ep. 50* (90).

118. The Benedictine editors placed this letter in sequence to *Ep. 50* (90) (although their numbering was different) and addressed it also to Studius. Some manuscripts, however, identify a different recipient, Irenaeus. Zelzer follows these, addressing the letter to Irenaeus and numbering it *Ep. 68* (84).

119. Ambrose, *Ep. 68* (84).

120. Ibid.

121. For a concise summary of Ambrose's pastoral ideas and the emergence of the pastoral treatise, see George Demacopoulos, *Five Models of Spiritual Direction in the Early Church* (Notre Dame, IN: University of Notre Dame Press, 2007), 16–17.

122. Ambrose, *Ep. 11** (3).

123. Although many commentators have emphasized Ambrose's political ambitions in the censure of Theodosius, if we are to believe that Ambrose took his pastoral responsibilities at all seriously, then we must take him at his word that his excommunication of Theodosius was designed for the emperor's spiritual benefit.

124. Ambrose, *De obitu Theodosii* 28, 34.

125. Ambrose, *Ep. 1a** (2).

126. Ambrose, *De obitu Theodosii* 34: "Quid, quod praeclaram adeptus victoriam; tamen quia hostes in acie prostrati sunt, abstinuit a consortio sacramentorum, donec Domini circa se gratiam filiorum experiretur adventu."

CHAPTER 7

LESSONS FROM MILITARY SAINTS
IN THE BYZANTINE TRADITION

JAMES C. SKEDROS

Located today in the museum of the Cathedral of St. Mark in Venice, Italy (Tesoro di San Marco), is a marvelously crafted portable enamel icon (45.5 x 35 x 2.7 cm) depicting the archangel Michael in Byzantine military attire holding in his right hand a sword and in his left an orb.[1] The icon is made of silver gilt on wood and makes liberal use of gold cloisonné enamel. The depiction of the archangel is typical. His entire body is gilded and only his face exposed. Michael stands erect and frontal, in a somewhat defensive or protective position. Behind him is a combination of thinly depicted architectural structures amidst a blue background with white dots suggesting a celestial context. His face is expressionless, even stern, as he gazes forward. The archangel is surrounded by a decorative gilded frame with inlaid precious stones. The top and bottom rows of the frame had been set with three circular medallions each; the bottom three, however, are missing. Depicted in the center of the top row is Christ in the traditional Pantocrator ("almighty") in bust, blessing with his right hand and holding the gospel in his left. To Christ's right in the top left corner is a circular medallion of the apostle Peter, and in the opposite top right corner a medallion of St. Menas. On the left and right sides of the frame are four oval medallions, two on each side, each of which contains a pair of saints whom the Byzantines remembered as early Christian martyrs and who, by the tenth century, were venerated as military saints. The eight martyrs (paired together in the following manner: Theodore Stratelates and Theodore Teron; Demetrios and Nestor; Procopius and George; Eustathios and Mercurios) are depicted in miniature full-body frontal positions, each carrying a sword in his right hand and a shield in his left. The workmanship of the icon is rather extraordinary: even the faces of the diminutive warrior saints are distinctive. Given its craftsmanship and content, the icon was most probably imperially commissioned in Constantinople. On stylistic grounds the icon is dated to about 1100, a particularly militaristic period for the Byzantine Empire.[2]

For the Byzantines, the archangel Michael represented heavenly protection. As leader of the heavenly hosts, Michael gave flesh to the biblical notion of God's ability to defend his people from their enemies.[3] Yet Michael was not alone. In addition to the variety of bodiless powers upon whom the Byzantines could call for protection was a select group of saints, almost always martyrs, who either served in the military during their lifetime or were believed to have done so by later Byzantines. This group of saints, commonly referred to as military or warrior saints (a modern label not used by the Byzantines), figures prominently within the religious landscape of Byzantium. These saints share many common characteristics and were often depicted as a group on the walls of Byzantine churches dressed in military attire with sword in hand.[4] The intention of this paper is not to present the specific "histories" or the development of the cults of individual military saints; this has already been done in special studies devoted to particular saints or to military saints collectively.[5] Rather, I am interested in placing into historical context the broad parameters of the development of the military saint in Byzantium as a distinct saintly "type," how such saints were remembered and venerated, and what, if any, conclusions one can confidently make regarding attitudes toward war, military service, and Christian lifestyle from the evidence of the veneration of these saints in Byzantium.

Issues of military service, support for the military, prosecution of war, and so on are not limited to the class of military saints but can be found in the lives of a variety of saints in Byzantium. In particular, the tradition of the imperial or kingly saint, beginning with Constantine, continued throughout the history of Byzantium and remained a prominent motif for Orthodox national churches down to the early twentieth century.[6] Although imperial and military saints share common characteristics vis-à-vis military issues, they are different in that none of the military saints honored in Byzantium ever served as head of an empire, kingdom, principality, or nation-state. A saint like Alexander Nevsky, grand prince of Novgorod (d. 1263), who defended his Orthodox people against Swedes and Germans, shares certain characteristics with the military saint, most especially that of participation in military combat. However, Nevsky was a prince who, like Byzantine emperors who were sainted, led men into battle as the leader of a state, not as a general who would ultimately have been under the orders of the emperor. Further, military saints did not meet their death in military battle, but voluntarily died instead of betraying their Christian faith. This paper does not deal with imperial saints, nor does it take up the issue of the passion-bearer saints within the Russian Orthodox tradition. An important hagiographic tradition, the passion bearers, exemplified most clearly by Sts. Boris and Gleb, did not form part of the Byzantine hagiographic tradition.[7] Although reference will be made to a variety of military saints, in what follows the arguments presented rely primarily upon the cults of the major military saints venerated by the Byzantines.[8]

WAR, BYZANTINE SOCIETY, AND MILITARY SAINTS

As in other medieval societies, war was part of the fabric of Byzantine society. The Byzantines knew only a few periods of prolonged peace, and throughout most of their thousand-year history the prosecution of war was common. Byzantine foreign policy included both offensive and defensive wars, wars for territorial gain (or the regaining of lost territory), wars for economic advantage, and numerous defensive struggles. It has been estimated that expenditures for the military during the period from

842 to 1025 were nearly three-quarters of the overall annual imperial budget.[9] Byzantine war strategists produced handbooks on military tactics while ecclesiastical authorities published liturgical protocols for use in military camps and on the battlefield. This does not mean, however, that Byzantine society was overtly militaristic. There is little to suggest that Byzantine culture was imbued with a military mind-set similar to, for example, that of the ancient Spartans. Yet neither was Byzantine imperial policy pacifistic; it was pragmatic and utilized diplomacy, ransom, and yearly monetary tributes, along with military might and tactics, to realize its foreign and domestic goals.[10]

It is not, therefore, surprising to find within ecclesiastical circles support for the military. Byzantine soldiers participated in an array of ecclesiastically sanctioned liturgical activities, including confession and the reception of the Eucharist prior to major military campaigns. Soldiers defending Thessaloniki against a Bulgarian attack anointed themselves with the *myron* of St. Demetrios, a sweet-smelling ointment believed to exude from the martyr's relics.[11] The oft-referenced rallying of the troops at Constantinople by Patriarch Sergios during the joint Persian-Avar siege of the city in 626 suggests that ecclesiastical figures were willing to support military enterprises, at least defensive ones. One of the most visible means by which the church was brought into the service of the military, and perhaps vice versa, was through the identification of a group of saintly intercessors, themselves having served in the Roman military and eventually been martyred for their Christian faith, who could assist the Byzantines in both their defensive and offensive military campaigns. These holy intercessors are often collectively referred to as "military saints" or "warrior saints," that is, saints who through their terrestrial military service, and their saintly lives as exemplified by their martyrdoms, formed part of the celestial military as intercessors for and protectors of the Byzantines.

The Byzantines venerated some seventy saints who, according to their hagiographic traditions, at some point during their lifetime were affiliated with the military. In addition to these seventy or so individuals, the Byzantines also venerated a handful of collective martyrs who were identified by the Byzantines as military personnel, most famously the Forty Martyrs of Sebasteia.[12] However, for most of these saints, very little historically verifiable information survives. Further, there are a handful of saints for whom no textual evidence exists, but whose surviving iconography in-dicates a military affiliation.[13] Only a handful of these seventy-plus mili-tary saints played any significant role among the Byzantine faithful, and some more than others. The main military saints for the Byzantines were Sts. Theodore Teron, Theodore Stratelates, Demetrios, Procopius, Mercu-rios, George, Sergius, Bacchus, Eustathios, the Forty Martyrs of Sebasteia, the martyrs of Melitene, Menas, Artemius, and Arethus.[14] This group will form the basis of this paper.

The trajectory from early Christian martyr to military saint is, at first glance, rather straightforward. By the end of the second century, there is sufficient evidence suggesting that Christians were serving in the Roman military.[15] At times, some of these Christians were required, either as part of their military obligation or as a result of imperial edict, to sacrifice to the emperor or a local pagan god. Refusing, some Christian soldiers paid with their lives. Christian communities remembered these martyred sol-diers as heroes of the Christian faith, and as early as the second quarter of the fourth century such communities began to build special edifices (*mar-tyria*) either to commemorate the places of martyrdom or, more often, to enclose the martyrs' remains (bones). The veneration of these martyrs who happened to have served in the Roman military was part of the larger phenomenon of the cult of the martyrs which was in full swing by the fourth century. An encomium by Gregory of Nyssa delivered at the tomb of Theodore Teron, a simple infantryman, lauds the martyr for his will-ingness to die for his faith but says little about his military affiliation and exploits. A few years earlier, St. Basil delivered a similar homily on the oc-casion of the feast of St. Gordios, a centurion in the Roman army, lifting up the martyr for his personal sacrifice (that is, his loss of life for his Christian faith) and not on account of his military service.[16] In the fourth century, the military record of a martyr was not singled out as playing any significant role in the martyr's commemoration. Rather, it was the fact of his martyrdom that brought about his veneration within the burgeoning cult of the martyrs.

The theme of martyrdom looms large in the development of the mili-tary saint. With very few exceptions, the military saints venerated by the Byzantines were martyrs.[17] Further, excluding Artemius (martyred under Emperor Julian) and Arethus (martyred in Najran in the sixth century), all were martyred prior to the peace of Christianity ushered in by Constantine. The Byzantine hagiographic tradition would eventually recognize these martyrs as having served in the Roman military (the two exceptions again are Artemius, who served as *doux* [governor] of Egypt, and Arethas, who was a leader [*exarchos*] of a group of Christians in southern Arabia). However, their path toward being identified as having a military career is unclear, and more often than not, historical evidence is lacking to confirm their military affiliation. In fact, of the major military saints, only Theodore Teron can, with any certainty, be said to have served in the Roman army.

On the contrary, Procopius did not serve in the military.[18] The authenticity of the military careers of Demetrios, George, and Menas is suspect primarily because the textual and iconographic evidence for their association with the military dates from, in most cases, no earlier than the sixth century, and several of these early sources say nothing about their military affiliation. For Demetrios and Menas, the earliest textual and archaeological evidence attests that these saints were commemorated for their healing powers, and their basilicas, respectively in Thessaloniki and at Abu Mena near Lake Mareotis outside of Alexandria, were major pilgrimage shrines.[19] In the case of St. George, Byzantine hagiographical texts place his martyrdom under Diocletian, identify him as a soldier, and locate his primary cultic center at Lydda in Palestine. Although miracles of healing and various interventions are associated with the saint, unlike the narratives of Demetrios and Menas, these miracle stories surfaced much later and never circulated as a collection.

Our knowledge of the development of the cult of the military saints in Byzantium is aided extensively by art-historical evidence. Images of the major military saints abound in Cappadocia, in the main church edifices of medieval Serbia (modern Kosovo), in the church of Christ in Chora, in the Monastery of Hosios Loukas, in churches in Kastoria, and on the walls of many of the churches of Meteora. Pre-iconoclastic representations of military saints rarely depict the saint in military uniform. Rather, the saint is represented in court dress, often holding a cross in one hand while the other hand is extended in the *orans* position of intercession. This depiction is rather typical of early Byzantine iconographic renditions of martyrs in general. It is not until after the end of iconoclasm and, in particular, during the tenth century, that we see an increase not only in the production of images of warrior saints but in their depiction in military attire.[20]

The artistic rendering of Byzantine military saints in military dress with shield and sword does not definitively emerge until the tenth century; nonethelesss, calling upon these saints for assistance in military affairs dates much earlier. In his encomium to St. Theodore Teron noted above, St. Gregory of Nyssa suggests that Theodore can be called upon for aid in battles. Archbishop John of Thessaloniki, writing in the second quarter of the seventh century, recounts three important miraculous interventions of St. Demetrios in the city's defense against a Slavic siege in 586. A prayer inscribed on the lintel of a military barracks at Ghour, Syria, and dated to around 525 calls upon the three military martyrs Longinus, Theodore Teron, and George for protection.[21] For Demetrios, a later miracle (dating to ca. 680) recounts how the saint, riding on a horse, led the defenders of Thessaloniki on a successful defeat of its attackers.

Though not novel, there is a noticeable shift in the number and portrait type of military saints after iconoclasm. It coincides with the militaristic ideal among Byzantine emperors during the second half of the tenth and first quarter of the eleventh century. During this time, medieval Byzantium was moving toward the apogee of its military and geographic success. Emperors such as Nikephoros II Phokas (963–69), John I Tzimiskes (969–76), and above all Basil II (976–1025) personally led their armies into battle and were highly successful on the battlefield. In particular, the Byzantines began to depict military saints not in isolation but in groups, either in monumental painting on the walls of churches (e.g., Hosios Loukas) or on portable ivory triptychs.[22] When writing about important military victories of the late tenth century, Byzantine historians of the following two centuries connect the dates on which these victories occurred to the feast days of the military saints Theodore Stratelates and George.[23] The emperor John Tzimiskes (969–76) frequently called upon St. Theodore Stratelates for aid in battle; the saint is said to have appeared on a white horse encouraging the Byzantine army in its fight against the Scythians at Dorystolon in Bulgaria.[24]

MILITARY SERVICE AND MARTYRDOM

The Byzantines had at their disposal various means by which to propagate the memory of their saints and to ensure their commemoration and veneration in the life of the church and society. The most common and encompassing means was the account of the martyrdom or life of a saint. Given that all of the military saints listed above were martyrs, most of what the Byzantines learned of these men came from the stories of their martyrdoms. Putting aside questions of the authenticity or accuracy of these accounts, they are nearly unanimous in the general narrative they convey. The martyr in question was invariably a member of the Roman army, often, as in the cases of Demetrios (at least in the more developed versions of his martyrdom), Sergios, and Theodore Stratelates, important leaders of high military rank. These texts do not raise the question of the morality of military service. However, the military careers of these saints were interrupted because their Christian faith became problematic with military service within a pagan context. The moral or religious dilemma faced by these Christians was not related to the violence of military service, nor to the fact that as soldiers they were required at times to take the life of another. Rather, the conflict surrounded their refusal to participate in pagan ritual practices, especially sacrificing to the emperor or to any of a number of pagan gods.[25] Once their Christianity was revealed, usually through their refusal to offer sacrifice, they were forced to either sacrifice or face death.

From the various "passions," or written accounts of the lives of the military saints, there is no indication that military service, per se, was frowned upon. In fact, St. John Chrysostom, St. Basil of Caesarea, and St. Gregory of Nyssa wrote encomia on early Christian martyrs who served in the Roman army. These sermons, delivered for the most part in the chapels which housed the particular martyr's relics, focus almost exclusively on these Roman soldiers as martyrs and are silent regarding the appropriateness or inappropriateness of their military service. Rather, the martyrs were to be emulated either for refusing to participate in the pagan aspects of military service often required in late imperial Rome or for maintaining their Christian faith to the point of death, or for both. In his panegyric on the martyr Gordios, Basil described the young martyr's military career in laconic yet positive terms: "He [Gordios] occupied a prominent position such that he was entrusted with the leadership of one hundred soldiers, and he was conspicuous among the military ranks for the strength of his body and the bravery of his spirit."[26] Basil went on to note that Gordios was not alone in his conversion to Christ since three centurions from scripture also turned to Christ while serving in the military. Yet in the end, Basil's homily focuses primarily upon Gordios's refusal to offer sacrifice to the pagan gods and his embracing of his public execution "as if he were delivering himself into the hands of angels."[27]

In several of the passions, the success of a martyr's military career is highlighted.[28] The example of St. Eustathios is instructive. The tenth-century encomium by Nicetas David Paphlagon identifies Eustathios as a Roman soldier who rose through the ranks of the Roman army during the reigns of Trajan and Hadrian, eventually becoming a prominent general.[29] While still a pagan, Eustathios was hunting with some of his fellow soldiers when he saw an image of Christ (some versions have Eustathios see a cross) appear between the antlers of a deer. The vision led to his baptism along with that of his wife and children. Later, during a raid of barbarians, Eustathios was called upon to lead the Roman army. After defeating the barbarians (Eustathios was a Christian by this time), he was summoned by Emperor Hadrian to Rome to be honored. Invited to visit the temple of Apollo with Hadrian, the saint refused and was put to death. In addition to the encomium by Nicetas, a life of Eustathios is contained in the Metaphrastic Menologion. Given the late date of these textual witnesses to the story of Eustathios, H. Delehaye concluded that the story, which reads much like Job, is fictitious.[30] Fictitious or not, the story is an example within hagiographic literature where success on the battlefield does not raise a moral dilemma.

The various written accounts (including sermons) of the military saints circulating in Byzantium take a negative view of military service only when such service involves the saint in immoral behavior (unrelated to one's military responsibilities) or apostasy. For St. Hieron and the Martyrs of Melitene, military service posed challenges since the company one keeps in the military is not very Christian. We are told that St. Hieron's initial refusal to serve in the military was motivated by his fear of the loose morals of his would-be fellow soldiers.[31] However, almost universally, it is the refusal of the saint to participate in pagan practices and the concomitant ritual sacrifices associated with military service that lead to the martyrdom of the saint. This is best exemplified in the martyrdom story of Sts. Sergios and Bacchus.

The earliest account of the martyrdom of Sts. Sergios and Bacchus dates to the fifth century.[32] Sergios held the high-ranking position of *primicerius* of the *schola gentilium*, that is, the leader of one of the units which formed the personal bodyguard of the emperor. His companion, Bacchus, served as *secundarius* in the same unit.[33] Jealousy among fellow soldiers led to their denouncement as Christians to the emperor. Not wanting to believe that two of his closest military guards were Christians, the emperor ordered them to enter a pagan temple, offer sacrifice, and eat the sacrificial meat. Refusing, the two soldiers were stripped of their military attire, dressed in women's clothing, and publicly mocked. Bacchus was the first to be put to death, in the border town of Barbalissus. Sergios was eventually martyred at Rusafa, Syria, which became the center of his cult. The martyrdom account is very specific about the military titles held by the two martyrs. The text often refers to the saints as "soldiers of Christ." Otherwise, the text is silent about the propriety of military service.

DEFENSIVE WARFARE AND DEFENDERS AGAINST ENEMIES

Hagiography tells us more about how people understood, venerated, and utilized the saints than about the saints themselves. As already noted, the texts which the Byzantines read about their saints, especially the military saints, offer very little historically verifiable information about these saints. What the texts do reveal, especially stories of the miraculous intervention of a saint within Byzantine society, is how the Byzantines made use of the power of the saints for their benefit. The texts, coupled with significant iconographic evidence, indicate that the military saints played an important apotropaic and defensive role for the Byzantines.

An early and stark example of calling upon a military saint for protection against enemies comes from Gregory of Nyssa's homily on Theodore Teron. Delivered on the saint's feast day (February 17) at his shrine at Euchaita (Pontus) sometime between 379 and 381, the encomium offers traditional exhortative language in which Gregory encourages his audience gathered for the feast to hold fast to their Christian faith and practice, as evidenced by Theodore's courageous yet selfless act of martyrdom. Gregory closes his sermon by entreating the intervention of the martyr:

> We are craving for many benefactions from you: intercede on behalf of the fatherland [τῆς πατρίδος] with our common King. After all, the fatherland of a martyr is the region where he suffered, and his [fellow] citizens [πολῖται] and relatives are those who buried him and are keeping and honoring him. We view afflictions with suspicion, we expect danger: it will not take long before the sinful Scythians are plunging us into the pains of war. As a soldier, fight for us; as a martyr, speak boldly [τῇ παρρησίᾳ] on behalf of your fellow-servants. . . . Beseech [God] for peace, so that these feasts may not stop, so that the furious and lawless barbarian may not attack churches and altars nor the profane trample upon the holy.[34]

As Gregory clearly points out, Theodore's ability to provide protection for the local citizenry depends, in part, on the location of his burial and the veneration afforded the saint by the faithful.

In addition to protecting the cities which housed their relics and assisting the military in its prosecution of war, military saints also served a more particularized role in aiding individuals. Certainly this is true in the numerous healing miracles associated with many of the warrior saints. Various Byzantine saints could heal, but few offered their beseechers physical force to defend an individual from specific danger as did the military saints. This unique function of the military saint is best observed in iconography. St. George and St. Theodore Teron are depicted killing dragons, often while riding horseback. Of the two, the image of St. George slaying a dragon is better known, but such imagery was not limited to him. In an iconographic type dating to no earlier than the thirteenth century, St. Demetrios, riding on a horse and dressed in military attire, spears the Bulgarian ruler Kalojan, who had besieged Thessaloniki in 1205. Though not particularly common for later Byzantines, the depiction of St. Demetrios killing Kalojan became popular among the Balkan Slavs.[35] The warrior saint, given his military role, offered the notable ability to defeat the recalcitrant beast or person.[36]

Examples could easily be multiplied which reflect the significant role military saints played in the life of Byzantine society, both at the popular and imperial levels. The fourteenth-century *Treatise on the Dignities and Offices*, which describes various Byzantine court ceremonials, notes that a banner of St. George on horseback was carried in imperial processions separately from a banner which included the four military saints Demetrios, Procopius, and the two Theodores.[37] The eleventh-century Byzantine historian John Skylitzes informs his readers of the intervention of St. Theodore Stratelates during a battle against the Rus' in 971 in which the Byzantines were victorious. Out of gratitude, the emperor John I Tzimiskes built a large shrine to house the saint's relics.[38] Patriarch Philotheos Kokkinos (1353–54, 1364–76) penned a hymn, to be sung for the emperor and his troops before battle, which invokes the protection and intercession of Procopius, Theodore, Mercurios, and Eustathios.[39] With the accession to the imperial throne of the military aristocracy of the Komnenian dynasty, Emperors Alexios I, John II, and Manuel I placed Demetrios, George, and Theodore Stratelates, respectively, on their coins.[40]

THE ETHICS OF WAR

In assessing the textual and iconographic data for the function of the military saint in Byzantium, one is struck by the ubiquity of the evidence for their veneration. Even if we account for the fact that hagiographic literature was, by sheer volume, the largest literary production of the Byzantines, the quantity of vitae, martyrdom accounts, miracle collections, synaxaria, and menologia notices referring to the major military saints remains impressive. Add to this the iconography that has survived, both monumental and portable, as well as icons on lead seals and imperial coinage, and the repertoire of material seems endless.[41] This abundance is explained in part by the importance given to saints in medieval Christendom and in Byzantium in particular. Further, given that the defense of the empire, along with other military engagements, monopolized the resources and energy of the state, it is not surprising that the warrior saint, in particular, figured prominently in Byzantium. From all of this evidence, can we reasonably arrive at some conclusions regarding the Byzantines' ethics of war as expressed in their veneration of military saints?

As stated earlier, almost every military saint was a martyr who had met his death either prior to the peace of the church or during the reign of the emperor Julian. None is female.[42] All the major military saints were thus commemorated as early Christian martyrs. They were martyrs first. This is reflected in the various lives and passions written about them, which pay scant attention to their military careers. The veneration of these saints during the fourth and fifth centuries is to be understood within the larger context of the cult of the martyrs. As martyrs, they had a special boldness (παρρησία) in the presence of God and were able to intercede on behalf of the faithful. Like other martyrs, the military saints (if we can even call them such at this early date) intervened in the individual lives of the faithful, most often providing healing from ailments. Sts. Demetrios, Artemius, and Menas each had a burgeoning healing cult associated with the place of their martyrdom or burial well before they were called upon by the Byzantines in times of military need. With the exception of George and Theodore Teron, prior to iconoclasm the major military saints were depicted in iconography wearing senatorial clothing. It is not until the tenth century that we can definitively identify a group of early Christian martyrs who are being collectively venerated by the Byzantines as warrior saints.

As a martyr, the military saint did not meet his death on the battlefield. He was not venerated as a slain soldier. Rather, he died at the hands of the leaders he once served, choosing death over apostasy. It is interesting that when Emperor Nikephoros II Phokas (963–69) requested that his slain soldiers be counted as martyrs, Patriarch Polyeuktos refused, citing St. Basil's recommendation that soldiers who killed in battle could not receive communion for three years.[43] Death in defense of the homeland did not result in sainthood. The commemoration of saints with military affiliation in Byzantium begins with their status as martyrs. Once their sanctity is established, through their martyrdom, then their additional characteristics will be exploited as the needs of society begin to be expressed through the veneration of the saints.

To try to develop a systematic ethic of war based on evidence from hagiography and the veneration of saints poses some serious challenges. Hagiography is anything but systematic. It is part history, part panegyric, and part epic. It is not the vehicle through which systematic theology is expressed or developed. As an epic, the saint's life displays traditional heroic elements. The hero is there to defend those in need through a variety of miraculous interventions and heroic measures (most especially martyrdom). The hero is not meant to articulate theological formulas or reason out ethical situations. At best, the saint as depicted in image and text is a type, a metaphor, a story of how God can act to help his faithful.

What the evidence for the veneration of military saints in Byzantium suggests is that, for the Byzantines, war was an unavoidable fact of life. Therefore, as in so many other moments of suffering and uncertainty, in time of war, both offensively and defensively, the Byzantines turned to their heavenly intercessors for assistance. In the fight against hostile military enemies, the Byzantines developed a cadre of saints who themselves had served in the military and invoked their assistance on the battlefield, behind the city walls, and for general protection. The cult of the military saints reflects the deep need of Byzantium for protection. If an ethics of war can be gleaned from this aspect of Byzantine society, it is that the military saint assists the state in its role as defender of the commonwealth.

NOTES

1. David Buckton, *The Treasury of San Marco Venice* (Milan: Olivetti, 1984), no. 19, 171–74.

2. On the reign of Emperor Alexios I Komnenos (1081–1118) and its military challenges, see Warren Treadgold, *A History of the Byzantine State and Society* (Stanford: Stanford University Press, 1997), 612–29.

3. The cult of the archangel Michael was ubiquitous in Byzantium; see Johannes Peter Rohland, *Der Erzengel Michael: Arzt und Feldherr* (Leiden: Brill, 1977).

4. One of the best examples of Byzantine military saints depicted as a group in Byzantine monumental art is found in the fourteenth-century *parekklesion* (side church) of the Chora Monastery (Kariye Camii) in Istanbul; see Robert Ousterhout, *The Art of the Kariye Camii* (London: Scala Publishers, 2002); Paul Underwood, *The Kariye Djami*, 4 vols. (New York: Pantheon Books, 1966), vol. 3.

5. See especially Christopher Walter, *The Warrior Saints in Byzantine Art and Tradition* (Aldershot: Ashgate, 2003).

6. See Alexander Webster's useful article "Varieties of Christian Military Saints: From Martyrs under Caesar to Warrior Princes," *St. Vladimir's Theological Quarterly* 24 (1980): 3–35. St. Ioannikios is a rare example of a Byzantine saint who enlisted in the army and after twenty years of military service retired to enter a monastery. Born in 754 in Bythinia, he left military service because he could no longer suffer to see the deaths of his fellow soldiers. He was remembered and venerated by the Byzantines as a holy man and not as a military saint most probably because he did not meet death through martyrdom. For his *vita*, see Denis F. Sullivan, "The Life of St. Ioannikios," in Alice-Mary Talbot, ed., *Byzantine Defenders of Images: Eight Saints' Lives in English Translation* (Washington, DC: Dumbarton Oaks Research Library and Collection, 1998), 243–351.

7. On Sts. Boris and Gleb, princes who allowed their brother to kill them rather than see others die in a civil war to preserve their rightful political positions, see R. M. Price, "Boris and Gleb: Princely Martyrs and Martyrologies in Kievan Russia," in Diana Wood, ed., *Martyrs and Martyrologies* (Oxford: Blackwell, 1993), 105–15. A more complete discussion of notions of war and pacifism in the Orthodox hagiographic tradition must include these saints and the tradition they represent.

8. I have chosen to use the adjective "military" as opposed to "warrior" in describing those saints the Byzantines depicted in image and text as armed soldiers.

9. Treadgold, *History of the Byzantine State and Society*, 576, table 13.

10. Edward N. Luttwak, *The Grand Stategy of the Byzantine Empire* (Cambridge, MA: Harvard University Press, 2009).

11. Walter, *Warrior Saints*, 82n57, as found in Hans Thurn, ed., *Ioannis Scylitzae Synopsis Historiarum*, Corpus fontium historiae Byzantinae 5 (Berlin: de Gruyter, 1973), 412–14. See also James Skedros, *Saint Demetrios of Thessaloniki: Civic Patron and Divine Protector, 4th–7th Centuries CE* (Harrisburg, PA: Trinity Press, 1999).

12. The earliest textual account of the Forty Martyrs, the *Testament*, makes no specific reference to their military status; for the Greek text and English translation, see Herbert Musurillo, *The Acts of the Christian Martyrs: Text and Translation* (Oxford: Clarendon Press, 1972), 354–60. By the time of the Metaphrastic Menologion (ca. 1000), their military affiliation is taken for granted.

13. In particular, three saints are depicted in the dome of the Rotunda (the Church of St. George) in Thessaloniki who each contain the title στρατιώτης (*stratiotes*). Recently, Charalambos Barkirtzis and Pelli Mastora, "Are the Mosaics in the Rotunda in Thessaloniki Linked to Its Conversion to a Christian Church?,"

in Miša Rakocija, ed., *Niš and Byzantium* 9 (Nis 2011): 42, have argued that the images in the lower band of the dome of the Rotunda are not saints but elite supporters of Emperor Constantine and that the Rotunda was built and decorated as a mausoleum for Constantine.

14. Hippolyte Delehaye, *Les legends grecques des saints militaires* (Paris: A. Picard, 1909), identified the two Theodores, Demetrios, Procopius, Mercurios, and George as constituting the major group of military saints in Byzantium. To this list, Christopher Walter, *Warrior Saints*, 145–211, adds Sergius, Bacchus, Eustathios, the Forty Martyrs of Sebasteia, the Martyrs of Melitene, Menas, Artemius, Arethas, Martin of Tours, and Phanourios.

15. J. Helgeland, "Christians and the Roman Army from Marcus Aurelius to Constantine," *Aufstieg und Niedergang der römischen Welt* (Berlin: de Gruyter, 1979), 2.23.1:724–834. For early Christian attitudes toward military service, see Louis J. Swift, *The Early Fathers on War and Military Service* (Wilmington, DE: M. Glazier, 1983).

16. For a discussion of Gregory's encomium, see Vasiliki Limberis, *Architects of Piety: The Cappadocian Fathers and the Cult of the Martyrs* (Oxford: Oxford University Press, 2011), 54–65.

17. Of the nearly exhaustive listing of Byzantine military saints (some seventy in number) indentified by Christopher Walter, *Warrior Saints*, only St. Martin of Tours, St. Ioannikios, and St. Eudocimus were not martyrs.

18. Our earliest reference to Procopius comes from Eusebius, *The Martyrs of Palestine* 1, who places the martyrdom of Procopius first in his collection. According to Eusebius, Procopius was a reader, interpreter of Syriac, and exorcist for the church of Scythopolis. For the critical edition of the short recension, see Gustave Bardy, SC 55 (Paris: Éditions du Cerf, 1993), 122.

19. For St. Demetrios, see Charalambos Bakirtzis, "Pilgrimage to Thessalonike: The Tomb of St. Demetrios," *Dumbarton Oaks Papers* 56 (2002): 175–92; Skedros, *Saint Demetrios of Thessaloniki*. For St. Menas, see Peter Grossman, "The Pilgrimage Center of Abū Mīnā," in *Pilgrimage and Holy Space in Late Antique Egypt*, ed. David Frankfurter (Leiden: Brill, 1998), 281–302. Artemius is another example of a military saint whose early veneration focused on his healing shrine in Constantinople, noted especially for healing of hernias and male genitalia.

20. For example, see the detailed discussion of the transformation of the portrait type of St. Menas in Warren T. Woodfin, "An Officer and a Gentleman: Transformations in the Iconography of a Warrior Saint," *Dumbarton Oaks Papers* 60 (2006): 111–43.

21. Elizabeth Key Fowden, *The Barbarian Plain: St. Sergius between Rome and Iran* (Berkeley: University of California Press, 1999), 4.

22. Walter, *Warrior Saints*, 275–76. The best known example is the Harbaville Triptych, a late tenth-century ivory measuring 24.2 x 28.5 cm and located today at the Louvre. See Adolph Goldschmidt and Kurt Weitzmann, *Die byzantinischen Elfenbeinskulpturen des X.–XIII. Jahrhunderts* (Berlin: B. Cassirer, 1930; repr., Deutscher Verlag fur Kunstwissenschaft, 1979), no. 85, pl. xxxiv. One of the earliest iconographic groupings of military saints is found in the Basilica of St. Demetrios in Thessaloniki. A recent cleaning of the mosaic on the west side of the northern pier has revealed an inscription identifying the saint with two children, most often taken as St. Demetrios, to be rather St. George. Thus, these pier mosaics represent a collection of three important military saints: Demetrios, who is depicted in several of the pier mosaics, the newly identified George, and St. Sergios. The mosaics date to ca. 630; see Skedros, *St. Demetrios of Thessaloniki*, 94–102. For the identity of St. George, see Charalambos Bakirtzis, "Προεικονομαχικό ψηφιδώτο του αγίου Γεωργίου στη Θεσσαλονίκη" [A preiconoclastic mosaic of St. George in Thessalonike], in *ΔΩPON: Τιμητικός τόμος στον καθηγητή Nίκο Nικονάνο* (Thessalonike: 10ē Ephoreia Vyzantinōn Archaiotētōn Chalkidikēs kai Hagiou Orous: D' Tomeas Tmēmatos Architektonōn tēs Polytechnikēs Scholēs tou A.P.Th., 2006), 128–29.

23. Michael McCormick, *Eternal Victory: Triumphal Rulership in Late Antiquity, Byzantium and the Early Medieval West* (Cambridge: Cambridge University Press, 1990), 170.

24. Leo the Deacon, *History*, ed. K. B. Hase, *Leonis diaconi Caloënsis historiae libri decem*, Corpus scriptorum historiae Byzantinae 30 (Bonn: Weber, 1828), 153.22–154.9.

25. In addition to idolatry, some Christians were also concerned with the immoral behavior and the evils of bloodshed that accompanied military service. Swift, *Early Fathers*, 32–79. For a balanced summary of the debate over whether pre-Constantinian Christianity was pacifist or promilitary see James J. Megivern, "Early Christianity and Military Service," *Perspectives in Religious Studies* 12 (1985): 175–83.

26. Basil, *On Gordius* 2 (PG 31:493); translation from John Leemans, Pauline Allen, et al., *Let Us Die That We May Live: Greek Homilies on Christian Martyrs from Asia Minor, Palestine, and Syria (c. AD 350–AD 450)* (London: Routledge, 2003), 60.

27. Basil, *On Gordius* 8 (PG 31:505); translation from Leemans, *Let Us Die*, 66.

28. The tenth-century metaphrastic version of the martyrdom of St. Demetrios identifies the martyr as the "proconsul [*anthypatos*] of Greece" (PG 116:1185). The term is used here anachronistically and most likely had the meaning of "governor," although by the tenth century it had become an honorific

title. Alexander Kazhdan, "Anthypatos," *The Oxford Dictionary of Byzantium*, ed. Alexander Kazhdan (Oxford: Oxford University Press, 1991), 1:111.

29. PG 105:379.

30. Hippolyte Delehaye, "La légende grecque de saint Eustache," *Mélanges d'hagiographie grecque et latine* (Brussels: Societé des Bollandistes, 1966), 212–39.

31. Walter, *Warrior Saints*, 178.

32. See the detailed study of the late antique cult of Sts. Sergios and Bacchus by Fowden, *The Barbarian Plain*. For an English translation of the martyrdom account, *Passio antiquior* (Bibliotheca hagiographica graeca, ed. François Halkin, 3rd ed. [Brussels: Société des bollandistes, 1969], 1624), see John Boswell, *The Marriage of Likeness: Same-Sex Unions in Pre-Modern Europe* (London: Fontana, 1995), 365–76. On the date of the *Passio antiquior*, see Walter, *Warrior Saints*, 148.

33. David Woods, "The Emperor Julian and the Passion of Sergius and Bacchus," *Journal of Early Christian Studies* 5 (1997): 344, has rightly noted the anachronistic use of the *schola gentilium* as forming part of the imperial bodyguard before Constantine.

34. Gregory of Nyssa, *Homily on Theodore the Recruit* (PG 46:748); translation from Leemans et al., *Let Us Die*, 90–91.

35. Walter, *Warrior Saints*, 88–90.

36. Christopher Walter, "The Intaglio of Solomon in the Benaki Museum and the Origins of the Iconography of Warrior Saints," *Deltion tes Christianikes Archaiologikes Etaireias* [Δέλτιον τῆς Χριστιανικῆς Αρχαιολογικῆς Ἑταιρείας] 15 (1989–90): 35–42.

37. J. Verpeaux, ed., *Traité des offices* (Paris: Éditions du Centre National de la Recherche Scientifique, 1966), 196; André Grabar, "Pseudo-Codinos et les cérémonies de la Cour byzantine au XIVe siècle," in *Art et société sous les Paléologues: Actes du colloque organisé par l'Association internationale des études byzantines à Venise en septembre 1968*, Bibliothèque de l'Institut hellénique d'études byzantines et post-byzantines de Venise 4 (Venice: Stamperia di Venezia, 1971), 201.

38. John Skylitzes, *Synopsis historiarum* 308.15–19; 309.29–33.

39. Walter, *Warrior Saints*, 132.

40. Michael F. Hendy, *Coinage and Money in the Byzantine Empire, 1081–1261*, Dumbarton Oaks Studies 12 (Washington, DC: Dumbarton Oaks Center for Byzantine Studies, 1969).

41. For images of saints on lead seals, see J. Cotsonis, "The Contribution of Byzantine Lead Seals to the Study of the Cult of the Saints," *Byzantion* 75 (2005): 383–497.

42. The Theotokos is the obvious exception. However, she provides a unique test case for Constantinople; see Vasiliki Limberis, *Divine Heiress: The*

Virgin Mary and the Creation of Christian Constantinople (London: Routledge, 1994), 124–32; Averil Cameron, "The Theotokos in Sixth-Century Constantinople," *Journal of Theological Studies* 29 (1978): 79–108.

43. The reference to Nikephoros's request is found in Skylitzes, *Historia synopsis* 14.18. The late Byzantine canonists Zonaras, Balsamon, and Blastares each discussed Polyeuktos's response and the legitimacy of Basil's canon. G. A. Rhalles and M. Potles, *Syntagma ton theion kai hieron kanonon*, 6 vols. (Athens, 1852–59; repr., Athens: Athenai Gregores, 1966), 4:132–33; 6:492–93. The episode has received some attention recently: see Tia M. Kolbaba, "Fighting for Christianity: Holy War in the Byzantine Empire," *Byzantion* 68 (1998): 204–7; Paul Stephenson, "Imperial Christianity and Sacred War in Byzantium," in James K. Wellman, ed., *Belief and Bloodshed: Religion and Violence across Time and Tradition* (Lanham, MD: Rowman and Littlefield, 2007), 83–95; and Ioannis Stouraites, "Jihad and Crusade: Byzantine Positions towards the Notions of 'Holy War,'" *Byzantina Symmeikta* 21 (2011): 52–58.

DEBATES ON JUST WAR, HOLY WAR, AND PEACE

Orthodox Christian Thought and
Byzantine Imperial Attitudes toward War

ALEXANDROS K. KYROU AND
ELIZABETH H. PRODROMOU

Grant Peace to Your world, to Your churches, to the clergy, to
those in public service, to the armed forces, and to all Your people.
—Prayer before the Ambo, Divine Liturgy of
St. John Chrysostom

This study constitutes an initial effort by the authors to situate Orthodox
Christian thought within contemporary scholarly inquiries and practi-
tioner discussions regarding the theological foundations and religious
bases for waging war. This work straddles multiple disciplinary boundaries, with a strong emphasis on history and political science, reflecting
the collaboration and respective expertise of the authors. Though centered

in the humanities and social sciences, this study aims to explore Orthodox thought on matters of war and peace with a goal of learning more about "how the Orthodox Church and theology have been, through innovation, a contributory cause to change in society and culture in different historic periods."[1] Our working assumption is that Orthodoxy indeed has something new to offer for how we think about the incendiary question of the relationship between faith and war, and, therefore, faith and peace.

We proceed in three parts. First, we outline the drivers of the current conversation in the West about the relationship between religion and war. Who are the defining religious and nonreligious voices that are shaping the discourse and argumentation about the ethics of war and peace in contemporary world affairs? What does the discussion about the religious ethics of war and peace, and more generally, about the role of religion in international relations, suggest about the viability of an international system that relies on an architecture of the state conceived over four centuries ago at the Treaty of Augsburg and the Peace of Westphalia?[2]

Second, though recognizing that debates about war versus peace include many religious voices, we focus on debates within Christianity. The analytic focus on Christianity leads to the claim that the conventional alternatives of the just war thesis (overwhelmingly associated with Roman Catholic thought) versus pacifism (largely derived from a Radical Protestant critique of Roman Catholicism) are largely confined to a Western Christian hermeneutic that differs in important respects from Eastern Christian ruminations on war and peace. Here we set out the state of the question in Western Christian thought and acknowledge the relative lack of a genuinely Orthodox contribution by Orthodox scholars who have internalized the Western paradigmatic polarities, and we offer a potential, uniquely Orthodox paradigm constructed not only on *theoria* but also on the *praxis* of the militarized Eastern Christian state—the Byzantine Empire.

In particular, it is plausible to propose a distinctively Orthodox Christian hermeneutic of war and peace by resuscitating the eschatological nature of Christianity. This, in turn, generates an irreconcilable tension between theological ideal and pastoral necessity that positions Orthodoxy between a categorical rejection of notions of just or holy war, on the one hand, and complete pacifism, on the other. So, what is the alternative? We outline an innovative Orthodox alternative, albeit one needing amplification.

Third, against the background of debates centered on holy war, we examine the conceptual formulation and practical implementation of an Orthodox view of war and peace in the Byzantine Empire, identifying the historic conditions and implications of the innovative features of Orthodox theological ruminations on war and peace. Here and in the conclusion, we take up the "so what" question. In other words, even if we make a plausible claim about the original position of Orthodoxy on war as defensive and as a mechanism of last resort after the failure of diplomacy, what does the consolidation of this theoretical position under the particular conditions of the Byzantine Empire mean for today's totally different conditions of war-making?

WHERE DOES RELIGION FIGURE IN CURRENT DEBATES ON WAR AND PEACE?

Where does religion figure in current debates on war and peace by scholar-practitioners of international relations? What accounts for the renewed vigor of debates about the religious justifications to support versus reject war and to delineate and delimit war-making in the twenty-first century?

The proximate causes for the engagement between theology and international affairs were the twin events of the 9/11 terrorist attacks against the United States and the American invasion of Iraq. Indeed, as al Qaeda framed its September 11 strike on the United States as an Islamic holy war against the infidel enemies of Islam, the administration of George W. Bush found support from American Christian theorists who cast Washington's "preemptive war" against Iraq as a just war. Bush's unfortunate reference to a crusade against evil was instructive, as well, but it was the resort to competing and comparative theologies to conceptualize and countenance violence in the international system that was striking for several reasons.

First, a religious pluralism was expressed by the multiple traditions— primarily Christianity and Islam, but with some input from Judaism—

that participated in the arguments about the causes and consequences of the 9/11 attacks.

Second, the subset of those events—which included America's initial military ouster from power of the Taliban regime in Kabul, the US overthrow of Saddam Hussein, and the protracted US occupation of Iraq and seething civil war conditions there—provoked what Alfred Stepan would call a multivocal discussion within Islam and Christianity regarding the moral and ethical features of war.[3] One need only note the proliferation of *jihadi* websites,[4] as well as the outpouring of just war literature and blog sites,[5] that have emerged since 2001 in order to recognize the extraordinary internal diversity in the religious explication of a rationale for and prosecution of war.

Finally, the engagement of religious voices in disputation over the theological grounds for war and peace reflected a broader phenomenon of interest for both the academy and the public policy sphere—namely, the unanticipated salience of religion in world affairs, in direct contradiction to the analytical, predictive, and normative conventions of the theory of secularization that had achieved hegemony in the social sciences.[6]

In this respect, the vitality and urgency of both just war and *jihadi* arguments about war, peace, and religion were part of the global manifestation of religious voice, activism, and interaction with secular actors at the closing of the twentieth century, in what amounted to a critical reassessment of the legitimacy of the state and the meaning of modernity. Therefore, both the just war and the *jihadi* interpretations of the 9/11 events, as well as the chain reaction generated therefrom, were expressions of and responses to the shortcomings of the contemporary understandings of the Westphalian state, built on sovereignty principles of territory and nonintervention and mythologized as the defeat of, divorce from, and inevitable disappearance of religion.

Regardless of the causal variables (ideas or interests) proposed to explain why the end of the Cold War had not ushered in an era of global peace built on the twin foundations of liberal democratic regimes and market-based economies, there was overwhelming empirical evidence that the international system needed serious adjustment. The signature events of the First Gulf War, the wars of Yugoslav succession, and the Rwandan genocide that closed out the second millennium offered shocking testimony to the crux of the problem: the growing contradictions and tensions between the axiom of nonintervention and the need to suspend that principle for humanitarian priorities and, at times equally important, material logic.

In short, the current historical expression of perennial debates about just war, holy war, and pacifism emerged within the combustive chrysalis of Islamic extremism and American imperialism.[7] Therefore, while indisputably voiced by Christian and Muslim thinkers frequently using reflexive, antagonistic categories of otherness, the deployment of theology for purposes of theorizing on world affairs reflected the shared concern, with Buddhist, Baha'i, Hindu, and other faiths, about how to remake the sovereign state system.[8]

WHERE IS ORTHODOX CHRISTIANITY?

Within this current historical conjuncture, where does Orthodoxy fit regarding Christian reflections on war and peace?

There is by now an extensive literature on what can reasonably be viewed as the two main tendencies in Christian thought on war and peace. The conventional historiography of these two tendencies pits Christian pacifism against just war militarism. On the one hand, the Christian pacifist tradition is narrated with roots in the theology that developed with the establishment and formation of the early church, dating from the time of Christ up through the early fourth century. Accordingly, the watershed of the Constantinian moment led to a series of events that supposedly pushed pacifism to the theological margins, supplanted by the alternative tendency toward activism and, arguably, militarism, which is associated with just war theory.

The dominant historiography of Christianity characterizes early modern, modern, and contemporary reiterations of the tension between Christian pacifism and just war militarism as the struggle between competing Radical Protestant and Roman Catholic hermeneutics of peace and war, respectively. Furthermore, this polarized representation of Christian thought and experience with war leads to what Orthodox theologian John McGuckin neatly summarizes as a "macro-picture of Church history as a sclerotic decline, where simple [pacifist] origins are progressively corrupted into [the] oppressive structures [of the imperial *Pax Constantina*]" by which the church seized ever greater amounts of territory, a condition from which the Protestant Reformation brought the first meaningful rediscovery of the authentic, exclusively pacifist core of Christianity.[9]

It is against this almost caricatured representation that we find Orthodoxy constructed by conventional historiography. Where does Orthodoxy fit into this narrative of Christian thought and church history? First, because the Byzantine Empire was, after all, indelibly linked to Constantine, the Eastern Orthodox Church becomes the institutional embodiment of and, therefore, object of criticism for the decisive shift away from the pacifist tendency toward the militarist tendency. Paradoxically, however, the theological bedrock of just war theory lies in the works of Augustine of Hippo and Thomas Aquinas, both thinkers associated with the Latin church. So, even though Orthodoxy is blamed for the rupture with pacifism, it is the works of Augustine and Aquinas, who had no direct influence on Orthodox theology, which express the turn toward just war.

Furthermore, insofar as the supposed rehabilitation of the pacifist tendency in Christianity is meant to originate with Protestant thinkers writing after Byzantium's fall and the Eastern Church's captivity behind the veil of Ottomanism, the revival of pacifism by some Orthodox thinkers is generally associated with argumentation by Protestant converts to Orthodoxy or Westernized (read, Protestantized) Orthodox Christians.

The conventional narrative of the Christian church on war and peace has been overwhelmingly accepted and internalized by many Orthodox theologians, as evidenced by their recent work on matters of war and peace. Not incidentally, this work has been largely an effort to catch up with Catholic and Protestant inquiries provoked by the chain of events detailed above.

Emblematic is Alexander Webster's endorsement of Augustine as the paradigmatic voice of just war theory, a position Webster supports so enthusiastically that he proposes a theological move beyond the notion of just war to a maximalist position of justifiable or virtuous war.[10] Not only does Webster argue that there is a "teleology of justice" that defines justifiable war as a lesser good.[11] He dismisses as counterfeiters and purveyors of a lesser morality those Orthodox thinkers who endorse either pacifism or war as a lesser evil, chalking up their interpretive and ethical "lapses" to forces of Protestant infiltration through ecumenical contacts, emigration to Western Christian countries, and conversion—this list includes scholars such as George Dragas, Vassilios Giultsis, and the entire group of scholar-practitioners who founded the Orthodox Peace Fellowship.[12]

David Bentley Hart is even more polemical in his claim that it is "a singular sort of delusion to imagine that the Eastern Orthodox tradition is any more hospitable to pacifism than the Western Catholic tradition, given the utter absence of pacifist tenets from Orthodoxy's teachings, liturgy, or history. [This] . . . delusion is particularly acute amongst . . . a not inconsiderable number of (Western) Eastern Christians," but overall, the problem stems from an obdurate "refusal to learn the meaning of unfamiliar terms with a magnificent indifference to historical fact."[13]

If the dominant historiographical narrative of Christian thought on war and peace has been internalized and embellished by Orthodox scholars, is it possible to discern the footprints of an alternative hermeneutical path in Orthodoxy when it comes to war—and, by extension, peace?

Our tentative "yes" begins with the claim about the historiographical weaknesses that limit the conventional view. These weaknesses include a reliance on a facile, linear rendering of church history that either omits or misunderstands conjectural events and branching paths; an Orientalist reading of church history divided artificially into a completely discrete, internally monolithic West and East; and an unwillingness to undertake the interdisciplinary work necessary to reveal the analytical limits and empirical errors of the previous two methods.[14]

A stronger affirmative claim that Orthodoxy offers a more nuanced—if discernibly ambivalent and not fully systematized—approach to the ethics of war and peace rests primarily on a reading of the sources in a manner that reveals a different conceptual apparatus from that deployed in the war-versus-peace reduction. This conceptual apparatus is contained in a hermeneutic of Eastern Christian, especially Byzantine, military history and reading of the various proof texts that, while taking into account the works of Augustine and Aquinas, rely on a far broader reading of sources that are given comparably greater emphasis in Orthodox Christianity—the works of Basil of Caesarea and Athanasius of Alexandria are instructive, although certainly not the only sources.

This point can be made clear by outlining the footprints of a distinctive Orthodox hermeneutic on war and peace. Taken together, Orthodox sources reflect a continuous, emphatic characterization of Christianity as eschatological—*ergo*, the mysterious nature of the church's place in history. Mining the sources shows that this eschatological conception of Christianity is the foundation of a distinctively Orthodox hermeneutic on war. For it is from this nonnegotiable, eschatological perspective that there emerges an apparently irreconcilable, unresolvable tension between the theological ideal (the prelapsarian condition and the kingdom to come), on the one hand, and pastoral necessity (postlapsarian reality), on the other, from which all rumination on war and peace derives.

Having acknowledged the tragedy of this unresolvable tension, for humanity and all creation, we must categorically reject any notion of war as good or war as the lesser good, and certainly of war as virtuous. Instead, we understand war as intrinsically evil, because it is a condition and praxis that is informed by our sinfulness. Indeed, from a eucharistic perspective, the sin of ego over the ideal of love not only explains the rupture in ideal communion between man and God, but is replicated most violently and grotesquely in the act of war—which is the mass expression of the postlapsarian reality of death.

By applying the conceptual tools of *apokalypsis* and applying the divine communion of eucharistic theology to produce an explanation and interpretation of war, Orthodoxy then moves to try, with admitted ambivalence, to classify the only acceptable form of war. Simply put, because of pastoral necessity, war will sometimes occur—albeit, as a last resort, after the exhaustion of all diplomatic efforts by the state. That condition is when the defenseless, the weak, or vulnerable believers are threatened: then, Orthodoxy admits that the state may wage one type of war and one type only—that is, the defensive war. And, finally, Orthodox theology offers a conceptual tool for specifying the only acceptable goal of war—namely, repentance, or *metanoia*.

It was during the millennium-long age of the Byzantine Empire that the conceptual architecture of Orthodox thought on war was clarified. Likewise, it was Byzantine theologians and statesmen who deployed that conceptual architecture to develop a sophisticated set of operational parameters, metrics, and methods for waging the defensive war.

HOLY WAR AND HOLY PEACE IN BYZANTIUM

One of the central problems affecting even some of the most rigorous scholarship on Byzantium and war is a recent trend toward ahistorical writing. Despite new and impressive advances in this field, some historians who have examined Byzantine attitudes toward war have approached their subject from a position that reflects a modernist materialist perspective, not accurately accounting for the intellectual, philosophical, and theological content and context of the Byzantine worldview and experience. Though recognizing the centrality and omnipresence of Orthodox Christianity in Byzantine society, such scholars have tended to detach and compartmentalize the Byzantine Empire's chief state instrument of power, the military, in ways that ignore, minimize, or misunderstand the role of religion in imperial war-making.[15] Some of this interpretive orientation reflects the natural outgrowth of research which has focused on the functional and technical aspects of Byzantine warfare, a scholarly direction promoted, not surprisingly, by the availability of corresponding thematic source materials.[16]

Inasmuch as conceptual issues have entered into these studies on Byzantium and war, the emphasis is squarely on the operational dimensions of strategic theory and practice.[17] Conversely, the theoretical underpinnings informed by Orthodox Christianity that critically shaped Byzantine attitudes toward war are sometimes sidestepped or misunderstood. Indeed, rather than demonstrating historical awareness of how Orthodoxy's ethical vision was applied to war in Byzantium—in the same sense that such a universal ontology informed the perceptions of every other interest and activity of the imperial state—some studies reveal an analytical approach influenced by Western preconceptions. Many of these works emphasize the role of religion, in general, and Orthodoxy, in particular, as an ideological structure that served the twin political purposes of legitimizing the Christian Roman Empire and, by extension, rationalizing and justifying war fought in the interests of the imperial state. Such views warrant serious examination, but by predicating their arguments on flawed interpretations of the historical evidence they contribute to the West's long and complex intellectual tradition of misunderstanding Byzantium, in general, and Orthodox attitudes toward war, in particular.[18]

The acute limitations and consequent problems stemming from an ahistorical and Western interposition on Orthodoxy and war in Byzantium are made clear in particular by the way the issue of holy war, a chronic Western religious and secular preoccupation, has been debated by Byzantinists. The twentieth century's most influential and widely revered Byzantine historian, Steven Runciman, identified a comparative Eastern-Western Christian dichotomy in attitudes toward war, which has, since the publication in the 1950s of his magisterial studies on the Crusades, more or less defined the parameters of the historiographical discussion on Byzantine and Orthodox sensibilities on war.[19] Runciman concisely juxtaposed the inherent philosophical ambivalence and complex working posture toward war found in the Orthodox East with the utilitarian views and uses of war in the Latin West. He effectively encapsulated Orthodox Byzantium's moral dilemma and responses by noting:

> The Christian citizen has a fundamental problem to face: is he entitled to fight for his country? His is a religion of peace; and war means slaughter and destruction. The earlier Christian Fathers had no doubts. To them a war was wholesale murder. But when the Empire became the Christian Empire, ought not its citizens to be ready to take up arms for its welfare? The Eastern Church thought not. Its great canonist, Saint Basil, while he realized that the soldier must obey orders, yet maintained that anyone guilty of killing in war should refrain for three years from taking communion as a sign of repentance. This counsel was too strict. The Byzantine soldier was not treated as a murderer. But his profession brought him no glamour. Death in battle was not considered glorious; and death in battle against the infidel was not martyrdom; the martyr died armed only with his faith. . . . Indeed, the Byzantine always preferred peaceful methods, as being morally superior and usually materially cheaper, even if they involved tortuous diplomacy and the payment of money. War was a last resort, almost a confession of failure.[20]

The medieval West's praise for aggressive war and cultural esteem for military prowess stands in stark contrast to the Byzantines' meditations on defensive war and peace. Runciman argued:

To Westerners brought up to admire martial valor, the Byzantine desire to avoid bloodshed seemed cowardly and sly. The Western theologians were less strict. Saint Augustine held that wars might be waged at the command of God; and the military society that had emerged in the West out of the barbarian invasions inevitably sought to justify its habitual pastime. The code of chivalry that was developing gave prestige to the military hero; and the pacifist acquired a disrepute from which he has never recovered. The Church could only try to divert this military energy into paths that were to its advantage. A war in the interests of the Church became a holy war, permissible and even desirable. Pope Leo IV in the mid-ninth century declared that anyone dying in battle for the Church would win a heavenly reward. Pope John VIII a few years later ranked soldiers dying in a holy war as martyrs whose sins would be forgiven.[21]

As Runciman makes clear, the various Western crusades—wars of annihilation against Muslims and Jews in Spain and Christian heretic populations in the Latin West, as well as wars of conquest against Orthodox "schismatics" in the Greek and Slavic East and against Muslims in the Holy Land—were holy wars invoked and blessed by the papacy. Indeed, "the idea of a holy war directed by the Papacy was very attractive to the great reforming pontiffs of the mid-eleventh century. The Papacy . . . was anxious to establish its authority over the whole Church and its independence from all lay control and, indeed, its superiority over all potentates."[22] Accordingly, in the West, holy war was put to use by Rome to mobilize large-scale military campaigns aimed at promoting the papacy's political ambitions and ecclesiastical pretensions.[23] The fact that such holy wars ennobled Western secular elites' bloodlust and adventurism only added to their allure, popularity, and ferocity.[24]

Runciman's understanding of attitudes toward war in Byzantium was equally clear. The role of the Byzantine emperor as God's viceroy made him responsible for the welfare and security of Christians, which sometimes, always regrettably, required him to lead wars of defense, but all wars, even those fought to protect the empire's people, were tragic and baneful. In summation, the concept of holy war, even the idea of glory in war, was completely alien to the thinking of Orthodox Christians in the Byzantine Empire.

Although Runciman's views on this subject continue to be reflected in the dominant currents in Byzantine studies, especially in the works of notable Byzantine military historians such as George Dennis,[25] challenges to this oppositional East-West dyad on holy war within medieval Christianity have become more common among some historians during the last two decades. The most thought-provoking revisionist scholarship on this issue is associated with the research of historian Tia Kolbaba, who posits that the consensus on holy war in the field's secondary literature conflicts with her reading of the primary sources.[26] Although Kolbaba concedes that the Byzantines did not fight crusades, she insists that they "were familiar with the idea of God commanding a war against the infidel and promising his soldiers rewards in the hereafter. They shared these ideas with western Christians."[27] In short, Kolbaba constructs an argument purporting the supposed acceptance and routine prosecution of holy war by the Byzantine Empire. Despite its historiographical importance, Kolbaba's interpretation is marred by serious methodological deficiencies, including a lack of sensitivity to contextualized rhetoric and an inordinate reliance on one seriously flawed Greek-language publication to support her position.[28]

The Byzantines, who carefully studied the world around them, were of course well aware of the invocation of "holy war" by some of their neighbors to justify violent actions. Indeed, the Byzantines had to often defend themselves against such inventions in the forms of expansionist Islam's jihad and the Latin West's aggressive holy wars, the Crusades.[29] Nonetheless, the Byzantines' awareness of such concepts is not synonymous with their adoption of such ideas. Kolbaba's conclusion that the Byzantines possessed an outlook similar to that of Catholic crusaders, one that folded the sacred into the profane to produce an oxymoronic view of war as holy, is ultimately based on both a parsed use of the historical record and a fundamentally ahistorical interpretation of Byzantine thought on war.

The argument that the Byzantines were proponents of holy war stems from a misunderstanding of the Byzantines' own ambiguities on war. In Kolbaba's view, the tensions between Christian pacifism and imperial war-making were not a function of a complex moral dilemma and attendant philosophical uncertainty between the two—a theological ideal and a pastoral reality, as pointed out earlier in this study—but the result of "ideological" inconsistencies between an "official position" of the church, on the one hand, and the actual practices and values of the Byzantine church, state, army, and society, on the other.[30]

The proposition that, in essence, Byzantium engaged in a kind of collective self-deception—officially condemning all war while unofficially prosecuting de facto holy wars—ignores entirely the moral and ideational principles that functioned as the foundations for Byzantine governance and the legitimate actions of the state. Indicative of this ahistorical approach, Kolbaba at no point in her work explores the crucial role of Orthodox Christianity in her discussion on holy war in the Byzantine Empire. The mistaken assertion that the Byzantines did not reconcile the "contradictions" on war that confronted them should not be interpreted as a sign that genuine tensions never existed or that they were merely the result of an insincere public display of obligatory church posturing contradicted by actual religious and political values and actions. Indeed, the profound existential nature of this weighty issue for the Byzantines should not be underestimated any more than it should be ignored or simplified.

What is overlooked in such scholarship is that the apparent ambiguity of the Orthodox, and hence Byzantine, perspective on war consciously reflected the dynamics of Orthodox canon law. Indeed, the conceptual source and operational practice for understanding Byzantine attitudes and approaches to war is to be found in the Orthodox principle of *oikonomia*.[31] As one of the ways of observing canon law, oikonomia involves the meditative and compassionate resolution of ecclesiastical and moral questions in accord with the spirit of God's love of humankind, wisdom, and will for the salvation of the person. Consequently, oikonomia, as a sanctified path for navigating problems and contradictions in an imperfect world, is not a mechanism for granting exceptions to dogmatic maxims, but the aim and goal of those rules themselves. By situating the constancy of oikonomia relative to war, Orthodox theologian Philip LeMasters posits:

> In Orthodox moral theology, one simply does not find theoretical justification for war as a good endeavor, let alone pronouncements that war is holy. Orthodoxy does not require nonviolence or pacifism

as essential characteristics of the Christian life; neither, however, does it sacralize war. Instead, the church merely tolerates war as a sometimes tragically necessary or unavoidable endeavor. . . . The peace of Christ—and the non-resistant, forgiving love by which Christ brought salvation to the world—as we know it inevitably relies on imperfect arrangements of political, social, economic, and military power, which both reflect and contribute to the brokenness of human souls and communities. . . . The church does not simply condemn these realities or ask Christians to pretend that they do not live in the world as we know it. Instead, Orthodoxy calls everyone to work toward peace, reconciliation and justice for their neighbors. When doing so requires involvement in warfare, the taking of human life, or other endeavors that damage the soul, the church provides spiritual therapy for healing and guidance for growth in holiness.[32]

The principle of oikonomia provided the Byzantines with both a moral and practical architecture to produce tolerable, albeit always imperfect, responses to war. Rather than disguising or rationalizing contradictions, this approach reflected both the gravity and moral consistency that actually characterized the Byzantines' normative attitudes.

In fairness to Kolbaba and other Byzantinists who share her views, there is a tendency among most modern scholars—historians and theologians alike—to oversimplify the early church's position on war. This dominant perspective posits that the church ruptured itself from its own three-century-long pacifist ideology in order to enter into a power-sharing relationship with the imperial state, an ideological revolution in church-state relations initiated by the Christian-convert emperor Constantine in the first half of the fourth century and concretized under Emperor Theodosius in the second half of the same century.[33] According to this popular narrative, when the church merged its interests with those of the state in the so-called Constantinian fall, the former's supposedly unqualified pacifism was betrayed in favor of political opportunism, resulting in the morally corrupting willingness of hierarchs to lend approval to wars waged to protect imperial and hence, after Constantine, church power.

Despite this generally unchallenged view of a cynical and rapid transformation of the early peace-loving church, a more nuanced approach reveals that early Christianity's moral engagement with the state was more complex and the development of its position on war was more gradual than is typically assumed. The New Testament, for example, offers no uniform guidance on the morality of soldiering, the basic human instrument for warring. While Christ warned his followers that "those who take up the sword are destroyed by the sword" (Matt. 26:52; our translation), John the Baptist, who told Roman soldiers to end their oppression of civilians, did not demand that they abandon their army careers or not uphold their military duty to defend the empire's defenseless people (Luke 3:14). Christ himself did not encourage soldiers to leave the army. Indeed, in another Gospel story, Christ held up a Roman centurion as an inspiring example of goodness and faith (Luke 7:9).[34]

Like the New Testament, the immediate postapostolic writings did not provide a simple, fundamentalist view of war.[35] Although many early Christian authors decried military service and all forms of violence, others maintained that good Christians, especially those already in military service at the time of their conversion, could play a role in the defense of the empire, whose very security and stability were crucial to the preservation of God's newly chosen people and the furtherance of their faith. Hence, perhaps not surprisingly, abundant textual and archaeological evidence demonstrates that a substantial number of Christian soldiers did, in fact, serve in the Roman army before the time of Constantine, that Roman military leadership not only tolerated but seems to have encouraged Christian worship in some areas, and that the Christian church did not shun or denounce its communicants who served and fought in the armed forces.[36]

The work of historian Timothy Miller points to a process of gradual and subtle formulation of Byzantine thought on war that paralleled remarkably the simultaneously steady and deliberative means, rather than some instantaneous manifestation of an absolute position, by which Christian theology, and Christology in particular, developed. Moreover, Miller reminds us that it was the Roman state far more than the church that was influenced and ultimately changed by Constantine's confederation of the two to produce the great transformation of the Roman Empire in the fourth century.[37] On the church's decisive influence in shaping the personality and values of the Byzantine state, Miller notes:

Byzantine Christian concepts regarding warfare and the proper role of the state in the governance of human society flowed directly from the pre-Constantinian tradition. Moreover, the Eastern government readily responded to the spiritual guidance of the church leaders in shaping its goals and adjusting its practices. Thus, the emperors claimed to reign in the name of Christ and considered it their duty to strive for the peace God had ordained for human beings. In many ways the Byzantine state used the political concepts worked out by early Christian and patristic thinkers as a blueprint for constructing what East Roman intellectuals considered the New Jerusalem.[38]

Furthermore, Miller makes it clear that Byzantine attitudes toward war did not represent an aberration from the historic views of the early church. Instead, such originally heuristic and heterodox, rather than definitive, views evolved in a continuous Christian environment to gradually become established "orthodox" positions. Consequently, it was in the Byzantine Empire, more than the Latin West—whose pre-Constantinian continuity with the early church was broken by the barbarian invasions— that this process, firmly rooted in consistency with the early church, was completed.

Miller concisely summarizes the inseparable connection of a Byzantine hermeneutic on war to the early church:

> In view of the direct link between later Byzantine civilization and the spiritual and secular traditions of the post-apostolic and patristic period of Christian history, it seems only natural to suggest that Byzantine opinions on the morality of warfare would shed additional light on the views held by earlier generations of Christians and show how certain seminal ideas evolved into more sophisticated theories concerning the morality of armed conflict. It is a fallacy of modern Western scholars to see Augustine of Hippo as the only [early] Christian intellectual to develop a theological framework for addressing the question of warfare in a systematic fashion.[39]

In short, despite the dominant Western historiographical narrative, the bridging of church and state in Byzantium did not produce a rupture in the church's supposedly well- and long-established views on war. Instead, as the development of a more cogent Christian theology would benefit from the new relationship between church and state, the same creative and empowering structure would contribute similarly to the maturation of a coherent approach to war in Byzantium. The failure to recognize and comprehend the Byzantines' subtle development of a lucid, rational system of thought on war rests with modernist scholars and not the Byzantines, who, after all, created, understood, and applied their own ideas about war for their very survival. Indeed, "the Byzantine Empire, more than most other societies, depended for its very existence on successfully waging war."[40]

Those scholars who claim the presence of a holy war ideology in Byzantium give little attention to the philosophy of just war, often conflating the two or taking for granted that the existence of one assumes the existence of the other, if any distinction at all is made between the two concepts. Some historians dismiss the holy war position but argue that the Byzantines fought what they themselves understood as just wars, in the sense that they were morally consistent with the accepted principle of self-defense, but did not develop a just war ideology such as that articulated by Augustine, which would later be marshaled as a rationale for wars of aggression by Western Christians.[41] Finally, another group of scholars, made up primarily of theologians and philosophers employing—implicitly, if not explicitly—Reinhold Niebuhr's distinction between "perfect" and "proximate" justice (the latter compromised by fallen reality), posit that the Byzantines viewed their wars as neither holy nor just, but unavoidable, *justifiable* in the face of invasion and mass murder but not actually *just*.[42] This distinction between justifiable and just wars is consistent with the Byzantines' agile Orthodox intellectual perspective.[43]

The Byzantines' military strategies, both theoretically and in practice, can illuminate their perspectives on the morality of war. Out of sheer necessity, the Byzantine Empire produced one of the world's most successful defense forces. During most of its long history, the Byzantine army was characterized by a remarkable resilience, recovering from many and often serious defeats to ultimately triumph and reassert itself century after century over countless adversaries. Indeed, the Byzantine army won incredibly complicated campaigns while almost constantly forced to fight several larger enemies simultaneously on multiple fronts. Because the Byzantines were continually beset by enemies from east, north, and sometimes west, it would have been easy for them to fall into a militaristic mentality. However, their moral foundation prevented such a drift. Unlike the much more famous, revered forces of Alexander, Hannibal, Genghis Khan, Frederick, or Napoleon—whose armies and high-flying campaigns were short-lived expressions of the individual military geniuses of their respective leaders—the sustained, many-centuries-long defense of Byzantium was the result of collective, continuously expanding knowledge, a military science, based on consistent strategic thinking and military doctrine acquired and studied across generations. In short, the Byzantines drew from the preceding centuries of Greek, Roman, and Near Eastern warfare, adapted such lessons to the changing conditions of war in Late Antiquity and the Middle Ages, and systematically applied their store of military knowledge through the prism of an Orthodox Christian view of war to produce one of the most effective fighting forces in history.[44]

Because the Byzantines did not romanticize fighting and approached warfare as a technical skill that required study and knowledge, a corresponding corpus of literature, largely in the form of military manuals known collectively as *strategika*, was written by them to help educate and train their officers.[45] Obviously, the military was regarded as crucial to the survival of society. Yet, despite the importance of generalship and soldiering, the military profession, like war itself, was not considered a noble endeavor.[46] Indeed, the sixth-century author of one of these military studies described war as the worst of all evils.[47] Conversely, the medieval Christian West's pervasive cult of chivalry elevated violence in war to a celebrated and noble act of honor—identifying it with delight and valor—and, when the opportunities for actual killing were limited, transformed it into sport for the demonstration of prowess.[48]

Although the military literature produced by the Byzantines is generally classified as a practical occupational genre—composed of manuals on strategy, battle tactics, logistics, and other operational issues intended for use by officers—these works are also valuable for scholars interested in the Byzantines' holistic approach to war. Many of the authors of these works ruminate on the morality of war, offering rich primary sources for understanding the Byzantines' attitudes toward war in historical context and from an experiential perspective.

It is instructive that these works reveal a near-uniform outlook. For the Byzantines, battle was only one aspect of war, and, indeed, was considered the least desirable aspect and one to be avoided whenever possible. War is abhorrent and is to be undertaken only when all other means of defense have been exhausted. In addition to moral and religious influences, the perspective of the empire's military establishment on war was shaped by a solemn, practical understanding of the inherent unpredictability of war. Formalizing this general view into the military principle and strategy of economy of force, the Byzantine army at war always favored maneuver and deception over battle.[49]

The idea of holy war is never mentioned or discussed in these works. This is not surprising, for the concept of holy war was incompatible with the Byzantines' moral and intellectual architecture. The Byzantines were well aware of the idea of holy war among foreign, barbarous peoples as well as among their own pre-Christian cultural ancestors, but such thought had no place in Byzantine civilization and Orthodox belief. It is significant and revealing that the Byzantines never developed a lexicon for "holy war." Rather, they applied the Greek term for holy war— ἱερὸς πόλεμος—only to their historical patrimony, limiting it to a historiographical usage to identify the three "sacred" Greek internecine wars fought for control of the sacred oracle of Apollo at Delphi in antiquity. The proposition that the literate, sophisticated culture of Byzantium would champion a distinct ideology of holy war without the benefit of corresponding language, concepts, or any writings to establish and communicate such a view is incredible.[50]

Nor are we limited to an argument *ab silentio* regarding the Byzantines' lack of an ideology of holy war. Illustrative of the enormous differences between Eastern and Western Christianity on this issue is an incident involving the emperor Nikephoros II Phokas (r. 963–69), a former general who had, before ascending the throne, recaptured the island of Crete from the Muslim Arabs. A pious man who wished to honor the soldiers and sailors slain under his command, he attempted to have the church "establish a law that those who fell during wars be honored equally with the holy martyrs, and be celebrated with hymns and feast days."

Instead, he was severely admonished by the church's hierarchy for impiety and subjected to a lengthy moral corrective based on patristic and scriptural sources.[51]

The *strategikon* written by Emperor Leo VI at the beginning of the tenth century, *The Taktika of Leo VI*, exemplifies the Byzantine approach to war. In the prologue to his widely read manual, Leo VI states:

> Honored by the image and word of God, all men ought to embrace peace and love for one another instead of taking up murderous weapons in their hands to use against their own people. But since the devil, the killer of men from the beginning, the enemy of our race, has made use of sin to bring men to the point of waging war against their own kind, it becomes entirely necessary for men to wage war. . . . With everyone embracing his own safety, peace will be cherished by all and will become a way of life.[52]

Leo expresses the Byzantine view that human beings—all of whom are created in the image of God according to Genesis 1:26–27—are by nature peaceful, and that the natural order of peace is disrupted by evil. The devil, who delights in the destruction of humanity, leads men to violence against each other through the greatest work of evil—war. In his reflection on Leo's writing, Timothy Miller underscores the conscious balance between acceptable self-preservation, on the one hand, and moral restraint in warfare, on the other hand, to reveal the Byzantines' approach to war, a theologically driven mind-set which limited Orthodox Christians and their empire to fight only defensive wars:

> A Christian emperor could legitimately undertake a war against those who had fallen under the spell of the evil one and had been incited to invade imperial territory. With God's blessing the emperor and his troops repelled such invaders. If the barbarians remained within their own territories, however, it was not right to begin an offensive war against them. A good emperor was to avoid not only spilling the blood of Christian subjects, but also uselessly shedding the blood of barbarians.[53]

Leo's views, repeated by numerous other Byzantine authors, were not meaningless platitudes. The emperor Constantine V, for example, a highly successful military leader, characterized as "noble" his campaign against the Bulgars in 772–73 because no soldiers perished in the operation.[54] The Byzantines' revulsion for war and bloodletting was not an "official" affectation—it was genuine and determined by their society's religious and moral values. Inseparable from Orthodoxy, Byzantine thought held that war was evil and its impact on *all* people—aggressors and defenders, guilty and innocent—was tragic and dehumanizing. For the Byzantines, the notion that war could be just or holy was anathema, inconceivable. Consequently, for the Orthodox Byzantines, unlike Arab and Turkish Muslim *gazi* warriors or Catholic crusaders, wars were not fought to destroy other faiths, expand the power of some secular or religious leader, or plunder foreign treasure—wars were fought out of necessity when diplomacy failed to preserve peace. In the final analysis, war in the view of Byzantine society could only be justified when in accordance with Orthodoxy and the continued existence of the empire.[55]

Inferential arguments that seek to identify the presence of holy war in Byzantium face considerable resistance from Byzantinists who have subjected such assertions to systematic analysis. Invariably, historians who support the position of holy war in Byzantium begin their discussions by questioning the terms involved in the debate, implying that there is no scholarly agreement on a comprehensive definition of holy war. This claim, however, ignores the fact that there is a broad historiographical consensus on at least the fundamental criteria necessary for the categorization of a conflict as a holy war. The leading authority on this issue as it relates to Byzantium, George Dennis, identifies three essential criteria in defining holy war. First, a holy war must be promulgated by a recognized religious authority, such as an Islamic caliph or a Catholic pope. Second, the objective of a holy war must be religious, such as the capture of sacred sites or the forced expansion of a religion. Third, the religious authority responsible for promulgating the holy war also promises a spiritual reward, such as an absolution of sins or a declaration of martyrdom for warriors, which assures them of entry into paradise. None of these ideas or practices, which resonated deeply throughout jihad and the Western Crusades, existed in Byzantium or could be found anywhere in Orthodox thought.[56] One other basic and crucial feature defining a holy war, which Dennis surprisingly overlooks, and which also was not present in Byzantium, is the clear conviction and collective belief among those waging war that they are, indeed, fighting a holy war.

The Byzantines assigned no holy, romantic, or glorious qualities to the human carnage, mayhem, and destruction that accompanied armed conflict. War was universally understood by the Byzantines as tragic and evil, especially by the soldiers most actively involved in fighting and killing. Indeed, this was a society in which retiring Orthodox soldiers frequently took up the monastic life as a means to recover spiritual well-being and work toward the remission of their sins, a life of *metanoia* (repentance) after war. War, when prosecuted, was an unavoidable calamity, fought as a last resort. But when war was undertaken, Byzantine society knew what it was defending and why.

Yet, despite its self-righteous convictions and the fact that the Byzantine Empire found itself almost constantly at war, it was not a warlike society. The moral certainties of the Byzantine ideology of war and peace—firmly rooted in Eastern Christianity's continuity with the early church and attendant Orthodox hermeneutic on armed conflict—bear much of the credit for this distinctive model of response to war that aimed to balance the physical demands of protecting the defenseless with the spiritual ideal of, and belief in, the natural condition of peace.[57] If in medieval Western Europe the problem of reconciling the rupture of the early Christian idea of peace with harsh political reality led to the development of the concepts of just war and holy war, Byzantium developed no such concepts because it experienced no such rupture. The elaboration of the idea that the empire sought peace but was also morally obligated to defend its people against aggression represented neither a philosophical contradiction nor a theological compromise as much as it marked a rational and ethical achievement in Byzantine meditation on war, an Orthodox innovation which offers possibilities for a different moral perspective on the problem of war and the preservation of peace in the present.[58]

Now, WHAT DOES ALL OF THIS MEAN for Orthodoxy and its value and innovative relevance for addressing the problem of war in our time? Even if we make a plausible argument about a distinctively Orthodox hermeneutic of war and peace, is this necessarily innovative, and, most urgently, does Orthodoxy offer anything original, new, or innovative in how scholar-practitioners can conceptualize and operationalize the problematic of war? And, most specifically, can a religiously grounded theory of war developed almost two millennia ago help to bring peace to the international order of today, a dramatically different cultural, political, and social context? Put differently, can we say that Byzantine Orthodox thought is a possible source of innovation for resolving the tensions between the (legal-ethical) human rights imperatives and (legal-institutional) principles of nonintervention and territoriality that vex the Westphalian world order?[59] Although in need of further amplification for a more robust response to these questions, our tentative answers are yes.

We think there is no question about the conceptual distinctiveness of Orthodoxy—its eschatological, eucharistic, and *metanoic* features. These lead in turn to what is a theological notion—unresolvable tragic tension—that is the window into the current crux of the matter (nonintervention versus intervention). They also point to the notion of defensive war and linkage to a *metanoic* requirement, but this is where a lot of work remains to be done and critical questions require further study in order to realize the innovative potential of the Orthodox Byzantine tradition.[60] How, for example, would we define defensive war? Who is to be defended when we can no longer talk about a Christian state or even an Orthodox commonwealth? And how is the *metanoic* ideal applied to the state itself—chaplaincy, war crimes tribunals, international human rights, and religious freedom law?[61] Can we consider these structures as institutional forms of *metanoia*?

This unresolvable tension and the limit of defensive war are keys to understanding the historicity of the problem of nonintervention for purposes of order of the state system versus intervention for the ethical imperative of protecting the weak and vulnerable. Here, perhaps, the Byzantine *strategika* offer a window into operational principles of defensive war and *metanoic* imperative.

All of this adds up to a very different notion of war—war is evil, and there are conventions (the Geneva Conventions, the US Army Field Manual, international human rights architectures, and the ICC) that express this view. What Orthodoxy can do—if it has some innovative potential—to realize this idea is to develop it more fully. In this sense, Orthodox Christian thought helps to historicize the relationship between religion and state in a way that offers a provocative history of the future.[62] Orthodoxy's theologically grounded alternative of defensive war, as developed and codified in the Byzantine period, deserves evaluation for its nuanced exegesis of the causes, conditions, mechanisms, and goals of war and peace.

NOTES

An earlier version of this paper was presented by Elizabeth H. Prodromou at the Interdisciplinary Symposium on Orthodoxy and Innovation in the Greek-Speaking World from Byzantium to the 21st Century, Copenhagen, June 2009.

1. From the Trine Stauning Willert prospectus appearing in "Preliminary Programme Version," June 1, 2009, *Interdisciplinary Symposium on Orthodoxy and Innovation in the Greek-Speaking World from Byzantium to the 21st Century*.

2. The Treaty of Augsburg was signed in 1555 between the Holy Roman Emperor Charles V and the alliance of Lutheran princes known as the Schmalkaldic League. Based on the compromise of *"cuius regio, eius religio"* ("whose realm, his religion," or "in the prince's land, the prince's religion"), the mapping of the division of Western Christendom onto the emergent state allowed the German princes to select either Roman Catholicism or Lutheran Protestantism as the official religion within their territories. In short, a region's ruler determined the religion of his people. The Peace of Westphalia was brokered with the 1648 signing of two treaties that ended the ongoing wars within Western Christianity, ending the Thirty Years' War in the Holy Roman Empire (the German lands) and the Eighty Years' War between Spain and the Republic of the Seven United Netherlands. The peace treaties deepened the territorialization of Western Christianity begun at the Treaty of Augsburg by defining the legal, territorial, and military dimensions of state sovereignty. For definitive treatments of the religious dimensions of the emergence of the state within the context of Western Christianity, see Dan Philpott, *Revolutions in Sovereignty: How Ideas Shaped Modern International Relations* (Princeton: Princeton University Press, 2001); Philpott, "The Religious Roots of Modern International Relations," *World Politics* 52 (January 2000): 206–45.

3. Alfred Stepan, "Religion, Democracy, and the 'Twin Tolerations,'" in *Journal of Democracy* 11, no. 4 (October 2000): 37–57.

4. See Jarret M. Brachman and William F. McCants, "Stealing Al Qaeda's Playbook," *Studies in Conflict and Terrorism* 29, no. 4 (2006): 309–21.

5. See JustWarTheory.com, http://www.justwartheory.com.

6. A growing, nuanced, interdisciplinary literature explains and critiques the hegemony of the epistemic categories of secularization theory. Representative treatments include José Casanova, *Public Religions in the Modern World* (Chicago: University of Chicago Press, 1994); Linda Woodhead, ed., *Peter Berger and the Study of Religion* (New York: Routledge, 2001). For two useful synopses by Elizabeth Shakman Hurd, see *Comparative Secularisms in a Global Age* (New York: Palgrave Macmillan, 2010); Shakman Hurd, *The Politics of Secularism in International Relations* (Princeton: Princeton University Press, 2008).

7. For cogent and compelling treatments of the debates on America's role as a post–Cold War hegemon using imperialist and militarist behaviors, see Andrew J. Bacevich's companion works, *American Empire: The Realities and Consequences of U.S. Diplomacy* (Cambridge, MA: Harvard University Press, 2004); *The New American Militarism: How Americans Are Seduced by War* (New York: Oxford University Press, 2006).

8. For example, see J. Daryl Charles, *Between Pacifism and Jihad: Just War and Christian Tradition* (Downers Grove, IL: InterVarsity Press, 2005).

9. John A. McGuckin, "Nonviolence and Peace Traditions in Early and Eastern Christianity," in *Religion, Terrorism and Globalization: Nonviolence; A New Agenda*, ed. K. K. Kuriakose (New York: Nova Science Publishers, 2006), 192.

10. See two articles by Alexander F. C. Webster, "Justifiable War as a 'Lesser Good' in Eastern Orthodox Moral Tradition," *St. Vladimir's Theological Quarterly* 47, no. 1 (2003): 3–57; "Just War and Holy War: Two Case Studies in Comparative Christian Ethics," *Christian Scholar's Review* 15, no. 4 (1986): 343–71. The most extensive articulation of Webster's arguments is found in Alexander F. C. Webster and Darrell Cole, *The Virtue of War: Reclaiming the Classical Christian Traditions East and West* (Salisbury, MA: Regina Orthodox Press, 2004).

11. Webster, "Justifiable War," 51.

12. See George Dragas, "Justice and Peace in the Orthodox Tradition," in *Justice, Peace and the Integrity of Creation: Insights from Orthodoxy*, ed. Gennadios Limouris (Geneva: WCC Publications, 1990), 40–44; Vassilios Giultsis, "An Ethical Approach to Justice and Peace," in Limouris, *Justice, Peace*, 56–69. For an emblematic treatment from the Orthodox Peace Fellowship, see Jim Forest, "Justifiable War: Response #2," *St. Vladimir's Theological Quarterly* 47, no. 1 (2003): 65–67. Noting its official appellation, the Orthodox Peace Fellowship (OPF) of the Protection of the Mother of God is an international, nonpartisan,

pan-Orthodox organization dedicated to the active pursuit of peace as understood and taught from an Orthodox Christian perspective. Leading Orthodox intellectuals associated with the OPF include Archbishop Anastasios (Yannoulatos) of Albania, Bishop Kallistos (Ware) of Diokleia, Rev. Fr. Anthony Coniaris, the late Rev. Dr. Thomas Hopko, the late Jaroslav Pelikan, and Albert Raboteau. In addition to Forest's response to Webster, several other critiques also appear in the 2003 *St. Vladimir's Theological Quarterly* special issue dedicated to the question "Justifiable war?" See the following in that issue: John Breck, "'Justifiable War': Lesser Good or Lesser Evil?," 97–109; Nikolas K. Gvosdev, "War and the Orthodox Statesman," 69–75; Philip LeMasters, "Justifiable War: Response #4," 77–82; David Pratt, "Dual Trajectories and Divided Rationales: A Reply to Alexander Webster on Justifiable War," 83–95; Joseph Woodill, "Justifiable War: Response #1," 59–64. For a comparative source which demonstrates the considerable extent to which Webster's stance reflects the most recent post-9/11 incarnations of the Western just war tradition, see Daniel M. Bell Jr., *Just War as Christian Discipleship: Recentering the Tradition in the Church Rather than the State* (Grand Rapids: Brazos Press, 2009).

13. Presumably, this is a reference to Orthodox Christians living in the West. See David B. Hart, "Ecumenical Councils of War," *Touchstone: A Journal of Mere Christianity* 17, no. 9 (November 2004): 40–43. Hart's publication is a review essay of Webster and Cole, *Virtue of War.*

14. See Maria Todorova's magisterial historical work on Balkanism, *Imagining the Balkans,* updated ed. (Oxford: Oxford University Press, 2009). There is a rich literature in political science and anthropology that works from and complements the Todorova perspective; for examples, see Milica Bakic Hayden, "What's So Byzantine about the Balkans?," in *Balkan as Metaphor: Between Globalization and Fragmentation,* ed. Dusan I. Bjelic and Obrad Savic (Cambridge, MA: MIT Press, 2002), 61–78; Philpott, "Religious Roots," 206–45; Elizabeth H. Prodromou, "Paradigms, Power and Identity: Rediscovering Religion and Regionalizing Europe," *European Journal of Political Research* 30, no. 2 (September 1996): 125–54.

15. A detailed organizational and administrative examination of the Byzantine military, which, nonetheless, ignores entirely the role of religion in the life, thought, and actions of the imperial forces, is found in Warren Treadgold, *Byzantium and Its Army, 284–1081* (Stanford: Stanford University Press, 1995). Conversely, for a highly informative collection of studies that take into account the important links between Orthodoxy and the Byzantine military, see Walter E. Kaegi, *Army, Society, and Religion in Byzantium* (London: Variorum Reprints, 1982).

16. A thorough review of the major currents in Byzantine military studies appears in the introduction to John Haldon, ed., *Byzantine Warfare* (Aldershot: Ashgate, 2007).

17. For a brilliant example of scholarship on the coordination of Byzantine military strategy with state intelligence and diplomacy, see Edward N. Luttwak, *The Grand Strategy of the Byzantine Empire* (Cambridge, MA: Belknap Press of Harvard University Press, 2009). An important study of the theoretical foundations of Byzantine strategic thought is found in George T. Dennis, "Some Reflections on Byzantine Military Theory," in *John K. Zender: A Festschrift*, ed. R. S. Calinger and Thomas R. West (Indianapolis: Perspective Press, 2007). A brief but invaluable distillation appears in the booklet by Walter E. Kaegi, *Some Thoughts on Byzantine Military Strategy* (Brookline, MA: Hellenic College Press, 1983). For research on a diverse set of topics involving Byzantine diplomacy, see Jonathan Shepard and Simon Franklin, eds., *Byzantine Diplomacy: Papers of the Twenty-Fourth Spring Symposium of Byzantine Studies, Cambridge, March 1990* (Aldershot: Variorum, 1992).

18. The problem of Western intellectual perception and historical ignorance of, and subsequent prejudice against, Byzantine civilization is meticulously analyzed in Dimiter G. Angelov, "Byzantinism: The Imaginary and Real Heritage of Byzantium in Southeastern Europe," in *New Approaches to Balkan Studies*, ed. Dimitris Keridis, Ellen Elias-Bursac, and Nicholas Yatromanolakis (Dulles, VA: Brassey's, 2003), 2–21.

19. See Steven Runciman, *A History of the Crusades*, vols. 1–3 (Cambridge: Cambridge University Press, 1951–54). Runciman's successful publications popularized awareness of Byzantium more than the works of any other twentieth-century historian. Although he was instrumental in setting the frontiers for the discussion of war in Byzantium, the beginnings of this scholarly dispute actually preceded Runciman's defining involvement in the debate.

20. Steven Runciman, *The First Crusade* (Cambridge: Cambridge University Press, 1951; repr., 2005), 33.

21. Ibid., 33–34.

22. Ibid., 36.

23. On this general subject, see Rebecca Rist, *The Papacy and Crusading in Europe, 1198–1245* (London: Continuum, 2009). The Fourth Crusade, culminating in the sacking of Constantinople and dismemberment of the Byzantine Empire by Latin forces in 1204, is widely viewed as more crucial than the ecclesiastical schism of 1054 in producing the final rupture between Eastern and Western Christendom. Moreover, the Fourth Crusade was not the only example of Western Christians making war against Eastern Christians and using

the schism as justification to attack and oppress Orthodox populations. Before the events of 1204, Orthodox Christians had already endured a more-than-century-long wave of multiple invasions and violence from Catholic Normans against Byzantine Southern Italy and the Balkans, as well as from Catholic Germans and Swedes against Russia. In contrast, the complete absence of any such activity by the Byzantines against Western Christian territories underscores the profound dichotomy between the West and Byzantium in their respective attitudes toward war. For information on papal plans against Orthodox Christians in the Byzantine territories occupied by Latin crusaders and the systematic preaching of anti-Greek crusading indulgences in the thirteenth century, consult Maureen Purcell, *Papal Crusading Policy, 1244–1291: The Chief Instruments of Papal Crusading Policy and Crusade to the Holy Land from the Final Loss of Jerusalem to the Fall of Acre, 1244–1291* (Leiden: Brill, 1975), 86–88. The protracted and brutal Catholic crusades against Orthodox Christians in Russia and the Baltic region is examined in Iben Fonnesberg-Schmidt, *The Popes and the Baltic Crusades, 1147–1254* (Leiden: Koninklijke Brill NV, 2007).

24. Ironically, as a result of the Fourth Crusade and earlier Western aggressions, more Orthodox Christians and Greek lands were subjected to Latin occupation than Muslim populations and Arab territories would ever be conquered by the Catholic crusades. For a lively example of the consequences of Western crusading adventurism for a Greek and Orthodox population, see George Jeffrey, *Cyprus under an English King in the Twelfth Century: The Adventures of Richard I and the Crowning of His Queen in the Island* (London: Zeno, 1973). A more critical, comprehensive study is found in Peter Lock, *Franks in the Aegean, 1204–1500* (London: Longman, 1995). In addition, see George T. Dennis, *Byzantium and the Franks: 1350–1420* (London: Variorum Reprints, 1982); Jonathan Harris, *Byzantium and the Crusades* (London: Hambledon and London, 2003).

25. See the following concise and seminal studies: George T. Dennis, "Defenders of the Christian People: Holy War in Byzantium," in *The Crusades from the Perspective of Byzantium and the Muslim World*, ed. Angeliki E. Laiou and Roy Parviz Mottahedeh (Washington, DC: Dumbarton Oaks Research Library and Collection, 2001), 31–39; Angeliki E. Laiou, "On Just War in Byzantium," in *To Hellenikon: Studies in Honor of Speros Vryonis, Jr.*, ed. Jelisaveta S. Allen, Christos P. Ioannides, John S. Langdon, and Stephen W. Reinert (New Rochelle, NY: Aristide D. Caratzas, 1993), 153–74.

26. Tia Kolbaba, "Fighting for Christianity: Holy War in the Byzantine Empire," *Byzantion* 68 (1998): 194–221. Reprinted in *Byzantine Warfare*, ed. John Haldon, The International Library of Essays on Military History (Aldershot: Ashgate, 2006), 43–70.

27. Ibid., 61 (reprint).

28. Much of Kolbaba's argumentation is derived from another author's Greek-language doctoral dissertation, which was published apparently without meaningful revision in 1991; see Athina Kolia-Dermitzaki, Ὁ βυζαντινός «ἱερός πόλεμος»· Ἡ ἔννοια καί ἡ προβολή του θρησκευτικού πολέμου στό Βυζάντιον [The Byzantine 'Holy War': The Idea and Propagation of Religious War in Byzantium], Historical Monographs 10 (Athens: S. D. Vasilopoulos, 1991). Kolia-Dermitzaki attempts and, according to rigorous academic review, fails to prove that the concept of holy war existed in Byzantium before the start of the Crusades; in fact, she situates the development of holy war in the fourth century, within the establishment of an official church-state ideology. The poorly informed historical discussion, theoretical superficiality, and acute analytic flaws that characterize this book are methodically detailed in an enlightening and important review of the book and, more broadly, the subject of holy war in Byzantium; see Walter E. Kaegi's review of Kolia-Dermitzaki's book in *Speculum* 69, no. 2 (1994): 518–20. Although Kolbaba adds considerable historiographical sophistication to her use of Kolia-Dermitzaki's thesis, Kolbaba's serious research has, ironically, spawned a flurry of English-language publications whose authors have been far less sober in their assessments than has been Kolbaba. The most egregious example of this derivative and irresponsible writing is to be found in Geoffrey Regan, *First Crusader: Byzantium's Holy Wars* (London: Palgrave Macmillan, 2003). In a misguided homage to Kolbaba's scholarship, Regan makes the extravagant claim that not only did the Byzantines aggressively develop the concept of holy war, but their systematic application of its principles against the Sassanid Empire in the seventh century represents the first Christian crusade, establishing the model for the future Western crusades. Byzantinists rightly ignored Regan's book when it was first published by a minor press in 2001. However, since it was republished by a prominent press in 2003, after being situated in the new debates on religion and the Crusades which followed the terrorist attacks of September 11, 2001, *First Crusader: Byzantium's Holy Wars* has garnered widespread praise from Western medievalists, and has consequently contributed to the perennial problem of misunderstanding of Byzantine civilization among nonspecialists. For an example of an even more troubling improvisation in historical invention which obfuscates rather than clarifies understanding of the complex nexus of early Christianity, violence, and war, see H. A. Drake, "Intolerance, Religious Violence, and Political Legitimacy in Late Antiquity," *Journal of the American Academy of Religion* 79, no. 1 (2011): 193–235. See also Thomas Sizgorich's "Sanctified Violence: Monotheist Militancy as the Tie That Bound Christian Rome and Islam," *Journal of the American Academy of Religion* 77, no. 4

(December 2009): 895–921; Sizgorich, *Violence and Belief in Late Antiquity: Militant Devotion in Christianity and Islam*, Divinations: Rereading Late Ancient Religion (Philadelphia: University of Pennsylvania Press, 2009). In both his article and his book, Sizgorich relies heavily on Drake's earlier book *Constantine and the Bishops: The Politics of Intolerance* (Baltimore: Johns Hopkins University Press, 2000), and argues that the conceptual roots of Islamic jihad may be found in late antique and Byzantine Christian praise by Ambrose and other Christian writers for the military exploits and religious persecution conducted by emperors such as Theodosius I and Heraclius (as well as in the ascetic struggles of monks). Sizgorich's article, however, shows little contextualization of the "proof texts" on which he relies; in particular, he draws no distinction between wars of defense or reconquest and wars of aggression and expansion. He provides a somewhat more nuanced approach, along with a more expansive adaptation of the social science theory of communal identity formation (in this case through militant forms of piety), in his book.

29. On the jihad's assault against Byzantium, see Walter E. Kaegi's two important volumes, *Byzantium and the Early Islamic Conquests* (Cambridge: Cambridge University Press, 1992), and *Muslim Expansion and Byzantine Collapse in North Africa* (Cambridge: Cambridge University Press, 2010).

30. Kolbaba, "Fighting for Christianity," 55 (reprint). A highly insightful analysis of the theological framework and applied principle that inform and enable Orthodox situational distinctions between acceptable/appropriate and unacceptable/inappropriate actions in war is found in Gayle E. Woloschak's essay "War, Technology, and the Canon Law Principle of *Economia*," ch. 11 in this volume.

31. For a thoughtful and rigorous analysis of the centrality and overarching importance of *oikonomia* in determining Orthodox Christianity's response to war, see Philip LeMasters, "Orthodox Perspectives on Peace, War and Violence," *Ecumenical Review* 63, no. 1 (March 2011): 54–61.

32. Ibid., 59–60.

33. For an informative and analytic biographical and historical study of Constantine, see Paul Stephenson, *Constantine: Unconquered Emperor, Christian Victor* (London: Quercus, 2009). Breaking from the standard Western trope on Constantine, Stephenson applies considerable evidence and analysis to present Constantine's reign as one dedicated to cultural and spiritual renewal of the Roman Empire through the idea of a unified Christian state and society, underpinned by a commitment to religious tolerance.

34. See Timothy S. Miller, introduction to Miller and Nesbitt, *Peace and War in Byzantium*, 9.

35. This is not to suggest that fundamentalist strains have not existed in the church's recent history, or that such views have not sometimes made their way into centers of power and influence. In particular, religious literalists were encountered in the wider Byzantine cultural commonwealth, especially in areas experiencing the very early stages of conversion to Christianity, before a fuller understanding of Orthodoxy would take root. In these cases, fundamentalist misunderstanding of Christian pacifism and evolving principles of self-defense often led to tragic consequences. See Mary Cunningham, *Faith in the Byzantine World* (Oxford: Lion Publishing, 2002), 39. For a succinct representative example of the traditional Western paradigm and approach to the history of medieval pacifism that completely ignores Orthodoxy and the Byzantine Empire, see Rory Cox, "The Medieval Pacifist," *History Today* 60, no. 8 (2010): 25–27.

36. Cunningham, *Faith in the Byzantine World*, 39.

37. Miller, introduction, 1–14.

38. Ibid., 10.

39. Ibid., 10–11.

40. Ibid., 4.

41. For a rigorous and absorbing example of this perspective, see Laiou, "On Just War in Byzantium," 153–74.

42. See the following Reinhold Niebuhr works: *Moral Man and Immoral Society: A Study of Ethics and Politics* (New York: Charles Scribner's Sons, 1932; new ed., Continuum International Publishing, 2005); *An Interpretation of Christian Ethics* (New York: Harper & Brothers, 1935; repr., Seabury Press, 1979); and *Beyond Tragedy: Essays on the Christian Interpretation of Tragedy* (New York: Charles Scribner's Sons, 1937).

43. For an elaboration of this view, as well as other Orthodox theological views on just war and defense, see Stanley Harakas, "No Just War in the Fathers," In Communion [website of the Orthodox Peace Fellowship], August 2, 2005, http://www.incommunion.org/2005/08/02/no-just-war-in-the-fathers/; David K. Goodin, "Just War Theory and Eastern Orthodox Christianity: A Theological Perspective on the Doctrinal Legacy of Chrysostom and Constantine-Cyril," *Theandros: An Online Journal of Orthodox Christian Theology and Philosophy* 2, no. 3 (2005), http://www.theandros.com/justwar.html; and Marian Gh. Simion, "Seven Factors of Ambivalence in Defining a *Just War* Theory in Eastern Christianity," in Marian Gh. Simion and Ilie Talpasanu, *Proceedings: The 32nd Annual Congress of the American Romanian Academy of Arts and Sciences* (Montreal: Polytechnic International Press, 2008), 537–43.

44. For a brilliant overview of the relationship between the Byzantines' methodical study of military science and the professionalism of their armed

forces, see the introduction in George T. Dennis, trans., *Maurice's Strategikon: Handbook of Byzantine Military Strategy* (Philadelphia: University of Pennsylvania Press, 1984). The military system established by the reforms of the early empire was so well conceived that the Byzantine armed forces would not require significant change at the tactical and operational levels for several centuries. The versatility and sophistication of the Byzantine army in its organization and tactical coordination of different types of troops produced significant advantages in battle over its many opponents who lacked comparable combined arms ability and organization. For a thorough history of the army of the late Byzantine Empire, see Mark C. Bartusis, *The Late Byzantine Army: Arms and Society, 1204–1453* (Philadelphia: University of Pennsylvania Press, 1992). A highly original study that places the Byzantine army in its social and political contexts is found in Walter E. Kaegi, *Byzantine Military Unrest, 471–843: An Introduction* (Amsterdam: Hakkert, 1981).

45. George T. Dennis's publication of *Maurice's Strategikon* in 1984 marked a major advance in making available to researchers a seminal primary source on the Byzantine approach to war. Although many other extant documents on war and warfare remain to be translated and published, several significant *strategika* have appeared since the publication of *Maurice's Strategikon*. For examples, see George T. Dennis, text, translation, and commentary, *The Taktika of Leo VI* (Washington, DC: Dumbarton Oaks Research Library and Collection, 2010); George T. Dennis, text, translation, and notes, *Three Byzantine Military Treatises* (Washington, DC: Dumbarton Oaks Research Library and Collection, 1985); John F. Haldon, introduction, edition, translation, and commentary, *Constantine Porphyrogenitus: Three Treatises on Imperial Military Expeditions* (Vienna: Verlag der Osterreichischen Akademie der Wissenschaften, 1990); Eric McGeer, *Sowing the Dragon's Teeth: Byzantine Warfare in the Tenth Century* (Washington, DC: Dumbarton Oaks Research Library and Collection, 1994); and Denis F. Sullivan, ed., *Siegecraft: Two Tenth-Century Instructional Manuals by "Heron of Byzantium"* (Washington, DC: Dumbarton Oaks Research Library and Collection, 2000).

46. Miller, introduction, 5. For a discussion of this issue and a review more generally of faith and religion among Byzantine troops, see Peter Schreiner, "Soldiers," in *The Byzantines*, ed. Guglielmo Cavallo (Chicago: University of Chicago Press, 1997), 74–94. Information on the entry of personnel into the military is detailed in John F. Haldon, *Recruitment and Conscription in the Byzantine Army, c. 550–950: A Study of the Origins of the Stratiotika Ktemata* (Vienna: Verlag der Osterreichischen Akademie der Wissenschaften, 1979).

47. Dennis, *Three Byzantine Military Treatises*, 20–21; Miller, introduction, 5.

48. An excellent source for this subject is found in Richard W. Kaeuper, *Chivalry and Violence in Medieval Europe* (Oxford: Oxford University Press, 1999).

49. John F. Haldon's *The Byzantine Wars* (Stroud, UK: History Press, 2008) and *Byzantium at War, AD 600–1453* (New York: Routledge, 2003) contain a wealth of information on the Byzantines' way of war. In addition, see the valuable volume edited by Haldon, *Byzantine Warfare* (Aldershot: Ashgate, 2007).

50. See Dennis, "Defenders of the Christian People," 33.

51. For a textual discussion of this famous episode, see Patrick Viscuso, "Christian Participation in Warfare: A Byzantine View," in *Peace and War in Byzantium: Essays in Honor of George T. Dennis, S.J.*, ed. Timothy S. Miller and John Nesbitt (Washington, DC: Catholic University of America Press, 1995), 33–40.

52. Dennis, *Taktika of Leo VI*, 3–5.

53. Miller, introduction, 4.

54. Haldon, *Byzantium at War, AD 600–1453*, xxx.

55. Ibid.; consult Dennis, "Defenders of the Christian People," 31–39. For an informative study that contrasts the Western Christian ethic of holy war with Orthodoxy's abhorrence of such thought, see Aristeides Papadakis in collaboration with John Meyendorff, *The Christian East and the Rise of the Papacy*, Church History 4 (Crestwood, NY: St. Vladimir's Seminary Press, 1994). For a seminal source-based investigation into Byzantine society's self-perception, see Deno John Geanakoplos, *Byzantium: Church, Society, and Civilization Seen through Contemporary Eyes* (Chicago: University of Chicago Press, 1984).

56. Dennis, "Defenders of the Christian People," 31; Laiou, "On Just War in Byzantium," 153. Along with examination of textual sources, the absence of holy war in Byzantium can be evidenced by the careful analysis of sacred Orthodox objects; see Nicholas Oikonomides, "The Concept of 'Holy War' and Two Tenth-Century Byzantine Ivories," in Miller and Nesbitt, *Peace and War in Byzantium*, especially 62–86.

57. John Haldon, *Warfare, State and Society in the Byzantine World, 565–1204* (London: Routledge, 2003), 275–80.

58. See Laiou, "On Just War in Byzantium," 30; Miller, introduction, 1.

59. Richard A. Falk dates the end of the Cold War and al Qaeda terrorist attacks on the United States as the defining events that have plunged the world into a struggle of competing visions of how to achieve world peace and global justice. Arguing that it is "no longer clarifying to act as if we still inhabit a Westphalian world organized around territorial units whose governing authorities

claim sovereign rights. . . . Instead, the framing of world order is a more tenuous and contested reality" that challenges the capabilities and legitimacy of the Westphalian state. For Falk, we are in a moment of transition to either a neo- or a post-Westphalian world order. See Richard A. Falk, *The Declining World Order: America's Imperial Geopolitics*, Global Horizons (New York: Routledge, 2004), ix.

60. For an interesting interpretive study which argues that the Divine Liturgy of St. John Chrysostom crystallizes Orthodox Christianity's views on war and communicates what should be appropriate responses to violence and aggression, see Philip LeMasters, "Peace in Orthodox Liturgy and Life," *Worship* 77, no. 5 (September 2003): 408–25. This article also contains considerable historical evidence outlining the Orthodox understanding of war as distinct from the just war tradition of Western Christianity. For additional related information, see Robert F. Taft, S.J., "War and Peace in the Byzantine Divine Liturgy," in Miller and Nesbitt, 17–32.

61. For a thoughtful discussion of Orthodoxy's historic engagement with human rights, see John A. McGuckin, "The Issue of Human Rights in Byzantium and Eastern Orthodox Tradition," in *Christianity and Human Rights: An Introduction*, ed. John Witte Jr. and Frank S. Alexander (Cambridge: Cambridge University Press, 2010), 173–90.

62. There is a growing interest in historical and comparative studies of empire, spawned by the measurable and observable problems of the Westphalian state and by the reality, perception, and implications of American hegemony in world affairs. See Craig Galhoun, Frederick Cooper, and Kevin W. Moore, *Lessons of Empire: Imperial Histories and American Power* (New York: The New Press, 2006).

PART THREE

CONSTRUCTIVE DIRECTIONS IN
ORTHODOX THEOLOGY AND ETHICS

CHAPTER 9

WAR AND PEACE

Providence and the Interim

PETER C. BOUTENEFF

Wars are a sin par excellence.

—Archimandrite Sophrony (Sakharov)

God heals in no more certain way than through suffering and humiliation.

—St. Gregory of Nazianzus

The logic of Christianity, specifically the logic of the cross, is one of reversal. Through the cross—an instrument of torture and death—joy comes into the world. "Unless a grain of wheat falls into the earth and dies, it remains alone; but if it dies, it bears much fruit" (John 12:24).[1] God works in his creation by means of humiliation, struggle, and finally death. Evil never has the last word, but becomes the instrument of good, and life ἐν Χριστῷ consists in our cooperation in this divine sublimation of evil. But can we go one step further and *affirm* the evil means of good ends? Furthermore, may we participate in the bringing on of evil in order to effect good? These questions loom large as we consider the theological implications of war, with all its complexity and ambiguity: war as source of suffering, violence, and death, war as victory over evil, war as an arena of glory and honor.

This essay will not address the questions surrounding the justifiability of war in general or of specific wars. It seeks rather to contribute to a contemporary reflection on war through the lens of divine providence, since—as I will argue—this is effectively the approach bequeathed to us by the church fathers. The fathers rarely address war directly; still less do they address it theologically.[2] When they do speak of war, they identify it both as an evil though apparently inevitable factor of our interim fallen reality, and also (more rarely) as a means of divine victory. We do not find in the fathers a "theology of war," but we do glean from them important insight on the underlying questions of the "logic" of evil. Not that the fathers involve themselves in theodicy as understood in modern terms; as I will show, their approach to questions of evil and its role within God's inscrutable will more often centers on God's ordering of the world and his ongoing care for it. It is the patristic reflections on *providence*, then, where I believe we properly seek the underpinnings of an Orthodox theology of war. In this essay, therefore, I will first address the ways in which war may be characterized as evil or good and take as my foil the characterization of justifiable war as a "lesser good" by Fr. Alexander Webster. Next, as a means of exploring more deeply the interplay between good and evil, I will endeavor a broad but purposeful survey of patristic thought about providence, which will elicit some concluding observations.

GOOD AND EVIL, WAR AND PEACE

Fr. Alexander Webster has argued that, contrary to the common casting of war as a "lesser evil," Orthodox tradition in fact presents war—at least potentially—as a "lesser good." The basic argument may be found in two of his publications, most notably the book he coauthored with Darrell Cole in 2004, *The Virtue of War*.[3] This book was built on an issue of the *St. Vladimir's Theological Quarterly* that featured Webster's essay "Justifiable War as a 'Lesser Good' in Eastern Orthodox Moral Tradition," together with six response essays, all critical of Webster's approach.[4] Webster's aim is to challenge the claim that no war is justifiable, because logically one cannot see something as both "evil" and at the same time "justified," and also because of his conviction of the justifiability of, for example, the Iraq war begun in 2003—hence his idea of justifiable war as "a lesser good."

The function of the present essay is not to engage with Webster's historical study or his own analysis, since that has already been done in the essays mentioned above and through subsequent book reviews. Furthermore, Webster's "lesser good" applies not to war in general but to those wars that are deemed justifiable. Still, in evaluating the Orthodox tradition on war through exploring traditional views on providence, I intend to use his "lesser good" trope as a phrase against which to articulate a more fitting way of looking at war generally speaking.

Although the patristic, canonical, and liturgical traditions do not present a simple unanimity on this subject, and although the tradition collectively can be seen to sanction battle under certain circumstances, it is clear that it views war as evil, while recognizing that the perverse conditions of a fallen world may make it tragically necessary, and that God can make evil into a vehicle of goodness. On the way to discussing divine providence in this light, I would set out a few areas for reflection to help evaluate the idea of war as a "lesser good." The first and simplest of these is the irony that calling war, or a particular war, a "lesser good" instead of a "lesser evil" in fact makes us *less* justified in engaging in it. One may conceivably opt for a lesser evil because it is by nature the better of two options in the face of an apparently inescapable evil. But why on earth would one ever choose a lesser good, if a greater good were available? Choosing a "lesser good" can only be the worse option, or a bad compromise. The greater, not the lesser good is what one must seek and choose, and that orientation will more likely involve moral authority and diplomacy, rather than the violent killing of human beings.

Ends and Means

Second, speaking of war as a "lesser good" invites reflection on the whole dynamic of means and ends. The age-old question of whether "the ends justify the means" is based on the implicit premise that "the means" are bad; otherwise they would not seek justification. It classically yields either the consequentialist claim that actions are not to be judged in and of themselves but solely on their outcome (wherein the ends *do* justify the means), or the deontological position that the action itself is what counts (wherein they do not). The idea of war as a lesser good would seem to rest on the idea that it is a bad (or at the very least ambiguous) means to a good end. Christian tradition on this question can seem ambivalent. On the one hand, St. Paul makes an unequivocal statement, echoed throughout the Christian tradition, that good ends can never justify evil means (e.g., Rom. 3:8; 12:17–21).[5] And yet we have the fundamental logic of the cross—a murderous means effecting a good end. The death of the Savior, like the death of the grain of wheat (John 12:24), would seem to be a means justified by the glorious end of resurrection and salvation.

The only way we can make sense of these apparently conflicting data is to point out that the cruciform logic of life-through-death, of growth-through-crisis, does not lead us to *celebrate* the death or the crisis itself, other than in a spirit of irony—or more precisely, in the faith that God can transform evil, "making it good by his goodness."[6] True, the tradition commonly speaks of death as a "mercy" in that it severs the cycle of sin. And we sing hymns of joy to the life-bearing cross of Christ. But it is one thing to accept a dreadful condition and its consequences, praying for God to transfigure it, and another thing to promote the condition itself into something "good." While we invoke, with canny irony, "joy through the cross" to celebrate our salvation and to help us understand our tragedies, we do not speak of calamities as "good." God, in his Christ and by his Holy Spirit, promises to make of any evil a victory, whether in this age or in the age to come, and this includes the evils that, with hindsight, seem to be "necessary." Judas Iscariot was, in a sense, a necessary agent for Christ's life-giving death, but the church's hymnography speaks of him and his betrayal *exclusively* in terms of evil, avarice, and wanton failure of perception,[7] and not as "good" in any way. Taking this logic into the sphere of moral decisions (and therefore closer to the subject of war), we would not speak of "abortion as a lesser good," even in those cases where it is argued as a justifiable decision, and this is because the tragic consequences of abortion are indelible.

Furthermore, while the tradition shows several ways in which people actually seek out hardship as a means of growth in godliness, we only have a right to do this in ways that affect ourselves alone. Neither do we act on our own initiative, but in response to the Divine. That is the spirit of ascetical renunciation: it is a personal affair, in consultation with a spiritual director and in consent with the community.[8] None of the suffering and humiliation in which Christians consciously (and cautiously) participate is done in such a way as to affect someone *else* and certainly not unto their death. Christ submitted himself to the pathological mentality of violence in allowing himself to be scourged and killed on the cross. He didn't kill other people, or force a "healing suffering" on anyone. He did warn that "the world" would be a context of tribulation (John 16:33), in ways that no one would celebrate as "good."

Therefore, while the "ends" of salvation are bound up with the "means" of suffering and death, and while suffering and death can even prove instrumental in the effecting of growth, glory, and goodness, the means are never seen as good (whether greater or lesser) in and of themselves, but only insofar as *God transfigures them*. Deontology and consequentialism both crumble under the inscrutability of God's providence.

What Is War?

Third, speaking of war as a "lesser good" invites a spelling out of the senses in which war can be described as "good." Identifying goodness within war is possible and important (as will be seen below), but within parameters that need to be thoughtfully defined. This in turn invites a brief definition of war, together with observations of how war is in fact engaged in in our world.

The status of war, as justifiable or not, as evil or not, and as inevitable or not, depends in part on the stage of a particular conflict under discussion. It is one thing to debate the justifiability or inevitability of entering into a conflict that is already at the point of crisis, such as where one's country is under attack, or where a dictator is slaughtering his own people. It would be difficult to speak of military involvement in such cases in terms of "evil." And one may well call such involvement "inevitable" and even "right," albeit tragically. However, this does not mitigate the fact that the totality of the dynamic that leads to such conflicts is evil, not just within the generalized dynamic of human brokenness, but as a particular series of death-dealing decisions and failures of creativity and wisdom—failures of communion with God and the other. Entering certain conflicts may indeed be inevitable and necessary, and one's behavior within such conflicts can be noble, honorable, and right, but the dynamic of war, taken as a whole, is pure evil. Let us review how it is so.

War is typically defined in the dictionaries as *the hostile contention by means of armed forces, or a state of armed conflict between nations, states, or groups within them.* The definition of war as "conflict" is neutral as to the question of whether a particular war is justified and as to which side of any given conflict is justified. Where the dictionaries are not neutral is in their near unanimous agreement on the use of the two descriptives "hostile" and "armed." Neither goodness nor justifiability is ruled out with hostility or armament, but these words indicate that war presumes the physical destruction of enemies.

War, as it is played out constantly all over the globe and throughout human history, is experienced through a broad constellation of synchronous and diachronous elements and phenomena. A list of components, not all of which are necessarily present in every war (indeed, some are illegal in NATO countries, e.g.), may include the following, once war is declared and set into motion:

- dehumanization of enemies;
- deployment of armed personnel;
- battle—ground, air, and naval, whether manned or unmanned, resulting in wounding, killing, and/or destabilization of combatants as well as noncombatants;
- further psychological destabilization through internment, possible threat and/or implementation of torture, and/or rape;
- the destruction of infrastructure (power facilities, educational facilities, medical facilities, economic structures);
- the deliberate destruction of natural resources so that land is no longer arable.

However its participants and bystanders actually experience war—and by nature people experience it in a very broad variety of ways—war is predicated upon the infliction of violent death, both by definition and by experience.

Apart from the psychological and ecological trauma inflicted through war, the morality of the destruction of lives by violence is made problematic by several factors, some of which are at play also in the moral debate about capital punishment. Few Orthodox theologians, past or present, have defended capital punishment; they reject it along the principles that (a) the decision as to whether another human being should live or die rests with God alone, partly owing to (b), the fact that no person is 100 percent evil, and that the killing of a person will inevitably result in the destruction of something good or of the potential for good, something perhaps known only to God. If this argument may hold for a single human being, would it not hold all the more for an entire body of people? Wars involve armies of people trying to kill each other. Combatants and noncombatants die. Families, cities, villages, fields, and forests are destroyed.

This is precisely why the canonical tradition prescribes repentance for *any* soldier who causes the death of another, even if a particular war is understood or framed as "inevitable," or even "justifiable" in some qualified, provisional way that would sanction its combatants: it is still the killing of human beings, and that is *bad*.

Well-known arguments are brought into play to justify certain wars (such as the Augustinian/Thomist *jus ad bellum* criteria), but we ought to note that these have the sole intention of *limiting* war, because it is obviously a horrible death-dealing thing. So, while acknowledging a certain kind of near-inevitability of war within a tragically fallen interim dynamic, and the concomitant need for a prepared military, I wish only to underscore the fact that is well known to combatants and noncombatants alike: insofar as it systematically and deliberately operates through violent death and destruction, war itself is evil. Indeed there is no better example for the fallenness, the brokenness, the perverse distortion of humanity, than that people are brought to burn or tear each other's flesh until they die.

Hard as it may be to believe, the above is not meant to advocate a radical pacifism, neither is it meant to instill guilt or moral paralysis in the men and women of the military, and this is because part of the evil of war is that it requires all nations to be prepared for it in order to defend just causes, and in order to defend themselves. This also means that understanding war and killing as evil does not mean that we see its participants, the armed forces, as necessarily evil. Although war's participants in some cases may be engaged in unequivocally evil acts, the armed forces—acting in obedience to their country and its leaders—must be supported physically, morally, and spiritually, so that they may participate in the good that God may bring out of evil, and so that they do not succumb to the temptations to brutality that wars bring in such abundance. The plight of the conscientious soldier can only be looked on with awe, gratitude, and prayer; a credible theological response to the tragedy of war can only serve to deepen that prayerful disposition.

War as Good

War is evil, but it must also be observed that—by God's grace—war can be a vehicle of goodness and a participation in God's redemptive work. Through war, evil can indeed be destroyed. Through war, people not only exhibit sadistic brutality, but also are frequently brought to their most noble selves. As Homer[9] and countless soldiers will testify, war is capable of bringing glory and honor, and martyrdom, in abundance.

In this way, war has furnished much of the church's imagery for the spiritual life, from the scriptures onward (cf. Isa. 1:17; Eph. 6:13–18; 1 Thess. 5:8; etc.). The shields, breastplates, helmets, and swords—even the violence by which the kingdom of God is to be taken, make for an apt set of metaphors for the combat against the passions within ourselves and real evil in the world. The military spiritual equipment serves "the gospel of peace" (Eph. 6:15). This imagery testifies both to the prevalence of war in the contexts that produced it and to the potential that war carries for glory and for the victory of good over evil.

And so, the ambiguity of war, the ways in which it is by definition evil and also potentially the bearer of good, brings us squarely into the realm of divine providence, and specifically the cruciform dynamic wherein God heals and gives life through suffering and death. To further set the stage for our reflection on providence, a few brief words about peace.

What Is Peace?

Peace, in one (secular) definition, may be understood simply as the absence of war or of any conflict. This is not necessarily a good thing. One may even be leery of such a peace: a relationship that is devoid of all disputes is unhealthy, especially if conflict is suppressed rather than resolved. As the saying goes, "Better genuine confusion than false clarity." A suspicious attitude toward "peace" as absence of conflict is given one of its most extreme utterances by the otherwise moderate twentieth-century theologian Paul Evdokimov, who attributes to Origen the idea that "a time of peace is propitious to Satan, who steals from Christ His martyrs and from the Church its glory."[10] Such a statement not only evokes the vital (though still tragic) role of the martyr in the life of the church; it portrays peace—as absence of struggle or conflict—as a spiritually dangerous place, a radicalization of the old aphorism that "idle hands are the Devil's workshop."

While such caution toward apparent "peace" is a mainstay of tradition, it reflects only a shallow definition of peace. For peace, more theologically speaking, is understood not as an absence but as a divinely instituted presence, specifically a state of reconciled communion. Silence is more than the absence of noise. For its part, peace—as a *presence*—is something given and defined by God, in such a way that our limited understandings of peace are confounded, as are our limited understandings of justice, goodness, and the other divine attributes. This is why St. Paul speaks of the peace of God as "passing all understanding" (Phil. 4:7), and why the Gospel of John records Jesus himself saying, "Peace I leave with you; my peace I give to you; not as the world gives do I give to you" (John 14:27). These New Testament understandings are surely influenced by the Hebrew *shalom*, which has to do with the wholeness, soundness, and fullness of life intended by the God of Israel: material, spiritual, relational, social, and cosmic.

Peace, as a presence, also has everything to do with unity, understood specifically as union with and in God. Dionysius, recalling the inscrutable nature of divine peace, reminds us also of its relationship to communion: "With reverent hymns of peace we should now sing the praises of God's peace, for it is this which brings all things together. This is what unites everything, begetting and producing the harmonies and the agreement of all things. All things therefore long for it, and the manifold and the divided are returned by it into a total unity; every civil war is changed into a unified household."[11] Peace, therefore, is properly reckoned along theological terms, and yet has deeply practical consequences that pose concrete challenges in the Christian life within the fallen world. War may indeed require and evince glory and honor, but as Thomas Merton reminds us, peace does so even more: "Peace," he wrote, "demands the most heroic labor and the most difficult sacrifice. It demands greater heroism than war. It demands greater fidelity to the truth and a much more perfect purity of conscience."[12]

Reckoned theologically and practically, peace in its deeper meaning is intrinsically, unambiguously good. War, on the other hand, is at root evil and death-dealing, and at best, by the grace of God, transfigured into a *means* of achieving peace and life and wholeness. In our interim age, war can tragically be something through which one must pass on the way to peace and reconciliation. Peace, however, remains the standard and the goal; war is neither. Peace is a name of God; war is not.

PROVIDENCE

In this world, God brings peace, and effects his essential will of our deification, and the union of all things in heaven and all things on earth (Eph. 1:10), through means that we can describe, with profound understatement, as counterintuitive. "Through the cross, joy comes into all the world."[13]

And so we turn to a more purposeful examination of the cruciform dynamic of divine providence that has undergirded everything that has been said so far. Because if war is indeed evil, if it can be seen as "sin par excellence,"[14] then it can properly be evaluated against this theological perspective.

From Providence to Theodicy

As we search the tradition on the subject of providence, we find vital contributions to modern reflections on this question, as well as surprising limitations, owing largely to the vast distance between our context and that of the first-millennium church, a distance that is perhaps felt with special acuteness on this very subject. The "problem of evil" is perennial, explored from the pre-Socratics to the present, yet the character of the inquiries has changed drastically over time. The common observation that the "theodicy question" took on a new character after the Jewish holocaust tells only part of the story, for the twentieth-century explosion of human suffering and death is but one important part of a larger picture. Indeed, one could not properly even speak of "theodicy"—understood as the justice of God, or rather the *justification* of God—during the church's formative centuries. Job's line of inquiry is made to sound timid, and its resolution facile, by the post-holocaust calls for God's justification and the concomitant challenges either to his omnipotence or his characterization as "good." What the early centuries do produce, as we shall summarize below, is a series of reflections on divine providence which follow a different line of inquiry from that common today.

Several modern authors identify this shift in perspectives with evolving socioeconomic and theological factors.[15] Perhaps the most relevant and fundamental of these has to do with people's expectations of both longevity (life expectancy has doubled since antiquity) and quality of life. Theologically, it is also argued that the Enlightenment engendered a weakened doctrine of original sin, such that eighteenth-century Westerners were less prone to feel that we all *deserve* to suffer. Reformed doctrines of total depravity make this case harder to argue. Yet there is no doubt that we moderns often feel an entitlement to happiness, and by extension to peace and tranquility, that was quite unknown in antiquity.

Widespread suffering and poverty remain as ever in modern times, yet to the extent that suffering and war become the exception rather than the rule of life, a certain traditional sensibility that fears prosperity and welcomes adversity is arguably more distant than it ever was. As a result, the question "why does God allow evil, war, and suffering?" is now framed in a way that places God on trial for the brazen audacity of allowing suffering and evil at all. In other words, once suffering is understood not as an inevitable companion but an unwelcome visitor, we arrive at "theodicy," rather than "providence."

With the goal of gleaning further insights from the tradition for a contemporary reflection on war, then, what follows is a broad and impressionistic survey of patristic currents on evil and providence, through a set of emblematic *topoi* dealing with the evident ambiguity of the world created by God and with God's providential vision for it. War itself will take an implicit rather than explicit role in these next pages, to emerge again in our concluding paragraphs.

Providence and Mystery

When Anthony the Great asks God why some people die sooner than others, why there are rich and poor, and why bad things happen to good people (and vice versa), he receives the following answer: "Anthony, keep your attention on yourself; these things are according to the judgment of God, and it is not to your advantage to know anything about them."[16]

It is a recurrent pattern particularly in the ascetical literature: a monk raises questions of providence and evil, and receives a rebuke—from God, from his Abba, or from nature itself—indicating that he has no business asking such questions. This powerful theme resonates throughout the early patristic treatises devoted to the subject of providence. John Chrysostom's *On Providence* is indicative:[17]

> Do not pose reckless questions, do not struggle to reason on the things that are, for you have a good enough witness concerning them. If this word is not enough, and if you want to occupy yourself with a detailed investigation, you are only throwing yourself into a violent sea, with whirlpools of reasoning, creating a great tempest. You will not increase in knowledge, but will only prepare a disastrous shipwreck for yourself.[18]

The scriptural roots of this trend run deep. Much psalmody is concerned with the humbling of the heart in order to put all trust in the Lord.

> O LORD, my heart is not lifted up,
> my eyes are not raised too high;
> I do not occupy myself with things
> too great and too marvelous for me.
> But I have calmed and quieted my soul,
> like a child quieted at its mother's breast;
> like a child that is quieted is my soul. (Ps. 131:1–2)

There is no plumbing the depth of God's plans, as he himself reminds his people: "My thoughts are not your thoughts, neither are your ways my ways" (Isa. 55:8).

For St. Paul too, God's will is ultimately beyond human comprehension. In God, worldly wisdom is overturned (1 Cor. 1:20–25). God's will, which is something we can only hope to understand through spiritual wisdom (Col. 1:9), is specifically spoken of in terms of mystery. "Mystery" for Paul carries several meanings, encompassing awesome depth as well as hiddenness. The mysteriousness of God's will, however, does not prevent Paul from discussing it. In Paul's view, God wills the union of all things in Christ (Eph. 1:9). God also wills (*providentially*) the "hardening of Israel" so that the full number of gentiles would come in (Rom. 11:25). He plans to reveal his wisdom through the church (Eph. 3:9). In each of these passages, God's will is an awesome mystery.[19]

Chrysostom remarks on Paul's awe, noting that even such a great, powerful, and wise man as the apostle is struck with amazement when confronted by the mystery of God's providence. Indeed, any other attitude is madness. The reason that people are spiritually ill, the reason they are scandalized by God's allowance of evil, is simply this: "a curious and reckless mind, the desire to know the cause of all that happens and to enter battle with the incomprehensible and ineffable providence of God."[20]

The call to humility in such matters does not cut off all inquiry, and even the early Christian writers' pious treatments of providence address difficult questions. The reader is only being shown that the starting point of inquiry into providence and divine dispensation ought to be one of faith. The authors of antiquity knew the tendency to conduct inquiries about evil in a spirit that was either predisposed to placing God on trial, or perhaps to an overly technical argumentation, relying on cold syllogisms that are liable to lead one astray from reality. Such were the lines of inquiry that the fathers sought to avoid, or to bring into a right perspective.

Indeed, the starting point for the fathers' inquiry is not only faith in God, but an *eschatological* vantage. The fathers interpreted history and the present in terms of a greatly broadened time-perspective. In the short term, there is the very practical sense that making sense of strangeness, the absence of justice, the existence of evil and of heresy, is often simply a matter of time: if you wait long enough, you will likely see reversals of fortune. But the fathers' sights are set further still, in the age to come, where everything is settled, where all reaches its rightful place, where evil is shown for what it really is: nonbeing.

The early treatises on providence are not designed to gain many converts from nonbelief. They seek rather to orient the faith of believers, and particularly those who know their Bible. That orientation begins with wonder and humility. Most reflections on providence from within the tradition stem from a place of conviction that God knows what he is doing, that he has the world in his care, on the universal and the particular levels. This cannot be argued logically or irrefutably; it is a faith position, an orientation. Indeed, the fathers were explicit that providence is often a matter of perception, dependent upon one's interpretation. Chrysostom is clear about the role of the disposition of the person in discerning providence. The cross, he writes, is a stumbling block only to the foolish mind. The thief, who never even saw Christ's miracles or heard his teaching, was of such a disposition that the cross was the vehicle of his conversion, whereas so many others rejected Christ precisely *because of* the cross.[21] Beauty, and scandal, are in the eye of the beholder.

The Marvel of Divine Management

The call to an awestruck humility in approaching questions of God's care for the world is related to another powerful and consistent current of reflection on providence: wonder. Several early church writings on divine providence take the form of extended meditations on the beautiful ordering of creation. The two characteristic examples below are from Basil of Caesarea and Theodoret of Cyrus. Each reflects upon God's attention to every detail of creation, even unlikely ones. From St. Basil:

> I have heard it said that the sea urchin, a little contemptible creature, often foretells calm and tempest to sailors. . . . No astrologer, no Chaldaean, has ever communicated his secret to the urchin: it is the Lord of the sea and of the winds who has impressed on this little animal a manifest proof of his great wisdom. God has foreseen all, he has neglected nothing. His eye, which never sleeps, watches over all.

He is present everywhere and gives to each being the means of preservation. If God has not left the sea urchin outside his providence, is
he without care for you?[22]

And then from Theodoret:

Mark another manifestation of [God's] providence. The body provides the natural couch of the buttocks so that you can make a seat
out of the ground or a stone and not be hurt by sitting on bare limbs.
You are ungrateful notwithstanding. You fail to recognize the gifts,
and rave and rant against this wisdom that makes such provision
for you.[23]

From the sea urchin to the human posterior, God has created things
thoughtfully, and continues to look after his world. This conviction
brings with it simultaneously a sense of praise and wonder, as well as outrage at the thought of alternate interpretations. To imagine that the universe was not created with wisdom beyond measure, and that it goes
unlooked-after by the creator, constitutes sacrilege. This indignation is
reminiscent of Plato, who, in his discussion on divine providence in the
Laws, considers it blasphemous to deny divine care for humanity, either
in the global or in the particular sense.[24]

The wonder at the supra-abundant knowledge and care with which
God created the world entails for the fathers a conviction about his ongoing involvement in subsequent history. In scripture, the recounting of
the formation of Israel is entirely wrapped up with the consciousness of
God's plan for Israel and of his acts for bringing this plan about. Scripture, in its primary function of recounting God's acts for the world, is
predicated on the dual conviction that God acts for his people and that
nothing happens in the world without God's willing or allowing it.[25] The
landmark passages which define Israel's identity are recitals of God's acts
in the Pentateuch and the Psalms. Similarly, Isaiah's prophecy portrays the
historic figure of Cyrus the Persian as the (unwitting) instrument of God
in liberating Israel from captivity (Isa. 44:28–45:7).

This same thinking endures in subsequent history. In the eyes of
the faithful, God is involved in history, hardening the hearts of some and

softening those of others, using people—and often their *wars*—as instruments of his ongoing care for his creation. A late eighteenth-century text takes its cue from this scriptural mind-set, positing that just as God hardened the hearts of Israel, so he may be understood to have providentially strengthened the Ottomans:

> [Our Lord] raised out of nothing this powerful empire of the Ottomans, in the place of our Roman [Byzantine] Empire which had begun, in a certain way, to cause to deviate from the beliefs of the Orthodox faith, and he raised up the empire of the Ottomans higher than any other kingdom so as to show without doubt that it came about by divine will, and not by the power of man, and to assure all the faithful that in this way he deigned to bring about a great mystery, namely salvation to his chosen people.[26]

And as God used Cyrus the Persian as his instrument, he now used the Sultan:

> For this reason he puts into the heart of the Sultan of these Ottomans an inclination to keep free the religious beliefs of our Orthodox faith and, as a work of supererogation, to protect them, even to the point of occasionally chastising Christians who deviate from their faith, that they have always before their eyes the fear of God.[27]

Because God is all-powerful, and because he cares for his creation, he is completely involved in the largest and the smallest particulars of the creation and sustenance of the world. The perception of God's providential care can extend to all dimensions of history. Indeed, writers with a taste for irony like to point out that one of providence's most compelling achievements is the way in which it uses the wicked, the haughty, the hardened of heart—and yes, wars and violence—in order to evoke the greater good.

Providence and Freedom

Many ancient and modern responses to the problem of evil revolve around human freedom—a freedom that was not undermined, in the fathers' understanding, by the guiding hand of God in the events of history. Freedom is the critical factor among the possible explanations for why evil and suffering are permitted by the good and all-powerful God. In order to allow humans to love him in a genuine and free relationship, God gives humans the freedom to move toward or away from him. God respects this freedom to the end, in effect cloaking his omnipotence. The twentieth-century Orthodox theologian Vladimir Lossky expresses it this way:

> The love of God for man is so great that it cannot constrain; for there is no love without respect. Divine will always submits itself to gropings, to detours, even to revolts of human will, to bring it to a free consent: of such is divine providence, and the classical image of the pedagogue must seem feeble indeed to anyone who has felt God as a beggar of love waiting at the soul's door without ever daring to force it.[28]

Yet the divine gift of freedom, together with God's ongoing respect of it, lies paradoxically at the root of ongoing evil and suffering. That the world which we know is at such a radical removal from the ultimately intended bliss is due to individual and collective human choices, made in freedom.

Human free will looms large in patristic writing on providence, but it also runs as a current through patristic reflection on anthropology. Freedom is seen as one of the primary characteristics which reflect the divine nature in the human person. Forming a critical aspect of the *imago dei*, freedom is taken with the utmost seriousness in patristic anthropology, and anything which stands in its way needs carefully to be addressed. This is why writings such as Gregory of Nyssa's substantial letter *Against Fate* strive to debunk astrological determinism: not only is it a misplaced faith in the stars, but determinism is also contrary to Christian understanding of the human person. In the face of all contextual deterministic factors (socioeconomic, physiological, nature or nurture, etc.), the human person is free to make good or bad choices, even unto perdition.

The sacred character of human freedom is also one of the reasons that the sixth-century church so strenuously rejected doctrines of universal salvation: they potentially limited both divine *and human* freedom. Just as God must be free to judge, so the human person must remain free to the end, even free to perish. The crux of morality, the hinge of that salvation which was irrevocably wrought through the cross of Christ, is human free choice—the choice to accept or reject divine life. As Lossky again has put it, a single will is required for creation, but two wills for deification.[29] God alone willed to create. But a person will not be saved and brought to the ultimate end of *theosis* without his or her assent.

One of the effects of this emphasis on human freedom is that it means that God is not the author of evil; the blame lies with our own freely made decisions. Such thinking precedes Christian thought.[30] Then, early in the Christian era, Origen appears to have suggested that free choice is a factor from before the beginning of our earthly life. The nature of our freely made choices—to rest in God, to hesitate in our love for God, or to reject God—determines where and how God "places" us within the material world, determines the ways in which our lives will be spelled out, in an interaction with God's ongoing providential care. More traditional schemes, while rejecting noetic preexistence, nonetheless emphasize human free will as the substrate upon which divine providence operates. The providential will of God allows the strange—allows evil—purely as a response to decisions made in freedom by persons. The existence of war, the apotheosis of evil, testifies to God's enduring and fearsome respect for human free choice.

"Irenaean Theodicy"

As suggested above, contemporary writers on theodicy are often frustrated when entire patristic treatises "on providence" (Chrysostom, Theodoret, and evil St. Basil's *Hexaemeron* homilies) go little further than to assert the unfathomable mysteries of the divine will and the wonders of creation. Indeed, if this had constituted the sole word from early Christian tradition on the problem of evil and suffering, we might consider that tradition to have been in deep denial concerning many legitimate questions, and painful groans of the heart, when it comes to God and evil.

Some church fathers took a philosophical-ontological approach to evil, one that has also not proven all that helpful today. Taking up the Platonic tradition, Sts. Gregory of Nyssa, Augustine, and Dionysius the Pseudo-Areopagite, among others, declared evil as an ontological void, having no existence in itself. Good alone can be said to truly exist, while evil is merely the privation or distortion of good, having no being in itself. This line of thinking, however logical, provides little satisfaction for those who suffer, nor does it significantly further an inquiry that is focused on the evils and goods of war. One imagines that the argument for the ontic nonexistence of evil falls tragically flat in the foxholes.

If modern reflections on evil have remained largely untouched by the church fathers, one voice has loomed large: St. Irenaeus of Lyons. The emergence of this second-century church father in contemporary theodical discourse owes largely to the writing of John Hick, one of the pioneers of contemporary Christian reflection on the problem of evil.[31] Hick sees Irenaeus's view as an antidote to the prevalent Western understanding of evil attributable to St. Augustine. In that view, the human person is understood as having been created in a finished state, falls of his own accord, and so elicits God's "Plan B": rescue by means of the incarnation, death, and resurrection of Christ. It is not surprising that Irenaeus has earned Hick's admiration, for in Irenaeus we find a vision that has yet to be either challenged or surpassed, even if it goes largely ignored by Western Christians (as well as a considerable number of Eastern Christians who, arguably, have absorbed the Augustinian understanding of the fall).

Irenaeus's vision rests on the basic principle that the fall (or as he prefers to call it, the "apostasy")—though tragic—plays a critical, necessary role in God's vision for humanity.[32] The Adam and Eve of Genesis 2–3 are not perfected human beings but are like children, who partake of the knowledge of good and evil ahead of their time. But this knowledge, for Irenaeus, is part and parcel of being in the divine image. God wills a humanity that is made to be what God himself is, but he wants humanity to participate in what will be a *process*, culminating in what would later come to be called theosis or deification. Humans are thus intentionally created in a lesser state and, through the knowledge of good and evil (and therefore through the process of falling down and getting up), approach the higher state of divinization that is indicated, emblemized, and recapitulated in the person and work of Jesus Christ.[33] This schema addresses the age-old question of why human beings were not created either divinized at the outset or as preprogrammed agents of virtue. Virtue is only genuine if it is chosen from among alternate possibilities. Hick aptly summarizes Irenaeus: "Virtues that have been formed within the agent as a hard-won deposit of right decisions in situations of challenge and temptation are intrinsically more valuable than ready-made virtues created within her without any effort on her part."[34] Human existence thus becomes, as Hick calls it, a vale of soul making.

Irenaeus's ideas are echoed in several other fathers. Theophilus of Antioch, Gregory of Nazianzus, and Ephrem the Syrian all posited the first parents in Eden as works in progress, as children who partake at an inappropriate time of something they were always meant to have. Furthermore, Irenaeus's framework gives a still greater meaning to the patristic currents on providence that we have been discussing: The "soul making" that is to take place in this world—specifically through suffering and its redemption, through sin and its repentance—yields precisely the perspective that the fathers collectively espouse, marveling at divine management and humility before his awesomeness. As the psalmist has it, "Before I was afflicted, I went astray; but now I keep thy word" (Ps. 119:67). "God heals in no more certain way than through suffering and humiliation [κακοπάθεια]," says Gregory of Nazianzus. He continues, "God's love for man is the counterpart of [our] tears."[35] Suffering is a part of soul making. This line of reasoning, which goes at least as far back as the Stoics, is central to patristic thought on providence. Suffering is a proving ground, showing forth righteous persons, revealing the glory of God. Suffering, while never an end in itself, is an opportunity for building faith, strength, humility, and peace of soul.

As we move now toward a conclusion, we are driven by the following question: as disciples of St. Irenaeus and his legacy, can we say that suffering, death, evil itself—and therefore war, which embodies all of these—are, in a manner of speaking, willed by God and, as such, "good"?

Providence and the Divine Will

"Providence is the care that God takes over existing things. Providence is the will of God through which all existing things receive their suitable direction." These two sentences, verbatim (in Greek), begin the reflections on providence of at least three of the most prominent ancient church authors, spanning three centuries.[36] If there is a stock definition of providence among the Greek-speaking fathers, this is it.

The two operative words in the definition are *care* and *will*. The term ἐπιμέλεια carries a primary meaning of "care." It suggests diligence, attention, looking after (cf. Acts 27:3). It also implies responsible management (cf. 1 Tim. 3:5), as well as engagement, involvement. Providence, according to the church's earliest consistent understanding, is God's attentive management and engaged involvement with creation.

The term βούλησις is one of the words which render "will" or "volition." Providence is not only an engaged care, but God's *volition*, through which things achieve their proper orientation. God *wills* the things that happen in the world in the way that is most propitious for the world. Yet Christian tradition is not prepared to say that God wills evil and suffering. There are different ways of reckoning with this. One way, which is identified with many writers, perhaps beginning with Irenaeus, is to distinguish will from permission—God *allows* suffering and evil in order to effect his *will* that humanity be brought into free communion with him. Origen, perhaps similarly, distinguishes between God's will (*voluntate*) on the one hand and "providence" on the other. "God concerns himself with mortals, and nothing is done either in heaven or on earth without his providence. Note that we say 'without his providence,' and not 'without his will.' For if many things happen without his will, nothing is done without his providence. Providence is that according to which God organizes, administers, and disposes all things; will is that according to which God wants or doesn't want something."[37] Origen seems to be positing a primary volition of God which gives way to and is somehow actualized by the disposition and administration of "providence."

It is St. John of Damascus who takes this dynamic of permission and volition to the next level, according both of them the status of "will."[38] He calls them the antecedent (or primary) will (προηγούμενον θέλημα) and consequent (or secondary) will (ἑπόμενον θέλημα). The primary will of God, his essential will, is his own (ἐξ αὐτοῦ)—it is, effectively, the will that all be saved, and come to his kingdom (cf. 1 Tim. 2:4). The secondary or consequent will, which John equates with permission and providence, comes into play through interaction with free human beings—its source or cause rests in us ourselves (ἐξ ἡμετέρας αἰτίας). This is important, for it shows that even if the cause/source rests in created human realities, saying that God "allows" evil is effectively no different from saying that he *wills* it.

The two registers of volition remain, of course. What God desires, in the primary sense, is that his human creation be in free and loving communion with him. But once you say "free and loving," you imply not one but two willing agents—in this case the divine and the human. The dynamic of fall, of evil, suffering, and death, is God's *willed* means of effecting this primary desire. Evil and suffering are not merely obstacles to salvation; God makes of them a *means* of salvation.

The church's tradition has always denied a Manichaean duality of gods, a good god who is the source of all good warring with an evil god who is the source of all evil. While the Christian God is by no means the author of evil, God willfully orders the world in a way that both allows and utilizes it. In this sense, then, the answer to our question is "Yes, in a properly qualified manner of speaking, evil is willed by God."

IF THIS IS THE CASE, might we not then be justified in calling war (or certain wars) a "lesser good"? Indeed, if we consider what the fathers say about evil and providence, can we say that *they* reckon war as a potentially "lesser good"? No, we cannot, for two reasons that we touched on above.

One is that evil in the world, however sublimated by God, is never *of itself* an object of praise, other than through self-consciously ironic and awestruck language of "joy-through-the-cross." What is praised, that is, what is accorded the attribute of "good," is God's work and his providential care, never the evil by which it is sometimes wrought. We praise God for his exceeding greatness. We praise glory and honor wherever they are to be found, whether on the battlefield or in the household. We celebrate redemption wrought by God. But God forbid we praise war itself, which is by definition the willful destruction by human beings of other human beings, cultures, and microclimates, none of which are unequivocally worthy of death, at least as far as we can judge.

The other is that, while God works good out of evil, while he "makes evil to be good by his goodness," the tradition does not encourage anyone to participate in evil in order to participate in its sublimation. Evil and temptations form a part of human growth toward God, but they are to be avoided at all cost: "It is necessary that temptations come, but woe to the man by whom the temptation comes!" (Matt. 18:7). Bringing on evil, in the trust that it will be overcome, is the equivalent of tempting God (cf. Matt. 4:7). In this sense, evil and temptations are in no way "good," apart from the good that comes by God's grace and in the struggle to overcome them. God heals in no more certain way than through suffering and humiliation, but it is not within our province either to praise them or subject others to them willfully.

This leads us to a final, sad observation: the "glory of war" is scarcely accessible to the contemporary American mentality. Homer praised war as a face-to-face contest in a spirit of valor, with clear-cut enemies. While the deep bonds between soldiers, the profound code of honor, and the spirit of self-sacrifice remain true today as ever, the fact is that many wars of the recent decades, so dependent on technology and machines (some of them even unmanned), so plagued by "collateral damage," and often with motivations that are scarcely even apparent, fail to live up to the Homeric ideal—that is, if actual wars *ever* lived up to that ideal. We must be proud to the point of awe, and grateful in the extreme, for the soldiers who go to the battlefield and fight and die in the service of their country, despite what may be ambiguous motivations and flawed planning on the part of their superiors. We can only feel the deepest esteem for their valor in times of the most extreme danger and peril imaginable, especially if we ourselves have never been so challenged. Because war is hell, war is evil, war is the worst thing that humanity has to say for itself. The miracle and mystery is that God, in his unsearchable judgments and supra-abounding love for us, makes use of something so horrific as war and violence to bring us to his likeness in glory.

NOTES

1. Unless otherwise noted, all quotations from the Bible are from the Revised Standard Version (RSV).

2. This reticence may owe in part to contextual factors that prohibited the fathers from undermining civil authorities and their policies. The tradition of civil disobedience is limited at best in the early Christian centuries.

3. Alexander F. C. Webster and Darrell Cole, *The Virtue of War: Reclaiming the Classic Christian Traditions East and West* (Salisbury, MA: Regina Orthodox Press, 2004).

4. *St. Vladimir's Theological Quarterly* 47, no. 1 (2003).

5. Webster cites these verses, but counters them with the example of the heart surgeon, who must break ribs and cut into a heart in order to heal it. *Virtue*

of War, 108. Paul's point is a greater one, addressed within the broader questions of the salvation of Jews and gentiles and the dynamic of "the law" and human actions. His point is that even if God's righteousness may be revealed by way of human sin, it only goes to show that no one is justified by their works, and that God alone is righteous. There is no "lesser good" logic involved here.

6. Cf. the anaphora of St. Basil the Great.

7. See, for example, the hymns of the Matins of Great and Holy Friday, on which Christ's passion is commemorated.

8. Even sexual renunciation is to be effected "by agreement" (1 Cor. 7:5).

9. It would be difficult to romanticize today's wars along the lines of Homer, as two recent studies by Jonathan Shay show: *Achilles in Vietnam: Combat Trauma and the Undoing of Character* (New York: Scribner, 1994) and *Odysseus in America: Combat Trauma and the Trials of Homecoming* (New York: Scribner, 2002).

10. *The Sacrament of Love* (Crestwood, NY: St. Vladimir's Seminary Press, 1985), 75.

11. Dionysius, *Divine Names* 11.1 (PG 3:948D–949A).

12. Thomas Merton, *Peace in the Post-Christian Era* (Maryknoll, NY: Orbis, 2004), 90.

13. Orthodox Resurrectional Matins hymn.

14. Archimandrite Sophrony (Sakharov), *Words of Life* (Maldon, UK: Stavropegic Monastery of St. John the Baptist, 1996), 9. (See the epigraph above.)

15. Kenneth Surin, *Theology and the Problem of Evil* (Oxford: Blackwell, 1986); Terrence Tilley, *The Evils of Theodicy* (Washington, DC: Georgetown University Press, 1991); Odo Marquard, "Unburdenings: Theodicy Motives in Modern Philosophy," in Robert M. Wallace, trans., *In Defense of the Accidental: Philosophical Studies* (New York: Oxford University Press, 1991), distilled helpfully in Mark Larrimore, ed., *The Problem of Evil: A Reader* (Oxford: Blackwell, 2001), xxvii–xxix.

16. Anthony, *Apophthegmata Patrum*, saying 2, in Benedicta Ward, trans., *The Sayings of the Desert Fathers*, Cistercian Studies 59, rev. ed. (Kalamazoo, MI: Cistercian, 1984), 2.

17. The subject of divine providence is a major theme in Chrysostom's work; it finds explicit and sustained treatment especially in the treatises *On Providence*, *On the Incomprehensibility of God*, and *To Those Who Are Scandalized by Adversity*.

18. *On Providence* 4, x (SC 79, 86).

19. See Peter Bouteneff, "Sacraments as the Mystery of Union: Elements in an Orthodox Sacramental Theology," in *The Gestures of God: Explorations in Sacramentality*, ed. G. Rowell and C. Hall (London: Continuum, 2004), 91–107.

20. John Chrysostom, *On Providence* 2.1 (SC 79, 60).

21. Ibid., 14.9; 15.4.

22. St. Basil, *Homilies on the Hexaemeron* 7.5.

23. Theodoret of Cyrus, *On Divine Providence* 3.21. See T. Halton, trans., *Theodoret of Cyrus on Divine Providence* (New York: Newman Press, 1988), 41.

24. Plato, *Laws*, 899–910. See T. J. Saunders, trans., *Plato: The Laws*, rev. ed. (New York: Penguin, 1975), 432–47.

25. G. E. Wright's *God Who Acts: Biblical Theology as Recital* (London: SCM, 1952), and his subsequent *The Old Testament and Theology* (New York: Harper and Row, 1969) both remain influential.

26. *Didaskalia Patriki*, being the "paternal exhortation" of Patriarch Anthimos of Jerusalem, issued in Constantinople, 1798. It is a reaction to the political reforms of the Enlightenment and of the French Revolution. Translated in Richard Clogg, ed., *The Movement for Greek Independence, 1770–1821: A Collection of Documents* (New York: Harper & Row, 1976), 56–62; the quotation is from 59.

27. Ibid.

28. Vladimir Lossky, *Orthodox Theology: An Introduction* (Crestwood, NY: SVS Press, 1978), 73.

29. See ibid.

30. Plato's *Republic*, e.g., ends with the myth of Er, a parable on the afterlife which focuses on the role of free choice in a person's destiny. The role of human freedom, writes Plato, is such that "the gods are blameless."

31. Hick's seminal work, *Evil and the God of Love*, rev. ed. (New York: HarperSanFrancisco, 1977; first published 1966), inspired further elaboration specifically in the essay "An Irenaean Theodicy," in *Encountering Evil: Live Options in Theodicy*, rev. ed., ed. Stephen T. Davis (Louisville: Westminster John Knox, 2001), 38–52.

32. Cf. Irenaeus, *Adv. Haer.* 4.37–39.

33. See Peter C. Bouteneff, *Beginnings: Ancient Christian Readings of the Biblical Creation Narratives* (Grand Rapids: Baker Academic, 2008), 79–83.

34. Hick, "Irenaean Theodicy," 43.

35. Gregory of Nazianzus, Or. 24.11 (SC 284:62).

36. John Damascene, *Expos.* 43.2 (Kotter II, 100); Nemesius of Emesa, *Nat. Hom.* 42, 343–44 (Morani 125); Maximos the Confessor, *Ambig.* 10.42 (PG 91:1189B). Maximos inserts the clause "according to our God-bearing fathers," by whom he must have meant at least Nemesius.

37. Origen, *Hom. in Gen.* 3.2 (SC 7bis:114–16).

38. Cf. Peter Bouteneff, "The Two Wills of God: Providence in St. John of Damascus," *Studia Patristica* 42 (2006): 291–96.

CHAPTER 10

A HELPER OF PROVIDENCE

"Justified Providential War" in Vladimir Solov'ev

BRANDON GALLAHER

> Providence certainly extracts good from our evil, but from our good it derives a still greater good. And what is of especial importance is that this second kind of good comes about with our direct and active participation, while the first, that derived from our evil, does not concern us nor belong to us. It is better to be a helper than a dead instrument of the all-merciful Providence.
>
> —Vladimir Solov'ev, *The Justification of the Good* [*Opravdanie dobra*][1]

An Orthodox approach to war and peace begins appropriately with praise and providence.[2] This is the sense of a prayer from *The Liturgy of Saint Basil* that runs: "Preserve the good in goodness, and make the evil be good by your goodness." We also learn prophetically from Joseph, as a type of Christ crucified by man but willed to be sacrificed by God, when he speaks to his own brothers who tried to kill him, that God can transform the most heinous action (e.g., fratricide or deicide) toward the goodness of life (Gen. 50:19–21).[3] It is also the approach to the notion of "just war" taken by Vladimir Solov'ev (1853–1900). For him, war was unarguably evil: "To the first question with regard to war there exists only one indisputable answer: *war is an evil.*"[4] However, he held that it was not an "absolute evil," such as eternal damnation or a deadly sin like adultery, but a "relative evil" which, being less than other evils, was, in relation to them, a "lesser good." It proved itself necessary insofar as it might prevent the arising of a "greater evil" or even could produce, paradoxically, a "greater good." But such an ethical approach merely imaged the providence of God. The evil that human beings do is permitted by God providentially for the purposes of his "justification of the Good," his perfecting of the cosmos, since God can, despite us, extract good out of our evil using us as "dead instruments." However, and far more importantly, an act which has evil consequences, such as physical violence in war, under certain clearly defined circumstances and with the right intention, can be deemed moral and indeed morally obligatory, and in such a situation, Solov'ev argues, we directly and actively work with God as his "helpers," transforming evil into a still greater good (*JG*, 278, 332–33 [*OD*, 356, 425–26]). In other words, Solov'ev espoused a providential version of just war theory, which might be called "justified providential war."

Solov'ev is today a neglected figure and deserves to take his place among the most important thinkers of the nineteenth century. He was a philosopher, theologian, poet, critic, and mystic, and a massively influential figure in late nineteenth- and early twentieth-century Russian thought and life.[5] A close friend of Fyodor Dostoyevsky (1821–81), and reputedly the model for both Ivan and Alyosha in *Brothers Karamazov*, he inspired figures in the arts (the Symbolist poets: Vyacheslav Ivanov [1866–1949], Aleksandr Blok [1880–1921], Andrei Bely [1880–1934]), philosophy and theology (Prince Sergei N. Trubetskoi [1862–1905], Nikolai Lossky [1870–1965], Sergii Bulgakov [1871–1944], Semyon Frank [1877–1950], Pavel Florensky [1882–1937], Lev Karsavin [1882–1952]), and even, with his late works, in liberal social philosophy (Prince Evgenii N. Trubetskoi [1863–1920], Pavel Novgorodtsev [1866–1924], Pyotr Struve [1870–1944], Bulgakov again). However, due to his focus in some of his most famous books (e.g., *Lectures on Godmanhood*, 1877–

81), essays, and poems on the quasi-divine mythical figure of "Sophia," his philosophy/theology ("sophiology"), and its continuation in figures like Florensky and Bulgakov, was rejected as heterodox by a younger generation of Russian émigré theologians (especially Georges Florovsky [1893–1979] and Vladimir Lossky [1903–58]), whose patristic-exegetical vision of theology has until very recently been all but unquestionable in contemporary Eastern Orthodox theology. Although he was admired by some figures in the West (notably, Hans Urs von Balthasar [1905–88], Louis Bouyer [1913–2004], and Thomas Merton [1915–68]), his influence was mostly limited to the few in the German- and French-speaking worlds who were sympathetic to his hybrid idiom of Kantianism, German Romanticism, the Greek fathers, Aquinas, and esoterica (e.g., Kabbalah). Yet large tracts of Solov'ev, especially his writings on ethics, law, and social issues, make no explicit reference to his sophiology, and it is in this area that he has much to teach us concerning the phenomenon of war.

THE GOOD

But one simply cannot understand how Solov'ev understands war without a broad awareness of what he meant by the "justification of the good" and how it relates to providence, the kingdom of God, Christ, the task of humanity, and evil. Solov'ev's version of just war theory is above all *wholistic*, such that one does violence to his thought by treating his theology (broadly understood) separately from his ethics. In his massive *Opravdanie dobra* (*Justification of the Good*; 1897; rev. 1899)[6] he writes that the book aims to show that the Good "as truth and righteousness" is the only right and consistent way to live in all things to the end of one's days (*JG*, lii [*OD*, 3]). The Good, for Solov'ev, is not the particular forms in which it is manifested, which are conditional upon circumstances and history and—in different circumstances—might actually be an evil or source of evil (lxvi [20]). Rather, the Good is the source of all virtues, of all particular goods and duties. These duties cohere in the Good beyond any conflict of powers, and the Good orders the moral nature of man. Human beings bear in their consciousness the Good as the unity of all the inner forms of the good given in our reason and conscience by which we discriminate between good and evil. Unusually, Solov'ev understands human

moral nature as structured by three fundamental feelings or moral sentiments: shame (the foundation of sexual shame), pity/compassion/charity
(the basis of altruism), and piety/reverence (as the moral basis of religion;
see 23–36 [49–65]). Much of the book consists of a sort of phenome-
nology of these ultimate foundations of the moral life, and he believes
that any moral teaching is nothing but a development of these data as
their demands cover all human relations (e.g., family) and organizations
(e.g., church, state, and economic and local civic society [*zemstvo*]). When
the three fundamental feelings are considered from different points of
view, we can arrive at corresponding virtues, rules of action, and the conditions of particular goods (81 [119]).

There are three essential attributes of the Good. As unconditioned,
it is "pure," giving us the ability in each case to draw absolute distinctions
between good and evil (deliberation) and in these cases to say *yes* or *no*
(action) by gifting us with free will. Second, as all-conditioning, it is "all-
embracing [*polnota*: completeness]" in that it is connected to all concrete
relations. Solov'ev explains this by showing the rational and ideal content
of the Good "through the concrete moral data in which it is contained"
(*JG*, lxviii–lxix [*OD*, 22–23]). He shows how the Good has been acted
upon in the whole of history and in society insofar as it is realized in the
family, the economy and local community, the state, the church, and
every area of life, growing "in completeness and definitiveness as the conditions of the historical and natural environment become more complex"
(lv [6]).[7] Lastly, as being realized through all things, it is "all-powerful [*sila
ili deistvennost'*: power or potency]" insofar as it is providence itself and
will ultimately triumph over all things, including death, revealing the
kingdom of God and accomplishing the universal resurrection (lxviii–lxix
[22–23]). The moral significance of life, therefore, is determined by the
Good, and it is the last court of appeal for all forms and events, which are
held up to it, are conditional, and are relative to it, as it is "not conditioned by anything, but itself conditions all things, and is realised through
all things" (lxviii [22]). The focus of Solov'ev's work is the second of these
attributes (i.e., the Good's completeness/integrality/all-embracing character), as he believed that Kant had already dealt well with the "formal
purity of the will" or deliberation and action, and, he opined, if one could
show that the Good conditions everything, then its purity and omnipo-

tence would become manifest. However, in focusing on this latter aspect, we often, as we shall see, are left guessing as to how, more precisely, Solov'ev understood both moral decision-making and choice, as well as the nature of providence. These latter themes are treated in passing, and one must piece together his opinions on them from different sources. Solov'ev's ethics, therefore, despite its great brilliance, seems somewhat like a fragment awaiting completion.

As should be apparent, the Good, for Solov'ev, is "from God" (*JG*, 117 [*OD*, 163]). Indeed, it is the same thing to say that I believe in it and its objective independent significance in the world as to say that I believe "in the moral order, in Providence, in God" (77 [115]), since the Godhead is "this perfect reality, this absolute or supreme good" (144 [195]). The Good, as the pure, all-embracing, and all-powerful way and end of God himself, justifies itself by remaining true to itself in all its varied paths, and Solov'ev tries to show this through giving an account of it in all of human life and history. In "showing" the "essential Good" as the only sure path for those striving to act morally, one does not then *individually* prove its reliability—as one would rationally prove in a theodicy that God is not responsible for evil—but merely allows it to show itself as sure and true since "it alone justifies itself and justifies our confidence in it," for (and here enters praise) God is the Good One to whom before the open grave (as repeated both at the Orthodox funeral service and in a *Panikhida* or memorial service) we call, "Blessed art thou, O Lord: teach me thy justification" (*nauchi mia opravdaniem Tvoim* [Slavonic; Hebrew and LXX: "thy statutes"]; Ps. 119:12; 118:12 LXX) (*JG*, lii [*OD*, 3]). In other words, the title of what is arguably the most substantial modern work of Orthodox moral philosophy/theology (*Opravdanie dobra*), written by a man often portrayed by the neopatristic founders of contemporary Orthodox theology as a "heretic," was inspired by the Orthodox Church's funeral services.

PROVIDENCE

But why should one, theologically speaking, care about this justification of the Good? Here enters providence. The Good is justified in the fact that in all the meandering paths of history, God can be shown to draw forth the good out of the most dire circumstances, out of evil itself, even the horror of war. Evil, for Solov'ev, is a "real *power*, ruling our world by means of temptations" and the passions, so to fight it—and he saw the world as a battleground between good and evil—one must seek assistance in "another sphere of being," working in conjunction with the Good in all its serene divinity as it justifies itself (Solov'ev, *Three Conversations*, 15 [*Tri razgovora*, 83]).[8] This co-working with God against the power of the evil one is part of God's perfecting of the world, his divinization of it, turning evil to good and letting goodness flourish in even the most awful places, and, as we shall see below, we can even cooperate with him in this task in the evil of war under certain strict circumstances and with the right intention.

The justification of the Good in history, therefore, is only ultimately obtained in the transfiguration, the perfection, of all things. All of reality and man in particular is imperfect, unlike God, who is perfect, and the task of creation is to become perfect, to become the "absolute moral order" or "the kingdom of God" (*JG*, 145–47, 165 [*OD*, 195–98]). God is at work in the world, which, as it is imperfect, is not the end of God's work but the means, the system of conditions, by which he accomplishes its perfection as the "kingdom of ends." What exists exists in virtue of God's approval of it either as being good as a "means" or as a "purpose" and an "end." In the consciousness and freedom of man lies the inner possibility for each human to stand in an independent relationship to God, to be his "direct purpose" in the kingdom of ends, voluntarily and consciously preferring good to evil in everything. All of history, therefore, is the realization of this possibility for all human beings: full, conscious, and free union with God, the approach to perfection whereby God is manifested in both man and matter, which is the unconditional good that God desires for every person, indeed all creation (158, 150 [211, 201–2]), or, "according to the patristic expression, the possibility of becoming divine (*theosis*)" (296 [379]).[9] What Solov'ev's thought is focused on above all, then, is what he referred to as the "spiritualization of matter and the materialization of spirit,"[10] or "free theurgy."[11] This union of heaven and earth, transfiguration of creation which is the revelation of the kingdom of God, the resurrection of all things and the perfect moral order in which the Good is justified, Solov'ev also describes—unsurprisingly, since evil cannot remain in existence if God is to be all in all—as the "universal resurrection and restitution of all things, *apokatastasis ton panton* [Acts 3:21]" (165 [220]; translation adapted).[12]

Human beings are not a passive instrument of the will of God in this process; they are, rather, the "voluntary ally and co-participant in his work in the universe," which is to bring it to perfection, in theological language, to divinize it (*JG*, 150 [*OD*, 202]). Such divinization, in its full accomplishment, being a reality where God is all in all, is the ultimate triumph of the Good, for all God's ways are then shown to be just and true even in the face of evil, suffering, and great horrors like war. However, it is not only crucial that we strive for perfection in ourselves; we must also recognize the possibility of good in all that is and work for it to be actualized, attempting to make love shine in even the darkest places. This possibility is above all manifested in all rational and free beings, so we must not only recognize ourselves as bearers of the consciousness of the absolute ideal of the Good (*imago dei*) but also strive to realize it completely (*similitudo dei*). We must recognize this possibility in all other persons, who have an absolute worth and can never be treated as only a means to an end (229, 231 [296, 298]), so that the attaining of perfection is not only an individual task but also a "world-wide work of history" that takes form in the family, the church, economic and local civic relations, and the state (152 [204]).

The obtaining of perfection, the revelation of the kingdom of God, as was said above, requires the cooperation of God and man. It is simply impossible for God to obtain his purpose in creation in fully perfecting it, turning evil into good, extracting peace from war, apart from human activity, because human beings themselves, as free beings, cannot attain perfection at once but only through a long and laborious process of becoming perfect. Perfection is a gift to humanity from God—the divine content of the unconditional Good—but it is nevertheless not something which can be simply gifted instantly since it is an "inner condition attainable only through one's own experience alone," and an absolutely crucial part of that experience is the capacity to receive it. Here what is needed is humanity's uniting of their will with that of God; but in order for this to happen there must be an inner *askesis* whereby humanity through experience is purged of all that is incompatible with the Good (*JG*, 150–51 [*OD*, 201–3]). The "unconditional principle of morality," therefore, is to work in synergy with God, recognizing all human beings as having absolute value as they too are made in the image and likeness of God, in order to perfect oneself, others, and creation *"so that the Kingdom of God may be finally revealed in the world"* (152 [204]).

But how can the ideal of the unconditional Good be obtained in human consciousness without some sort of divine aid? If the Good is borne as an ideal in human consciousness, as the call to perfection, then is it not possible that that ideal of the Good, the actual possession of absolute perfection, might actually exist in a person? But if such a realized ideal exists, it cannot be merely human, but must be divine-human—the God-man in whom and through and to whom we are all called (*JG*, 167 [*OD*, 222]). The purpose of the world process, the meaning of history, then, lies at the center of history, and this is the ultimate justification of the Good, which is the revelation of Jesus Christ as the "all-embracing [*vseedinoe*: all-one] Word of the Kingdom of God," understood as the "perfect moral order realized by a new humanity *which spiritually grows out of the God-man*" (168 [224]).[13] Christ realizes the meaning of everything, the perfect moral order, by embracing and connecting together all things, gathering the universe together in reality, by the "living personal power of love" (165 [220]). He is both the absolute principle of the Good and its fullness, and he founds the perfect moral order by the universality of his spirit (169 [225]). This spirit is capable of embracing and regenerating all things, and as its perfection is complete and absolute, fully realized, it is even victorious over death itself in the resurrection; how much more, then, over the evil of war. Christianity reveals to human beings the absolutely perfect and immortal "personality" in the "event" of the revelation of Jesus Christ, and it promises a society built after the pattern of that revelation. Since such a society cannot be built by external force, as then it would negate the perfection of Christ, the "promise" of it is set before us as a "task" for each individual and for all people (213–14 [276–77]). We are "tasked" to accept Christ and regard all things in his spirit, and this means to enable this spirit to become incarnate in all things, Christifying all of reality from family relationships to geopolitical unions (169 [225]). Christ is the "event" of the revelation of the Good, and with this revelation comes the "promise" of a community conformed after him—the kingdom of God. But the "task" of this community, of enacting the absolute and final revelation of the truth that is Christianity in the world, is in our hands since the "moral regeneration of our life must be brought about by ourselves" (214 [277]).[14]

When Solov'ev spoke of a "task" of humanity, he meant no less than a "Christian politics" which was tasked with fulfilling the promise given to us in Christ and his church by elevating and transubstantiating all social and political forms into the kingdom.[15] This means the transformation or "humanization" of the society, material life, nature, and the individual in the spirit of Christ.[16] But if there is such a "Christian" politics, then there certainly could be a state that was also "Christian" and embodied such politics (*JG*, 382–83 [*OD*, 484–86]). Indeed, Solov'ev saw political organization, the body politic, as absolutely crucial to the good of both the individual and society and believed that it was as necessary to human flourishing as the human body. With the coming of Christ and the good news of the kingdom, the animal, vegetable, and mineral kingdoms did not disappear, he argued, and so too there is no reason that the "human kingdom" seen in political organization and in civil and juridical order—the state, in short—should be abolished, as it is as necessary to historical progress as the others are to "cosmical" progress (382 [485]).

Along with the order summarized in the state comes not only political office and law but the military, and Solov'ev pointed out that if the centurion Cornelius (Acts 10) could become a Christian and not renounce his service as a soldier, then it must be possible to have not only a "Christian soldier" but a collection of such soldiers as a "Christian army," and if an army is the "extreme expression and the first real basis" of the order of the state, then a "Christian state" is also surely possible (*JG*, 378–80 [*OD*, 480–82]). Christ came not to abolish but to confirm—and by confirming, to transform and complete—the civic and juridical order embodied in the state (382–83 [484–86]). The Christian state is, he argued, "*collectively organized pity*" raised from a limited and powerless individual feeling to a historically organized social force and activity which can (and this will sometimes involve military force) give help and protection to countless people instead of dozens or a few hundred (385 [488]). The organized pity of the state is needed for working toward the revelation of the kingdom, which requires the preservation of social life and the improvement of the conditions of human existence so that human creativity is liberated for the work of perfection (392 [496]), and as long as the kingdom is not yet attained, there will be need for people to be cared for and defended, possibly with force, and there will be the moral demand for organizing this well and on a wide scale (386 [489]). We will return to this issue below.

Solov'ev's politics was in no way a quietist or reactionary conservatism, for he fought not only for the rights of ethnic Poles and religious minorities in Russia, like the Jews and the Old Believers, but against capital punishment and for a more equitable role for women in society.[17] Politics for him was the living out of the kingdom of God in the world through striving for unification with God in Christ "by means of an internal divinization [*obozhenie*] through an experience of the cross, through moral *podvig*,[18] through self-abnegation both personal and national."[19] Indeed, his call for the realization of the kingdom of God on earth through realizing divine law in the human world and embodying the heavenly in the earthly took the form in the 1880s of a rather utopian proposal for a free, true, universal, and Christoform "theocracy" as a *symphonia* of independent but mutually dependent centers of power: the church, state, and local economic and civic society (*zemstvo*), each headed by its respective organ of king/emperor, priest/pope, or prophet/independent preacher and teacher, as Christ himself is a priest, a king, and a prophet.[20] Solov'ev, in true Russian messianic fervor and despite his stringent critique of Russian nationalism and of the Russian Orthodox Church,[21] saw the Russian empire as a providential reality that embraced the three peoples best able to exemplify what he would call "the social Trinity"[22]—the Poles as Roman Catholics under the pope, the Russians with their czar, and the Jews with the law and the prophets.[23] The high priest of the church is the highest expression of piety as the church embodies this feeling (as "collectively organized piety," *JG*, 385 [*OD*, 488]), the Christian monarch is the summation of mercy/pity and truth as seen in the state, and the true prophet is the highest attainment of shame and conscience as heading the local economic and civil society (402 [509]). As recent scholarship has shown,[24] Solov'ev never abandoned this theocratic ideal (see esp. 351–403 [447–509]), but it is arguable that his awareness of human fallibility and blindness when faced with counterfeit goods, the emphasis on the coming of Christ, and the focus on the freedom of prophecy moved him "ever further away from seeking his ideal"—as the late Oliver Smith has observed—"in concrete human institutions and authorities."[25]

EVIL

Now that we have a broad overview of Solov'ev's vision of the Good—of social, ecclesial, and political society and providence and Christ—how does this rather elaborate vision relate precisely to the existence of evil? Evil, for Solov'ev, may be either absolute, such as "mortal sin" and damnation, or relative, which is to say less or greater than some other evil. Since all evil is a privation of good, and God is the Good, some evils may be regarded, in comparison to others, as good in a relative sense; for example, if one has cancer, an operation can be a "necessary evil" to save one's life, or if one has the flu, fever, shivering, cough, and so on, those can be an expression, a symptom, of the body's fight against the illness, although such a state is far from being a happy condition (*JG*, 331–33 [*OD*, 423–26]). God, we are told, neither approves of evil—for then it would be good—nor denies it unconditionally, for in that case it would not exist at all. Evil—and here Solov'ev is building on a well-known patristic teaching—exists by the providence of God.[26] God denies it a final and abiding existence, so in the end it will perish and God will be all in all. He *permits* evil, then, as a "*transitory condition of freedom*" or for the sake of a "*greater good*." On the one hand, God permits evil inasmuch as the annihilation of it would violate human freedom, making for a "greater evil," thereby making free and perfect goodness, which must be chosen, impossible in the world. On the other hand, the cause of the existence of evil is God's permission insofar as in his wisdom he can "extract from evil a greater good or the greatest possible perfection." Evil, quite simply, is in the providential service of God or is "subservient" to him so that an unconditional rejection of it would be contrary to the will of God. It is crucial, therefore, that we begin to regard evil in God's fashion, which is not to be "indifferent" to it but to rise beyond "absolute opposition to it and allow it—when it does not proceed from us—as a means of perfection insofar as a greater good can be derived from it." Here Solov'ev is very careful, for having said that, like God, we must allow for evil "when it does not proceed from us," he then qualifies this statement by saying that such an approach involves the recognition of the "possibility," indeed, the "potentiality," of good in all that exists, and the obligation follows to "work for that possibility to become an actuality" (152 [203–4]).

The trouble with this sort of providential thinking on evil is that it is most vague, because one is unclear when evil is evil as such and when it might in fact harbor some possibility or potentiality of good as a further consequence which God providentially draws out. This ambiguity is exacerbated by Solov'ev's adaptation of the notion of metaphysical evil, with God being absolutely good and everything less than him being relatively evil, and so a lesser good than something better, with only mortal sins being absolutely evil.[27] The temptation is to think that one is not bound by ordinary morals and that one can do an evil act, which is probably a lesser good anyway, for the sake of the good that may emerge from it, thus bringing Paul's condemnation on oneself: "And why not do evil that good may come?—as some people slanderously charge us with saying. Their condemnation is just" (Rom. 3:8 RSV).

Solov'ev was well aware of this "mistaken view" such that providence might derive wonderful results from a person's drunkenness or other immorality. He gives the example of a drunk, who from the motives of abstinence does not go to the pub. However, had he followed his evil inclination, on his way stumbling back drunk he would have found a half-frozen puppy which he would have warmed back to life, and this puppy, having grown up into a big dog, would have saved a drowning girl in a pond, and the girl would have grown up to be the mother of a great man. The misplaced good deed of abstinence would have "interfered with the plans of providence," because through this chain of consequences, a great man would remain unborn. But if evil (and "relative," being drunkenness) might lead to good, the same might be said for good leading to unforeseen evil. For example, we might hypothesize that a man having saved another man's life from a robber might have inadvertently allowed a terrible murderer to survive, so, the reasoning goes, he should not have saved him in the first place (*JG*, 275–76 [*OD*, 353–54]). Of course, such mad providential thinking, Solov'ev contended, would make morality impossible in that we could never abstain from any evil act or even do a good act that was morally obligatory, because it might just lead to some evil consequence we cannot foresee. In order for Christian moral reasoning to function, acts must be bad or good in themselves, whatever consequences they may have. Otherwise one would end up with a form of utilitarianism that would be simply morally unworkable. Despite this acknowledgment, it seems that Solov'ev's notion of the relativity of good and evil—and we shall return to this matter below—contradicts the notion that he also wishes to hold that all acts must be good or bad in themselves.

All things considered, Solov'ev held that such faulty thinking ultimately implodes, since clearly the series of unknown events with bad or good consequences might go on forever, and moral calculation would become impossible, as we can never know the whole series of consequences right down to the end of the world. One cannot, therefore, act or not act on the basis of indirect consequences but only on the basis of the "impulses *directly* following from the positive demands of the moral principle." We must trust that reason and conscience are aligned with providence such that when in each concrete case our reason and conscience tell us what direct good one can do independent of all indirect consequences, providence will not let these actions ultimately lead to evil (*JG*, 276–77 [*OD*, 354–56]). Solov'ev argues, therefore, that providence can and does extract good from evil, but that this does not require our participation and does not concern us. However, there is a second form of providential action that does concern us, which is when from the good we do, a good that may in fact have an unintended evil consequence (to which we shall return), God can derive a "still greater good." This latter, greater good drawn out by providence requires "our direct and active participation," for "it is better to be a helper than a dead instrument of the all-merciful Providence" (278 [356]).

We must, as was said earlier, look for the good that can be done in all circumstances, even in and during the evil of war. This type of providential thinking is resolutely Christoform and ecclesial. Although Christ has through the cross and the resurrection finally conquered evil at the center of the cosmos—namely, *in* himself—the victory over evil in the circumference of the world, *within* the rest of humanity, has to be accomplished through humanity's own experience in conjunction with God. Those in the church have, as it were, been baptized into Christ but have not yet put on Christ. This ecclesial cooperation with God's victory over evil in Christ is twofold: (a) by struggling on the side of good against evil even until the very end of the age, and (b) by seeing evil providentially and attempting to actualize the potential good in what is merely a possibility. But how might one precisely actualize the potential good in the midst of evil?

We are given the germ of Solov'ev's response in the context of his discussion of crime and punishment—the principle of double effect. Without getting too deeply into the complexities of this issue, this is the teaching, stated classically by Thomas Aquinas (1225–74),[28] of how an act can be morally permissible when it involves a side effect that is a bad result.[29] There are many classic examples. A surgeon amputates a person's limb as the patient is suffering from a flesh-eating disease. The doctor who removes a woman's uterus, which is cancerous, so saving her life, ends up killing her unborn child. A pilot shoots down a hijacked plane that is hurtling toward a tall building in a metropolis, saving those in the building and the city but killing those in the plane. A crazed killer attacks you with a knife, and in attempting to save your own life, you kill him instead.

There exist various classic conditions under which the principle of double effect can be called upon in moral evaluation: (1) the act must be good or indifferent; (2) the evil (side) effect is not intended, only permitted or tolerated, but the good effect is intended; (3) the good effect is not produced by means of the evil effect, thus meaning that the agent intends the evil as a means to the good; and (4) there must be a proportionally grave reason for permitting the evil effect.[30] Solov'ev discusses the question whether it is moral to use physical violence to prevent a criminal from murdering someone when the evildoer is unaffected by "words of rational persuasion." He argues that it is not only permissible but binding on a person to defend someone in such a case, for, despite the necessary violent effect of such action, one not only preserves the life of the victim but actively respects and supports the perpetrator's human dignity by preventing him from carrying out his evil intention, and thus saves him from sin (*JG*, 273–74 [*OD*, 350–51]). Physical violence in itself is not bad or immoral. It is in a sense morally neutral, and what gives it its character is one's intention—evil (e.g., vengeance, hatred of the evildoer) or good (e.g., restraining the evildoer for the sake of the victim and the evildoer)—and the circumstances of the case. If "the application of muscular force" were bad in itself, then even a good intention would not justify an action, for then one would be applying the immoral rule that the end justifies the means. Physical force rationally used is a "good means" as long as it is "used for the real good of others," and in such an application of it, it is "directly prescribed by the moral principle." As long as our attitude is moral in that we are thinking of the evildoer's own good, there is nothing immoral in the violence; it will simply be the "inevitable condition of our helping the man, just like a surgical operation or the locking up of a dangerous lunatic" (274 [351–52]).

This of course has problems, including how we can so neatly separate our good intention from any intent to will the side effect,[31] which requires a detailed account of action and deliberation that Solov'ev simply does not mention. But Solov'ev's basic point could not be clearer. What is ostensibly evil is actually good under certain circumstances and with the right intention: "The dividing line between the moral and immoral use of physical compulsion may be a fine one, but it is perfectly clear and definite" (*JG*, 274 [*OD*, 352]). With the principle of double effect, we can see how, in the midst of evil, we might be able to do good, working consciously with God in the growth of a greater good. Here finally enters the issue of war, and with war, as we shall see, things become much more ambiguous.

WAR

Solov'ev was absolutely clear that war was an evil, yet, following his understanding of physical violence, he regarded the participation in war in certain circumstances and with the right intention as morally obligatory and, furthermore, as part of the human work toward the revelation of the kingdom and the future resurrection. In order to understand his position we now need to turn to a discussion of his famous *Tri razgovora* (*Three*

Conversations [1900]), which we shall supplement by his chapter on war in *Justification of the Good* (*JG*, 331–50 [*OD*, 423–46]). This final work of Solov'ev, as can be seen from its usual subtitle ("On War, Progress, and the End of History), is eschatological in theme and consists of three conversations between five upper-class Russians (the General, the Politician, the Prince, a middle-aged Lady [who says very little that is substantive], and a "Mr. Z") in the garden of a French villa on "the struggle against evil and the meaning of history from three different standpoints" (*TC*, 20 [*TR*, 87]). The last conversation concludes with Mr. Z reading from a manuscript written by a monk called "Fr. Pansophii" (usually latinized as Pansophius: "all-wise"), entitled "A Short Story of the Anti-Christ," which is on the end of the world or the *eschata* (last things or events).[32] This story is much better known than the rest of *Three Conversations* and is often published separately a bit like Fyodor Dostoyevsky's "The Legend of the Grand Inquisitor," told by the character Ivan in *Brothers Karamazov* (1880). The work as a whole, however, is really a dramatic meditation on the ultimate or final things that matter, from war to salvation.

Solov'ev gives, in the three conversations and the concluding "Short Story of the Anti-Christ," multiple portraits of different approaches to war. In the first conversation, we have a sketch of "holy war" in the speeches of the General, followed by the second conversation, where "the ideas of culture and politics" prevailing in the mid-to-late nineteenth century are expressed and defended by the Politician. This latter position roughly overlaps with Realpolitik. These first two conversations are interrupted by the pacifist viewpoint dramatized by the character of the Prince, who is portrayed as both dissenting and shrill. Solov'ev concludes the work with a third conversation in the speeches of Mr. Z and his relation of Father Pansophius's tale. These last two sections of the work present the "absolutely religious" point of view which Solov'ev claims will show "its decisive value in the future." This is his own position—although he acknowledges the "relative truth" of the other positions—and I want to argue that it is a version of "just (or "justifiable") war" from the point of view of the justification of the good or providence (*TC*, 20 [*TR*, 87]).

The first conversation, especially as seen in the speeches of the General, gives prominence to the "religious conception of the everyday life" characteristic of the past (*TC*, 20 [*TR*, 87]). The General portrays the view known in the literature surrounding the ethics of war as "holy war." He argues that the Russian Army is, following a slogan of that day, "a glorious band of Christ-loving warriors," each of whose members knew from earliest times till that very day not only that the army served a "good and important cause" but that war was a "holy cause" and was part of a service that was good, honorable, and noble and, above all, sanctified and exalted by the church and glorified by the nation (31, 32, 34; and see 37 [93, 94, 95; and see 98]). He upholds the opinion that all the saints mentioned in the *Synaxarion* are either monks or warriors, so, he says, it seems implausible that the soldiers who are saints could have been glorified if military occupations (let alone war) were regarded as a "necessary evil" something like "liquor traffic" (35–36 [96–97]).

In one of the most dramatic moments in the work, he tells a grisly tale about the ethnic cleansing in Armenia during the Russo-Turkish War of 1877–78 carried out by Turkish and Kurdish irregular soldiers, the Bashi-Bazouks, who were known for their brutality and lack of discipline and who, not being salaried, lived off of their plunder (*TC*, 52–59 [*TR*, 109–14]). This episode in Russian history was fresh in the memory of the public due to the Armenian Massacre of 1895.[33] This tale is a moving witness to Solov'ev's opinion that war is evil. During one of the campaigns, the General and his Cossacks came across the remains of a caravan of Armenian refugees, many of them women and children, who had been tied to the axle wheels of their carts by the irregulars—some by their heads, some by the feet, and some by their waists. The General recounts that the irregulars, after mutilating many of their victims (cutting off breasts, disembowelling), "slowly grilled" them by setting the carts on fire. One scene remains vivid in the General's memory: a woman was tied to a wheel by her head and shoulders so she could not move. She bore no wounds and was unburnt, but on her face was sheer terror; indeed, the General believes she had died of horror: "And before her dead, staring eyes was a high pole, firmly fixed in the ground, and to it was tied the poor little naked body of a baby—her son, most likely—a blackened, scorched little corpse, with protruding eyes" (54 [110]). Through one survivor, the General and his troops track down the irregulars and in vengeance for their actions butcher them all in turn. He says that the memory of killing over a thousand men in fifteen minutes is his "best and purest": "It was not with my own sinful hands that I killed, but with six pure, chaste steel guns, which poured forth a most virtuous and beneficent rain of shells" (52–53 [109]). He believes—and here talk of "intention" seems somewhat quaint in the face of such mad sacralizing of vengeance—that he was acting as the means of God in wiping the irregulars off the face of the earth: "Well, God was with us. The whole thing was over. And I felt in my soul Pascha, the bright Resurrection of Christ. . . . I have in my soul the same bright feast. A silence I knew not from whence and an incomprehensible lightness rested upon me. I felt that all worldly stains were washed away, and that all the burden of earthly trouble had fallen from my shoulders. I was in Paradise—I was feeling God, and there was the end of it" (57–58 [113]; translation revised).[34]

The second conversation, where the speeches of the Politician are in the foreground, exhibits notions of culture and progress, which were characteristic of the educated people of that day (*TC*, 20 [*TR*, 87]). The Politician's views are (by and large) a summary of the sort of Realpolitik concerning war that can be seen in the classic treatise *Vom Kriege* (*On War* [1832]) of Carl von Clausewitz (1780–1831). For Clausewitz, war is not merely a political act, but also "a real political instrument, a continuation of political commerce, a carrying out of the same by other means."[35] War is, then, the means of violence by which one forces one's opponent to achieve one's political object or end; and here it would seem to contravene the moral rule that the end never justifies the means (*JG*, 230–31, 241, 274 [*OD*, 297–98, 310–11, 351–52]). The Politician says that from history one can see that "war" is the "main, if not only, instrument" by which the state has both been created and gradually consolidated (*TC*, 77 [*TR*, 129]). One cannot, *pace* the anarchism of the Prince—who is a stand-in for the great novelist and political philosopher Count Lev N. Tolstoy (1828–1910) (see below)—establish a stable human community outside the "compulsory forms" of the state; so it remains a "colossal fact" that war has a supreme historical importance in the existence of stable human community (78 [129]). All things considered, war, though politically necessary and never to be ruled out entirely as a political tool, is horrific and increasingly politically "useless" in comparison with diplomacy (83–84 [133–34]). Indeed, the Politician argues that war is gradually becoming obsolete with the disappearance of "militancy" and "national *pugnacity*," to be replaced by parliamentary struggles and a general new international order (90–92; and see 109 [138–40; and see 152–53]).

The Politician's views are, on the one hand, the product of his atheism—a general (now quite contemporary!) feeling that religion should be sidelined and one should have as little of it as possible in public life. One is reminded here of the famous interruption of an interview of Prime Minister Tony Blair by his powerful political strategist, Alastair Campbell, when a reporter asked Blair about his Christian faith: "We don't do God."[36] This is coupled with a moral relativism that believes that there are no absolute rules but only *necessary* rules that are the product of either societal conventions or a utilitarian calculation based on cause and effect (*TC*, 64, 67, 69, 87, 95, 111, 137, 149 [*TR*, 118, 121, 122–23, 136, 142, 154–55, 175–76, 185]). On the other hand, in the place of God, the Politician has set up a belief in progress, by which is meant European high culture and peace whose major characteristic is "politeness," which is understood as the necessary condition of all cultured activity and conduct (111–12 [154–55]). Wars, then, are not so much evil but "horrid" and "repulsive" to a civilized nation founded on *politesse* (113 [155–56]). The Europeanization (or perhaps a version of Walter Benjamin's "aestheticization of politics"?)[37] of Russia and all "barbarian" peoples like the Turks, by which is meant the spreading of the virtue of politeness, is the ultimate aim of political action insofar as "real culture" requires the cessation of all fighting between people and nations (97, 100–101, 103–8 [143, 146–47, 148–52]). This "progress" is the "peaceful, 'polite,' universally profitable settlement of all international relations and conflicts" (114 [157]).

Though this point of view rules out the religious life and is morally vacuous, Solov'ev acknowledges its relative truth (*TC*, 21 [*TR*, 87–88]). As we shall see below, he held that peace in history has been achieved through war and that the security of the state has been secured by it as well; so war could and can serve, under certain conditions, the purposes of goodness. Nevertheless, Solov'ev saw that the fundamental blindness of this view was its failure to acknowledge evil as a real power in the world which was at war with the good. The adherents of this view held a naïve faith in progress and human perfectibility (without grace or an acknowledgment of sin) that led them to deny, so close to the catastrophe of

World War I, that their "children [would] ever see a great war—a real European war," and led them to suppose that their "grandchildren [would] learn only of little wars—somewhere in Asia or Africa—and of past wars from historical works" (80; and see 102 [130; and see 147–48]). Even if peaceful cooperation between "Christian nations and states" is not only possible but also a necessary way to prevent the "salvation of the Christian world" from being devoured up by "lower elements," nevertheless, the cessation of war in general, Solov'ev opined, seems "impossible before the final catastrophe is over" (24 [90]).

Here a brief excursus on Solov'ev's vision of this final catastrophe is in order. Dating back as far as 1890, Solov'ev speculated that there would be at the end of the age a military clash between Western Christian civilization ("Europe") and a new Mongol onslaught ("Asia"), in the form of China (about whose civilization he was extremely hostile and dismissive) or sometimes a Pan-Asian menace led by Japan. The defeat of this Asian onslaught was all that was necessary to bring about Christian (i.e., European and Western) world domination. He often referred to this eschatological "yellow peril" threat as "Pan-Mongolism"[38] and wrote a celebrated poem (1894) with the same title, prophesying the fall of Russia, as the Third Rome, to the Chinese

> regiments
> As innumerable as locusts
> And just as insatiable
>
> . . . .
>
> O Rus! Forget your bygone glory.
> The two-headed eagle is shattered
> And scraps of your banners are given
> For amusement to the yellow children.[39]

A few lines from this poem form the epigraph for his "Short Story of the Anti-Christ" in *Three Conversations* (*TC*, 159 [*TR*, 193]). He tells the reader that he left out the "'conjecture'" from the tale in order to avoid making the story "too long and too complicated" (24 [90]). This is not entirely correct, as the tale relates that, before the rise of the Anti-Christ and the end of the age with the unity of all the churches against him, a united East Asia under Japanese leadership defeats Russia and Europe, though the Asian alliance ultimately suffers a "crushing defeat at the hands of the All-European army" (164 [196]). Solov'ev wrote numerous other works (e.g., *China and Europe* [1890], *Enemy from the East* [1892]) that elaborate this frankly racist and civilizational nationalist apocalyptic vision.[40]

At the end of his life, Solov'ev was much concerned by the Chinese Boxer Rebellion (1899–1901), where early Chinese nationalists fought against Western colonialism, foreigners, and Christian missionary work (tens of thousands of Christians and hundreds of missionaries were slaughtered during these events). He saw the Boxer Rebellion as proof of his apocalyptic fears for the future menace from the East and for the need for Western powers (including Russia) to divide up China and prevent its growth as a rallying point for all East Asia.[41] However, military action was not enough to combat a united Asia, for, in his last days, Solov'ev confided to his disciple Prince Sergei N. Trubetskoi (1862–1905), a philosopher and historian of ancient Greek philosophy, that one cannot fight China without having first overcome one's own internal "Sinomorphosis" or internal Asiaticism.[42] Solov'ev's speculations on Asia and eschatology had considerable influence in Russia, and they were often combined with various forms of Russian messianism that argued that Russia had a special mission of expansion into the East.[43] Versions of these sorts of messianic, nationalist, militarist, and racist ideas have been revived and recombined in post-1991 Russia. Since 2009, under Patriarch Kirill I (Gundaev) (b. 1946), the Moscow Patriarchate has developed a quasi-phyletist form of *symphonia* to support its vision of the Russian Federation under President Vladimir Putin as the "third Rome" which is a beacon to the West of Christian morality and rectitude: *Russkii mir'* (the Russian world).[44] The ideology of *Russkii mir'* forms the ideological basis for the collaboration of the Russian state and church with the evangelical wing of the US Republican Party (including the engagement of Putin and the Moscow Patriarchate with Donald Trump).[45]

Returning to our main analysis, the Prince, representing pacifism in *Three Conversations*, is generally acknowledged as a caricature of the views of Lev Tolstoy with his suspicion of the state, questioning of the resurrection, holding that violence was the greatest evil, and propounding of vegetarianism, chastity, teetotalism, and the evils of tobacco.[46] Contrary to the views of Solov'ev, the Prince holds that war and militarism are "absolute" and "utter evils" which humanity must get rid of "at any cost" and "immediately." The suppression of the "barbarism" of war "in any case" would be a "triumph for reason and good." War is simply "murder" under another name, and as murder it breaks the commandment "Thou shalt not kill!" (*TC*, 39–41 [*TR*, 99–101]). One must not only refuse to take part in war but persuade others to do likewise (*JG*, 346 [*OD*, 440]). From the standpoint of morality, what is of greatest import is not the one who is killed but only the one who kills and listening to one's conscience (confirmed by the divine law) that says "Don't kill!," so there can be no exceptions in regard to the evil of killing (*TC*, 46, 49 [*TR*, 105, 107]; and see *JG*, 346 [*OD*, 440]). The "essence of the Gospel" is the principle of "not resisting evil by force" (*TC*, 144 [*TR*, 181]).

If we have a true Christian spirit, then the "kingdom of God" will be established on earth and humanity will achieve the "greatest good that they are capable of securing." However, this kingdom is actually destroyed by our various states, armies, courts, universities, and factories. We act like the workers in the parable of the husbandmen (Matt. 21:33–46), who do not carry out their master's will (*TC*, 135–36 [*TR*, 174]). In the case of the mercenaries slaughtered by the General, the Prince opines that someone with true Christian spirit would have "found some means, even in this case as in every other, to awaken in those dark souls the good which lies hidden in every human being" (62–63 [116–17]). In a sense, evil exists only insofar as we are resistant to it and by the measures we take against it, but it has no real power on its own, and so in a sense it does not exist and only appears to because of our wrong beliefs (145 [181]).[47] Of course, if evil does not exist, then one does not need to fight it. However, the central problem with the "moral optimism" of this approach to war is that evil exists as a real power in the world, not just as a deficiency of the good (63 [117]). It is the positive resistance and predominance of the "lower qualities" or passions over the high ones or virtues in every sphere of being, so there is quite simply evil in the majority of people (147 [183]). If one does not oppose evil, in some cases by force if necessary, it will triumph over the good. Indeed, in the very Gospel parable (Matt. 21:33–45) that the Prince cites, the tenants eventually kill the son of the master/householder, and so the master goes and destroys them and gives the vineyard to others (141–42 [178–79]). Furthermore, if a true Christian spirit is one which can awaken even in the darkest of souls the inherent good in them, then it would seem that Christ himself was lacking in this spirit, given his betrayal by Judas and his crucifixion through the actions of the Jews and the gentiles alike (63–64 [117–18]). The views of the Prince are not only counter to the gospel but also false in terms of the justification of the good, because their quietism leads to the triumph of evil.

The third conversation is dominated by the speeches of a "Mr. Z" and is capped off by his reading of the "Short Story of the Anti-Christ" by Fr. Pansophius, which tells of the political and spiritual rise of the humanist Anti-Christ, the most extreme manifestation of evil in history, who is ultimately toppled by the reunified Christian Church (of Protestants, Roman Catholics, and Orthodox) and unassimilated Jews. Solov'ev considers this third standpoint to be that of the "absolutely religious," which he holds to "unreservedly" (*TC*, 20 [*TR*, 87]). If the viewpoints of the General and the Politician represent the past and the present, respectively, then Mr. Z's standpoint is, for Solov'ev, the word of the future and one that is particularly sensitive to the battle of good against evil through providential cooperation with God. This apocalyptic vision of the struggle against the mystery of iniquity, a vision of its short-lived triumph and ultimate destruction, is above all expressed in the tale of the Anti-Christ. Broadly speaking, the perspective of Mr. Z is that of "just war" or, what might be more precise, "justified providential war," and we shall return below to a closer analysis of this view (which is that of Solov'ev).

Almost in Hegelian fashion, Solov'ev acknowledges the "relative truth" contained in the first two standpoints seen in the General and Politician. However, he believes that the "higher absolute truth" expressed by Mr. Z does not exclude or deny the relative truth of his interlocutors; indeed Solov'ev considers that truth's initial realization to be found in the conditions expressed in their opinions, but he believes the higher truth instead raises them up to fullness and in this manner "justifies, appreciates, and sanctifies them" (*TC*, 20–21 [*TR*, 87–88]). Indeed, the Politician's view that wars can lead to peace is also that of Solov'ev himself (*JG*, 342 [*OD*, 436]). All of world history is God's judgment of the world, and it involves a struggle between good and evil historical forces culminating in the apocalypse. For this struggle to be finally resolved, before Christ can come in glory dressed in "royal apparel, and with the wounds from the nails in his outstretched hands" (*TC*, 193 [*TR*, 220]), there must be a great battle between these forces, and this takes place firstly in the field of the internal (and so peaceful) development in the common forms of our culture, some of which are examples of "collective evil" such as (as Solov'ev saw it) economic injustice, nationalism when it degenerates into jingoism, a penal system based on "retribution," and capital punishment (*JG*, 239 [*OD*, 308]). Only the power of evil is "absolutely wrong," and Solov'ev can see how the sword of the soldier and the pen of the diplomat could be equally useful "tools" for fighting the power of evil according to circumstances. The "good," then, as we saw earlier with the discussion of the providential use of evil for good, "finds its expression in many various forms and fashions" (*TC*, 21 [*TR*, 88]).

In regard to the evil of war, he uses *religious* examples taken from a decisive period during the Mongol or Tatar Yoke of Rus' (1240–1480) to illustrate how God can providentially use the relative truths of Realpolitik and holy war. On the one hand, we see the perspective of the Politician providentially at work in St. Alexis, Metropolitan of Moscow and all Russia (ca. 1292–1378), who peacefully pleaded numerous times with the Mongol Golden Horde while acting as regent for St. Dimitrii Donskoi, Prince of Moscow (1350–89) during the latter's minority. On the other hand, in the person of Sergius of Radonezh (1314–92) we see the perspective of "holy war" when he blessed the arms of Dimitrii Donskoi before the Battle of Kulikovo (1380), in which Donskoi defeated the Tatar general Mamai (ca. 1335–81) (*TC*, 21 [*TR*, 88]). The perspective that is not granted by Solov'ev to have a relative truth is that of the pacifism of the Prince (a stand-in, as we argued, for Tolstoy). Indeed, the Anti-Christ's principle claim is that unlike Christ, who brought the sword, he will bring "peace," and he is proclaimed as the "Great Peacemaker" (166, 172–73; and see 169–71 [199, 203–4; and see 201–3]). The book itself ends with the characters saying that the Prince "ran away" at the point in the tale when the Anti-Christ is confronted by the Elder John, who symbolizes the Orthodox Church, because "[the Prince] couldn't stand it" (194 [221]). Thus Solov'ev identifies the great humanitarian Anti-Christ—whose "goodness" is a distortion that hides evil understood as a parody of the Good (120, 193–94; and see 157, 165 [162, 220; and see 191, 197–98])—with the representative of pacifism in the story. Pacifism, it is as if we are told, not only capitulates to evil but also actively encourages it.

"JUSTIFIED PROVIDENTIAL WAR"

As was said above, the views of Mr. Z are those of justified providential war. The justified war tradition is often identified with the West, but Byzantine scholars, Slavists, and even (controversially) some Orthodox theologians have argued that there is a form of this tradition both in Byzantium and in "Orthodox" cultures more generally.[48] In the Western just war tradition, for a war to be "justified" it is broadly acknowledged that it must meet the following criteria: (1) the war must have a just cause; (2) attempts at peaceful resolution should have been exhausted so that it is a "last resort"; (3) the decision to go to war should have been made by an appropriate and clearly defined authority; (4) it should be known that going to war will not make the situation worse than it is, but possibly better; (5) there should be a reasonable prospect of the war achieving its aims; and (6) the war should be motivated by the right intention.[49] However, Solov'ev's version of just war is less interested in the criteria—though he presupposes many of the classic conditions—which make a war to be a justified undertaking (*jus ad bellum*, as opposed to the just nature of how the war is fought, or *jus in bello*) than in arguing more broadly that war is part of the justification of the Good or the ongoing providential perfecting of all creation in Jesus Christ crucified and risen from the dead.

His approach to war, which he considers evil (*JG*, 332 [*OD*, 425]), begins with an acute sense of the reality of evil. Evil is not only a "natural defect," an imperfection that will disappear by itself with the "growth of good"—in the patristic terminology, a *privatio boni*—but a "real power" which rules over the world by appealing to the worst in us, so that to fight it, to side with the good against evil, one needs divine aid (*TC*, 15 [*TR*, 83]). In every human being is a "beast"; what distinguishes the "bestial human being" is their willingness to act against the goodness in them in the form of their intellect and conscience. Some keep the "beast" tightly chained, whereas the bestial person has a chain but does not use it (47; and see 147 [105–6; and see 183]). Moral evil can only be overcome through the "inspiration of the good," which is the direct and positive action of the good power on us—grace—in holding up and transforming our reason and conscience, leading to "real life in the good." Such life is the organic growth of the whole person—internally in himself, in his role in the family and society, in the nation, and in humanity itself—so that one might attain graciously "the vital unity of the risen past" which is life in the resurrected Christ (of which more below) in conjunction with "the evolving future in that eternal present of the kingdom of God which will be, though on earth, the new Earth, joined in love with the new Heaven" (152–53 [187]). There is also "social evil" when the crowd, each person enslaved by the beast of evil personally, resists the few righteous people and overcomes them (147 [183]).[50] This can take many forms, from political tyranny, as in fascism and Stalinism, to institutional injustice, such as sexism. Finally, there is the last evil, which is "physical," when the baser elements of the human body resist the "living and enlightening power that binds them together into a beautiful form of organism," shattering the form and destroying the basis of the higher life. We are speaking, of course, of the most extreme evil called death (148 [183]).

Since evil seems to threaten the good at every level, something more than individual moral transformation or political reform—however important they are for the realization of the kingdom—is needed, something divine beyond ourselves but also intimately human: the resurrection of the God-man, but a resurrection not merely "metaphorical" but "literal" or factual (here Solov'ev takes a swipe at liberal Protestantism) (*TC*, 155, 148 [*TR*, 190, 184]).[51] In looking to the personal resurrection of Christ, we see one victory of the good power of life over evil of all types, and this gives us hope that we will have future victories over evil in the collective resurrection of the dead. Evil in this context actually enhances the triumph—the ultimate justification, realization, and power—of the Good, since, if it is more powerful than our mortal frame, God's goodness in the resurrection to eternal life is even more powerful than both the evil of death and the gift of mortal life (148–49 [184]). God's testimony of himself, his justification of the Good, is then seen in the triumph of goodness in the accomplished resurrection of Christ, which opens the gates of the kingdom of God, heralding the resurrection of all, trampling down death by death (149 [184]). It is not an accident then that the whole of the *Three Conversations* ends with a tale concerning the apocalypse, the triumph of the Good of the church, the Jews and Christ, the kingdom of the resurrection, over the evil of the devil and the Anti-Christ, the kingdom of death, as the last things, the *eschata*, are the final justification of the Good.

But how do we apply this to the evil of war? Where does this fit into Solov'ev's understanding of providence? War is a relative evil, less than some other evil and, being compared with it, even good. It is necessary for the preservation of the good order of the state under certain conditions, just as if, using the principle of double effect, when one has cancer, an operation can be a "necessary evil" to save the patient's life (*JG*, 332–33 [*OD*, 424–25]). One cannot, therefore, simply and absolutely reject war under the negative definition of it as an evil and calamity. This definition does not exhaust it, for there can be a positive element within it, not in the sense that is "normal" but that it may be actually "necessary" in "given conditions" so that (a) a moral ideal can be upheld under abnormal circumstances, and (b) through doing good amidst evil, one might cooperate with God's providence in its revelation of the kingdom, which not only can draw good out of evil we do but, through the good we do, can create an even greater good (333 [425]).

Solov'ev uses various metaphors and examples to bring across this justified providential understanding of war, some of which (as we saw with the image of "surgery") presuppose the principle of double effect and the various classical criteria for a just war. War, he argues, is like the symptom of the fever in a sick body that is struggling for health; as long as there is "moral disturbance" in humanity, external wars can actually be helpful and necessary in cleansing the body politic (*JG*, 332 [*OD*, 424]). Another example is found in a mother throwing her child out of a window. Everyone agrees that throwing children out of a window onto the sidewalk is evil. However, if in the case of a fire there is no other way of saving the child, this action becomes "permissible and even obligatory," since it prevents a greater evil, which would be the death of the child. Solov'ev argues that the moral principle here is not throwing children out of the window in extreme cases but saving those in danger, and this is the only motive of action, that is, the intention to save another human being. But the moral norm in this extreme case, which may have the side effect of a child being either hurt or even killed, can only be realized in a way that, while not a deviation from it, or, say, in contradiction to the moral ideal, is "dangerous and irregular," but proves from real necessity to be the only way to achieve the norm in specific conditions. Thus, just as a mother in a burning building might save her child by throwing it out the window onto the pavement, so too it may be necessary or even obligatory to enter into a war, with the consequent loss of human life, itself an evil (side) effect, in order to preserve human life and avoid extreme suffering by preventing a worse evil of, say, genocide, mass torture, and the arising of fascism (333 [425]). Thus the war would be a relative evil, in comparison to genocide; war might be regarded as good in comparison to genocide, so war is, in this limited sense, a lesser good. So man, working with God's providence, can, in certain situations where evil is rife, actually do good from which God can create an even greater good. War, then, is an abnormal phenomenon, which depends upon a necessity, which makes it permissible and obligatory under strictly defined conditions, but, for Solov'ev, it is never straightforwardly virtuous as some would have it in their polemic against pacifism.

If war is a "relative" evil, not all black, then its "opposite" in peace cannot be said to be perspicuous in character, or pure white (*TC*, 40–41 [*TR*, 100]). It is true neither that war is an "absolute evil" nor that peace is an "absolute good," since it is possible to have (relatively speaking) "*a good war*" and an "*evil peace*" (39 [99]). An "external peace" is not good in and of itself, and it only becomes good in connection with the inner regeneration of humanity. Once this external union is known to be insufficient by experience, then, we are told, the time will be ripe for "spiritualizing the united body of the universe" and for realizing within it "the Kingdom of Truth and Eternal Peace" (*JG*, 345 [*OD*, 439–40]). More practically—and the genius of Solov'ev is to veer back and forth between the facts of history in all their minutiae and their spiritual/providential meaning—Solov'ev affirms the relative truth of the observations of the Politician by arguing that it is a fact that war gave rise to rights and treaties as a security of peace. War, then, as the organization of the state, is the first important step toward the establishment of peace (335 [428]), which is a view that can be traced back to Aristotle.[52] Moreover, external wars between states have created more complex bodies possessing a unity of culture, which has led to the quest for peace and balance within their limits (345 [440]). War does not only disunite but unites peoples so that war and peace are like the two inseparable faces of Janus (337; and see 338–43 [430; and see 431–38]). Furthermore, Mr. Z says he thinks that after the introduction of universal military service, the abolition of armies and eventually individual states is only a matter of time not far from the present, given the fast pace of events (*TC*, 38 [*TR*, 99]). In antiquity, Solov'ev argues, not only did war serve the purposes of peace (e.g., *Pax Romana*), but also fewer active military forces were needed to obtain the peace as time went on, "while the peaceful results became . . . more and more important and far-reaching" (*JG*, 338 [*OD*, 431]). Even in his own day, Solov'ev held—and here he is reminiscent again of the Politician— one could see how the wars of the Revolution and the Napoleonic wars led to the process of the gathering together of scattered lands by means of a "single material culture," and this one culture, fashioned through wars of rebellion and empire, allowed for the "advance and the dissemination of universally European ideas which conditioned the scientific, technical, and economic progress" of the nineteenth century, bringing about the "material unification of humanity" (342 [436]).

The state, as I argued earlier, can serve as a positive good in the gradual perfecting of all creation, and, furthermore, if humanity has an unconditional worth, this worth lays upon us an unconditional duty to realize the good not only in our own personal lives but in other people. We can perform this task only if we look to the collective whole of humanity for completion, no longer living in isolation. I have a moral duty, therefore, to protect and care for others who are a part of the same collective, and this may mean, as we saw earlier, service in the military, especially if the life of the state is threatened (*JG*, 347–49 [*OD*, 442–44]). This is simply the broader extension of one's moral duty, in seeking to protect a helpless victim threatened with danger by a "villain," to first use persuasion and, if this does not succeed, then even to use "force" (*TC*, 48 [*TR*, 106]). Killing in the context of war is not murder because in most instances no "evil intention" is directed at the person whose life is taken.

An evil intention only arises in the circumstances of hand-to-hand combat, and there the decision of guilt or innocence must be left to the individual conscience, which is at liberty. Murder in such circumstances, if it can be called such, is "accidental"; that is, it is the unintended effect of an action whose intention is just—for example, to protect one's fatherland, to save the innocent. If one refuses military service in order to avoid accidental murder, one actually may commit a more serious evil, since another recruit will have to take one's place, and then one consciously forces one's neighbor, otherwise free, to the life of the military with the very same burden of accidental killing that one suffered previously (*JG*, 346–47 [*OD*, 440–42]). The state, the so-called clearly defined authority that wages war as a "collectively organized pity" (385 [488]), therefore, plays a crucial role in cooperating with providence, being its conscious corporate helper in the revelation of the kingdom. The defense of the state is so important for Solov'ev because only through preparatory state organization, with its actualization of altruism, can the ideal of truth and peace (i.e., the inward unification of humanity) or the kingdom of God be gradually and painfully revealed in the world. The final revelation of the kingdom of God and the resurrection from the dead are a corporate task to which all human beings are called in synergy with God, and in certain cases war is the extraordinary means through which this task can be accomplished.

THE CHALLENGE OF SOLOV'EV TO ORTHODOX MORAL THEOLOGY

All things considered, despite the beauty of a vision of man's cooperation in Christ for the task of revealing God's kingdom, a task that involves working with God to bring a greater good out of the moral morass of war, in the end one is left with considerable ambiguity and a vague idealism by Solov'ev's version of justified providential war. War, he argues, has been the direct means of the external and the indirect means of the internal unification of humanity, and God has blessed and used it in his perfecting of all of creation. Reason, therefore, forbids us to give it up as long as it is needed (so short of the last things). However, our conscience compels us to strive that war should no longer be needed by the natural organization of humanity, which is divided into hostile camps. Instead, we strive for perfection, and, as the full justification of the Good envisions, we attempt to actualize in world history the ideal of humanity as "a moral or spiritual organization." And the description of what precisely this "moral organization" consists of is the "totality of the moral conditions which justify the good in the world" and, therefore, the ultimate end or conclusion of moral philosophy, which itself forms the final idealistic chapter of Solov'ev's *The Justification of the Good* ("The Moral Organization of Humanity as a Whole") (*JG*, 350 [*OD*, 446]).

More troubling than the pervasive vagueness and idealism of Solov'ev's system is its failure to provide an adequate response to over a century of seemingly perpetual war. Since Solov'ev's death in 1900, we do not seem any closer to the revelation of the kingdom despite two world wars, the proxy wars of the Cold War period, and the perpetual war on terror which seems to be the motor of the world economy. War in the twentieth century does not seem to have established a lasting peace, as he believed it would. Furthermore, he does not give clear criteria to distinguish between those unjust states which are on the wrong side of providence or simply passive instruments of it (e.g., Nazi Germany, Stalin's Soviet Union) and those states that are genuinely working consciously with providence toward the revelation of the kingdom (e.g., the Russian Federation, the United States of America). In fact, one would be hard pressed to point to any state in all of history that lives up to his ideal, let alone a "Christian state" in today's postsecular age. Thus the distinctive element of his just war theory, which is its reimagining of the tradition in light of providence, seems more a utopian fiction than a vision of the Christian moral life as it might in fact be lived.

The fictive element of the whole project becomes more apparent the closer one looks, for the conditions under which war is justified are not always clearly delineated by Solov'ev; in fact he mostly mentions them in passing. One wonders, furthermore, why, if war can be justified in certain conditions and with the right intention, he even bothers to call it a relative evil or lesser good, for this only obscures the salient point that in certain cases it is actually "virtuous" to be violent. War can be good, and to say that this is a good which is relative to some worse evil simply obscures the paradox. It is as if he is torn between asserting the evil of war and asserting the fact that it might actually be good. Here the problem lies with his Platonic metaphysics, with God as the Good being on a sliding scale and all other being as a falling away into evil. Yet if everything—short of God—is tacitly evil, then on what basis do we say that one act is less evil or more good than another? One might argue that all morality is in the context of the fall, so one is faced with trying to work for goodness within the context of more or less bad choices; but this does not seem like a good basis for ethics, which should give clear moral direction.

This brings out what is the central difficulty of Solov'ev's ethics, and indeed of the very few Orthodox attempts at Christian ethics in this last century: it does not have an account of what precisely counts as a moral act, what an intention is, and how one might distinguish in deliberation between indirect and direct motivation. His ethics, as we said at the beginning, focuses on the "all-embracing character" of the Good, how it is seen in every aspect of human life from the individual in relation to his family to the state, but he steps back from giving any account of the "purity" of the Good, which requires an account of the unconditionality of the human will and how that will can be said to be at work freely in any action. Yet to give an account of the good in all aspects of reality without describing what it is to act at all means that one has shaped a human being but left them without a head and legs, so that they are a mere torso that cannot move toward anything. Finally, we are left with a challenge. Orthodox moral theology must provide a detailed account of the nature of moral deliberation and action, one which engages with the whole tradition in East and West as well as contemporary philosophy, and here Solov'ev has shown us the entrance; for, as he has expressed so well, the answer lies within the cooperation of the divine and the human in Christ, the synergy of wills, which is the creative co-revelation of the kingdom.

NOTES

For comments on earlier drafts and assistance, I am indebted to the members of the LOGOS group as well as Metropolitan Kallistos Ware, Professor Nigel Biggar, Professor David Pratt, and Dr. Christopher Stroop.

1. *The Justification of the Good: An Essay on Moral Philosophy* [= *JG*], trans. Nathalie A. Duddington, ed. Boris Jakim (Grand Rapids: Eerdmans, 2005; first published 1918), 278. Subsequent references to *JG* are in the text and are followed by a reference to *Opravdanie dobra* [= *OD*] (*Opravdanie dobra: Nravstvennaia filosofiia*, in *Sobranie sochinenii Vladimira Sergeevicha Solov'eva* [= *SSVSS*], ed. S. M. Solov'ev and E. L. Radlov, 10 vols. [St. Petersburg: Prosveschenie, 1911–14; repr., 12 vols., Brussels: Izdatel'stvo Zhizn' s Bogom/Foyer Oriental Chrétien, 1966–70]). The quotation cited here appears in *OD*, 8:356.

2. For a complementary account see Peter Bouteneff's essay, ch. 9 in this volume, "War and Peace: Providence and the Interim."

3. Cf. Ambrose, *De Joseph patriarchia* (CSEL 32, pt. 2, §§2.8 and 12.69 [PL 14:644, 667]); Melito of Sardis, *On Pascha*, trans. Alistair Stewart-Sykes (Crestwood, NY: St. Vladimir's Seminary Press, 2001), §§59, 69.

4. Solov'ev, like many Russian writers of the nineteenth and early twentieth centuries, liberally uses italics and other visual means (e.g., stretching out words) for stylistic emphasis. I have reproduced his italicization in all quotations.

5. See Nathaniel Wood, "Deifying Democracy: Liberalism and the Politics of Theosis," Ph.D. diss., Fordham University, May 2017; Wood, "'I Have Overcome the World': The Church, the Liberal State, and Christ's Two Natures in the Russian Politics of Theosis," in *Christianity, Democracy, and the Shadow of Constantine*, ed. George E. Demacopoulos and Aristotle Papanikolaou (New York: Fordham University Press, 2017), 155–71; Jeremy Pilch, *"Breathing the Spirit with Both Lungs": Deification in the Work of Vladimir Solov'ev*, Eastern Christian Studies 25 (Leuven: Peeters, 2017); Oliver Smith, *Vladimir Soloviev and the Spiritualization of Matter* (Brighton, MA: Academic Studies Press, 2010); Randall A. Poole, "Vladimir Solov'ëv's Philosophical Anthropology: Autonomy, Dignity, Perfectability," in *A History of Russian Philosophy, 1830–1930: Faith, Reason, and the Defense of Human Dignity*, ed. G. M. Hamburg and Randall A. Poole (Cambridge: Cambridge University Press, 2010), 131–49; Modris Lacis, *La divino-humanité du Christ comme fondement du processus social: Une étude sur la christologie de Soloviev* (Saarbrücken: Éditions universitaires européennes, 2010); Judith Deutsch Kornblatt, intro., trans., ed., with Boris Jakim and Laury Magnus, trans., *Divine Sophia: The Wisdom Writings of Vladimir Solovyov* (Ithaca, NY: Cornell University Press, 2009); Brandon Gallaher, "The Christological Focus of Vladimir Solov'ev's Sophiology," *Modern Theology* 25, no. 4 (October 2009): 617–46; Manon de Courten, *History, Sophia and the Russian Nation: A Reassessment of Vladimir Solov'ëv's Views on History and His Social Commitment* (Bern: Peter Lang, 2004); Paul Valliere, *Modern Russian Theology: Bukharev, Soloviev, Bulgakov; Orthodox Theology in a New Key* (Grand Rapids: Eerdmans, 2000), 109–223; A. F. Losev, *Vladimir Solov'ev i ego vremia* (Moscow: Molodaia Gvardiia,

2000); Wil van den Bercken, Manon de Courten, and Evert van der Zweerde, eds., *Vladimir Solov'ëv—Reconciler and Polemicist* (Leuven: Peeters, 2000); Kristi Groberg, "Vladimir Sergeevich Solov'ev: A Bibliography," *Modern Greek Studies Yearbook* 14–15 (1998–99): 299–398.

6. See note 1 above.

7. See Paul Valliere, "Vladimir Solov'ev (1853–1900): Commentary," in *The Teachings of Modern Orthodox Christianity: On Law, Politics, & Human Nature*, ed. J. Witte Jr. and F. S. Alexander (New York: Columbia University Press, 2007), 52–55.

8. Vladimir Solov'ev, *War, Progress and the End of History: Three Conversations Including a Short Story of the Anti-Christ* [= *TC*], trans. Alexander Bakshy and Thomas R. Beyer (Hudson, NY: Lindisfarne Press, 1990), 15 (*Tri razgovora* [= *TR*] [1899–1900], *SSVSS*, 10:83). Subsequent citations to this work are in the text and include a *TC* reference followed by a *TR* reference.

9. Here see Jonathan Sutton, *The Religious Philosophy of Vladimir Solovyov: Towards a Reassessment* (Basingstoke: Macmillan, 1988), 51–86; Smith, *Vladimir Soloviev*, 91–144; and especially Pilch, *"Breathing the Spirit with Both Lungs."*

10. Vladimir Solov'ev, *Kritika otvlechennykh nachal* (1877–80), *SSVSS*, 2:174, and see v–xvi; and see Solov'ev, *Dukhovnye osnovy zhizni* (1882–84), *SSVSS*, 3:379 (*God, Man and the Church: The Spiritual Foundations of Life*, trans. Donald Attwater [Cambridge: James Clarke, 1974], 134 [use with caution]).

11. Solov'ev, *Kritika*, 352, and see the texts in Vladimir Wozniuk, trans. and ed., *The Heart of Reality: Essays on Beauty, Love and Ethics by V. S. Soloviev* (Notre Dame, IN: University of Notre Dame Press, 2003); see Smith, "The Sophianic Task in the Work of Vladimir Solov'ëv," *Journal of Eastern Christian Studies* 59, no. 3–4 (2007): 167–83; Smith, *Vladimir Soloviev*.

12. On universalism see Kallistos Ware, *The Inner Kingdom* (Crestwood, NY: St. Vladimir's Seminary Press, 2000), 193–215; Hans Urs von Balthasar, *Dare We Hope "That All Men Be Saved"?*, trans. David Kipp and Lothar Krauth (San Francisco: Ignatius Press, 1996).

13. See Gallaher, "Christological Focus of Vladimir Solov'ev's Sophiology."

14. Compare *Dogmaticheskoe razvitie tserkvi v sviazi s voprosom o soedinenii tserkvei* (1886), *SSVSS*, 11:21–22. Also see "On the Decline of the Medieval Worldview" (1891), in *Freedom, Faith, and Dogma: Essays by V. S. Soloviev on Christianity and Judaism*, ed. and trans. Vladimir Wozniuk (Albany, NY: State University of New York Press, 2008), 160, 164 ["Ob upadke srednevekovago mirosozertsaniia," *SSVSS*, 6:382, 387].

15. "On Counterfeits" (1891), in *Freedom, Faith, and Dogma*, 156 ["O poddelkakh," *SSVSS*, 6:337–38].

16. "The Jews and the Christian Question" (1884), in *Freedom, Faith, and Dogma*, 88 ["Evreistvo i khristianskii vopros," *SSVSS*, 4:185].

17. See de Courten, *History, Sophia and the Russian Nation*, 275–486.

18. *Podvig* is an untranslatable Russian word usually rendered in English along the lines of spiritual/ascetic "struggle," "exploit," "attainment," and "feat." For discussion see the essay of Sergii Bulgakov, "Heroism and Spiritual Struggle [*Podvichnichestvo*]," in *Sergii Bulgakov: Towards a Russian Political Theology*, ed., trans., and introd. by Rowan Williams (Edinburgh: T & T Clark, 1999), 69–112, with Williams's discussion in his introduction at 65–66.

19. "Jews and the Christian Question," 64 (revised translation) ["Evreistvo i khristianskii vopros," *SSVSS*, 4:158]. See also "On Counterfeits," 150, 155–56 ["O poddelkakh," *SSVSS*, 6:330–31, 337–38].

20. "Jews and the Christian Question," 66–88 ["Evreistvo i khristianskii vopros," *SSVSS*, 4:160–85]. See especially the unfinished *Istoriia i budushchnost' teokratii* [History and future of theocracy] (1885–87; *SSVSS*, 4:241–633) and its résumé, *La Russie et l'église universelle* (1889), in *La Sophia et les autres écrits français*, ed. François Rouleau (Lausanne: La Cité, 1978), 123–297 (*Russia and the Universal Church*, trans. Herbert Rees [London: Geoffrey Bles, 1948]). See van den Bercken, de Courten, and van der Zweerde, *Vladimir Solov'ëv—Reconciler and Polemicist*, 411–60, 473–83.

21. See Vladimir Wozniuk, ed. and trans., *Politics, Law and Morality: Essays by V. S. Soloviev* (New Haven: Yale University Press, 2000); *Freedom, Faith, and Dogma*, 17–31, 33–41, 121–70, 191–227.

22. "L'Idée Russe" (1888), in *La Sophia et les autres écrits français*, 102.

23. "Jews and the Christian Question," 66–88 ["Evreistvo i khristianskii vopros," *SSVSS*, 4:160–85].

24. See Smith, *Vladimir Soloviev*, 176–206.

25. Ibid., 206.

26. See Bouteneff, "War and Peace."

27. Solov'ev does not state clearly the criteria for a "mortal sin."

28. See Thomas Aquinas, *Summa Theologica* II-II.64.7.

29. Here see T. A. Cavanaugh, *Double-Effect Reasoning—Doing Good and Avoiding Evil* (Oxford: Oxford University Press, 2006).

30. Ibid., 26; and see David Pratt, "From Just War Fictions to Virtues of Benevolence: Renovating the Just War Theory," *Louvain Studies* 31, no. 3–4 (2006): 292.

31. For the difficulties inherent in the use of this sort of reasoning, see Pratt, "Just War Fictions," 291–98.

32. On eschatology and Solov'ev in the context of the Russian Silver Age, see Judith Deutsch Kornblatt, "Eschatology and Hope in Silver Age Thought,"

in *A History of Russian Philosophy, 1830–1930: Faith, Reason, and the Defense of Human Dignity*, ed. G. M. Hamburg and Randall A. Poole (Cambridge: Cambridge University Press, 2010), 288–95; David M. Bethea, *The Shape of Apocalypse in Modern Russian Fiction* (Princeton: Princeton University Press, 1989), 110–16.

33. Valliere, "Vladimir Solov'ev (1853–1900): Commentary," 58.

34. Ibid., 57–58.

35. Carl von Clausewitz, *On War*, new and rev. ed., 3 vols., trans. and ed. J. J. Graham and F. N. Maude (London: Kegan Paul, Trench, Trübner, 1918), bk. 1, §24, p. 42.

36. See Colin Brown, "Campbell Interrupted Blair as He Spoke of His Faith: 'We Don't Do God,'" *Daily Telegraph*, 4 May 2003, http://www.telegraph .co.uk/news/uknews/1429109/Campbell-interrupted-Blair-as-he-spoke-of-his -faith-We-dont-do-God.html.

37. See Walter Benjamin, "The Work of Art in the Age of Mechanical Reproduction," in *Illuminations*, ed. Hannah Arendt, trans. Harry Zohn (New York: Schocken, 1968), 242; see Lutz Peter Koepnick, *Walter Benjamin and the Aesthetics of Power* (Lincoln: University of Nebraska Press, 1999).

38. On Solov'ev's ideas on Pan-Mongolism, see Alena Eskridge-Kosmach, "Russian Press and the Ideas of Russia's 'Special Mission in the East' and 'Yellow Peril,'" *Journal of Slavic Military Studies* 27, no. 4 (2014): 662–65; Harsha Ram, *The Imperial Sublime: A Russian Poetics of Empire* (Madison: University of Wisconsin Press, 2003), 221–25.

39. Solov'ev, "Appendix B: Panmongolism," in *Politics, Law, & Morality: Essays by V. S. Soloviev*, ed. and trans. Vladimir Wozniuk (New Haven: Yale University Press, 2000), 294 (lines 25–27, 30–33) ["Panmongolizm," *SSVSS*, 12:95–96].

40. Solov'ev, "The Enemy from the East," in *A Revolution of the Spirit: Crisis of Value in Russia, 1890–1924*, ed. and trans. Bernice Glatzer-Rosenthal and Martha Bohachevsky-Chomiak and trans. Marian Schwartz (New York: Fordham University Press, 1990), 43–52 ["Vrag s Vostoka," *SSVSS*, 5:452–65]; Vladimir Wozniuk, ed. and trans., *Enemies from the East? V. S. Soloviev on Paganism, Asian Civilizations, and Islam* (Evanston, IL: Northwestern University Press, 2007).

41. See Solov'ev, "Po povodu poslednikh sobytii: Pis'mo v redaktsiiu" (1900), *SSVSS*, 9:222–26; and see Ram, *Imperial Sublime*, 264n31.

42. Oliver L. G. Smith, "Is Humanity King to Creation? The Thought of Vladimir Solov'ev in the Light of Ecological Crisis," *Journal for the Study of Religion, Nature and Culture* 2, no. 4 (2008): 468–69n11.

43. See Eskridge-Kosmach, "Russian Press and the Ideas of Russia's 'Special Mission in the East' and 'Yellow Peril,'" 664–75, and Ram, *Imperial Sublime*, 226–34.

44. See Sergei Chapnin, "A Church of Empire: Why the Russian Church Chose to Bless Empire," *First Things*, November 2015, https://www.firstthings.com/article/2015/11/a-church-of-empire; Brandon Gallaher, "A Tale of Two Speeches: Secularism and Primacy in Contemporary Roman Catholicism and Russian Orthodoxy," in *Primacy in the Church: The Office of Primate and the Authority of the Councils*, vol. 2, *Contemporary and Contextual Perspectives*, ed. John Chryssavgis (Crestwood, NY: St. Vladimir's Seminary Press, 2016), 807–37; Gallaher, "The Road from Rome to Moscow," *The Tablet*, February 20, 2016, 8–9.

45. Christopher Stroop, "Between Trump and Putin: The Right-Wing International, a Crisis of Democracy, and the Future of the European Union," *Political Research Associates*, May 11, 2017, http://www.politicalresearch.org/2017/05/11/between-trump-and-putin-the-right-wing-international-a-crisis-of-democracy-and-the-future-of-the-european-union/#sthash.yabTSawE.cvjvDDWy.dpbs; "Pence Meets with One of Putin's Top Clerics: Strange Bedfellows at BGEA's World Summit in Defense of Persecuted Christians," *Religion Dispatches*, May 12, 2017, http://religiondispatches.org/pence-meets-with-one-of-putins-top-clerics-strange-bedfellows-at-bgaes-world-summit-in-defense-of-persecuted-christians/; Casey Michel, "The Rise of the 'Traditionalist International': How the American Right Learned to Love Moscow in the Era of Trump," *Right Wing Watch*, March 2017, http://www.rightwingwatch.org/report/the-rise-of-the-traditionalist-international-how-the-american-right-learned-to-love-moscow-in-the-era-of-trump/.

46. See Sergey M. Solovyov, *Vladimir Solovyov: His Life and Creative Evolution*, trans. Aleksey Gibson, 2 vols. (Fairfax, VA: Eastern Christian Publications, 2000; previously published 1977 but finished 1923), 2:496. See also Lev Tolstoy, *On Civil Disobedience and Non-Violence* (New York: Bergman 1967); cf. Solov'ev, *TC*, 135–36, 142–51, 155 [*TR*, 174, 179–86, 189–90].

47. This is Mr. Z's summary of the views of the Prince with which the Prince agrees.

48. See Angeliki Laiou, "The Just War of Eastern Christians and the Holy War of the Crusaders," in *The Ethics of War: Shared Problems in Different Traditions*, ed. Richard Sorabji and David Rodin (Aldershot: Ashgate, 2007), 30–43; David K. Goodin, "Just-War Theory and Eastern Orthodox Christianity: A Theological Perspective on the Doctrinal Legacy of Chrysostom and Constantine-Cyril," *Greek Orthodox Theological Review* 48, no. 3–4 (2004): 249–67; George Dennis, "Defenders of the Christian People: Holy War in Byzantium," in *The*

Crusades from the Perspective of Byzantium and the Muslim World, ed. Angeliki E. Laiou and Roy Parviz Mottahedeh (Washington, DC: Dumbarton Oaks Research Library and Collection, 2001), 31–39; Alexander F. C. Webster, "Justifiable War in Eastern Orthodox Christianity," in *Just War in Comparative Perspective*, ed. Paul Robinson (Aldershot: Ashgate, 2003), 40–61; Paul Robinson, "The Justification of War in Russian History and Philosophy," in Robinson, *Just War in Comparative Perspective*, 61–75; Alexander Webster and Darrell Cole, *The Virtue of War: Reclaiming the Classic Christian Traditions East and West* (Salisbury, MA: Regina Orthodox Press, 2004); David Bentley Hart, "Ecumenical War Councils: On Webster and Cole's *Virtue of War*," in *In the Aftermath: Provocations and Laments* (Grand Rapids: Eerdmans, 2009), 148–55.

49. See Richard Sorabji, "Just War from Ancient Origins to the Conquistadors Debate and Its Modern Relevance," in Sorabji and Rodin, *Ethics of War*, 14; Paul Robinson, introduction, *Just War in Comparative Perspective*, 1.

50. Here see Gregory Baum on personal and social/systemic sin: *Religion and Alienation: A Theological Reading of Sociology* (New York: Paulist Press, 1975), 197–208.

51. See "Vladimir Solovyov's Letter to L. Tolstoy: On the Resurrection of Christ," *Sobornost'*, n.s., no. 1 (March 1935): 8–12 (translator not listed) [Letter of Vladimir Solov'ev to Lev Tolstoi: "O Voskresenii Khrista," *Put'* 5 (1926): 97–99].

52. Aristotle, *Politics*, trans. Ernest Baker (London: Oxford University Press, 1958), 7.14, §13, 1333a39, 317.

CHAPTER 11

WAR, TECHNOLOGY, AND THE CANON LAW PRINCIPLE OF *ECONOMIA*

GAYLE E. WOLOSCHAK

This article aims to provide a better understanding of Orthodox perspectives on war and particularly war technologies as they relate to decisions to go to war, decisions to use particular technologies, and decisions on how to handle war in the context of the loss of life that ensues. My central thesis is that Orthodox Christians can assume appropriate attitudes to war and war technologies only on a case-by-case basis, much like the canon law principle of *economia*, which is used in decisions to permit certain practices under unique circumstances while still realizing that the practice itself is wrong. In this case, we can still make global statements about killing people and fighting wars, noting that these are wrong while acknowledging that there could be circumstances when war would be appropriate. This is exemplified by Orthodox attitudes to other forms of killing, most notably contrasted in Orthodox attitudes toward abortion, where multiple lives are at risk and the church has had predominantly one attitude throughout history, as well as capital punishment, when only one life is at stake and when the church has taken different positions at different times in history. The International Orthodox Consultation held at Saidnaya, Syria, in 2010 concluded that "the mission of the church is to live in and preserve God's peace and, despite human failure, to communicate prophetically the peace of God to the world as a blessed peacemaker."[1] Similarly, from a technology perspective it can be noted that just as developing technologies that could be used for abortion are most often a result of technologies that were developed for other purposes, the same can be said of technologies that are used for war. In the case of unique technologies that are developed only for abortion or only for war purposes, one could argue that as long as there is a moment when either could be appropriate, the development of such technologies could be conceived as acceptable even if not something that could be easily embraced.

WAR AND TECHNOLOGY: THE NUCLEAR PROBLEM

Angst about humanity destroying itself has existed through the history of the world. During the last century, this concern expressed itself predominantly through dread of a global holocaust caused by all-out nuclear war. The bombs dropped at Hiroshima and Nagasaki demonstrated to the world the horrific consequences of nuclear bombs and the overwhelming destruction that humankind can cause. Museums established in Hiroshima and Nagasaki today help to show the damage caused by the uranium and plutonium bombs dropped, respectively, on these two cities, and both cities have taken the lead in nuclear nonproliferation activism working toward the elimination of all nonpeaceful use of nuclear materials. Despite this, there is general concern among the Japanese population that "just war" models have been used to justify the dropping of the bombs on Japan, and that this leads to a general lack of understanding of the nuclear holocaust that overwhelmed Japan during World War II.[2] To ameliorate some of this (and perhaps because of US interests as well), to this day by treaty the US government is obligated to study the children and grandchildren of radiation-exposed individuals from these two cities. The Radiation Experimental Research Facility (RERF) was established jointly by the US and Japan to examine health consequences of nuclear explosions, including such endpoints as cancer, cardiovascular disease, mental retardation, and others, all of which were increased as a result of the nuclear bomb detonation.[3] During the same era, the United States also bombed Tokyo in a series of large-scale raids that also led to the destruction of a huge number of civilians; a single raid on March 10, 1945, killed one hundred thousand civilians, far more than those that died as a result of the dropping of the nuclear bomb on either Hiroshima or Nagasaki. Nevertheless, it was the new nuclear capabilities with long-term effects and possibilities for instant mass destruction that drove fear of war technologies for the coming decades, resulting in the Cold War, the development of the United States as a superpower, and other similar events.

The development of the nuclear bomb is perhaps one of the most interesting technology campaigns in modern history because the drive for the technology essentially involved a race to win World War II. While Germany invested large efforts in long-range rockets, the United States pursued the development of the atomic bomb. Funds and scientists were mobilized into the "Manhattan Project," a huge war effort that was eventually considered to be successful by the United States. Most of the scientists were civilians and not associated with military facilities, and eventually the bomb was assembled through a series of national laboratories run at that time by the Atomic Energy Commission (the predecessor of today's Department of Energy). At the conclusion of the war, rocket scientists from Europe were moved to the United States to continue the development of long-range weapons, leading to cross-fertilization with nuclear weapons into long-range nuclear rockets that were the key weapons proliferating during the Cold War era. The utilitarian attitude toward war technologies appears to be an important component of many governments' views on war technology development.

The bombs dropped on Hiroshima and Nagasaki were the only nuclear weapons used in war, but numerous other bombs have been detonated as "tests," causing disastrous consequences. Most notable was a fifteen-megaton test detonation termed BRAVO by the United States in the Marshall Islands in 1954; this blast resulted in the highest radiation exposure to people of any nuclear test and high-risk exposure of the population as far as 550 kilometers from the detonation site. While this event is not a direct consequence of war, one could argue that the reason to test the bombs was war driven. Similar detonations (with milder consequences) have been conducted by at least five nations worldwide—the United States, the United Kingdom, Russia, China, and France.[4] These nuclear bomb uses must be contrasted with "peaceful" applications of nuclear materials for nuclear energy and fuel and medical applications (including radiation therapy and diagnostic procedures). Nevertheless, not all radiation is human-made; humans are daily exposed to low doses of radiation from natural sources, including radiation in our food, our atmosphere, and from the earth's crust.[5]

To prepare humanity for possible consequences of nuclear disaster, nations made huge investments of funds, animals, and expertise in Cold War studies of radiation effects on animals (mostly dogs, rats, and mice). My own laboratory houses data and tissues from approximately forty-nine thousand mice, fifteen thousand dogs, and twenty thousand rats exposed to external beam radiation, plutonium, uranium, radium, and other radioactive substances yielded by these studies conducted from 1950 to 1988, although tissues from some of the earlier studies were discarded as irrelevant. These experiments were part of a huge national project carried out at over five universities and five national laboratories across the United States to understand long- and short-term consequences of radiation exposure. At the same time, the Soviet Union was conducting similar studies at their South Urals Biophysics Institute (SUBI) near the closed city of Ozyorsk with plutonium exposure to large numbers of rats, dogs, and other animals. Although both the Soviet Union and the United States terminated these studies soon after the end of the Cold War, in both cases the vastness of the costs in animals, money, and human-power that went into the work points to the fear and foreboding that hung over both nations in the post–nuclear bomb era.[6] Even today, the specter of the 9/11 atrocities hangs over humanity, renewing fears of "dirty bombs" (combinations of radioactive materials with infectious or toxic agents), "loose" radioactive materials being sold on the black market, and possible exposure of an unwitting population to harmful radiation doses. This has led to renewed efforts to develop countermeasures for radiation exposure.

Throughout history, technology has changed war. One can look back at the "Greek fire" which was used in ancient Byzantium as a new technology to enhance opportunities for winning battles,[7] or the development of the rifle in the 1850s,[8] which significantly changed the ways individuals engaged the enemy. According to Martin Van Creveld, after 1830 military advances changed drastically, and military-technological innovations came more rapidly and became more institutionalized and permanent.[9] He notes, "As each successive generation of sophisticated weapons and weapons systems appeared on the scene, all its predecessors were either thrown onto the garbage heap or sold to some less developed country. . . . A process of technology competition arose, one that was sometimes relaxed but never halted, generating a treadmill effect in which all countries were compelled to run for fear of standing still."[10]

A key moment in war technology proliferation came in World War II, starting with massive aerial bombing, the use of meteorological conditions to boost the effects of convention bombs, and the eventual development of rockets and nuclear weapons at the end of the war. All of these novelties have resulted in a constant "upping of the ante" until today, when we can wage biological warfare, make chemical and radiological weapons, and more. War, through the hasty development of new technologies, has become rapid and impersonal and can lead to unheard-of mass annihilation. In addition, because of other technologies (such as communication technologies, rapid transportation, and global positioning capabilities), information about the war is no longer confined to the realm of the media. Soldiers develop blogs to discuss their wartime exploits, and post photo galleries on the web to record their adventures, and with improved air flights they can now meet their families at airbases in Europe to catch up on life's joys and difficulties. The wars of today are sharply different from those fought only decades ago.

ORTHODOX PERSPECTIVES ON WAR

The Orthodox attitude toward war in general has been ambiguous at best. One can find examples in the literature at both extremes, with some writers claiming that Orthodox are pacifists and others stating that Orthodox support war in some forms and circumstances. This essay does not aim to discuss comprehensively the various views of war and peace to be found in Orthodoxy, but the range of views needs to be acknowledged.

While it seems that all Orthodox note that war is tragic and is to be avoided as much as possible, the disagreement appears to be based on just how inescapable war can be. Some contend that there can be a just war and base this on Western "just war" concepts, a position perhaps best articulated by Alexander F. C. Webster, who asserts that while war is never considered good or right, going to war is a matter of permitting a necessary evil for the overall good, or in other words that war can be justified for the good of humanity. Webster uses a variety of sources which he has identified as important to support the "just war" model, including comments from scripture, the church fathers, the saints, and the canons. [11]

Critics of Webster's views have noted that some aspects of this thinking are flawed, while others, including the Orthodox Peace Fellowship, take a more pacifist view and explicitly reject "just war" thinking.[12] These groups note that Orthodox are opposed to killing in all forms and that this is an evil that perhaps could be permitted under very rare circumstances but is never really justified. Overall, all forms of killing are perceived as disruptive of communion with God; killing another human being affects the person deeply and disturbs one's relationship with God. The church has often looked for healing of the break by expecting a period of penitence (confession, refraining from the Eucharist, etc.) from the person who has engaged in killing, even if the death is the result of an accident or involuntary act. This is true for all acts that lead to the death of another—acts of war, abortion, and other similarly tragic deeds.

What then is the Orthodox perspective on the development of technologies to be used exclusively for the purposes of war? Nuclear bombs are the example listed above, but in today's world new war technologies have been escalating. They range from new types of arms and automatic weapons to chemical warfare (such as napalm) to biowarfare agents and even to recent discussion about the use of performance-enhancing drugs for soldiers. Views on war and views on the development of war technologies should be distinguished, although the questions are tightly linked. Theoretically, one could support a defensive war and support only defensive technologies. Or, it could be theoretically conceived that a strong war technology could serve as a functional deterrent from any war, and that a nation could develop such technology without ever intending to use it. In today's world, a failure to develop new technologies is tantamount to losing the war since it is technologies in the hands of soldiers that actually fight the war. It is interesting that in Russia a link has been made between nuclear arms and the church, albeit by politicians and publicists rather than by theologians and church officials. For example, in 2007 Egor Kholmogorov, a publicist in Russia, commented, "In order to remain Orthodox, Russia must be a powerful nuclear state, and in order to remain a powerful nuclear state, Russia must be Orthodox."[13] While not so tightly tied to church perspectives, many in the United States government are convinced that military superiority is contingent upon the development of new technologies by a combination of strong funding to scientists in military and civilian facilities (including universities) and maintaining a strongly trained military machine. If the Orthodox attitude toward war is that it is always wrong, then perhaps it would be a logical conclusion that the development of war technologies is always inappropriate. However, a clear view on Orthodox attitudes toward the ethics of war is just not to be found, so it is impossible to dismiss the question of the ethics of war technologies as irrelevant.

ORTHODOX PERSPECTIVES ON TECHNOLOGIES

As a possible approach to the question of war technologies, it is worthwhile to explore the Orthodox perspective on the ethics of technologies. In recent times, a number of Orthodox scholars and ethicists have attempted to examine the ethics of different technologies, but the expressed views again lack unity. Most such questions explored in recent times are medical-ethical issues such as beginning- and end-of-life technologies, genetic manipulations, stem cell approaches, and others. There are no blanket statements about technology in general in the Orthodox literature, and many recent scholars note the need to evaluate each technology in context.[14] As noted above, the criticisms of technology come into two major categories: (1) concerns about the technology itself and (2) concerns about the application of the technology. For stem cell technologies, for example, some Orthodox writers have concerns about approaches used to generate the stem cells (whether embryos will be sacrificed, how to define the embryo, etc.), while others are more concerned about possible applications of the technologies for unethical purposes such as cloning and raising embryos for organ harvesting.

The church fathers certainly did not write about modern technology such as atomic bombs and nuclear fuel, so it is impossible to pick up a volume off the shelf and read a quote that will enlighten us directly on the issue. Instead, the general Orthodox approach seems to be that one must develop the mind of the fathers and examine how they answered their questions of the day in hopes of helping us solve the questions of today. St. Basil the Great in *The Greater Rules* wrote, "All the different species and techniques have been given us by God to make up for the deficiencies of nature. . . . Not by chance does the earth produce plants that have healing properties. It is clearly evident that the Creator wants to give them to us to use." Consider also this passage from the Wisdom of Solomon (7:17–22 NRSV):

> For it is he [God] who gave me unerring knowledge of what exists, to know the structure of the world and the activity of the elements; the beginning and end and middle of times, the alternations of the solstices and the changes of the seasons, the cycles of the year and the constellations of the stars, the natures of animals and the tempers of wild animals, the powers of spirits and the thoughts of human beings, the varieties of plants and the virtues of roots; I learned both what is secret and what is manifest, for wisdom, the fashioner of all things, taught me.

Based on these and other expressions in scripture and in the fathers of the church, it seems safe to conclude that knowledge and technology in and of themselves are not bad; rather, the more important question in determining whether a technology is acceptable is how the technology is used. Radiation technologies have been developed for peaceful (nuclear fuel, medical) and war (bombs) purposes. It would then be a very straightforward conclusion that peaceful applications of nuclear energy would be acceptable and nonpeaceful applications would not be. One can look at the disaster that accompanied the nuclear accident at the Chernobyl plant in April 1986 to note how errors in technology, design, and engineering can lead to loss of lives and to a radiation problem affecting multiple nations that is not yet resolved. However, it was technology again that helped to solve this problem. Arguably the greatest difficulty associated with the accident was the induction of thyroid tumors that occurred in children exposed to radioactive iodine. The very same technology which was used in the nuclear reactor, radioactive iodine, was used to cause tumor ablation and treat the children that developed thyroid cancer. Of the four thousand children that developed thyroid cancer, the radioactive iodine successfully cured all but ten of their thyroid cancers. Here we have a case where the technology could be abused and lead to cancer or could be used properly and lead to cures for cancer. Again, knowledge and technology coupled with a proper mode of use are considered to be good and acceptable vehicles for understanding and harnessing nature.

Not all cases of technology use are as obvious as this one, and this is where the problem lies—it is very difficult to discern whether a particular application of a technology is appropriate and that another is not. Nevertheless, the approach to solve this concern lies in using discernment to define what is right and what is not, what is true and what is false. This discernment is well exemplified by the ascetic fathers and mothers of the desert who spent their lives practicing and teaching discernment, and by a host of church fathers who wrote books and provided opinions through the centuries on issues that were as complex in their day as the issues we face today. This heritage has been passed to the church and can be used to apply to issues that impact the world today. Anthony Bloom, in his final encyclical, wrote, "Our task is not merely to imitate what was done by the saints of previous eras, but somehow to appropriate at a much deeper level the way in which they engage their own historical environment, seeking to respond as they would have responded had they lived in our day."[15]

While most technologies are science driven, they are usually generated with a goal in mind, an application for which the technology will be used. Nevertheless, there are often "spin-off" technologies that were unintended at the time of development and later come to be recognized as additional important use(s). For example, tools developed to help astronauts survive better in the confines of a space capsule were later found to be ideal for helping patients with heart arrhythmias and eventually led to the current-day pacemaker. This is also the case with some war technologies. The drug amifostine is a radioprotector and was initially developed at Walter Reed Military Hospital as a means of protecting military combatants from the effects of radiation encountered during a nuclear or radioactive attack; it is still carried in the field packs of some military personnel. The same drug was later found to have broad radioprotective capabilities and was carried by NASA astronauts into space to protect them against cancer induction caused by high energy radiation that is encountered in the space environment.[16] More recently, amifostine is being used clinically to protect patients receiving radiotherapy for head and neck cancers against normal tissue radio-toxicities, most notably loss of salivary function.[17] It is hard to imagine "peaceful" applications that can come from the development of better automatic weapons or heat-seeking missiles, but perhaps they are possible.

Some technologies, of course, follow the other direction—they were identified first in a nonmilitary setting for a "peaceful" application and then later were found to have a military benefit. Nuclear fission is perhaps the most important recent example—it was developed for wartime uses, but the concept for it has been used for the development of nuclear power reactors. A recent, more questionable example of this falls within the category of the "enhancement" technologies. Scientists were looking for a drug that could cure Alzheimer's disease and found one agent that causes a fivefold enhancement in the response times of mice with the disease.[18] Imagine a soldier with a fivefold-enhanced response time! A wide variety of news reports have documented the development of tools to permit the paralyzed to move computer cursors with brain impulses instead of using the mouse or to move a wheelchair with a sniff of the nose.[19] Can this technology allow a soldier to fire a gun with a thought instead of by pulling a trigger? These enhancement technologies have already become questionable in the civilian population, as we have outlawed the use of steroids and other enhancing drugs in sports. What is the ethics of their use in military situations? In general, the Orthodox Church has been shy about putting forth positions on most technologies. Although a few statements have been published on specific technologies, most technology questions tend to be handled individually by individual bishops. For example, while the Orthodox Church as a whole has not taken a specific position on in vitro fertilization, bishops have chosen to either give a blessing to it or not depending upon the situation; in a sense, the bishops are choosing to handle the technology problem by economia, by considering the spiritual implications in each person's unique circumstances, rather than by offering a blanket blessing for use of the technology across the board.

ATTITUDES TOWARD KILLING

A possible approach to evaluate Orthodox attitudes toward war technologies is perhaps to examine Orthodox attitudes toward killing. As noted elsewhere in this volume, several church canons clearly state the Orthodox Church's unwillingness to bless the killing of people.[20] The rules imposed on the clergy are often the stated ideal of the church, and the fact that clergy are not supposed to have been involved in the killing of anyone, even by accident, in self-defense, or in defense of others, is a clear statement of the church's unwillingness to sanction killing as an acceptable behavior. However, care for our neighbor is one of our sacred duties and in some circumstances may mean protecting the lives of others in a life-threatening situation. Elsewhere in this volume is a discussion of military saints and the conceptual way in which their lives have impacted church thinking on war.[21] While there are examples of military saints, pacifist saints who sacrificed their own lives to save others, and saints who died willingly to perpetuate peace, I cannot find an example of a saint who stood by and watched while others were killed. In the saints venerated in the church, omission is also an important means of expression. In this, perhaps, is a recognition that defense of others is an appropriate means of caring for others.

Perhaps one of the most articulated examples of killing defined in the canons is abortion. This paper will not discuss issues raised by abortion (such as when human life begins, when abortion is considered appropriate, etc.). The broad attitude of the church as reflected in canon 91 of the Quinisext Ecumenical Council (691) decreed that people "who furnish drugs for the purpose of procuring abortion, and those who take fetus-killing poisons, are made subject to the penalty prescribed for murderers." The same canonical position, along with the opinions of individual church fathers compiled in the *Photian Collection*, which was adopted by the church in 883, states that abortion of a fetus is not acceptable in most circumstances.[22] Nevertheless, under unusual circumstances, a woman can be permitted to have an abortion, but this is usually decided by "economia."

The concept of economia is based on the idea that there are rules that govern the church but that in order to appropriately manage the "household" (*oikos*) of the church, sometimes those rules must be reconsidered. There is a tension within church life between the real and the ideal, and economia is used to bridge the gap between the two. In some respects, it may be said that the explicit church rules are defined to provide grounds for careful consideration of actions and to emphasize the need for discernment, rather than to invoke blind obedience. When the canons are disregarded in favor of economia, it is done on a case-by-case basis with the decision of a spiritual father or bishop, and the rule itself is not overturned by the decision.[23] Discernment and knowledge of the facts are prerequisites of economia, and decisions to employ economia are made only after deep consideration and understanding. While the teaching of the church on the concept of economia is not precisely defined, Georges Florovsky has put into words much of the thinking that has gone into its practice:

> In the broadest sense "economy" embraces and signifies the whole work of salvation. . . . The vulgate usually translates it by *dispensatio*. In canonical language "economy" has not become a technical term. It is rather a descriptive work, a kind of general characteristic; οἰκονομία is opposed to ἀκρίβια as a kind of relaxation of church discipline, an exemption or exception from the "strict rule" (*ius strictum*) or from the general rule. The governing motive of "economy" is precisely "philanthropy," pastoral discretion, a pedagogical calculation—the deduction is always from working utility. "Economy" is a pedagogical rather than a canonical principle; it is the pastoral corrective of the canonical consciousness. "Economy" can and should be employed by each individual pastor in his parish, still more by a bishop or council of bishops. For "economy" is pastorship and pastorship is "economy."[24]

Joseph Allen similarly expressed the view that economia is a principle which is used to overcome difficulties encountered when the rules are themselves inflexible:

Economia is *the* means by which the hierarchs of the Eastern Church can face—and bypass—certain rigid and narrow restrictions imposed by the letter of canon law. It allows them to accommodate ecclesial regulations to each particular context as it arises. Economia is never considered for use in cases touching upon the basic doctrines—the dogmas—of the faith. Its function is to respond to those regulations inherited from the past whose time and relevance are past.[25]

Abortion is a classic example of this situation. The church has a general rule that abortion is considered wrong and inappropriate, because it involves the killing of life; Stanley Harakas notes that abortion is considered murder,[26] and John and Lyn Breck similarly comment that the Orthodox Church's respect for the sanctity of life leads to a rejection of abortion and other forms of murder.[27] Nevertheless, when it is in the best interests of "managing the household" (such as concern for the life of the mother), then a decision in favor of an abortion can be made. In all cases, the abortion itself is still considered to be wrong, but in the face of the difficult situation it is a decision that is made out of love and concern for the mother, her family, and others involved. In the case of abortion, it is clear that more than one life hangs in the balance of the decision—both the mother's and the child's lives are at risk and must be considered.

In contrast to abortion, the church has taken different positions on capital punishment through different periods of history. Unlike for abortion, no canon specifically forbids capital punishment, and we may suppose opposition to such punishment to be one of the implicit rules of the church household. The early church was opposed to capital punishment, a stance expressed by Lactantius (240–320):

> When God prohibits killing, He not only forbids us to commit brigandage, which is not allowed even by the public laws, but He warns us not to do even those things which are regarded as legal among men. . . . And so it will not be lawful for a just man . . . to accuse anyone of a capital offence, because it makes no difference whether thou kill with a sword or with a word, since killing itself is forbidden. And so, in this commandment of God, no exception at all ought to be made to the rule that it is always wrong to kill a man, whom God has wished to be regarded as a sacrosanct creature.[28]

Over time, the church in accommodation to the state has permitted capital punishment, but in recent years this has been challenged. Both the Greek Archdiocese of America and the Orthodox Church in America have issued statements opposing capital punishment on the grounds that it is considered to be killing for vengeance in most circumstances.[29] The one issue that distinguishes capital punishment from both war and abortion is that it usually involves the death of only one person, while in both war and abortion two or more lives are at stake. This distinction is important because a decision for or against capital punishment, while affecting many people, still involves the life of only one person, and therefore decisions about life or death in this situation are more straightforward. For abortion, the lives of two (or more if the mother has conceived twins or triplets) need to be considered; decisions cannot be straightforward because the child(ren) and mother all must be considered. In the case of war, decisions are even more difficult; the lives of soldiers, noncombatant troops, and civilians on both sides of the conflict need to be considered.

This difficulty is apparent from Orthodox perspectives on killing and war situations. While a few authors attempt to accept the concept of a "just war" and the claim that a war can be determined just at some moments in history, a more common reading of the existing literature is that war and killing are never good and always evil, albeit under some circumstances war can be an accepted evil because of what is at stake, because of the threat to life, or because of the need to defend the defenseless. I contend that a view that is more consistent with the Orthodox tradition is one similar to that used in exercising economia for abortion—killing and war are evils that under certain circumstances can be permitted because of the necessity of a given situation. This differs significantly from an Orthodox version of the "just war" concept, the "necessary evil" done in the interest of the overall good articulated by Alexander Webster.[30]

There are a number of reasons why it would be difficult to directly apply the economia approach to instances of war. Usually, economia applies to a single person and a single situation in the structure of the church and under the spiritual authority of a bishop. The war scenario does not really permit economia because, while it involves individuals, the decisions to go to war are made by nations, most of which are not in an Orthodox context and do not recognize any authority of the church. This paper does not discuss the pros and cons of Orthodoxy as a state religion; in the world today, even in predominantly Orthodox nations, decisions to go to war are made with little consideration of what religious leaders or others in positions of religious authority consider appropriate. Stanley Harakas has noted that what existed in the state/church relationship in predominantly Orthodox nations does not exist today: "On the part of the Orthodox . . . there must come an acceptance one day of the truth that the old means of state/church accommodation will never return. This means that the means available to the Orthodox Church are those that it had available to it in the pre-Constantinian period."[31] Nevertheless, there are, in fact, situations where Orthodox leaders, while perhaps falling short of blessing a war, have read prayers of blessing over weapons to be used in battle. The fact that prayers for blessing of weapons exist shows that the church has used them at various times throughout history.[32] Many of these blessings were employed by Orthodox Churches in the Communist era. One need only read Aleksandr Solzhenitsyn's comments on the "great solitaire," which selected against certain types of clergy in the Soviet Union, to appreciate that the Soviet gulags were full of Russian Orthodox priests who would not have blessed bombs and other military devices.[33] While not as widespread or as well known as the Soviet purging of "uncooperative" clergy, similar imprisonments were observed in Romania and other countries of Eastern Europe during the Communist era.[34] His Holiness Patriarch Pavle of Serbia, while noting that prayers for the blessing of weapons existed, requested that the Synod "require that no use be made of a service for blessing weapons included in an addition of the Book of Needs published in Kosovo in 1993. In the context of the events in former Yugoslavia, the blessing of weapons can only be regarded as sanctioning the use of weapons in a fratricidal war."[35]

A similar argument, although perhaps not with the direct use of economia, has previously been expressed by Philip LeMasters.[36] LeMasters likens Orthodox attitudes toward war to those of the church on a second marriage: "The Church's teaching is not that a second marriage is a lesser good in a theoretical moral sense; indeed, the traditional marriage service in such cases is penitential. The focus here is on healing and growth in holiness before God, not on some alleged level of moral purity."[37] LeMasters then argues that war, similarly, is a concession to death, to the fallen nature of the world, to a situation for which we must repent. While the comparison of war with a second marriage is not ideal, it too argues for the use of economia in the spiritual interest of those involved.

Both LeMasters and I, thus, argue for the stretching of a personal application of economia (abortion, second marriage) to a more global or community-based arena. While this is a radical and perhaps even provocative concept, there are personal aspects not only to marriage, but also to war. Persons make decisions to go to war, persons drop the bombs that kill others, persons kill other persons. In addition, blanket economia has sometimes been exercised one way or another toward groups. When economia was granted to the reception of heretics into the church, for example, this was granted to the entire community and not on a case-by-case basis. In Serbia following World War II, all deacons and priests were given blanket permission for a second marriage because so many had lost their wives during the war; this concession to the needs of the clergy was considered appropriate by the bishops for the orderly conduct and the spiritual well-being "of the household."[38]

CONCLUSIONS: ECONOMIA AS A MODEL

I contend that while the concept of economia is difficult to apply amidst the complexities of war, economia nonetheless provides a helpful model for thinking about an Orthodox attitude toward war and war technologies. For multiple reasons, economia as a functional mode of operation is difficult to apply to war—wars are initiated by nations and not individuals, the facts about a war are rarely known in advance of the fighting and usually only become unraveled by history, and the broad question of who would grant such economia is unclear. Nevertheless, economia illuminates the moral complexity of war in helpful ways since war can be judged only on a case-by-case situation, it is complicated and requires the use of discernment, war is judged as being an evil that can be accepted only as an "exception" rather than a standard rule, and it requires prayer and contemplation to understand whether it is appropriate or not. The same can be true about the development and deployment of war technologies. Again, no blanket statement can be made that a particular technology is inappropriate in and of itself unless the means to develop it are considered unethical. Nevertheless, the applications of that technology, again, can be considered on a case-by-case situation and discerned to be appropriate or not using an approach similar to that used for economia in traditional canon law contexts. If one considers the model presented here, it becomes clear that the complexities of the science and technology involved make it difficult for bishops to possess the requisite knowledge in all areas in order to make sound decisions regarding economia. Thus, when reflecting on war and war technologies, Orthodox bishops must dialogue with scientists, physicians, mental health professionals, historians, and others so that decisions can be made that truly support the spiritual health and salvation of the "household."

NOTES

1. This perspective is reflected in the entire statement of the International Orthodox Consultation held on October 22, 2010, and available in *Just Peace: Orthodox Perspectives*, ed. Semegnish Asfaw, Alexio Chehadeh, and Marian Gh. Simion (Geneva: World Council of Churches Publications, 2012), xxii–xxv.

2. Katsuhiro Kohara, "Hiroshima and the Pacifism/Just War Debate," *Interface* 6 (2003): 95–106.

3. E. Hall and A. Giaccia, *Radiobiology for the Radiologist*, 6th ed. (Philadelphia: Lippincott Williams and Wilkins, 2006).

4. Steven L. Simon, Andre Bouville, and Charles E. Land, "Fallout from Nuclear Weapons Tests and Cancer Risks," *American Scientist* 94, no. 1 (2006): 48–57.

5. Hall and Giaccia, *Radiobiology for the Radiologist*.

6. Qiong Wang, Tatjana Paunesku, and Gayle E. Woloschak, "Tissue and Data Archives from Irradiation Experiments Conducted at Argonne National Laboratory over a Period of Four Decades," *Radiation Environment and Biophysics* 49, no. 3 (August 2010): 317–24.

7. Mark C. Bartusis, *The Late Byzantine Army: Arms and Society, 1204–1453* (Philadelphia: University of Pennsylvania Press, 1992), 340–41.

8. Martin Van Creveld, *Technology and War: From 2000 B.C. to the Present* (New York: Free Press, 1989), 83–86.

9. Ibid., 223.

10. Ibid., 224.

11. See Alexander F. C. Webster, "Justifiable War as a 'Lesser Good' in Eastern Orthodox Moral Tradition," *St. Vladimir's Theological Quarterly* 47 (2003): 3–57; Webster, *The Price of Prophecy* (Washington, DC: Ethics and Public Policy Center, 1993); and Alexander F. C. Webster and Darrell Cole, *The Virtue of War: Reclaiming the Classic Christian Traditions East and West* (Salisbury, MA: Regina Orthodox Press, 2004).

12. See readings published by the Orthodox Peace Fellowship on their website and journal entitled *In Communion*, http://www.incommunion.org/. See also Hildo Bos and Jim Forest, eds., *For the Peace from Above: The Syndesmos Resource Book on War, Peace and Nationalism* (Bialystok, Poland: Orthdruk Printing House, 1999).

13. This is quoted in Alexei Bodrov, "Relations between the Russian Orthodox Church and the Military," in Asfaw, Chehadeh, and Simion, *Just Peace: Orthodox Perspectives*, 47.

14. See Stanley Harakas, *Wholeness of Faith and Life: Orthodox Christian Ethics*, part 3, *Orthodox Social Ethics* (Brookline, MA: Holy Cross Orthodox Press, 1999); Gayle E. Woloschak, "What Is on the Horizon? What Is Science Likely to Be Doing in the Upcoming Years?," in *Theological Foundations in an Age of Biological Intervention*, ed. David C. Ratke (Minneapolis: Lutheran University Press, 2007), 25–40.

15. Bloom, Anthony, *The Comforter: Our Support and Strength for Mission; The Gift of the Holy Spirit: The Church as a Continual Pentecost* (St. Stephen's Press, 2000), 11–22.

16. Hall and Giaccia, *Radiobiology for the Radiologist*.

17. William Small Jr. and Gayle E. Woloschak, eds., *Radiation Toxicity: A Practical Medical Guide* (New York: Springer, 2006).

18. John F. Disterhoft and M. Matthew Oh, "Pharmacological and Molecular Enhancement of Learning in Aging and Alzheimer's Disease," *Journal of Physiology Paris* 99, no. 2–3 (2006): 180–92.

19. *Rhode Island News*, June 10, 2009. See also Anton Plotkin, Lee Sela, Aharon Weissbrod, Roni Kahana, Lior Haviv, Yaara Yeshurun, Nachum Soroker, and Noam Sobel, "Sniffing Enables Communication and Environmental Control for the Severely Disabled," *Proceedings of the National Academy of Sciences of the United States of America* 107, no. 32 (August 2010): 14413–18.

20. See, for example, Valerie Karras's essay "Their Hands Are Not Clean, " ch. 5 in this volume.

21. See James C. Skedros, "Lessons from Military Saints in the Byzantine Tradition," ch. 7 in this volume.

22. *NPNF*[2] 14:404 (Council of Trullo, canon 91).

23. For a helpful overview of this theme within canon law, see Francis Thomson, "Economy," *Journal of Theological Studies* 16, no. 2 (1965): 368–420.

24. Georges Florovsky, "The Boundaries of the Church," in *Ecumenism 1*, vol. 13 in *Collected Works* (Belmont, MA: Nordland, 1989), 38.

25. Joseph J. Allen, "Economia as the Critical Principle in Making Decisions of Priesthood and Marriage," in *Vested in Grace*, ed. Joseph J. Allen (Brookline, MA: Holy Cross Orthodox Press, 2001), 4.

26. See, for examples, Stanley S. Harakas, *Health and Medicine in the Eastern Orthodox Tradition* (New York: Crossroad, 1990), 156–57. See also his *Let Mercy Abound: Social Concern in the Greek Orthodox Church* (Brookline, MA: Holy Cross Orthodox Press, 1983), 142–44.

27. John Breck and Lyn Breck, *Stages on Life's Way: Orthodox Thinking on Bioethics* (Crestwood, NY: St. Vladimir's Seminary Press, 2005).

28. Lactantius, *Divine Institutes* 6.20.15, quoted in Stanley Harakas, *Contemporary Moral Issues Facing the Orthodox Christian* (Minneapolis: Light and Life Publishing, 1982), 155–56.

29. Harakas, *Let Mercy Abound*; Thomas Mueller, "Capital Punishment and the Gospel," in *Resource Handbook for Lay Ministries*, ed. Arlene Kallaur (Syosset, NY: Orthodox Church of America, 1995).

30. See especially Webster, "Justifiable War as a 'Lesser Good'" and *Price of Prophecy*.

31. Stanley S. Harakas, *Wholeness of Faith and Life: Orthodox Christian Ethics*, part 2, *Church Life Ethics* (Brookline, MA: Holy Cross Orthodox Press, 1999), 110.

32. See Bos and Forest, *For the Peace from Above*, 120–21.

33. See, for example, Aleksandr Solzhenitsyn, *The Gulag Archipelago* (New York: Harper and Row, 1973).

34. Lucian N. Leustean, *Orthodoxy and the Cold War: Religion and Political Power in Romania, 1947–63* (Basingstoke, UK: Palgrave Macmillan, 2009).

35. Bos and Forest, *For the Peace from Above*, 120.

36. Philip LeMasters, "Justifiable War: Response #4," *St. Vladimir's Theological Quarterly* 47, no. 1 (2003): 77–82.

37. Ibid., 79.

38. Bishop Irinej (Dobrijevic), Serbian Orthodox Church of Australia, personal communication.

CHAPTER 12

JUST PEACEMAKING AND
CHRISTIAN REALISM

*Possibilities for Moving beyond the Impasse
in Orthodox Christian War Ethics*

PERRY T. HAMALIS

From South Korea to the United States, aspects of Eastern Orthodox Christianity are gradually being acknowledged both inside and outside the academy in countries where Orthodox Christians constitute a very small percentage of the population. Notwithstanding this growth in visibility, most people—including many Orthodox—are not clear about the stances on ethical issues that the Orthodox Church derives from its theological and spiritual resources. When confronting, for example, the immense spiritual, moral, and political challenges presented by war, questions quickly arise: *Which of the major ethical approaches to war does the Orthodox Church embrace: pacifism? just war theory? political realism? holy war? some other option? How does one or more of these approaches express Orthodoxy's distinctive theological tradition and way of life? And what—if anything—does the Orthodox Church have to add to current reflection on the issue of war?*

335

While there are significant reasons that the Orthodox ethical tradition, in general, has not developed as quickly or as systematically as the ethical traditions of many other Christian communities,[1] articulating a coherent Orthodox response to the ethical challenges of war is especially important today for three main reasons. First, war is a matter of life and death that presently and perennially impacts the Orthodox community in many of the same ways that it impacts other human communities. From the physical, emotional, and spiritual dangers of serving one's country as a soldier to the unpredictable specifics of collateral damage, war changes and ends human lives on all sides of a conflict.[2] Therefore, war is a social reality that demands normative moral reflection within every religious tradition, including Orthodox Christianity. Second, war is an inescapably public issue, one that typically is discussed and debated among a nation's citizens and is declared, financed, and executed by a government. While nonstate actors in wars have become immensely significant in recent decades,[3] the public nature of war remains, for even wars involving nonstate actors impact and implicate masses of people simultaneously. Unlike, for example, the bioethical decision to sign off on a "do not resuscitate" order for a loved one, ethical decisions about war are large-scale group decisions with implications for even larger numbers of persons. Therefore, an ethical response to the challenges of war demands language and concepts that can be heard and understood by a wide audience. And third, representatives of the Orthodox tradition have not, to date, provided a response to the ethical challenges of war that the Orthodox faithful and the broader public find coherent, authentically "Orthodox," and constructive.[4] Confusion over Orthodoxy's ethical teachings on war among both Orthodox and non-Orthodox who are studying Orthodoxy is not due to a lack of care in looking for resources; it is due to a lack of clear resources.

My argument, in what follows, begins by demonstrating that while there are several Orthodox thinkers who contend that Orthodoxy embraces neither pacifism nor just war theory and neither holy war nor political realism, there are few, if any, Orthodox who have developed coherent and ethically robust alternative responses to the challenges of war. Given this absence, and in light of the acute need for such a response, I advance the view that Orthodoxy should look beyond the four predominant ethical positions to two established but lesser-known responses, those of "Just Peacemaking" and "Christian Realism." Just peacemaking and Christian realism, I contend, are valuable to the Orthodox community for two overarching reasons. First, they cohere more organically with Orthodoxy's theological-ethical tradition than the four predominant stances (pacifism, just war theory, holy war, and political realism). Second, they are established stances that are recognized in the scholarly literature and in the broader public sphere, and thus provide language and concepts that are already familiar to many thinkers and political leaders. For these reasons, explicitly and deliberately affirming the just peacemaking and Christian realist traditions provides a way out of the impasse that has prevented the Orthodox Church from participating visibly and meaningfully in public deliberations and scholarly debates surrounding the challenges of war. Furthermore, building a coherent Orthodox stance in this way promises to enhance just peacemaking and Christian realism, contributing distinctively Orthodox insights to these two ethical traditions and widening their ecumenical support.

ORTHODOXY AND THE CURRENT LANDSCAPE OF WAR ETHICS

Several Eastern Orthodox theologians have expressed dissatisfaction with all four of the predominant ethical stances that structure responses to the challenges of war in the West—the pacifist, just war, holy war, and political realist traditions of reflection—arguing that none of them fits comfortably with an Orthodox theological-ethical vision. For example, four Orthodox theologians from the United States—Frs. Stanley Harakas, Alexander Webster, John McGuckin, and Philip LeMasters—have insisted upon the distinctiveness of Orthodoxy's teachings on this issue vis-à-vis other Christian communions. Harakas stresses the Orthodox tradition's general affirmation of "the peace ideal" and writes, "[there are, however,] great difficulties for the Church in dealing with [the Christian faith's] pro-peace bias in a world fraught with sin, evil, and injustice. My point is that the East has responded to the issue in a way that is different from that of the West."[5] Webster, in contrast, contends that "[Orthodox] tradition is, amazingly to Western Christians, bifurcated. Orthodox moral tradition simultaneously recognizes *both* absolute pacifism and what I would prefer to term . . . the 'justifiable war ethic' (instead of the more elaborate, systematic 'just war theory' that evolved in the Christian and post-Christian West)."[6] McGuckin notes that "even when the situation of war seemed unavoidable, and might be said to be for reasonable and defensible goals, the Orthodox Church has never endorsed it with anything comparable to the theory of the 'just war' that has played such a large part in the consciousness of Western Christianity."[7] And LeMasters, reporting the results of recent international conferences on Orthodox peace ethics, states, "Though the consultations revealed diversity on many dimensions of the application of Orthodox tradition, a point of consensus was that Eastern Christianity interprets issues of war and peace in distinctive ways that do not align perfectly with the dominant categories of Christianity in the West."[8] While their own accounts of Orthodoxy's teachings on war lack uniformity, Harakas, Webster, McGuckin, and LeMasters proclaim in unison that Orthodoxy's teachings differ *in some fundamental way* from the main stances articulated in Western (Roman Catholic and Protestant) churches. Put differently, "We're not all on the same page about Orthodoxy's teachings on war," say the Orthodox, "but we know we're *not* of the same mind as Roman Catholics and Protestants."[9]

To be sure, the lack of harmony among Orthodox voices, coupled with a univocal rejection of Western teachings, merits a skeptical reaction; yet some legitimate factors contribute to this perceived "East-West difference" on the topic of war. Historically, in the Christian East, there was no single church father who wrote extensively and systematically on the subject. From the fourth through the fourteenth century, none of the greatest theologians of the Byzantine church—St. John Chrysostom, St. Maximos the Confessor, St. John of Damascus, and St. Gregory Palamas, just to name a few—ever addressed the issue of war in the focused manner that St. Augustine, Gratian, St. Thomas Aquinas, or Erasmus of Rotterdam did.[10] Neither was there a controversy in the Orthodox Church like the one between the Reformers (Luther, Calvin, etc.) and the Radical Reformers (Müntzer, Menno Simons, etc.), in which the question of whether or not Christians can or should use the sword was a central point of contention.[11] Furthermore, and very significantly, the Orthodox Church never endorsed or practiced "crusades."[12] As McGuckin writes, "The medieval Eastern Church under the Byzantine emperors never erected a theology of holy war, or just war, despite the many temptations to do so as the borders of Byzantium were systematically eroded by Islamic forces."[13] LeMasters agrees with McGuckin, noting that Orthodox military saints were not canonized because of their military prowess or death in battle, as they would be if Orthodoxy endorsed "holy war," but rather because of the ways they imitated Christ's example of nonviolence and mercy despite finding themselves amidst the horrors of war.[14] In short, different historical factors and the different theological styles of Western and Eastern Christianity led to different approaches to the challenges of peace and war. Holy war and political realism, as well as pacifism and just war, as moral concepts that developed outside of Orthodox Christianity, do not seem to cohere organically when applied within the Orthodox tradition. They constitute a foreign moral language, one that Orthodox Christians speak—at best—with a thick accent. Where, then, does this leave the Orthodox?

Orthodoxy's rejection of the four major stances within war ethics presents a situation where, I believe, only three viable options remain: (1) the Orthodox Church defines its own stance, using language, concepts, and sources appropriate to Orthodoxy, and then communicates its stance to the broader public (academic and nonacademic); (2) the Orthodox Church identifies closely with one or more of the lesser-known but already existing approaches that have carved out some room within the discourse on war, and then builds constructively and distinctively from this starting point; or (3) the Orthodox Church effectively excuses itself from the table, deciding either to remain silent or to critique other churches' positions without offering a coherent alternative.

The third option, I believe, is a disgrace and a betrayal of the church's mission in the world. Orthodoxy has theological-ethical resources to offer, and to refuse to articulate a substantive response on an issue of such gravity opens the Orthodox Church to accusations of pastoral negligence and ethical laziness, if not to *misanthropia*. The first option is appealing in some ways as the most "organic" to the Orthodox tradition, but—given the current reality—it seems quixotic, politically ineffective, and unecumenical. This leaves the second option, embracing one or more existing approaches that lie outside the "big four" and then building from there. I believe this is the most promising direction for the Orthodox Church in the near future. By identifying—even conditionally—with at least one lesser-known but already existing approach, the Orthodox gain visibility, a seat at the table, and a substantive set of core concepts and principles. The main challenge, of course, is finding an appropriate "Western" partner.

PARTNERING OPTION #1: JUST PEACEMAKING

Among the lesser-known traditions of reflection on the challenges of war, two approaches hold particular promise as partners for the Orthodox. The first of these is "just peacemaking," an approach that is best known through the work of Baptist ethicist Glen Stassen, but which has also been developed by other Protestant ethicists, by several Roman Catholic scholars, and—most recently—by numerous Jewish and Muslim authors working in peace studies.[15] Its distinctive contribution is to redirect attention from casuistic arguing about the morality of specific wars to actively preventing war.

Taking Jesus' words in the Sermon on the Mount (Matt. 5:9), "blessed are the peacemakers," as their driving principle, proponents of just peacemaking articulate and seek to apply a set of approximately ten broadly construed practices that effectively reduce the probability and reality of war. Examples include supporting nonviolent direct action, taking independent initiatives to reduce threat, using cooperative conflict resolution, acknowledging responsibility for conflict and injustice while seeking forgiveness through repentance, fostering just and sustainable economic development, advancing human rights and democracy, working with emerging cooperative forces, reducing offensive weapons/weapons trade, and encouraging grassroots peacemaking groups.[16]

Just peacemaking proponents regard their mission in essentially practical terms. As Stassen writes, "The test of the truth and realism of just peacemaking theory is not whether war nevertheless sometimes breaks out, especially where these practices are not used; it does, and it will. The test is whether the empirical claim is true that each of these practices is preventing some wars."[17] The unambiguous aim of just peacemaking is to identify and employ individual and communal practices that effectively prevent wars. The moral grounding for just peacemaking is, therefore, pragmatic and teleological in nature. The practices it identifies and employs are normative because history confirms that they work; they have, in fact, yielded more peaceful states of affairs. Buttressing just peacemaking's practical character is the fact that many of the just peacemaking practices were developed and are endorsed by veterans—men and women whose direct experiences of war have led them to seek constructive alternatives.[18]

By identifying the core of their teachings as "practices," not "principles" or "ideals," proponents of just peacemaking are underscoring a pragmatic grounding and calling people of faith to action. The practices of just peacemaking are *transforming initiatives*. As initiatives, they require more than passive speculation and theorizing; they require forward movement, leadership, and action in the world by persons and communities. As transformative practices, they are limited to those initiatives that reshape relationships among persons, groups, and nations. Of course, not all practices are transformative, and not all transformative practices are reshaping relationships toward peace; however, the practices endorsed by just peacemaking are initiatives that change the dynamic between conflicting parties and yield less violence and destruction.[19]

The practical core of just peacemaking, however, is not theologically empty. As Stassen has articulated, just peacemaking's transformative initiatives express an incarnational Christology, and its current paradigm grew out of a "thicker interpretation of Jesus' Sermon on the Mount."[20] While the practices themselves are not necessarily limited to confessing Christians, they are described and defended by Christian theological and ethical convictions about the person, example, and teachings of Christ. These are not secularized or watered-down initiatives; they are initiatives that faithful Christians can endorse as genuine expressions of what it means to be a member of the church.

As the above account suggests, proponents of just peacemaking see themselves as providing an alternative to the divide among Christians between pacifism and just war on at least two levels. First, they have shifted the focus of Christian moral reflection to an *earlier* point in the phenomenon of war by attending to the social factors that often lead to the outbreak of war and to the practices that slow or stop such outbreaks. In essence, just peacemaking teaches that regardless of whether one believes that wars are never morally justifiable (pacifism) or sometimes justifiable (just war theory), we can agree that *preventing* wars is, at least, morally praiseworthy, if not a moral responsibility.[21] Its proponents thus emphasize the point that both pacifists and just war advocates can support just peacemaking since it attends to a different question and a different moment within the phenomenon of war. Second, just peacemaking provides an alternative to the identification of pacifism with "doing nothing" (except protesting) and of just war theory with "doing something [violent]" (through military action). It advocates an *active* approach to *peace*—"waging peace"—which provides a way for people and communities to get involved with constructive social/political practices that are nonviolent.

While a comprehensive account of just peacemaking or of its compatibility with Eastern Orthodoxy lies beyond our present scope, I believe that Orthodox Christians can and should embrace the just peacemaking tradition as part of the Orthodox Church's response to the challenges of war.[22] First, as a relatively new stance within war-and-peace ethics, just peacemaking does not bring with it the historical and confessional baggage many Orthodox associate with both pacifism and just war theory. Developed by an ecumenical and interdisciplinary group of scholars, just peacemaking is not wedded to a single denomination or to a reified theological tradition. Practically, this helps Orthodox leaders and scholars avoid accusations of being "too Catholic" or "too Protestant" in their response to war, regardless of the legitimacy of such labels. Furthermore, as a paradigm that is still maturing and that has been ecumenical from the start, just peacemaking is more open to incorporating Orthodox insights into its teachings and recommended practice through involvement in the World Council of Churches and other ecumenical and interfaith dialogues.

Second, just peacemaking's pragmatic moral grounding and emphasis upon practices for effectively preventing war resonate deeply with Eastern Orthodoxy's approach to ethics. Orthodox ethics tends to work more personally and contextually, from the ground up, than theoretically and abstractly, from the top down.[23] While Orthodox doctrines are understood as universally true, Orthodox ethics pays close attention to and privileges the uniqueness of each person and community.[24] We see this characteristic expressed by the Orthodox hierarchs and scholars gathered at recent conferences on peace ethics who together agreed that, while Orthodoxy's tradition and experience do not cohere organically with the predominant categories of pacifism, just war, and holy war, they do "provide pastoral resources for the pursuit of a dynamic praxis of peace, the manifestation of which takes various forms in light of the set of circumstances that the Orthodox community faces."[25] The spiritual resources within Orthodoxy for responding to the challenges of war constitute more of a "dynamic praxis of peace" than an abstract, systematic formula for assessing the moral legitimacy of violence.[26] This practical and contextual quality of Orthodox ethics fits much more comfortably with just peacemaking than with any of the four predominant stances.

Third, incarnational Christology and commitment to Jesus' teachings in the Sermon on the Mount, the theological-ethical claims that are most deeply intertwined with just peacemaking,[27] are fully compatible with Orthodox theology. For example, a recent statement by the Orthodox representatives for the International Ecumenical Peace Convocation of the World Council of Churches employs incarnational Christology when it states, "In every dimension of life, the faithful are called to embody the way of Christ as fully as possible in the circumstances that they face: to forgive enemies; to work for the reconciliation of those who have become estranged; to overcome the divisions of race, nationality, and class; to care for the poor; to live in harmony with others; and to use the created goods of the world for the benefit of all."[28]

Orthodoxy's traditional affirmation of Christ's full divinity and full humanity implies the belief that Christ's sovereignty extends over all dimensions of life and that Christians' membership in the body of Christ carries imperatives for Christlike action in the world, here and now. Strikingly, the document quoted above is entitled "Called to be 'Craftsmen of Peace and Justice,'" drawing its language from St. Nicholas Cabasilas, the fourteenth-century sacramental theologian who taught that "Christians, as disciples of Christ who made all things for peace, are to be 'craftsmen of peace.'"[29] While these passages suggest a compatibility between Orthodox theology and the theological claims shaping just peacemaking, they also provide a glimpse into how just peacemaking could be enhanced through Orthodoxy's rich theological and hermeneutical tradition. From Orthodoxy's sacramental and environmental theology to its insights on the dynamics of repentance and forgiveness, there is extraordinary potential for mutual enhancement between the just peacemaking and the Orthodox theological-ethical traditions.

Finally, Orthodoxy should embrace the just peacemaking approach to peace and war ethics because many—if not most—of just peacemaking's ten endorsed practices are already part of Eastern Orthodoxy's social witness, and those that are not should be. Consider the way in which International Orthodox Christian Charities (IOCC), the humanitarian aid agency of the Assembly of Canonical Orthodox Bishops of North and Central America, fits with the "foster just and sustainable economic development" practice. Just peacemaking advocates see this practice as vital to preventing wars for several reasons. Sustainable development provides opportunities for meaningful work that are part of a just social order; it combats the despair and disorder that can lead to war; and it provides a constructive response to the greed, sin, and violence that have typically fueled obstacles to just economic development.[30] Since its inception, IOCC has provided over $500 million in humanitarian relief, sustainable development, and self-help programs to people in need across the globe.[31]

Similarly, just peacemaking's "encourage grassroots peacemaking groups" practice has been a transforming initiative in many Orthodox contexts. In fact, Orthodoxy boasts a level of lived experience in this area unmatched by any other Christian communion because of its presence as the largest Christian church in the eastern Mediterranean and the Middle East. For example, youth "peace camps," which bring together young people from different religious and/or ethnic backgrounds, have been sponsored and offered by Orthodox communities in Lebanon, Syria, Jordan, Bosnia and Herzegovina, Greece, and Cyprus, all countries where Orthodox have long histories of tension and conflict with members of other faith and ethnic communities.[32] Other efforts include the establishment of the Institute for Peace Studies in Eastern Christianity (IPSEC) and of local and national chapters of the Orthodox Peace Fellowship (OPF), a grassroots organization that conducts theological research, publishes the journal *In Communion*, provides practical assistance in conflict areas, and promotes a range of peacemaking practices by drawing from the Orthodox tradition.[33] Initiatives like these need to be supported and expanded by Orthodox advocates for peace. As Fr. Emmanuel Clapsis has eloquently urged, "Advocacy for peace must not stop with praying the litanies of the Liturgy. We can pray these petitions with integrity only if we offer ourselves as instruments for God's peace in the world, only if we live them out in relation to the challenges to peace that exist among peoples and nations."[34]

The just peacemaking tradition, while still not one of the "predominant" stances within contemporary ethical discourse on war, provides an alternative approach that seems to cohere much more organically with Orthodox Christianity. Notwithstanding the fact that there have been several statements by the Orthodox Church within the context of ecumenical dialogues and international peace conferences that echo the spirit of the just peacemaking approach, Orthodox leaders and scholars have not yet fully embraced the language and specific recommendations of this tradition. I strongly recommend that we do so. The just peacemaking tradition offers fresh insights and a shift in focus that would enhance Orthodoxy's witness in the face of the challenges of war, and explicitly embracing this approach would provide a way for Orthodox leaders and scholars to participate in both the public and scholarly discourse on war more effectively. Conversely, the just peacemaking paradigm will benefit from the rich theological and spiritual resources of Orthodoxy if we openly and directly engage with its non-Orthodox advocates.

PARTNERING OPTION #2: CHRISTIAN REALISM

While the Orthodox Christian ideal is to avoid war and promote peace through prayer, diplomacy, and just peacemaking practices, the Orthodox tradition also offers resources that can illuminate the spiritual roots and challenges of war and that can help shape a normative Christian response once a war has begun. Here, a second lesser-known Western approach, "Christian realism," also seems to cohere in important ways with Orthodoxy. This ethical tradition mines the writings of St. Augustine and of twentieth-century public theologian Reinhold Niebuhr, and emphasizes the value of reconnecting theological anthropology to moral reflection on war. While St. Augustine is traditionally claimed by proponents of just war theory, Christian realists find his theology of history, his distinction between the earthly city and the city of God, and his realistic account of human corruption to be salient to present-day social ethics. Reinhold Niebuhr, writing in the aftermath of World War I and throughout the entirety of World War II, was dissatisfied with both pacifism's tendency toward detached idleness and just war theory's tendency toward rationalizing war. While he never considered himself to be a systematic moral theorist, a point Orthodox may view as more of a strength than a weakness, Niebuhr's ethical vision has since been called "Christian realism."[35] It is an ethical approach that engages a wide range of issues and has emerged as another option within the scholarly and political discourse on war.[36]

Religious ethicists such as Robin Lovin, Jean Bethke Elshtain, and John Carlson have looked to Augustine and Niebuhr for robust accounts of humanity's fallen condition and for the application of such accounts to critiques of both pacifist and just war stances. Lovin constructively examines the significance of Niebuhr's work *The Nature and Destiny of Man*, wherein Niebuhr describes human beings in terms of "freedom and finitude" and links finitude with an "anxiety" that drives human violence and injustice.[37] Similarly, Carlson underscores Augustine's and Niebuhr's preoccupation with "sin's noetic effects," that is, the ways in which fallen nature and both personal sins and sinful social structures impair human reason and judgment.[38] Niebuhr, he contends, was particularly concerned with such effects' pervasive impact on international politics and war, and resisted both pacifism and just war approaches as being naïve about the depth of sin's impact on human perception, thinking, and agency, both at the personal and political levels. Complementing Lovin and Carlson, Jean Bethke Elshtain, of blessed memory, highlights the inescapability of "dirty hands" in the political realm and the critique of earthly utopias expressed by both Augustine and Niebuhr.[39]

Returning to this essay's main question, why should Orthodox thinkers and leaders look to the Christian realist tradition when articulating normative responses to the challenges of war? What is it about Christian realism that makes it a more appealing stance than pacifism, just war theory, holy war, or political realism? A limited analysis of the affinities between Christian realism and Eastern Orthodoxy and the potential fecundity of pairing the two should prove sufficient for my present argument; however, I hope the suggestive claims I offer below will also inspire subsequent studies of Christian realism from an Orthodox perspective that are more detailed and developed.

First, unlike political realism, both Christian realism and Orthodoxy stress the essentially spiritual nature of the roots of war and the need for a robust theological anthropology—for a nuanced and honest account of who we are as human beings, both fallen and redeemed—if we are to respond appropriately and effectively to war's challenges. Edmund Santurri provides a concise account of Christian realism's perspective when he states, "For the Christian realist, political life displays in a peculiarly transparent way the fallen condition of the world."[40] Describing the theology of the fall's significance within Orthodox thought, Christos Yannaras writes, "The fall of man is not simply a particular twist to [Orthodox] anthropological theorizing, but the axis or 'key' to understanding man, the world and history. On the one side the truth of the fall and on the other side the truth of the deification of man define the fact of the Church itself and give meaning to its existence and its historical mission."[41] Yannaras rightly notes that the fall, with its consequences for humanity and all of creation, is a hermeneutical "key" to the Orthodox faith. Furthermore, if we think about Orthodoxy within a therapeutic framework—the church as "hospital" and God as "physician"—then a theology of the fall provides nothing less than a diagnosis of humanity's illness, the accuracy and illuminative force of which is paramount to understanding and following the way to healing, or salvation.

Second, Orthodoxy shares Christian realism's emphasis on the belief that both freedom and finitude characterize humanity's fallen condition.[42] For the Orthodox, this means that human beings retain our free will (*autexousia*) as well as our dignity as beings made "in the divine image" (Gen. 1:26), even after the entrance of death and sin into the world. Put differently, while the reality of sin and of the tendencies within us toward violence, oppression, and injustice are acknowledged in their horrific depths (the "realist" part), there is within both Orthodox and Christian realist thinkers an abiding hopefulness about humanity's potential for goodness and holiness through God's grace and the right use of human freedom (the "Christian" part). Reinhold Niebuhr links human freedom and finitude to the divine image and the fallen condition in a way that resonates with Orthodoxy's theological anthropology: "The high estimate of human stature implied in the concept of 'image of God' stands in paradoxical juxtaposition to the low estimate of human virtue in Christian thought. Man is a sinner. His sin is defined as rebellion against God."[43] For Niebuhr and other Christian realists, an honest assessment of human beings demands an affirmation of our extraordinary status as creatures made "in God's image" and capable of self-transcendence, as well as an acknowledgment of our proclivity for rebelling against God. Responding faithfully to the challenges of war requires that we recognize both poles of human possibility.

Third, affirming humanity's capacity for both extremes on the personal level leads Christian realists and Orthodox theologians to a sober realism about political possibilities within history. Consider the following anecdote from Orthodoxy's ascetical tradition:

> Two monks had this conversation: The first said, "I cannot understand why the Lord does not grant peace to the world even if only a single person implored him to do so." The second replied, "And how could there be complete peace in the world if but a single malicious man remained?"[44]

This short narrative reveals several insights: it affirms the reality of human freedom both for seeking God's help and for rebelling against God; it provides a brief but striking theodicy; and it expresses a healthy skepticism about any promises for heaven on earth. One of the most valuable contributions of the Christian realist tradition is its critique of utopian visions of every type. As Jean Bethke Elshtain argues, this thread within Christian realism goes back—at least—to St. Augustine's *City of God*, and it is as relevant today as it was when Augustine developed it within the context of the fifth-century Roman Empire.[45] Niebuhr takes up Augustine's understanding of history and eschatology and incorporates them into his discussion of "judgment."[46] In addition to affirming the reality of malicious persons in a fallen world, Niebuhr claims that, since God is the only one who can render a verdict on history, our judgments are necessarily limited. Political systems, however, tend to deny that our assessment of historical developments, and moments, is never the last word; they eschew acknowledging the limits of human judgment. Nonetheless, Niebuhr contends, Christians must reject such idolatry.

In critiquing this political tendency, Niebuhr primarily had Stalin and Hitler in mind, but he insisted that the same temptations extend to democracies and to every other type of human community. No political system is immune to idolatrous efforts to self-identify with the apex of historical accomplishment, whether the substance of this claim is a "classless society" or the "establishment of freedom and democracy." Within the context of war's ethical challenges, this thread within Christian realism serves as a vital reminder that, while human judgments on the meaning of history are never absolute, the deaths that wars bring are.

One might wonder whether Orthodox Christians, who have endorsed close ties between church and state/empire in multiple historical contexts, can embrace this dimension of Christian realism. While a case can be made that there were many important differences between Byzantium, tsarist Russia, and other collaborative efforts between the Orthodox Church and civil authorities, on the one hand, and the absolutist regimes of the twentieth century, on the other hand, the Christian realist tradition would help strengthen the thread within Orthodoxy that insists upon the limits of historical judgment on eschatological grounds. Again, the valuable insight of Christian realism is the reminder that, while some political systems are undoubtedly more just than others, and while the collapse of many totalitarian systems in the final decades of the twentieth century dramatically improved the lives of millions, there is no political community that is entirely free of idolatry.[47]

Fourth, like Niebuhr and other Christian realists, Orthodoxy sees "anxiety," or the fear of death, as well as the "noetic effects of sin," as consequences of humanity's fall and as forces within human agency and human perception that fuel violence and war. Before considering this connection more directly, we should note that, for the Orthodox, the fall is nothing less than an ontological catastrophe. It ushers in separation from God (or spiritual death), mortality (physical death), and the loss of communion with one's fellow human beings and all creation. Here, I believe, Orthodoxy has something to offer to Christian realism and to the broader conversation, namely, the categorical rejection of death's "goodness," "blessedness," or "acceptability." For the Orthodox, death is the enemy: it is contrary to God's will and essentially tragic.[48] As Metropolitan John (Zizioulas) of Pergamon puts it, "The [Orthodox] Christian view is that death is never good; it is always an outrage."[49] This point is vital to reflection on war. For the Orthodox and for Christian realists, even if war is the best available option, it is *always* tragic, *always* destructive, *always* a cause for mourning and for repentance.

Furthermore, the Orthodox Church teaches that the ontological consequences of the fall (separation from God, mortality, and human division) generate a corrupting form of the "fear of death" and a distorted perception of ourselves and others, consequences with grave social effects. Drawing upon Romans 5:12, Hebrews 2:14–15, and patristic sources, twentieth-century Orthodox theologians like Fr. John Romanides, Fr. John Meyendorff, and Archimandrite Sophrony of Essex develop the teaching that, under the power of death, human interactions are marked by competition for survival, jealousy for honor, exclusivism, mistrust, and strife.[50] Mortality, they contend, fuels fear and anxiety, which in turn fuels conflict and violence.

In a passage that pulls together several affinities between Christian realism and Orthodoxy, and that also highlights some areas through which Orthodoxy can make a constructive contribution, Archimandrite Sophrony, a contemporary of Niebuhr, writes:

> One of the first consequences of the primordial Fall was fratricide. And ever since then that sin has been the principal sin throughout history. The nature of man as a whole was torn to shreds—people, meeting with their like, do not recognize themselves, do not see our common unity of life. Struggling for their own individual existence, they slay their fellows, not understanding that thereby they plunge themselves into death in common with them. Baneful passion has ousted the bonds of love in people's souls, and [replaced them with] the urge to repress one's neighbour for the sake of a comfortable life for oneself and one's offspring. Because of this benightedness our whole world is plunged in an ocean of blood, a hostile atmosphere,

a nightmare of mutual destruction. The sin of our forefathers brought about universal dissolution. To this day mankind has not only failed to release itself from the spirit of fratricide but continues to plunge ever deeper into lethal delirium. The experience of centuries has taught man nothing. Victory through violence is always and inevitably short-term in this world. Translated into eternity, it will prove a never-ending disgrace. "All ye are brethren," said the Teacher—Christ. "One is your Father, which is in heaven" (Matt 23:8–9).[51]

For Fr. Sophrony, and for the Orthodox tradition more broadly, the implications of the fall are manifested day in and day out in the oppression, violence, and overall perversion of human relationships. Reminiscent of Augustine's *City of God*, Fr. Sophrony notes that Cain inherited corruption, was prideful and jealous of his brother, and—by murdering him—inaugurated the "fratricidal wars that crowd the history of our world."[52] His contention here that *all* wars—indeed, all acts of human killing—are "fratricidal" is crucial. It reflects the church's affirmation of the unity of human nature, a teaching that Fr. Sophrony reiterates above in his reference to the Lord's Prayer. This claim is not intended to suggest that all acts of killing are morally equal (a soldier killing in the context of battle is not the same as a murderer killing a child on a playground); rather, Fr. Sophrony's intent is to acknowledge that, regardless of the circumstances, killing another human person is killing one's brother or sister, since all human persons share equally in human nature and all are children of God.

The passage also suggests that the fear of death—"anxiety"—drives the desire to dominate and the tendency toward exclusivism. The fear of death carries profound social implications in part because, "struggling for [one's] own individual existence," one is urged "to repress one's neighbour for the sake of a comfortable life for oneself and one's offspring." This is, I believe, a teaching that merits long consideration and that can be applied both to war and to many other present-day ethical challenges. As Fr. Sophrony describes it, the proper pursuit of one's own preservation tends easily to sinful and abusive extremes both at the personal and the political levels, a claim that resonates deeply with Niebuhr's view. Consider, for example, the following passage from Niebuhr's *Moral Man and*

Immoral Society: "Every group, as every individual, has expansive desires which are rooted in the instinct of survival and soon extend beyond it. The will-to-live becomes the will-to-power. Only rarely does nature provide armors of defense which cannot be transmuted into instruments of aggression."[53] Both Niebuhr and Fr. Sophrony interpret the fallen human condition in a way that acknowledges the insidious effects of anxiety and the fear of death upon social life.

Finally, there is a dimension to Fr. Sophrony's teaching in the above-cited passage that pertains to the fall's noetic effects—a point shared with many other Orthodox and one that connects importantly with the Christian realists. As Fr. Sophrony puts it, "People, meeting with their like, *do not recognize* themselves, *do not see* our common unity of life." The willingness to oppress and destroy one another can be attributed, at least in part, to human beings' deficient perception. That is, on account of clouded vision, fallen human beings do not see reality truly; we do not recognize humanity's ontological unity.[54] In short, we do not know that the other—every other—is our brother or sister. Recall that, for Fr. Sophrony, killing is *always* fratricide, and he here suggests that fallen humanity's inability to see the truth of our ontological unity is a contributing cause to the tragedy of violence and war. In a related passage, he writes, "Those who do not see in themselves and, worse, do not see in their brethren any permanent worth become like wild beasts in their mutual relations, and readily take to slaughtering each other."[55]

In his insightful analysis of Niebuhr's ethics, John Carlson notes that Niebuhr did not believe human reason and perception were exempt from "the disease of sin."[56] In fact, Niebuhr's core critique of both natural law ethics in general and just war theory in particular builds upon this conviction. "Not all wars are equally just and not all contestants are equally right," Niebuhr writes. "Distinctions must be made. But the judgments with which we make them are influenced by passions and interests, so that even the obvious case of aggression can be made to appear a necessity of defense."[57] According to Niebuhr, the flaw at the heart of just war theory is its overconfidence in (fallen) human beings' ability to see clearly and judge accurately. Politics, that realm which displays the fallen condition of the world in a peculiarly transparent way, is messy. Niebuhr's rejection of both just war theory and pacifism traces back to his deeply held

Christian conviction that life in history leaves no space for human beings with absolutely "clean hands" or absolutely pure judgment. Orthodoxy concurs. Even the saints venerated within the Orthodox Church are never regarded as sinless. Such purity belongs only to the one whom Christians worship as God and Savior.

Before closing, it is worth reiterating that the point of an honest, realistic assessment of the human condition—for both Orthodoxy and Christian realism—is to provide a *diagnosis*. It allows us to see the raw truth of war's ugliness and of human beings' propensity for violence along with the hope of enabling peace and community. For both Christian realists and Orthodox thinkers, the only real and lasting cure to our violent predicament comes from the Holy Trinity. This solution, we believe, will not ever be fully realized on earth (because of our freedom and finitude), but we still have a responsibility to work toward progress in peace. Through the practices of just peacemaking, through authentic repentance which corrects our distorted perception and heals our fears and anxiety, through faithful and humane political leaders making good decisions amidst inescapably ambiguous circumstances, and through God's universal invitation to participate in Christ's victorious resurrection, we have cause for genuine hope.

GIVEN THE FACTS THAT (1) war impacts soldiers and noncombatants daily in deadly and life-changing ways, (2) war is a public issue that impacts entire communities and engages them in dialogue, and (3) Orthodoxy has distanced itself from the four predominant approaches to war ethics, yet has not provided a cohesive response to the challenges of war, I have argued that Orthodox leaders and thinkers should embrace two lesser-known approaches within peace and war ethics: just peacemaking and Christian realism. Embracing these two traditions is significant for two overarching reasons. First, as I have sought to demonstrate above, both just peacemaking and Christian realism display close affinities with basic elements within Orthodox Christianity's theological-ethical tradition. While I do not mean to suggest that there are *no* differences or points of contention between these ethical traditions and Orthodox ethics, I believe the points of shared conviction and teaching are plentiful and are sufficient both to merit mutual endorsement on a general level and to justify focused efforts to examine further connections. Second, by embracing the just peacemaking and Christian realist traditions, Orthodoxy would gain not only two rich sets of ethical resources, but also two sets of concepts and language *that are already recognized* within the public and scholarly discourse on peace and war; furthermore, this can be done without compromising Orthodox convictions. Put differently, just peacemaking and Christian realism can move Orthodox Christianity beyond the impasse it currently confronts: they provide a way for Orthodoxy to avoid the Scylla of "leaving the table" of discourse and the Charybdis of pacifism's, just war theory's, holy war's, and political realism's incompatibility with its historical and theological tradition. May Orthodox leaders and scholars have the courage, the humility, and the resolve to *explicitly* and *deliberately* embrace just peacemaking and Christian realism, offering the treasures of our tradition to their advocates with generosity and accepting their treasures with gratitude.

NOTES

1. These reasons include historical, cultural, intellectual, and theological factors. For an extended discussion of the historical development of Orthodox ethics, see Perry Hamalis, "Ethics," in *The Orthodox Christian World*, ed. A. Casiday (London: Routledge, 2012), 419–31.

2. See Aristotle Papanikolaou's essay "The Ascetics of War: The Undoing and Redoing of Virtue," ch. 1 in this volume.

3. The biggest factor here has been terrorist organizations that do not have formal ties to any nation-state, as well as groups like *Daesh* that wage war in support of a demand to be recognized as a legitimate state by the international community.

4. For an example of the public confusion over Orthodox teachings on war, see Andrew Walsh's essay on Orthodox responses to the 1999 Kosovo war, ch. 2 in this volume.

5. Stanley Harakas, "The Teaching on Peace in the Fathers," in *Wholeness of Faith and Life: Orthodox Christian Ethics*, part 1, *Patristic Ethics* (Brookline, MA: Holy Cross Orthodox Press, 1999), 158.

6. Alexander F. C. Webster, "Non-Revisionist Orthodox Reflections on Justice and Peace," *Greek Orthodox Theological Review* 37 (1992): 264.

7. John McGuckin, *The Orthodox Church: An Introduction to Its History, Doctrine, and Spiritual Culture* (Malden: Blackwell, 2008), 402.

8. Philip LeMasters, "Orthodox Perspectives on Peace, War and Violence," *Ecumenical Review* 63 (2011): 54.

9. For several excellent and critical analyses of the tendency among Orthodox authors to identify their teachings as sharply different from those of their Western counterparts, see the contributions in George Demacopoulos and Aristotle Papanikolaou, eds., *Orthodox Constructions of the West* (New York: Fordham University Press, 2013).

10. See the discussion in Valerie Karras's essay, "'Their Hands Are Not Clean': Origen and the Cappadocians on War and Military Service," ch. 5 in this volume. See also Fr. John McGuckin, "Nonviolence and Peace Traditions in Early and Eastern Christianity," in *Religion, Terrorism and Globalization: Nonviolence; A New Agenda*, ed. K. K. Kuriakose (New York: Nova Science Publishers, 2006), 189–202. McGuckin writes (193): "In the perspectives of the eastern Christian tradition, not only do these two monumental figures [Augustine and Aquinas] not feature but, needless to say, neither does their theory on the moral consideration of war and violence which has so dominated the western imagination. Eastern Christianity simply does not approach the issue from the perspective of 'Just War,' and endorses no formal doctrine advocating the possibility of a 'Just War.'"

11. See the helpful discussion in Owen Chadwick, *The Reformation* (London: Penguin Books, 1990). See also A. James Reimer, *Christians and War* (Minneapolis: Fortress Press, 2010), especially 88–110, as well as James M. Stayer, "Anabaptists and Future Anabaptists in the Peasant's War," *Mennonite Quarterly Review* 62, no. 2 (1988): 99–139.

12. On this point, McGuckin, "Nonviolence and Peace Traditions," 200, writes: "The sight of [Catholic] 'warrior-bishops' in full military regalia, passing through the streets of Constantinople in the Fourth Crusade, left its mark on contemporary Greek sources as one of the greatest 'shocks' to the system, and one of the incidentals that were taken by the Greeks as proof positive that Latin Christianity in the 13th century had a serious illness at its center."

13. McGuckin, *Orthodox Church*, 406.

14. LeMasters, "Orthodox Perspectives," 59. For an extended analysis of "military saints" in the late antique and Byzantine periods, see the essay by James C. Skedros, "Lessons from Military Saints in the Byzantine Tradition," ch. 7 in this volume.

15. For an example of non-Christian contributions to just peacemaking, see Susan Brooks Thistlethwaite, ed., *Interfaith Just Peacemaking: Jewish, Christian, and Muslim Perspectives on the New Paradigm of Peace and War* (New York: Palgrave Macmillan, 2012).

16. See Glen H. Stassen, ed., *Just Peacemaking: The New Paradigm for the Ethics of Peace and War*, rev. ed. (Cleveland: Pilgrim Press, 2008). The official list

of ten practices is as follows: (1) support nonviolent direct action, (2) take independent initiatives to reduce threat, (3) use cooperative conflict resolution, (4) acknowledge responsibility for conflict and injustice and seek repentance and forgiveness, (5) advance democracy, human rights, and religious liberty, (6) foster just and sustainable economic development, (7) work with emerging cooperative forces in the international system, (8) strengthen the United Nations and international efforts for cooperation and human rights, (9) reduce offensive weapons and weapons trade, and (10) encourage grassroots peacemaking groups and voluntary associations.

17. Glen H. Stassen, "The Unity, Realism, and Obligatoriness of Just Peacemaking Theory," *Journal of the Society of Christian Ethics* 23, no. 1 (2003): 173.

18. Cf. Stassen, *Just Peacemaking*, 11.

19. Cf. ibid., especially 34–37.

20. Glen H. Stassen, "How Incarnational Discipleship Led to Just Peacemaking," *Baptistic Theologies* 4, no. 2 (Autumn 2012): 89.

21. Just war theory is not the only approach to war ethics that regards some wars as morally justifiable; holy war, political realism, and Christian realism are all additional examples. I limit the point here to just war theory because this is the manner in which proponents of just peacemaking frame their position.

22. A few other Orthodox thinkers have begun to reflect on just peacemaking's compatibility with Orthodox Christianity, although the rationale here presented has not previously been developed. See, for example, Rev. Emmanuel Clapsis, "Peace and Peacemaking as an Interfaith and Ecumenical Vocation: An Orthodox View," paper presented at the Inter-Orthodox Consultation of the International Ecumenical Peace Convocation in Leros, Greece (September 2009), http://www.goarch.org. Clapsis makes a similar case for Orthodox involvement in peacemaking initiatives in his essay "The Peaceable Vocation of the Church in a Global World," in *Just Peace: Orthodox Perspectives*, ed. Semegnish Asfaw, Alexios Chehadeh, and Marian Gh. Simion (Geneva: WCC Publications, 2012), 163–74.

23. See the discussion in Gayle Woloschak's essay "War, Technology, and the Canon Law Principle of *Economia*," ch. 11 in this volume.

24. For example, in contrast to Roman Catholic theology and practice, Orthodoxy does not define dogma in the area of ethics.

25. LeMasters, "Orthodox Perspectives," 54.

26. Christos Tsironis, "Peace-War-Ecclesia in Modern Greece: Fragments and Continuities," in Asfaw, Chehadeh, and Simion, *Just Peace*, 138, reiterates the nonsystematic and nonlegalistic approach to moral issues within Orthodox ethics in his discussion of Orthodox war-and-peace teachings.

27. See the discussion in Stassen, *Just Peacemaking*, especially 17–32.

28. *Inter-Orthodox Preparatory Consultation towards the International Ecumenical Peace Convocation (IEPC)*, §19, Ecumenical Patriarchate, http://www.ec-patr.org/docdisplay.php?lang=gr&id=1125&tla=gr.

29. Nicholas Cabasilas, *The Life in Christ*, bk. 6 (PG 150:676–77); English translation in Gennadios Limouris, ed., *Orthodox Visions of Ecumenism* (Geneva: WCC Publications, 1994), 125.

30. Stassen, *Just Peacemaking*, 134–35.

31. See the website of International Orthodox Christian Charities, http://www.iocc.org/about.

32. One example of a grassroots peace organization of this type in Cyprus is "Mahallae" (http://mahallae.org/). In Lebanon, summer camps for Christian and Muslim youth have been led by alumni of "YES" (The Kennedy-Lugar "Youth Exchange and Study" program) in coordination with the Orthodox community of the Patriarchate of Antioch. See "Christian, Muslim Youth Connect in YES Alumni–Led Summer Camp," Kennedy-Lugar Youth Exchange and Study Program, September 30, 2012, http://yesprograms.org/impact/story/christian-muslim-youth-connect-yes-alumni-led-summer-camp. Also, Orthodox Christian individuals and communities in numerous countries have collaborated with the well-known organization "Seeds of Peace" to support youth peace camps, "Cooperation Circles," and the youth peace magazine *The Olive Branch*.

33. For information on IPSEC, see http://www.orthodoxpeace.org/. For information on the Orthodox Peace Fellowship, see http://www.incommunion.org/.

34. Clapsis, "Peace and Peacemaking as an Interfaith and Ecumenical Vocation."

35. For a helpful account of the historical development of "Christian realism," see Robin Lovin, *Reinhold Niebuhr and Christian Realism* (Cambridge: Cambridge University Press, 1995).

36. While some scholars have identified Niebuhr as a proponent of just war theory, John Carlson has demonstrated forcefully that such a categorization of Niebuhr's teachings does not hold up under scrutiny. Instead, Niebuhr's teachings should be regarded as constituting a discrete stance on the ethics of war. See John D. Carlson, "Is There a Christian Realist Theory of War and Peace? Reinhold Niebuhr and Just War Thought," *Journal of the Society of Christian Ethics* 28, no. 1 (2008): 133–61.

37. Lovin, *Reinhold Niebuhr*.

38. Carlson, "Is There a Christian Realist Theory?," 136, 150.

39. See Jean Bethke Elshtain, *Augustine and the Limits of Politics* (Notre Dame, IN: University of Notre Dame Press, 1995).

40. Edmund Santurri, "Global Justice after the Fall: Christian Realism and the 'Law of Peoples,'" *Journal of Religious Ethics* 33, no. 4 (2005): 784.

41. Christos Yannaras, *Elements of Faith: An Introduction to Orthodox Theology*, trans. Keith Schram (Edinburgh: T & T Clark, 1991), 75.

42. While a further exploration of this topic lies beyond my present scope, Andrew Flescher, "Love and Justice in Reinhold Niebuhr's Prophetic Christian Realism and Emmanuel Levinas's Ethics of Responsibility: Treading between Pacifism and Just-War Theory," *Journal of Religion* (2000): 61–82, has offered an analysis of Reinhold Niebuhr's and Emmanuel Levinas's theological anthropologies that suggests important points of connection and comparison with many of the teachings on "personhood" developed by recent Eastern Orthodox theologians.

43. Reinhold Niebuhr, *The Nature and Destiny of Man: A Christian Interpretation*, vol. 1, *Human Nature* (Louisville: Westminster John Knox Press, 1996), 16.

44. Archimandrite Sophrony (Sakharov), *Saint Silouan the Athonite* (Essex: Stavropegic Monastery of St. John the Baptist, 1991), 200.

45. See Elshtain, *Augustine*, especially 89–112.

46. For a discussion of "judgment" in Niebuhr's thought, see Robin Lovin, "Christian Realism for the Twenty-First Century," *Journal of Religious Ethics* 37, no. 4 (2009): 669–82, especially 671–77.

47. Oliver O'Donovan, *The Ways of Judgment* (Grand Rapids: Eerdmans, 2005), especially 67–83, provides a compelling analysis of this teaching within the thought of Augustine and Niebuhr.

48. For a more complete discussion of Orthodox teachings on death, see Perry T. Hamalis, "The Meaning and Place of Death in an Orthodox Ethical Framework," in *Thinking through Faith: Perspectives from Orthodox Christian Scholars*, ed. A. Papanikolaou and E. Prodromou (Crestwood, NY: St. Vladimir's Seminary Press, 2008), 183–217. See also my forthcoming monograph *Formed by Death: Insights from Ethics for Eastern Orthodox Christianity* (Notre Dame, IN: University of Notre Dame Press).

49. John D. Zizioulas, *Lectures in Christian Dogmatics*, ed. Douglas H. Knight (London: T & T Clark, 2008), 100.

50. John S. Romanides, "Original Sin according to St. Paul," *St. Vladimir's Theological Quarterly* 4 (1955/56): 20–21, writes, for example,

The power of death in the universe has brought with it the will for self-preservation, fear and anxiety (Heb 2:14–15), which in turn are the root causes of self-assertion, egoism, hatred, envy, and the like. Because man is afraid of becoming meaningless, he is constantly endeavoring to prove, to himself and others, that he is worth something. He thirsts after compliments and is afraid of insults. He seeks his own and is jealous of the success of others. He likes those who like him, and hates those who hate him. He either seeks security and happiness in wealth, glory, and bodily pleasures, or imagines that his destiny is to be happy in the possession of the presence of God by an introverted and individualistic process which excludes any real and active selfless love for others.

51. Archimandrite Sophrony (Sakharov), *On Prayer*, trans. Rosemary Edmonds (Crestwood, NY: St. Vladimir's Seminary Press, 1998), 111–12.

52. Sophrony, *On Prayer*, 117.

53. Reinhold Niebuhr, *Moral Man and Immoral Society: A Study in Ethics and Politics* (New York: Charles Scribner's Sons, 1932), 18.

54. Cf. Sophrony, *On Prayer*, 74.

55. Archimandrite Sophrony (Sakharov), *We Shall See Him as He Is*, trans. Rosemary Edmonds (Essex: Stavropegic Monastery of St. John the Baptist, 1988), 40.

56. Carlson, "Is There a Christian Realist Theory?," 136.

57. Niebuhr, *Nature and Destiny of Man*, 1:283.

CONTRIBUTORS

Peter C. Bouteneff is professor of systematic theology at St. Vladimir's Orthodox Theological Seminary. He received his D.Phil. in theology from Oxford University (1997). Dr. Bouteneff's broad interests within systematics include Christology, ecclesiology, and sacred arts. He contributed the chapter "Christ and Salvation" to the *Cambridge Companion to Orthodox Christian Theology*, and the chapter "Ecclesiology and Ecumenism" to the Routledge volume *The Orthodox Christian World*. He conceived of and edits St. Vladimir Seminary Press's Foundations Series, which includes his book *Sweeter Than Honey: Orthodox Thinking on Dogma and Truth* (St. Vladimir's Seminary Press, 2006). He has also published *Beginnings: Ancient Christian Readings of the Biblical Creation Narratives* (Baker Academic, 2008), and most recently *Arvo Pärt: Out of Silence* (St. Vladimir's Seminary Press, 2015), a theological exploration of the great Estonian composer. Dr. Bouteneff's work in ecumenical dialogue has led to many publications; to participation in global and local forums, where he represents the Orthodox Church in America; and to membership on multiple advisory boards, including the Tantur Ecumenical Institute for Theological Studies in Jerusalem.

George E. Demacopoulos holds the Fr. John Meyendorff & Patterson Family Chair of Orthodox Christian Studies and is professor of historical theology at Fordham University, where he is the co-founding director of the Orthodox Christian Studies Center. He received his Ph.D. in religious studies from the University of North Carolina at Chapel Hill (2002). Dr. Demacopoulos's research and teaching interests are in the fields of early Christian and Byzantine church history. He specializes in the relationship between Eastern Orthodox and Roman Catholics during the Middle Ages, expressions of authority within Christian communities, and the application of critical theory to the analysis of the Eastern Christian experience. He has published scholarly articles in many journals, including *Theological Studies, Journal of Late Antiquity,* and *The Journal of Religion*. His monographs include *Gregory the Great: Ascetic, Pastor, and First-Man of Rome* (University of Notre Dame Press, 2015), *The Invention of Peter: Apostolic Discourse and Papal Authority in Late Antiquity* (University of Pennsylvania Press, 2013), and *Five Models of Spiritual Direction in the Early Church* (University of Notre Dame Press, 2006). He has coedited (with Aristotle Papanikolaou) *Orthodox Constructions of the West* (Fordham University Press, 2013) and *Orthodox Readings of Augustine* (St. Vladimir's Seminary Press, 2008), and is the translator of *Gregory the Great: Book of Pastoral Rule* (St. Vladimir's Seminary Press, 2007).

JOHN FOTOPOULOS is associate professor in the Department of Religious Studies at Saint Mary's College, Notre Dame, Indiana. Dr. Fotopoulos received his Ph.D. from Loyola University Chicago (2001). His area of specialization is the New Testament and early Christian literature within the context of Greco-Roman society and culture, focusing in particular on the letters of Paul the apostle by using social-historical and rhetorical-critical methods of interpretation. He is a member of numerous academic associations in the United States and Europe, including the prestigious Colloquium Oecumenicum Paulinum, an ecumenical group of international Pauline scholars that meets regularly in Rome to discuss aspects of Paul's letters. Dr. Fotopoulos has published *Food Offered to Idols in Roman Corinth: A Social-Rhetorical Reconsideration of 1 Corinthians 8:1–11:1* (Mohr Siebeck, 2003), which was published in Greek as *Τα θυσιαστήρια δείπνα στη ρωμαϊκή Κόρινθο* (Pournaras, 2006); edited *The New Testament and Early Christian Literature in Greco-Roman Context: Studies in Honor of David E. Aune* (Brill, 2006); and coedited (with Eugen J. Pentiuc and Bruce N. Beck) *Studies in Orthodox Hermeneutics: A Festschrift in Honor of Theodore G. Stylianopoulos* (Holy Cross, 2016). Dr. Fotopoulos has also written numerous articles on the letters of Paul the apostle and on the Greco-Roman world that have been published in reference books such as *Blackwell's Companion to the New Testament* and *The Westminster Dictionary of the New Testament and Early Christian*

Literature and Rhetoric, and in academic journals such as the *Catholic Biblical Quarterly*, *Novum Testamentum*, and the *Greek Orthodox Theological Review*.

BRANDON GALLAHER is lecturer of systematic and comparative theology at the University of Exeter (Devon, UK) and former British Academy postdoctoral fellow in the Faculty of Theology and Religion, University of Oxford, and visiting fellow at the Institute for Advanced Study, University of Notre Dame, and at the Center for Interdisciplinary Study of Monotheistic Religions (CISMOR), School of Theology, Doshisha University (Kyoto, Japan). He received his D.Phil. in systematic theology from the University of Oxford (2011), where his research explored the tension between Christocentrism and the affirmation of divine freedom in the Trinitarian theologies of Sergii Bulgakov, Karl Barth, and Hans Urs von Balthasar. This work is published as *Freedom and Necessity in Modern Trinitarian Theology* (Oxford University Press, 2016). He has published historical articles, archival material, and translations on modern Orthodox theology—especially on Sergii Bulgakov, Georges Florovsky, Vladimir Lossky, Vladimir Solov'ev, John Zizioulas, and Christos Yannaras—in numerous book collections and academic journals. He has also coauthored (with Christopher Hays, Julia Konstantinovsky, Richard Ounsworth, and Casey Strine) the collaborative monograph on eschatology *When the Son of Man Didn't Come: A Constructive Proposal Regarding the "Delay of the Parousia"* (Fortress, 2015) and coedited with Paul Ladouceur a Georges Florovsky reader, *The Patristic Witness of Georges Florovsky: Essential Theological Writings*, which is forthcoming from Bloomsbury T & T Clark. He served as a subject expert in the Press Office of the Ecumenical Patriarchate during the Holy and Great Council of Crete in June 2016. For the last five years, he has been engaged in interreligious dialogue, especially with Islam and Zen Buddhism, and is currently writing a monograph reflecting on this activity entitled *Orthodoxy and World Religions in a Secular Age*.

PERRY T. HAMALIS holds the Cecelia Schneller Mueller Chair in Religion and is professor of religious studies at North Central College in Naperville, Illinois. He earned his Ph.D. in religious ethics at the Divinity

School of the University of Chicago (2004), focusing his research on the ethical teachings of Archimandrite Sophrony Sakharov and Thomas Hobbes. His broader interests include the themes of death and fear of death, politics and religion, and applied ethics. Dr. Hamalis's works have been published in *Studies in Christian Ethics,* the *Journal of Religion, Journal of the Society of Christian Ethics,* the *Greek Orthodox Theological Review,* and numerous encyclopedias. He also contributed the chapter "Ethics" to the Routledge volume *The Orthodox Christian World,* and chapters on ethics-related topics to *Christianity, Democracy and the Shadow of Constantine* (Fordham University Press, 2017), *Toward an Ecology of Transfiguration* (Fordham University Press, 2013), and *Thinking through Faith* (St. Vladimir's Seminary Press, 2008). His monograph *Formed by Death: Insights for Ethics from Eastern Orthodox Christianity* will be published by University of Notre Dame Press. Dr. Hamalis has lectured on topics pertaining to Orthodoxy and ethics across the country, in Greece, and in the Republic of Korea. In 2015–16, he was awarded a Fulbright Senior Research Fellowship and named Underwood Visiting Professor of Religion at Yonsei University (Seoul, Republic of Korea). In addition, Dr. Hamalis serves as a consultant to the Faith and Order Commission of the World Council of Churches and is a member of the board of trustees of Hellenic College Holy Cross Greek Orthodox School of Theology.

VALERIE A. KARRAS was a professor of church history, theology, and religious studies for over twenty years, having held teaching, research, and administrative positions at several institutions, including Southern Methodist University; University of California, Irvine; Saint Louis University; and Hellenic College and Holy Cross Greek Orthodox School of Theology. Dr. Karras received a Th.D. in patristic theology from the Aristotle University of Thessaloniki (1991) and a Ph.D. in church history from The Catholic University of America in Washington, DC (2002). Her research interests include women in the early and Byzantine church, gender in Greek patristic and Byzantine theology, and Greek patristic anthropology and soteriology. Dr. Karras has published articles, translations, and book reviews in such scholarly journals as *Church History,* the *Greek Orthodox Theological Review,* the *Journal of Early Christian Studies,* the *St. Vladimir's Theological Quarterly,* and *Theological Studies,* and in books published by scholarly presses such as Cambridge University Press, Dumbarton Oaks, Indiana University Press, and Liturgical Press. She is completing revisions to her book *Women in the Byzantine Liturgy*, which will be published by Oxford University Press. Dr. Karras has participated in several international ecumenical and interfaith dialogues and has served as secretary of the Orthodox Theological Society in America, on the boards of the North American Academy of Ecumenists and the Society for Buddhist-Christian Studies, and on the steering committees of the American Academy of Religion's Eastern Orthodox Studies Group and History of Christianity Section. She is currently a member of the board of the Interfaith Partnership of Greater St. Louis.

ALEXANDROS K. KYROU is professor of history and director of the Program in East European and Russian Studies at Salem State University in Salem, Massachusetts, where he teaches on the Balkans, Byzantium, and the Ottoman Empire. He received his Ph.D. in East European history at Indiana University (1993) and completed his postdoctoral work as a visiting research fellow in the Program in Hellenic Studies at Princeton University. He is also a former research fellow of the Kokkalis Program on Southeastern and East-Central Europe at Harvard University, as well as a past senior research scholar at the former Institute on Religion and World Affairs at Boston University. The author of numerous publications on Greek America and Balkan diasporas, international humanitarian relief in Axis-occupied Greece, and US foreign policy in southeastern Europe, Professor Kyrou is also the associate editor of the *Journal of Modern Hellenism*.

ARISTOTLE PAPANIKOLAOU is professor of theology and the Archbishop Demetrios Chair in Orthodox Theology and Culture at Fordham University. He is also a co-founding director of the Orthodox Christian Studies Center at Fordham, as well as senior fellow at the Center for the Study of Law and Religion at Emory University. He received his Ph.D. in theology from the Divinity School at the University of Chicago (1998). His published articles appear in many journals, edited volumes, and reference books, including *Modern Theology*, the *Journal of the American Academy of Religion*, the *Journal of the Society of Christian*

Ethics, the *Cambridge Companion to Orthodox Christian Theology*, the *Cambridge Companion to the Trinity*, and *The Oxford Handbook on the Trinity*. He is author of *The Mystical as Political: Democracy and Non-Radical Orthodoxy* (University of Notre Dame Press, 2012) and *Being with God: Trinity, Apophaticism and Divine-Human Communion* (University of Notre Dame Press, 2006), and coeditor of *Political Theologies in Orthodox Christianity* (Bloomsbury, 2017), *Orthodox Constructions of the West* (Fordham University Press, 2013), *Christianity, Democracy and the Shadow of Constantine* (Fordham University Press, 2012), *Orthodox Readings of Augustine* (St. Vladimir's Seminary Press, 2008), and *Thinking through Faith: New Perspectives from Orthodox Christian Scholars* (St. Vladimir's Seminary Press, 2008).

ELIZABETH H. PRODROMOU is Visiting Associate Professor of Conflict Resolution at The Fletcher School of Law and Diplomacy at Tufts University. She is a senior fellow in National Security and International Policy at the Center for American Progress (Washington, DC) and a nonresident fellow at The Hedayah International Center of Excellence for Countering Violent Extremism (Abu Dhabi). Prodromou served as vice chair and commissioner on the US Commission on International Religious Freedom (2004–12), and she was a member of the US Secretary of State's Religion and Foreign Policy Working Group (2011–15). Her research interests focus on the intersection of religion, democracy, and security. Published widely in scholarly and policy journals, such as *Social Compass*, *Orbis*, and *Journal of Democracy*, she is a frequent commentator and contributor on matters of religion and geopolitics in US and international media. She is coeditor and contributor for *Eastern Orthodox Christianity and American Higher Education* (University of Notre Dame Press, 2016) and *Thinking through Faith: New Perspectives from Orthodox Christian Scholars* (St. Vladimir's Seminary Press, 2008). She holds a Ph.D. (1993) and an S.M. in political science from the Massachusetts Institute of Technology.

NICOLAE RODDY is professor of theology at Creighton University in Omaha, Nebraska, teaching in the area of Hebrew Bible/Older Testament. He received his Ph.D. from the University of Iowa (1999), having completed his dissertation research as a Fulbright Scholar to Romania during the 1994–95 academic year. For the past twenty years, Dr. Roddy has served as codirector and area supervisor for the archaeological excavations at Bethsaida, Israel, and also codirects the *Virtual World Project* (www.virtualworldproject.org). Since 2003, he has been a faculty associate of the Goren-Goldstein Center for Hebraic Studies at the Faculty of Letters of the University of Bucharest, Romania. Dr. Roddy serves on the board of the Orthodox Center for the Advancement of Biblical Studies (OCABS) and formerly served as senior editor of the *Journal of the Orthodox Center for the Advancement of Biblical Studies*. Dr. Roddy has authored *The Romanian Version of the Testament of Abraham: Text, Translation, and Cultural Context*, published in the Early Judaism and Its Literature series of the Society of Biblical Literature (2001); edited *Words of a Shepherd: The Life and Writings of Protostavrophor Vojislav Dosenovich* (Holy Trinity Monastery, 2006); edited *Festschrift in Honor of Professor Paul Nadim Tarazi*, volume 1, *Studies in the Old Testament*, in the Bible in the Christian Orthodox Tradition series (Peter Lang, 2013); and written numerous book chapters and articles in journals such as the *Journal of Religion & Society*, *Biblische Notizen*, and *Studia Hebraica*. He is past president of the Rocky Mountain/Great Plains Region of the American Academy of Religion/Society of Biblical Literature, and formerly served on the steering committee of the Biblical Studies in the Eastern and Oriental Orthodox Traditions Section of SBL. Dr. Roddy has also served as regional coordinator for the American Schools of Oriental Research (ASOR).

JAMES C. SKEDROS is the Michael G. and Anastasia Cantonis Professor of Byzantine Studies and professor of early Christianity and dean of the School of Theology at Hellenic College and Holy Cross Greek Orthodox School of Theology, Brookline, Massachusetts. He received his Th.D. in the history of Christianity from Harvard Divinity School (1996) after receiving a Fulbright fellowship for doctoral research in Greece. From 1996 to 1998 he was assistant professor of Orthodox Studies at the Graduate Theological Union in Berkeley, California. Dr. Skedros's research areas include popular religious practices in late antiquity, Byzantine Christianity, the lives of early Christian and Byzantine saints, pilgrimage, and Christian and Muslim relations. He authored *St. Demetrios of Thessaloniki: Civic Patron and Divine Protector, 4th–7th c. CE* (Harvard University Press, 1999). His publications also include articles in journals such as *Studia Patristica* and in such edited volumes as *Byzantine Christianity: A People's History of Christianity* (Fortress Press, 2006) and *Philostratus's Heroikos: Religion and Cultural Identity in the Third Century C.E.* (Society of Biblical Literature, 2004).

ANDREW WALSH is associate director of the Leonard E. Greenberg Center for the Study of Religion in Public Life at Trinity College in Hartford. He holds a Ph.D. in American religious history from Harvard University (1996). His scholarly work focuses on religion and public life in the United States and the historical experience of Orthodox Christians in this country. Dr. Walsh coauthored with Mark Silk *One Nation Divisible: How Regional Religious Differences Shape American Political Life* (Rowman & Littlefield, 2008), summarizing the eight-volume Alta Mira Press series "Religion by Region"; he coedited the series Religion and Public Life in New England: Steady Habits, Changing Slowly and the volume by the same title. Andrew Walsh and Mark Silk are coeditors of the recently announced Columbia University Press series The Future of Religion in America, projected at twelve to fourteen volumes. Dr. Walsh is completing work on a book entitled *Orthodox Christianity in America*, which will appear in Columbia University Press's series Contemporary American Religion.

GAYLE E. WOLOSCHAK is professor of radiation oncology, radiology, and cell and molecular biology and associate director of the Centers of Cancer Nanotechnology Excellence in the Feinberg School of Medicine, Northwestern University; prior to 2001 she and her research group were at Argonne National Laboratory in the Biosciences Division. She is also adjunct professor of religion and sciences at Lutheran School of Theology at Chicago. Dr. Woloschak received a Ph.D. in medical sciences with a specialization in immunology from the University of Toledo, Medical College of Ohio (1980), and she completed her postdoctoral training in the Departments of Immunology and Molecular Biology at the Mayo Clinic, where she later became an assistant professor. Dr. Woloschak's scientific interests are predominantly in the areas of molecular biology, radiation biology, and nanotechnology studies. She has authored over two hundred scientific papers and received numerous grants. Dr. Woloschak received her D.Min. from Pittsburgh Theological Seminary and is on the editorial boards of several science-religion journals, including the joint publication board for *Zygon: A Journal of Science and Religion*. She is a member and currently associate director of the Zygon Center for Religion and Science, and director of its Epic of Creation and Future of Creation Science programs.

INDEX

CPSIA information can be obtained
at www.ICGtesting.com
Printed in the USA
LVOW13*1235171117

556596LV00005B/7/P